Language Development and Learning to Read

Language Development and Learning to Read

The Scientific Study of How Language Development
Affects Reading Skill

Diane McGuinness

A Bradford Book
The MIT Press Cambridge, Massachusetts London, England

MIT Press books may be purchased at special quantity discounts for business or sales promotional use. For information, please e-mail special_sales@ mitpress.mit.edu or write to Special Sales Department, The MIT Press, 5 Cambridge Center, Cambridge, MA 02142.

This book was set in Janson and Rotis Semi-sans on 3B2 by Asco Typesetters, Hong Kong. Printed and bound in the United States of America.

Library of Congress Cataloging-in-Publication Data
McGuinness, Diane.
  Language development and learning to read : the scientific study of how language development affects reading skill / Diane McGuinness.
     p.   cm.
  "A Bradford book."
  Includes bibliographical references and indexes.
  ISBN 0-262-13452-7 (cloth : alk. paper)
  1. Reading—Research. 2. Language acquisition—Research. I. Title.
LB1050.6.M34   2005
428.4—dc22   2004062118

10 9 8 7 6 5 4 3 2 1

Contents

Contents

Preface

Five thousand years ago, Egyptian and Sumerian scholars designed the first full-fledged writing systems. Though these systems were radically different in form, with the Egyptians marking consonants and whole-word category clues, and the Sumerians marking syllables, both were complete and self-contained. Any name, any word, or any word yet to come could be immediately assigned the appropriate symbols representing that word's phonology.

Schools were established for the sons of the elite—the rulers, priests, administrators, and wealthy farmers, plus the obviously gifted—and not much changed in this regard until the nineteenth century, when the universal-education movement began gathering momentum. Up to this point, no one kept track of which children were more or less successful in mastering this extraordinary invention. But with children sorted by age, and every child in attendance, individual differences in learning rate and skill were hard to ignore. In many European countries, individual differences were minor, and when problems did occur, they affected reading fluency and reading comprehension. In English-speaking countries, by contrast, individual differences were enormous. Some children were learning to read quickly but others were not learning to read at all, despite years of teaching. And this applied across the board—to decoding, spelling, fluency, and comprehension. Was this due to the teaching method, the nature of the written code itself, or something inherent in the child?

Answering this question took most of the twentieth century, and now that the answers are in, there are some huge surprises. Reading and spelling are easy to teach if you know how to do it. Influential theories driving much of the research on the language-reading connection over the past 30 years are not supported by the data. Meanwhile, the volume of research has snowballed to such an extent that the quantity of studies has become unmanageable. The huge and formidable databases on almost every topic related to reading are an impediment to progress.

To get a sense of the actual size of these databases, and the quality of the studies in them, the National Reading Panel (NRP) decided to keep score. They reported that of the 1,072 studies carried out over the past 30 years on methods of reading instruction, only 75 studies met a preliminary screening consisting of these criteria: publication in a refereed journal, comparison of at least two methods, random selection of subjects into comparison groups, and statistical analysis sufficient to compute effect sizes (National Reading Panel, 2000). On further scrutiny, only 38 studies were found to be methodologically sound. It was the same story for each area of reading instruction. The NRP uncovered a whopping 19,000 papers on the theme that "reading a lot" helps children learn to read. (It does not, but only 14 studies survived the final screening to prove it.) The training studies on phoneme awareness, reading fluency, vocabulary instruction, and methods of teaching reading comprehension all suffered a similar fate.

I faced the identical problems when I set out to write a book intended to review the research on reading in the twentieth century. Trying to squeeze all this material into one volume, while adjudicating between reliable and unreliable studies for the reader, proved impossible. The result was two complementary, but independent, books. One book deals with the historical and scientific research on reading instruction per se, including a detailed analysis of the NRP report (*Early Reading Instruction*). This book, *Language Development and Learning to Read*, focuses mainly on reading predictors—whether or not individual differences in specific perceptual, linguistic, or cognitive skills influence children's ability to learn to read. The proof (or lack thereof) for many of the popular theories in this area of research lies outside the field, in the mainstream research on language development carried out by developmental psychologists, psycholinguists, and researchers in the speech and hearing sciences, and this adds another level of complexity to the mix.

The table of contents for *Early Reading Instruction* follows this preface. The two books are self-contained and don't have to be read in any particular order. However, they do reference one another whenever a greater exposition (or proof) of a statement or argument is provided in the other volume.

A pronunciation key is provided in the accompanying table. It should be noted that this key does not conform to the International Phonetic Alphabet. Instead, it represents the most common spelling in English for each phoneme. IPA is a particularly poor fit to the English spelling system compared to other European alphabets, which are more directly tied to the Latin sound-symbol code. As such, IPA is confusing to people unfamiliar with it. For example, IPA marks the sound "ah" with the letter a. In English, this letter typically stand for the sounds /a/ (*cat*) or /ae/ (*table*), while "ah" is marked with the letter o (*hot*), which is the symbol for the sound /oe/ in IPA. This muddle obtains for most vowel spellings.

A glossary of terms is provided at the end of the book. I encourage readers to use the glossary, because there are many technical and specialist terms in the book.

English Phonemes and Their Basic Code Spellings
Sounds are indicated by slash marks.

Consonants

Sound	As in	Basic code spelling
/b/	*big*	b
/d/	*dog*	d
/f/	*fun*	f
/g/	*got*	g
/h/	*hot*	h
/j/	*job*	j
/k/	*kid*	k
/l/	*log*	l
/m/	*man*	m
/n/	*not*	n
/p/	*pig*	p
/r/	*red*	r
/s/	*sat*	s
/t/	*top*	t
/v/	*van*	v
/w/	*win*	w
/z/	*zip*	z

These consonant sounds are spelled with two letters.

/ch/	*chin*	<u>ch</u>
/ng/	*sing*	<u>ng</u>
/sh/	*shop*	<u>sh</u>
/th/	*thin*	<u>th</u>
/*th*/	*then*	<u>th</u>
/zh/	*vision*	—

These consonant combinations have special spellings.

| /ks/ | *tax* | <u>x</u> |
| /kw/ | *quit* | <u>qu</u> |

Vowels

Sound	As in	Basic code spelling
/a/	*had*	<u>a</u>
/e/	*bed*	<u>e</u>
/i/	*hit*	<u>i</u>
/o/	*dog*	<u>o</u>
/aw/	*law*	<u>aw</u>
/u/	*but*	<u>u</u>
/ae/	*made*	<u>a–e</u>
/ee/	*see*	<u>ee</u>
/ie/	*time*	<u>i–e</u>
/oe/	*home*	<u>o–e</u>
/ue/	*cute*	<u>u–e</u>
/o͝o/	*look*	<u>oo</u>
/o͞o/	*soon*	<u>oo</u>
ou	*out*	<u>ou</u>
oi	*oil*	<u>oi</u>
Vowel + *r*		
/er/	*her*	<u>er</u>
/ah/–/er/	*far*	<u>ar</u>
/oe/–/er/	*for*	<u>or</u>
/e/–/er/	*hair*	<u>air</u>

There are nine vowel + *r* phonemes, and all but one (/er/) are diphthongs —*two* sounds elided that count as one vowel. Those listed above have special spellings and need to be specifically taught. The remainder use more conventional spellings and can be taught in the usual way, as two phonemes: /eer/ /ire/ /ure/ /oor/ /our/ as in *deer, fire, cure, poor, our.*

Table of Contents to the Companion Volume: Early Reading Instruction

Acknowledgments

My grateful thanks to Steven Pinker and to my editor, Tom Stone, for their perceptive analysis of this book and wise suggestions. Without their help, this book would have been far more difficult to digest.

A very special thanks to the Sanibel Public Library for their generous help in locating hard-to-find papers and books.

Introduction

Two major questions guide the research on reading. The first and most obvious has to do with methods of reading instruction: What works best, and why? This is the topic of the companion book, *Early Reading Instruction*. The second question, and the topic of this book, is more subtle and complex. It stems from the fact that there are striking individual differences in reading skill even when children are taught in the same classroom with the same method by the same teacher. Why do some children learn to read easily and quickly, while others don't learn to read at all?

Three explanations have been put forward to explain the wide disparities in reading skill among children of all ages. These explanations split along nature-nurture lines. Briefly, they go like this:

1. Reading instruction is to blame. If reading instruction is vague or confusing, this opens the door for children to try out whatever strategy makes sense to them. For example, whole-word methods lead some children to believe that they can memorize each word as a random string of letters. This makes learning to read exactly like trying to memorize the telephone directory.

2. Impaired speech perception is to blame. The reason children have reading problems is that there is a delay or impairment in the development of "phonological processing," which ultimately leads to difficulties hearing phoneme sequences in words. Unless this aptitude falls into place *developmentally*, it will be difficult to impossible to teach the alphabet code.[1]

---

1. The terms *phonological* and *phoneme* are often used interchangeably in this field. To avoid confusion, I will use the term *phonological* to refer to speech

3. Delays or impairments in core language functions like receptive and productive vocabulary, syntax, and semantics are to blame. This will depress overall reading skill and hamper academic progress.

I want to explore each of these explanations in more depth to put them into a context. Because methods of reading instruction are not the topic of this book, I will devote more space here to the environmental explanation. The strongest evidence for an environmental explanation for reading skill is that individual differences in decoding and spelling skills are not found in countries with a transparent alphabetic writing system.

Reading Skill Varies from One Country to Another

The scientific study of reading is about the mastery of a human invention, not the study of natural laws like those in chemistry, physics, and biology. This complicates things. To begin with, there's no universal thing called "reading" independent of a particular language and a particular solution for how that language was written down. A reading problem in one country is not necessarily a reading problem in another. In English-speaking countries, the main test of reading success is decoding accuracy, the ability to read isolated words one word at a time. In many European countries, decoding accuracy is of little concern because *every child reads accurately.* Instead, the measures of reading success are reading fluency and reading comprehension.

This discrepancy is due to the way speech sounds (phonemes) are mapped to symbols in the different alphabetic writing systems. In a "transparent" alphabet, like the Italian, Spanish, German, and most Scandinavian alphabets, there is mainly one way to write each phoneme in the language, and one way to decode each letter or *digraph* (sh in *ship*). Transparent alphabet codes are transparent in the sense that it is obvious how they work, making them easier to teach and learn. (This does not mean they are immune to misleading forms of reading instruction.)

---

units in general (words, syllables, rimes, phonemes), and the term *phoneme* in its correct usage, as the smallest unit of sound in words—the individual consonants and vowels. To complicate matters, *phonological* is used in the speech and hearing sciences as the general term for all aspects of speech production.

In a highly opaque writing system like the English alphabet code, there are multiple spellings for the same sound and multiple decodings for the same letter or digraph. Opaque writing systems are hard to teach and learn, and unless teachers use methods that mitigate these difficulties, children can easily become confused and fail to learn to read.

If success in learning to read is intimately bound to the form of the script, no universal laws can be applied to it. This rules out the popular notion that "dyslexia" is due to some inherent (brain-based) flaw in the child. In English-speaking countries, the primary measure of dyslexia is decoding skill. If decoding skill was influenced by some biological predisposition, dyslexia ought to appear in all populations at the same rate. But dyslexia is virtually nonexistent in the countries listed above. All children (no exceptions) decode and spell at very high levels of accuracy. If biology (genes) isn't the culprit, then the problem is environmental. There is no other option. We will see how this complicates the interpretation of the data as the book progresses.

The second piece of evidence is more direct. In my research on children's reading strategies (McGuinness 1997a), I found that by the end of first grade, children in whole-language classrooms were using three different decoding strategies. A small minority were decoding primarily by phonemes (one sound at a time). Another group, whom I call "part-word decoders," searched for recognizable little words or word fragments inside bigger words. The third group ("whole-word guessers") decoded the first letter phonetically, then guessed the word by its length and shape—the overall visual pattern made by the letter string. Very few children used a pure sight-word strategy (the telephone-number strategy), and the children who did usually stopped reading before the end of the school year.

Reading test scores reflected these strategies, with the phonemic decoders superior, part-word decoders next, and whole-word guessers the worst. When these children were followed to third grade, the whole-word guessers had not changed their approach and were the undisputed worst readers in the class. Some part-word decoders had graduated to phonemic decoding, but the majority of the third graders remained primarily part-word decoders. Once more, phonemic decoders were far and away the best readers. This shows that children are active learners, and when confronted with vague or misleading guidelines for how to read, they try out strategies to overcome this difficulty. The fact that the strategies are different, and that they tend to stay constant over such a long period of time, is strong evidence against a developmental explanation.[2] The most successful methods teach the phonemic basis of the alphabet code from day one. Children taught with these methods were 1 or more years ahead of control groups and national norms. Remedial programs based on the same principles can correct a child's decoding strategy and improve reading scores by 1 to 2 years in about 12 hours or less (C. McGuinness, D. McGuinness, and G. McGuinness 1996). There is little support in these examples for a biological explanation for reading failure. (Where do the bad genes go in 12 hours?)

However, the question remains as to whether some type of delay or abnormality in language development compounds the problem. I turn next to the first biological explanation, the theory that individual differences in reading skill are caused by differences in the development of phonological awareness. This theory has been the mainstay of reading research and has influenced early reading instruction in the schools. To find out why reading researchers adopted a biological framework rather than an experiential one, we need to review a little history.

A Potted History of How We Got Where We Are

Several important historical events led us to this point. Two are critical to this story. The universal-education movement had the inadvertent effect of shutting down the first real breakthrough in how to teach our complex alphabet code, fostering the implementation of whole-word ("sight-word") teaching methods. Whole-word methods have dominated our classrooms for nearly 100 years and continuing.

The second event was an accident of fate. In the 1960s, Bond and Dykstra (1967) carried out the definitive study to end the "reading wars" between whole-word methods and phonics. Unfortunately, the data were handled incorrectly, with the result that no reading method appeared to be better than any other. This had far-ranging consequences, not the least

---

2. The inefficient and error-prone part-word decoder doesn't disappear with time. About one-quarter of my college students read this way.

of which was the diversion of research funding from the study of reading methods to studies with a clinical focus, addressing the problem: What's wrong with poor readers?

The initial breakthrough occurred in the mid-nineteenth century, when Isaac Pitman, a self-taught linguist and inventor of the famous "shorthand" method, had a flash of insight about how to teach our complex writing system. He observed that children in many other European countries had the benefit of a transparent alphabet while English children did not. Pitman's solution was to level the playing field, at least in the initial phase of reading instruction, by setting up what I call an "artificial transparent alphabet." Pitman's alphabet consisted of a one-to-one correspondence between the forty English phonemes and the letters of the alphabet plus new symbols for the leftover sounds. A one-to-one correspondence between phonemes and symbols provides children with critically important information about how alphabet codes work:

• They are based on the unchanging sounds (phonemes) in our speech. The number of these speech sounds is finite, providing an end point for managing the code.
• Letters are not the units of the code but are *arbitrary symbols* for those units.
• All codes are reversible. Reading and spelling (decoding/encoding) are mirror images of one another and should be taught together.

Pitman and a colleague, A. J. Ellis, worked to implement this new approach in the classroom, but the definitive program based on this idea was developed in the late 1890s by a classroom teacher named Nellie Dale. Instead of using arbitrary symbols, Dale set up what I call a *basic code*. This consists of forty phonemes, each represented by its most common spelling.

This not only makes the code transparently easy to teach, but spelling alternatives can easily be added later with no change in logic. Once the forty sounds and their forty basic spellings are mastered, teachers can move on to say: "There's another way to spell this sound. I'll show you how to remember when to use this spelling." This way, phonemes remain constant as the spellings expand. Phonemes form the basis for the code— an end point—around which the code can reverse. This preserves the true nature of a code in which encoding and decoding are two sides of the same coin.

This contrasts with the more typical phonics programs where the learning is letter-driven and phonemes are nowhere in sight. Children are told that letters can "make" sounds or "say" sounds. As reading progresses, these magic letters make more and more different sounds. Because letters and digraphs can be decoded in over 350 different ways, there is now no way to get back to the 40 phonemes, which voids the logic of an alphabet code.

The universal-education movement brought this breakthrough to a halt and plunged us into a century of whole-word methods. Fortunately, these insights weren't lost entirely. Programs similar to Dale's began to reappear in the 1960s and got some attention. Pitman's grandson designed the "initial teaching alphabet" (i.t.a.), which was launched in a vast experiment in the United Kingdom. In the United States, McCracken and Walcutt (1963) developed a program based on earlier work, which is now known as "Lippincott" after the publisher. Modern research on reading began in the 1960s, with the new tools of statistics and the publication of two ambitious projects. One mainly involved an observational analysis of reading instruction in the schools (Chall 1967), and the other was Bond and Dykstra's (1967) study, the largest experiment ever conducted on the efficacy of different types of reading instruction.

Although Chall's book contained much valuable information, it created a central contradiction. On the one hand, her largely anthropological account of classroom practices gave the impression that a teacher's skill was as important as, or more important than, the method. She observed on many occasions that a good teacher could make a potentially boring lesson interesting, while a poor teacher could make an interesting lesson dull. On the other hand, her use of simple tallies to summarize the results of the studies on reading methods dating back to the early 1900s gave the strong message that the method was overwhelmingly more important than the teacher. (That there were huge methodological problems with most of these studies goes without saying, and this provided a field day for critics.)

Bond and Dykstra (1967) measured the progress of over 9,000 first graders who were either taught some type of phonics, such as i.t.a. or Lippincott, or one of the whole-word "basal" programs of the day. This project was extremely well designed and well controlled, so it is all the more surprising that the data were handled incorrectly. Instead of using the test scores of the individual children, the investigators converted the data to classroom means. This dramatically reduced statistical power, changing the focus of the study (the study design) from one comparing *children* learning different methods to one comparing *classrooms*—teachers perhaps?[3]

As a result, outcomes were wildly erratic, varying from classroom to classroom and school to school, and seemed to show that no method was consistently superior to any other method on any measure. Yet when I reassessed the data, the Lippincott program, the method most similar to Dale's, was the outright winner. It was superior to every other program on every reading test (decoding, word analysis, fluency, and comprehension) by a constant 6-month advantage in gains across the board.

Unfortunately, no one knew this in 1967. Instead, because no method appeared consistently better than any other method, the inescapable conclusion was that *methods didn't matter*. Rather than solving the "reading wars" between whole-word methods and phonics, which was the intended goal of their project, Bond and Dykstra created a void. As Pearson said in his commentary on the recent reprinting of this study (1997, 431). "The First-Grade Studies were a dismal failure, for they (in conjunction with Chall's book) marked the end of the methodological comparisons in research on beginning reading."

(An analysis of this history and related themes is provided in *Early Reading Instruction*.)

How Reading Research Got Off Track

The void was filled by a new approach to reading instruction, and a new focus for reading research. Although one can never know the precise historical factors that shape future events, it seems likely that if everyone believed the definitive study to end all studies showed no special benefit for any type of method, the conclusion must be that all methods of reading instruction will have equal success. And if the teacher is at least as

---

3. In technical terms, this meant that the "within-subjects variance" was coming from the classrooms and not from the *children* within classrooms. For an analysis of this issue, see *Early Reading Instruction*.

important as the method, as Chall's classroom observations seemed to indicate, then any method will do.

Among the various whole-word methods being touted at the time, the one that endeared itself most to teachers' hearts was the notion that children could teach themselves to read by mere exposure to good children's literature—guessing words by visual memory and "context cues." And, if children engage in creative writing from the outset, they can teach themselves to spell by inventing their own spelling system ("invented spelling"). This approach became known as *whole language* (*real books* in the United Kingdom). It took the English-speaking world by storm with disastrous consequences, leading to functional illiteracy rates as high as 60 percent in the countries or states where it was mandated (see NAEP reports in Mullis, Campbell, and Farstrup 1993; Campbell et al. 1996).

Meanwhile, with funding withdrawn from research on reading methods, scientists had to look elsewhere. The focus shifted to children with reading difficulties, and mainstream reading research was largely reoriented to the study of reading predictors. The predominant question was reframed from "How should we teach children to read?" to "What is wrong with poor readers?"

In the 1960s, researchers had little idea which natural endowments (if any) give rise to an ability or inability to learn to read. One important finding in Bond and Dykstra's study did command attention. This was the discovery that phoneme discrimination was strongly correlated to subsequent reading skill, whereas visual perceptual skill (pattern recognition) was not. This directed researchers' attention toward an investigation of the language-reading connection, and to the gradual abandonment of the notion that poor readers were "word blind," suffering from some as-yet-unidentified visual perceptual impairment.

The Phonological-Development Theory Is Born
The shift from experimental research on reading methods to the correlational-type research on the nature of individual differences had unexpected consequences. Early on, the field was captured by the first coherent theory that appeared on the horizon. This was the theory that phonological awareness follows a prescribed developmental path from words to syllables to phonemes, and this determines when and how to teach reading.

The theory was first proposed in 1973–1974 (I. Y. Liberman 1973; Liberman et al. 1974). It has dominated the landscape for 30 years and continues to drive every area of the field, from research funding, to the choice of a thesis topic, to the development of phonological-awareness training programs and the implementation of these programs by the schools.

Unfortunately, this theory is not supported by the data. The original study which gave rise to the theory did not measure what it purported to measure. Two decades of research in the field shows that awareness of phonological units larger than the phoneme is irrelevant to learning alphabetic writing systems. Subsequent research on language development carried out by scientists in other disciplines provides no support for the particular sequence outlined in the theory. Despite this, the theory has not been abandoned.

Incorrect theories are part and parcel of the scientific process, and, as a rule, theories are revised when contradictory data come in. But incorrect theories can be dangerous when they turn into dogma and have practical and social consequences. The theory that phonological awareness develops in a specific way matters enormously when it purports to provide a complete account of individual differences in reading skill. This model has been used to determine when children should be taught to read. It pretends to explain "dyslexia," along with dire prophecies of continued failure. It has led to changes in early reading curricula that are remote from the logic and structure of the successful reading programs outlined in the National Reading Panel report.

In the new curricula spawned by the phonological-development theory, children are taught to discriminate and analyze every sound unit in speech (words, syllables, rhyming endings, phonemes) under the misguided assumption that this mimics the developmental sequence in speech perception. Even the ancient scholars who designed writing systems as long ago as 5,000 BC didn't make this mistake! All writing systems, past or present, are based on one type of phonetic unit below the level of the word, and *never more than one*. If sound units were mixed in a writing system, this would make it far too difficult to learn. Nor does it make any sense to teach an array of irrelevant sound units as preparation for learning a different sound unit. Children need to learn which sound unit the letters mark, not all the sound units the letters *don't* mark. This is tantamount to teaching several writing systems at the same time.

In part I, I will be reviewing the scientific research on the development of speech recognition and early productive language. Most of this research comes from disciplines outside the field of reading, and provides an objective test of the theory.

A Methodological Trap

Another problem in reading research is a consequence of the change in focus from reading methods to the study of poor readers. In any new field of inquiry, descriptive and correlational methodology guide the way, serving the function of mapping the territory or the "domain of inquiry." This is the tried-and-true means of discovering what might predispose a child to reading difficulties—though correlations can never prove causality. In this type of study, a large group of children is given a variety of tests, including a reading test, to find out which skills are most highly correlated to reading and which are not. Subsequently, these skills can be studied in carefully designed experiments.

But there's another way, one that involves a fatal shortcut. Taking this path has led reading researchers into a methodological quagmire. In this type of research design, a large number of children are given a standardized reading test as before. On the basis of how they scored, the children are assigned to "good" and "poor" reader groups, and the remaining children are dismissed from the study. The two groups are given more tests thought (or known) to be related to reading skill and then compared statistically. This, in essence, pits two segments of a normal distribution against one another, while at the same time heavily weighting one of these segments (poor readers) out of proportion to their actual numbers in the population.

I have christened this the *isolated-groups design* for obvious reasons. The isolated-groups design can't be found in any book on research design or statistics, because it violates every assumption of the mathematics of probability on which statistics is based (normal distribution, equal variances, random assignment to groups). This means that the vast majority of the scientific papers on reading published over the last 30 years (the most common studies in the refereed journals) are invalid, correlational-*type* studies in which groups of good and poor readers are compared on a variety of perceptual, motor, linguistic, and cognitive tasks. I use the word *type* to refer to the fact that these studies often masquerade as "experiments" (and employ the inferential statistics used for experimental research designs) when they are really bogus correlational studies in disguise.

The isolated-groups design has had the effect of plunging modern research on reading back in time, back to the days before statistical tests were available for the behavioral sciences. All that can be reliably reported from this kind of study are average scores, with no way to infer anything beyond this. (The isolated-groups design and other key methodological issues are discussed in chapters 9 and 11.)

Research on Language Development

The phonological-development theory is based on a putative developmental sequence for receptive language from infancy to childhood. Yet, despite the fact that this sequence is central to the theory, it has never been tested directly by the authors of the theory, or anyone else in the field. Meanwhile, language development has been assessed and mapped quite thoroughly by scientists in other disciplines.

Unlike reading research, mainstream research on language development has continued apace with no setbacks and is one of the great success stories of the behavioral sciences. There has been extraordinary progress due to innovations in how children are tested, technological advances in stimulus control and presentation, and a uniform set of goals within each field of study. By and large this research provides a different perspective on which language functions matter most for reading and academic success. I have divided this research into two parts. The first part includes studies on the early development of receptive language and bears directly on the validity of the phonological-development theory. This work is presented in part I.

The second group of studies includes the research on expressive and general language development, including higher-order language functions like syntax and semantics. The impact of delays or impairments in these core language skills on academic progress has been revealed in longitudinal studies largely carried out by researchers in the speech and hearing sciences. These studies are covered in part II. They reveal a tantalizing connection between core language functions, reading skill, and academic success.

Overall, a broad range of studies from a variety of disciplines show that no child, short of being deaf, mute, or grossly mentally disabled, is prevented by a language delay or deficit from learning "reading mechanics"—the ability to master the code sufficiently to read (decode) and spell (encode). Cossu, Rossini, and Marshall (1993) have shown that children with Down's syndrome (with an average IQ of 44) can master the transparent Italian alphabet code with sufficient skill to read words at a third- or fourth-grade reading level, even though they don't understand what they read and fail dismally on phonological-awareness tests.

The longitudinal studies, on the other hand, show that serious delays in core language functions like expressive vocabulary, syntax, and semantics put a child at high risk for difficulties with more advanced reading skills, like reading comprehension. This is due to a complex interaction of factors that, so far, have not been teased apart. Core language functions are a product of heredity, "shared environment," and "unshared environment," such as a school system. There is certainly compelling evidence implicating educational practice in this equation.

Here is one small piece of the puzzle. Beitchman and his colleagues in Toronto followed a large number of children with language delays and/or speech-motor problems from age 5 to age 19. Initially they were matched by sex, age, and classroom to a control group of children who were normal in every way. One of the more intriguing findings was that 9 percent of the control group subsequently fit the diagnosis "language impaired" by age 19. Vocabulary scores had plummeted to a standard score of 80 or worse (100 is average), and this was accompanied by seriously impoverished reading skills and academic test scores. How does one explain this? I submit that it is just as likely that poor reading instruction leads to maladaptive decoding strategies and poor reading comprehension, which in turn *cause* language skills and academic progress to stagnate over time, as it is likely for a child's once-normal language skills to take a nosedive for no apparent reason. (Beitchman's research is covered in chapter 8.)

Reading researchers and educators know little about the research on language development, just as the scientists who study language development know little about reading research. With rare exceptions, the two groups don't communicate or share research findings. They publish in different journals, attend different academic meetings, and scarcely know of one another's existence. One of my goals is to remedy this situation as well as appeal to the general reader interested in these important and fascinating studies.

The Goals of Science

The fact that the majority of studies in reading research over the past 30 years are limited to the phonological-development framework means this book is as much about the nature of scientific inquiry as it is about the connection between language development and learning to read. It is a story of the extraordinary success of one scientific endeavor and the sad failure of another. It is a testament to how and why modes of inquiry can lead either to greater knowledge or to increasing obfuscation.

Success in science begins with asking the right questions in the right order and knowing how to answer them. Failure is more likely to follow a pattern of presupposing something to be true ahead of time and setting out to prove it. The beauty of the scientific method is that it is the only system devised that shows us there's a real world out there, one that might not conform to what we believe. The trick comes in changing our thinking to accommodate the data, and not in further attempts to prove what we think we know.

By and large, mainstream research on language development and language acquisition carried out by scientists in a variety of disciplines is methodologically sound and rigorous. Research on the putative causes of success or failure in learning to read is not. This is a serious state of affairs, because false theories continue to drive research as well as what goes on during early reading instruction. It will come as a surprise to many readers familiar with this literature that not one of these popular theories is supported by the data:

1. The theory that explicit awareness of the phonological structure of language develops in the following sequence: words, syllables, phonemes. (Nor does this sequence fit the development of implicit perceptual abilities of the infant and toddler.)
2. The theory that children become poor readers because they have phonological or phoneme-processing deficits.
3. The theory that poor readers have a speech-motor disorder or developmental delay.

4. The theory that poor readers have a general (nonspecific) auditory-processing disorder.

5. The theory that poor readers have slower "naming speeds" than good readers.

In essence, *Language Development and Learning to Read* provides an inductive analysis of the data that leads to the conclusion that new theories, as yet unformulated, must replace old theories that have dominated the landscape for 30 years. This requires a major shift in our thinking, one that can only occur if there is a detailed (and fair) explication of the facts. Some of these facts are bold and obvious (even breathtaking). But most of the time, "facts" are more like fleas or gremlins, minor methodological quirks that can sink a study. They may hinge on technical details or on how well a study measures what it purports to measure.

For these reasons and more, my analyses of many studies (some high profile, some unknown) are very detailed in order to make specific and important points. Readers are welcome to skip "the proof" and go on to the summaries, but don't blame me if you don't agree with the conclusions. I strongly advise readers *not* to skip the two chapters on methodology at the beginning of part III. They are the most important chapters in this section. They spell out the three key problems in reading research that seriously undermine the field. Without this background, the research presented in part III can't be adequately evaluated.

On the Problem of Deductive Theories in Science

Because this book is largely cast in an inductive framework—evaluating current theories in light of the true facts—and reading research is mainly deductive in orientation, I need to address the problem of deductive theories in science. Reading research abounds with deductive theories, like those listed above. They continue to drive the field despite the mounting evidence against them. Often these theories are spawned from one or two studies, or even constructed *prior to* doing any research. A deductive theory has some validity for guiding future research, but not if you think it provides the answer before you have it. If universal education set us back to the mid-nineteenth century, and an invalid research design to the mid-twentieth century, unsubstantiated deductive theories take us out of the realm of science altogether.

There is no more illuminating assessment of the danger of deductive models in science than Francis Bacon's *Novum Organum* ([1620] 2004). His words are as valid today as they were nearly 400 years ago.[4]

Particularly relevant here is Bacon's analysis of the reasons people (and the scientists among them) can easily become seduced by what he called "undemonstrated speculations or hypotheses." In his colorful language, Bacon identified these reasons as a set of "Idols" that correspond roughly to mental fallacies.

The Idols of the Tribe reflect human nature in general, which tends to make us "suppose the existence of more order and regularity in the world than it finds" (Bacon, in Urbach 1987, 86). This creates a tendency to close off prematurely on a theory with a "simple pattern" and then become dogmatic about it: "The human understanding when it has once adopted an opinion ... draws all things else to support and agree with it. And though there be a greater number and weight of instances to be found on the other side, yet these it either neglects and despises, or else by some distinction sets aside and rejects" (p. 86).

The Idols of the Cave reflect a person's state of mind—a consequence of his or her constitution, education, and training: "Men become attached to certain particular sciences and speculations, either because they fancy themselves the authors and inventors thereof, or because they have bestowed the greatest pains upon them and become most habituated to them" (p. 88).

As a result, scientists will fail to look for remote, heterogeneous, or contradictory examples, and cling to what they know: "The human understanding is moved by those things most which strike and enter the mind simultaneously and suddenly, and so fill the imagination; and then it feigns and supposes all other things to be somehow similar to those few things by which it is surrounded" (p. 89).

Bacon offered this good advice: "Generally let every student of nature take this as a rule,—that whatever his mind seizes and dwells upon with peculiar satisfaction is to be held in suspicion" (p. 90).

Idols of the Marketplace refer to "following the crowd" and/or adopting lay language or terms that are imprecise (unscientific) to describe or

4. I have used the translations of Bacon's works in Urbach 1987.

explain scientific phenomena. This tends to commit the user to their corresponding theories and leads to two types of semantic fallacies: (1) assuming everyone means the same thing by the same term, and (2) assuming that naming something explains it or solves the problem of defining what it is. Again, as Bacon pointed out, this makes it difficult to look at the data in new ways: "Whenever an understanding of greater acuteness or a more diligent observation would alter those lines to suit the true divisions of nature, words stand in the way and resist the change" (p. 92).

Instead, Bacon argued, the proper way of science is through induction, which begins with the gathering of facts through rigorous observations and experiments, and ends with a systematization of those facts: "The true method of experience ... first lights the candle, and then by means of the candle shows the way; commencing as it does with experience duly ordered and digested, not bungling or erratic, and from it educing axioms, and from established axioms again, new experiments" (p. 33).

The scientist should provide, within reasonable limits, systematic observations and experiments that show the same effect in different contexts, plus experiments that attempt to *disprove* the premise or hypothesis before any theory is framed. Once all reasonable objections to any hypothesis have been ruled out, a theory is constructed that is faithful to the data. This is the essence of inductive theory building, the classical model in science. The inductive process, truth in reporting, and staying within the limits of the data are the backbone of the scientific method, and the reasons for its success.

Even Darwin ([1892] 1958, 55) confessed he was not immune to the Idols, and issued a stern warning against deductive theorizing in his autobiography:

I have steadily endeavored to keep my mind free so as to give up any hypothesis, however much beloved (and I cannot resist forming one on every subject), as soon as facts are shown to be opposed to it. . . . For with the exception of the Coral Reefs, I cannot remember a single first-formed hypothesis which had not after a time to be given up or greatly modified. This has naturally led me to distrust greatly deductive reasoning in the mixed sciences.

This fascinating, personal validation of Bacon's great insights is especially significant coming from a genius who carried out the greatest feat of inductive reasoning in the history of science—integrating thousands of facts, observations, and empirical data into one great theory that, so far, has not been defeated by any one of them.

In the following chapters, I will be putting several of the more influential deductive theories under the microscope to see how they hold up when research outside the field is brought to bear on them.

The Structure of the Book

This book is divided into three parts. Part I reviews the theory that phonological awareness develops in a particular sequence and affects the ability to learn an alphabetic writing system. It explores the research evidence on the development of speech perception and receptive language that provides a direct test of the theory. By and large, the studies come from disciplines outside the field, including developmental psychology, psycholinguistics, and psychophysics. The findings consistently refute the theory that the development of speech perception over childhood follows the pattern predicted by the phonological-development theory.

If the theory is incorrect, so too are the phonological-awareness training programs based on it, which explains why they are so ineffective. The NRP report shows that phonological training programs have a much smaller impact on reading skill (if any) than does a well-designed linguistic phonics program that teaches phoneme-letter correspondences at the outset. Furthermore, reading instruction based on rhyme and analogy are no more effective than garden-variety basals or whole-language programs. The final chapters in part I address the evidence on young children's skill in the analysis of phonemes and phoneme sequences, along with the implications of these findings for how and when reading should be taught.

Part II is devoted to the longitudinal studies on the development of general language functions, and the connection between speech production, receptive and productive vocabulary, semantics, syntax, and subsequent reading and academic skills. This work has largely been carried out by phoneticians, linguists, psycholinguists, and the research arm of the speech and hearing sciences. It is virtually free of deductive thinking and has the goal of mapping the impact of language development on academic success over extended periods of time. These scientists have uncovered a language-literacy connection that is far more complex and more important than anything found so far.

Part III focuses on the mainstream reading research that attempts to link reading ability to specific language skills. The areas of interest here are vocabulary, verbal memory, syntax, and naming speed or fluency. The more systematic and better controlled studies help answer the following question: If core language functions are intimately connected to levels of literacy and to academic success (as part II shows), which language aptitudes matter most? There are serious methodological problems with a majority of studies in this field due to the ubiquitous isolated-groups design. For this reason, two short chapters (chapters 9 and 11) are devoted to an analysis of methodology.

A final summary of the important evidence in this book, and what it means, is provided in chapter 17.

Basic research on language development is technically and conceptually complex, yet addresses questions that are focused and highly systematic. Reading research, on the other hand, is technically and conceptually simple, but addresses questions that are unsystematic and disconnected. I have done my best to organize this broad range of material around certain themes, but this has not been an easy task. If I haven't quite succeeded, I apologize in advance. In a very real sense *I am the messenger more than the author of this book.*

I

THE THEORY THAT PHONOLOGICAL AWARENESS DEVELOPS

THE ORIGIN OF THE THEORY OF PHONOLOGICAL DEVELOPMENT

Not long ago I tuned into the local weather channel to pinpoint the precise location of the thunderstorm I could hear rumbling in the distance. I was heading out for dinner with a friend and didn't want to get caught in a downpour. During Florida summers, these ministorms circulate around the landscape in whimsical fashion like little whirling dervishes, dumping an inch of rain in one location and none only blocks away. As I gazed at the enhanced radar, time-lapse illustration of the path of this storm, the weatherman began to speak. I call him Walter. Walter had been broadcasting the weather for several years, and he was announcing a special new event in his peculiar, flat voice, which is seriously deficient in prosody:

THE WEA-THER SER-VICE AT RUS-KIN WID LIKE TO A-NNOUNCE THAT IT WILL BE IN-STALL-ING A NOO COM-POO-TER VOICE SYS-TEM IN THE NEAR FOO-CHER. THIS WILL BE A GRIT IM-PRUV-MENT O-VER THE VOICE YOU ARE CURR-ENT-LY LIS-TEN-ING TO. THIS NOO SYS-TUM WILL BE A-BLE TO PRU-NOUNCE THE NAMES OF FLOR-I-DA CI-TIES MORE AC-RATE-LY THAN THE VOICE YOU ARE HEAR-ING NOW.

This was stunning. Walter, who over the years had won a soft spot in my heart, was indifferently casting doubt on his ability to pronounce words. He was, in effect, announcing his own demise without a shred of emotion. What a guy!

Walter is, of course, the weather robot, the computer-activated voice that reads off printed weather reports on the fly. The fact that computer voice recognition, and in this case, computer translation from text to voice, has not been a great success so far, tells us something about the complexity of speech perception, speech production, and reading, topics of the first six chapters of this book.

Walter is a product of two attempts at simulation. First, he had to be trained on pronouncing individual words (voice recognition/voice production). This is accomplished via an electronic analysis of the auditory signals in normal human speech, plus techniques for transforming those signals back into recognizable speech electronically. Walter goes one better, by being able to *read*, translating (transforming) printed text into his peculiar speech. Walter's mispronunciation problems are partly due to poor speech production (absence of melody, incorrect syllable stress, and mangled phonemes) and partly due to the fact that, so far, no electronic device can replicate natural speech or fill in the gaps created by our unpredictable spelling system. How could a computer, for example, handle changes in pronunciation caused by shifts in syntax?

Walter *read* the weather report for 3 years.
Walter can *read* the weather report without pausing for breath.

What Walter can't do, human infants and toddlers *can* without effort or special external programming. The issue for us here, is how speech recognition (receptive language) develops, and whether there is any evidence that individual differences in this developmental process affect learning to read.

Signs of the Times

To set the stage for the origin of the theory that phonological awareness develops in a specific sequence and manner, we need to go back to the late 1960s. The most significant event in the history of reading research was the failure of the largest study ever conducted on reading methods (Bond and Dykstra 1967). This had the inadvertent effect of reorienting research on reading away from a study of methods toward a more clinical focus, largely because that's where research funding was available.

Bond and Dykstra had more success with the correlational part of their study. They found that reading skill was significantly correlated to phoneme discrimination, but not to visual pattern recognition. This shifted people's thinking away from the popular visual model of reading difficulties toward a phonological explanation. Success in learning to read appeared to have something to do with a child's aptitude for analyzing sound sequences in speech. The fact that phoneme discrimination measured at the start of the school year predicted reading test scores measured at the end of the year added more credibility to this idea. Lag correlations are about as close as one can come to causality in correlational research, using the logic that time doesn't run backward. (This finding, of course, can't rule out other possibilities. For example, children who are taught to read at home generally enter school with superior phoneme-analysis skills.)[1]

In the same year, another landmark study was published by A. M. Liberman and his colleagues at the Haskins Laboratories (A. M. Liberman et al. 1967). This was a major review of the research on speech recognition in adults, heralding exciting new discoveries. These studies will be reviewed in the next chapter, but one of the most significant findings was that phonemes appear to have no physical identity. They overlap each other in speech to such an extent that there is no way to isolate them electronically. According to the laws of acoustics, a phoneme is an impossibility, even though it is quite real psychologically. This problem is still unsolved, which is why Walter the Weatherman can't be programmed to speak properly.[2]

Not long after this review appeared, researchers studying early language development discovered that infants a week or two old can discriminate between CV syllables that differ by one phoneme, like "ba" and "pa" (Eimas et al. 1971). This extraordinary result shows that newborns have a built-in phonetic discriminator, one that electronic machines

---

1. As noted earlier, I will use the term *phonological* to refer to all sound units in the speech stream, including the word. The term *phoneme* is reserved for its proper meaning: the individual consonants and vowels in a language. A phoneme is the smallest unit of sound in speech that human listeners can be aware of. Alphabetic writing systems mark phonemes and no other phonological unit.

2. I should add that Walter wasn't fired after all. He got a colleague instead. But while his colleague sounds more mellifluous and less robotic, he has an annoying 'abit of 'ropping his initial 'onsonants.

can't emulate. This discovery launched a flood of new research on neonate and infant language development.

It was in the context of these events that a group of American researchers developed the phonological theory of reading acquisition. According to this theory, there is a slow process of phonological development from infancy through early childhood that influences a child's ability to be aware of phonemes. For this reason, children with impoverished phonological skills, or a slow development of these skills, are likely to have difficulty learning an alphabetic writing system. Over the next decade, similar points of view were expressed by English researchers studying auditory perception, phonological awareness, and reading.

Today, the "phonological-awareness development" theory permeates every facet of reading research from the study of reading predictors, to protocols for prereading curricula and reading instruction, to the nature of "dyslexia" and guidelines for remedial reading programs. This is remarkable in view of the fact that the theory has never been tested directly. That is, no one in the field has actually studied the development of speech recognition in infancy and childhood. The scientific evidence in support of the theory consists of one behavioral study with a seriously flawed premise. Despite this, the theory has dominated the field for over 30 years with negative consequences for the field as a whole, as well as for educational practice.

The Cast of Characters

The phonological-development theory of reading acquisition was initially proposed as a hypothesis by Isabelle Liberman (1973; Liberman et al. 1974), the wife of A. M. Liberman cited above. The theory's longevity is due to the fact that it sounds credible, was persuasively argued, and has been promoted via the extensive research efforts of Liberman, her colleague Donald Shankweiler, and the many students they trained. To ensure that their ideas are represented as accurately as possible, I will quote from the 1974 paper.

The hypothesis links the evolution of writing systems to the developmental aptitude of children for learning to read an alphabetic writing system, with the caveat that children's difficulty in learning to read is largely due to problems with phonological analysis. This is a biological theory of speech perception.

An analogy between the evolution of writing systems and children's receptive language development appears in the abstract to the paper: "Writing systems based on the meaningless units, syllables and phonemes were late developments in the history of written language.... The present study provides direct evidence of a similar developmental ordering of syllable and phoneme segmentation abilities in the young child" (p. 201).

The notion that writing systems "evolve" comes from Gelb (1963), whose evolutionary model was hailed by reading researchers, even though it was regarded with considerable skepticism by his colleagues in paleography (Coulmas 1989). Here is Liberman et al.'s understanding of Gelb's theory:

In the historical development of writing, systems that used meaningful units came first.... Something like the word was the segment most commonly represented, at least in those systems that have a transparent relation to speech. One thinks of Chinese writing ... as a present-day approximation to this method in which the segment represented is the word.... Writing with meaningless units is a more recent development.... The segment size that was represented in all the earliest examples was ... that of the syllable. An alphabet representing segments of phonemic size was developed later. It is clear, moreover, that the alphabet developed historically out of a syllabary, and that this important development occurred just once. (p. 202)

Gelb has a lot to answer for, because none of these statements is true. A writing system based on meaningless elements is the *only* way a writing *system* can work (as opposed to a system of accounting or inventory control). Meaningful units (word symbols) were tried during the initial development of several writing systems. This solution was abandoned early on, because no one can memorize thousands of word-symbol pairs, not even the Chinese. "Writing with meaningless units" is not a "recent development," unless 3,000 BC (Egyptian consonant symbols) is considered "recent." Writing systems do not evolve into syllabaries and then into alphabets. Syllabaries are rare among writing systems, living or dead (Coulmas 1989; Daniels and Bright 1996; McGuinness 1997b; see *Early Reading Instuction* for an analysis of writing systems).

Based on these misconceptions, Liberman et al. argued by analogy to children's aptitude for segmenting units of speech, speculating that this aptitude would develop in the same order as writing systems: *word*, *syllable*, *phoneme*. This is a strange analogy, coming perilously close to "ontogeny recapitulates phylogeny," as if the capacity to design a writing system was a biological process that evolved over thousands of years, and learning how to decode a writing system reflects that process. The hidden inference in Gelb's theory is that humans not only evolved but got *smarter* over time, and writing systems became more sophisticated as a result. By adopting this model, Liberman et al. imply that children mimic this evolution developmentally. Framing this process in historical terms doesn't solve the problem: "We are tempted to suppose that the historical development of writing might reflect the ease (or difficulty) with which explicit segmentation can be carried out.... More to the point—we should suppose that for the child there might be the same order of difficulty, and, correspondingly, the same order of appearance in development" (p. 202).

Unfortunately for the theory, there is persuasive evidence from the comparative analysis of writing systems that ancient scholars must have been aware of the phonemes in their language, otherwise they could never have designed them, regardless of which phonological unit was involved (see *Early Reading Instruction*). There is no evidence of any historical sequence due to difficulty hearing phonemes. Quite the contrary. This is not to say that the ease of hearing specific phonological units didn't play a role in choosing the ultimate form of the writing system. For the most part, this choice was based on the structure of the language and on the *principle of least effort*: choose the largest unit (most clearly audible) that fits the linguistic/phonological structure of the language but that doesn't overload memory.

The fact that the languages themselves can't be carved up neatly into word-syllable-phoneme divisions is also a major problem for the evolutionary theory and the phonological-development theory alike. The majority of the world's languages are largely based on concatenations of CV units (diphones), taking the form CVCVCV, as in the word *potato*. In Hamito-Semitic languages like Arabic and Hebrew, consonant sequences frame the meaning of the word (semantics), while vowels swap in and out signifying changes in grammar. Some languages are largely composed of vowel sequences, including vowel duplication, and very few consonants (Hawaiian has only seven: /k/ /h/ /l/ /m/ /n/ /p/ /w/). Some languages, like Chinese, are tonal languages, built on a small corpus of syllable units that are reused again and again with different tonal inflections (the word *tang* has nine meanings). No one-size-fits-all biological or evolutionary scheme fits these facts. If the phonology of natural language doesn't obey any hard-and-fast rules, it is highly unlikely that inventions to represent natural speech in symbols do either.

The critical fact about alphabets, and another strong argument against Gelb, is that they are far less common among the world's writing systems than those based on the CV diphone. Also, there is clear proof that the authors of three major writing systems (the Brahmi script, Old Persian, and Korean Han'gul) created an alphabet and *chose not to use it*, opting for the CV unit instead. Why? Here, the answer is identical to Liberman et al.'s, but for different reasons. The phoneme is the smallest (briefest) unit of sound a human listener can hear. Due to "coarticulation," phonemes flip by so fast that most of us aren't aware of them. There seem to be two main reasons why ancient scholars opted for a larger phonetic unit if the language allowed it:

1. *Auditory analysis.*   Larger units are easier to hear and extract from the speech stream.
2. *Efficiency.*   The more phonetic information that is packed into a single symbol, the faster it is to read and write text.

It is obvious from these examples that no biologically predetermined form is ordained for the specific phonology of a language. Furthermore, so few languages are syllable based, in the sense that the syllable provides consistent phonological information, that the syllable is unlikely to play a major role in phonological development.

Because most children learn a language with little apparent effort, what do they focus on to enable them to do this? If children couldn't hear phonemes, but just a blurry moosh of syllables, they would never understand speech, much less learn how to produce it, a fact that Liberman et al. were aware of:

It must be emphasized that the difficulty a child might have in explicit segmentation is not necessarily related to his problems, if any, with ordinary speech perception.... Indeed there is evidence now that infants at one month of age discriminate ba from pa (and da from ta); moreover, they make this discrimination categorically, just as adults do, when the physical difference between the phonemes is very small [a 40 ms difference].... But it does not follow from the fact that a child can easily distinguish *bad* from *bat* that he can therefore respond analytically to the phonemic structure that underlies the distinction, that is, that he can demonstrate an explicit understanding of the fact that each of these utterances consist of three segments and that the difference lies wholly in the third. (p. 203)

This adds a new wrinkle to the theory and sets up a major contradiction. Liberman et al. couldn't ignore this new research, and had to weave it into their theory. To do this, they made a distinction between *implicit* sensitivities and the *explicit* awareness of them. However, if phoneme awareness comes first in implicit development, but last in explicit development, this would mean that the "basic unit of speech perception" is unrelated to the development of an explicit awareness of the "basic unit speech perception"!

This runs counter to all we know about perceptual-motor development. Generally speaking, what you can respond to (orient to) indicates what you're aware of; the more attention you pay to whatever that is, the more "explicitly aware" of it you become. However, if the target of an infant or toddler's interest is no longer relevant due to the acquisition of some requisite skill, these perceptual events drop below the level of consciousness. (This doesn't mean they can't be recovered.) The classic example of this phenomenon is the difference between the novice and the experienced driver. Just because an individual is not consciously aware of something (putting on the brake), doesn't mean the brain isn't processing it.

Although Gelb's theory provided a convenient (and compelling) platform for framing Liberman's ideas, the real impetus for the theory was a training study reported in the same paper. This study, and a similar study carried out by Fox and Routh (1975), specifically address the issue of children's implicit knowledge of sounds in speech segments versus their explicit awareness of them.

Phonological-Awareness Tests May Not Measure What You Think
Phoneme analysis is difficult for the reasons stated above, but, according to Liberman et al., syllable segmenting is easy. The syllable stands out, be-

cause, as they put it, it has a "vocalic nucleus," a "peak of acoustic energy" (strong and weak beats). For this reason, young children should have greater success in learning to segment words into syllables than into phonemes. This idea had some support from the suggestion by A. M. Liberman et al. (1967) that speech recognition was organized at the level of the syllable and not the phoneme.

The study involved preschoolers, kindergartners, and first graders in the age range 5 to 7 years. The children were given instructions on how to tap out syllables (or phonemes) using a wooden dowel, and then were trained on either the syllable task or the phoneme task. Syllable tapping was by far the simpler task. The proportion of children meeting the criterion of six correct in a row was 46 percent for 5-year-olds, 48 percent for 6-year-olds, and 90 percent for 7-year-olds. In the phoneme-tapping task, the success rate was zero for 5-year-olds, 17 percent for 6-year-olds, and 70 percent for 7-year-olds, and even then, the successful children took about twenty-five trials to reach criterion.

The authors speculated on whether the sudden improvement between ages 6 and 7 was due to being taught an alphabetic writing system or to a developmental shift in language and greater intellectual maturity. They favored the developmental explanation but stated that more research was needed.

The following year, a similar study appeared that produced the opposite results. Fox and Routh (1975) were concerned about explicit awareness as well, and, like Liberman et al., they tended to view this as developmental. But they had quite a different notion about what this meant. They believed that children may be able to show you what they know implicitly, if the task is designed to make this knowledge *explicit for them*. In other words, children may know more than they know they know, or know more than they can show. Fox and Routh felt this couldn't be demonstrated in tasks with a high cognitive load. Their goal was to develop a task where all the child had to do was listen carefully and segment speech. (When this paper was published, Fox and Routh were unaware of the Liberman study, and did not comment on the tapping task.)

They set up a series of tasks requiring increasing levels of analysis of words in sentences. The instructions were always the same. The children were asked to "say just a little bit of it"—depending on what they heard.

First, the examiner read a sentence, and the children were asked to say a little bit of it (any part would do). Then they were asked to isolate each word from what remained. Next, they had to say a little bit of the two-syllable words, and finally a little bit of single syllables (phonemes). For syllables with three phonemes, there was a two-step process. The children were asked to say a little bit of *win*. If they said /w/, the tester said: "Now say a little bit of *in*." If the children said *wi*, they were asked to say a little bit of *wi*.

Fox and Routh tested fifty children age 3, 4, 5, 6, and 7 years old. The children were taught to repeat sentences verbatim along with the rules of the segmenting game (with a raisin for each success) before the tests began. The results showed that performance on sentence- and word-segmenting tasks was identical. Out of eight possible correct, 3-year-olds averaged five correct, and the other children got nearly perfect scores. The children also did well on segmenting a portion of a two-syllable word. However, when the responses were scored according to whether the syllable was segmented at an appropriate syllable boundary, they did not do so well. Average scores were 43, 58, 44, 66, and 75 percent across the age range.

The phoneme-segmentation test was another story. A perfect score was 32 (one for each phoneme correct). Three-year-olds didn't do too badly, scoring 28 percent correct (9 out of 32). Four-year-olds jumped ahead, scoring 63 percent correct. Five-year-olds were better still (78 percent correct), and the 6- and 7-year-olds had nearly perfect scores (90 percent correct).

These results show that when no complex cognitive operations are required, and the test is developmentally appropriate, very young children can do something "explicitly" even though they only knew it "implicitly." They can segment initial phonemes at high levels of accuracy after simple training in a short space of time. And though the 3-year-olds did poorly on the phoneme test, they didn't do nearly as poorly as the 6-year-olds in the Liberman study. Equally important, Fox and Routh found that the proportion correct on the phoneme task was much higher than the proportion correct for the strict scoring on the syllables task! Plus, they found no abrupt shift in accuracy on the phoneme task between ages 6 and 7. Instead, the biggest shift was between ages 3 and 4.

If you only read the Liberman paper, you would be convinced that syllable segmenting was far simpler than phoneme segmenting. If you only read the Fox and Routh paper, you would be convinced that phoneme segmenting was far simpler than syllable segmenting. This is about as clear an example as one can find of how the nature of the task controls the outcome. If you relied on Liberman et al.'s developmental interpretation of their data, you would begin to teach reading at age 6 or 7. If you relied on Fox and Routh's data, you could begin to teach reading at age 4.

To make sense of these contradictory results, let's look at what the child actually had to do. The title of the Liberman et al. paper begins "Explicit Syllable and Phoneme Segmentation...." But their task didn't require the child to segment syllables explicitly, only to identify syllable "beats" and tap them out. If you say the words *elephant*, *telephone*, *garden*, you can hear the strong and weak beats in each word. You don't have to be aware of which units are syllables to do this, any more than you need to be aware that a song is written in 2/4, 3/4, 4/4, or 6/8 time in order to clap in rhythm with the music.

Fox and Routh's syllable task did require segmenting. In the strict scoring method, children got credit only if they segmented words at an appropriate syllable boundary. If a child segmented *baby* as /b/ or *bab*, this was scored as an error. The child wasn't asked how many syllables there were.

There are no beats in phonemes, so Liberman's tapping task becomes an entirely different kettle of fish. To work out how many times to tap, the child has to say the word, segment each phoneme in sequence, hold this sequence in mind, and repeat it in synch with tapping the dowel, a difficult task with a heavy memory load. Fox and Routh's phoneme task isn't so much a segmenting task as a "phoneme-isolation" task. The child has to pull the initial phoneme (first sound) off the front of a syllable (CV, VC, or CVC). She doesn't have to hear or say the remaining phonemes in sequence, a much easier task. The unanswered question is which task (if either) is an appropriate measure of what a child needs to be able to do to learn an alphabetic writing system.

Fox and Routh concluded that children have much better phonological skills than people give them credit for, and felt their task provided a way to access children's capacity to exhibit these skills. They did not propose a theory on the basis of these results, but instead called for more research to discover which method of phoneme-analysis training would be most useful for beginning readers. It is of considerable interest that Fox and Routh's results were largely ignored. And as time passed, this study was actually cited *in support* of the findings of Liberman et al!

The phonological-awareness theory was framed on the basis of Liberman et al.'s single study plus the various ad hoc assumptions identified above. For the authors, "explicit phonological awareness" didn't mean implicit knowledge made conscious, but awareness that is fully cognitive and analytic. Children should be able to count phonemes in sequence and keep track of their precise location in order to decode an alphabetic writing system.

This theory has had profound implications. The notion that children gradually become aware developmentally that words are made up of individual phonemes means there is some optimum time to teach reading. Because Liberman et al. decreed that this optimum time occurs around the age of 6, this was taken as scientific affirmation of the status quo. Meanwhile, programs were written to introduce kindergartners to a potpourri of phonological units to prepare them for the difficult task of segmenting phonemes in words.

The mere existence of these phonological training programs is actually contradictory to the theory, which shows how mindless this has become. If phonological development is "biological," developing in a fixed sequence as is claimed, why do these phonological skills need to be trained? More to the point, *how could they be trained*? Forty years of research in developmental psychology shows that you can't train young children to learn to talk, nor correct their errant grammar; you can only model it. And when all is said and done, why direct children's attention to speech units like syllables that play no role in the writing system?

The phonological-development theory had a powerful, hypnotic effect on its authors. If you truly believe that reading acquisition depends entirely on the development of phonological awareness, there is a temptation to look at other correlates of reading skill as inevitably linked to phonological processing (human understanding "feigns and supposes all other things to be somehow similar").

This led to a one-cause-fits-all approach that appeared early on in a highly influential paper by the same group:

Since differential effects of phonetic confusability on good and poor readers occurred regardless of whether input was to the eye or to the ear, we suspect that difficulties of poor readers are not limited to the act of recoding from script, but that they are of a more general nature. A benefit of this hypothesis is that it permits us to bring together a number of previously unrelated findings regarding the cognitive characteristics of poor readers and permits us to view the findings as related manifestations of a *unitary underlying deficit.* (Shankweiler et al. 1979, 541; emphasis mine)

These "cognitive characteristics" included phonetic confusions and an abnormal verbal memory span. And despite the fact that good and poor readers in this study did not differ on any tests of speech perception or production, perhaps by probing deeper, such deficits may be found: "Subtle deficits might be demonstrated by children with reading disabilities in their perception of the acoustic cues for speech" (p. 543).

None of this is to say that Liberman and her colleagues believed that children couldn't be taught: "If it should be found that explicit segmentation of this kind is an important factor in reading disability, we should think ... that it should be possible (and desirable) to develop this ability by appropriate training methods" (Liberman et al. 1974, 211).

It isn't clear here whether this means that children with reading problems should get special remedial help, or whether appropriate training should be used in the first place for all beginning readers.

Update
Over the next decade, research accumulated that showed that performance on phoneme-awareness tests is significantly correlated to subsequent reading skill, while tests of visual memory or pattern recognition are not. The big question was whether this was a product of innate differences in phonological development, or a result of being taught to read an alphabetic writing system. In 1985, Liberman and Shankweiler provided an update of their theory, taking this new research into account. (It is worth

noting that Gelb's evolutionary model was conspicuously absent from this paper.)

Here's how they viewed the theory at this time: "We know that the child's awareness of phonological structure does not happen all at once, but develops gradually over a period of years" (p. 9). Liberman et al.'s 1974 study is the sole reference in support of this conclusion: "It was clear from these results that awareness of phoneme segments is harder to achieve than awareness of syllable segments, and develops later, if at all" (pp. 9–10).

In their discussion of the more recent research, the general term *phonological structure* is used to describe these results, despite the fact that most of the studies in their minireview showed that *phoneme awareness* was the critical factor in decoding skill. They devoted considerable space to their finding that kindergartners' scores on the syllable-tapping task partially predicted which reading group they were in at the end of first grade, as well as to a training study on rhyme analysis by Bradley and Bryant (1983):

Together, this pair of experiments—combining longitudinal and training procedures—offer the strongest evidence to date of a possible causal link between phonological awareness and reading and writing abilities. At the very least, they support other studies showing that there are methods for training phonological awareness that can be used successfully with young children.... They also indicate that this training can have beneficial effects on children's progress in learning to read and spell. (Liberman and Shankweiler 1985, 11)

Liberman and Shankweiler, so eager to emphasize the importance of global phonological awareness, raised doubts about whether phoneme awareness was even relevant. They observed, due to coarticulation, that phonemes are so hard to distinguish there can never be any direct correspondence between the underlying phonological structure of a word and the sound of the word. Rather, phonological segments "are recovered from the sound by processes that are deeply built into the aspect of our biology that makes us capable of language"— processes that go on "automatically, below the level of conscious awareness" (p. 9).

But if this is true, how does anybody learn an alphabetic writing system? Apparently with the greatest difficulty, because "there is no way to produce consonant segments in isolation" (p. 9). In fact, Liberman and Shankweiler argued, it is impossible for teachers to illustrate how the alphabet code works. The word *drag* was used as an example: "Though the word 'drag' has four phonological units, and, correspondingly, four letters, it has only one pulse of sound, the four elements of the underlying phonological structure having been thoroughly overlapped and merged.... The teacher can try of course to 'sound out' the word, but in so doing will necessarily produce a nonsense word" (p. 9).

In other words, *drag* can only be segmented as "duh-ruh-aa-guh," not as /d/ /r/ /a/ /g/.

The problem with this assertion is that, as any good phonics teacher knows, it isn't true. In fact, the only phonemes in English that are difficult to produce in isolation are the voiced consonants /b/ /d/ /g/ /j/. Yet even these phonemes can be segmented quite nicely by keeping the voicing brief.

Curiously, Liberman and her colleagues never commented on the discrepancy between their results and those of Fox and Routh. That study was either ignored or described as supporting their position (As Bacon remarked: "And though there be a greater number and weight of instances to be found on the other side, yet these it—by some distinction sets aside and rejects.") Here's a quote from one of Liberman's colleagues: "It is now well documented that preschoolers cannot tell you that *'pat'* has three separate sounds (Liberman et al. 1974), produce *'just a little bit of man'* (Fox and Routh 1976), or say *'pat without the /p/'* (Rosner and Simon 1971)" (Fowler 1991, 99).

The interesting question is how Liberman et al.'s theory could accommodate Fox and Routh's results. Certainly the developmental time lines would have to be redrawn, to say nothing of the developmental sequence. And while Fox and Routh did find that the ease of segmenting proceeds from larger to smaller units, they also discovered that there is no integrity of the syllable as a consistent or definable unit of sound, a fact pointed out by Venezky (1999) as well.

Overall, the phonological-development theory is unconvincing. There are too many facts and anomalies the theory can't explain—Fox and Routh's data among them. Processing and producing speech require a period of learning, though certain properties of receptive language are "hard wired," as Liberman et al. (1974) pointed out. Some type of phoneme sensitivity is up and running early on and undoubtedly plays an important role during early speech production. However, there is no reason why phoneme awareness would became more and more conscious and analytic. Adults are certainly not aware of phoneme sequences when they carry on a conversation. In fact, no one needs to be explicitly aware of phonemes *unless they have to learn an alphabetic writing system.* If explicit awareness of phonemes was truly part of a developmental (biological) sequence, this would only occur in countries with an alphabetic writing system. Cross-cultural studies show that adults who are illiterate or learn a different type of writing system have little or no awareness of phonemes. These cross-cultural studies were reviewed by Liberman and Shankweiler, then promptly explained away.

More Fuel

Equally influential players have become part of the history of the phonological-development theory. They are the English researchers Paula Tallal (at least English trained), and Lynette Bradley and Peter Bryant. Tallal's research and her theory of language development are presented in chapter 4. Her theory is based on nonverbal auditory processing. Here is the gist of her thinking on this issue:

The ability to process non-verbal auditory stimuli rapidly and the capacity to discriminate phonemes develops with age, reaching an assymptote ... by the age of $8\frac{1}{2}$. (Tallal and Piercy 1974, 92)

A broad body of research now suggests that phonological awareness and coding deficits may be at the heart of developmental reading disorders.... There may be a continuum between developmental language disorders and the types of reading disorders which are characterized by deficits in phonological awareness. (Tallal, Sainberg, and Jernigan 1991, 369–370)

Bradley and Bryant (1983, 1985) included an additional phonological step between the syllable and the phoneme, at a word's "onset" and its "rime" (initial consonant(s) + rhyming ending, as in *l-and, b-and; fr-ight, n-ight, s-ight*). According to Bradley and Bryant, all children spontaneously engage in word play and rhyming games. This play is a precursor to phoneme awareness and predicts the ability to master an alphabetic writing system. For this reason, they advocate training in the manipulation of words that start with the same consonants and share rhymes *prior to* learning to read. Bradley and Bryant's own research does not support the conclusion that this strategy would be useful, nor does anyone else's. This work is covered in chapter 6.

A Theory Becomes Dogma

And so a working hypothesis became theory, the theory became dogma, and The Dogma will not go away despite the accumulation of data that call it into question. The Dogma is alive and well in Adams's well-known book *Beginning to Read* (Adams 1994, 294–295):

In the earliest writing systems, meaning was depicted directly ... [and] evolved gradually in both time and levels of abstraction—first words, then syllables, then phonemes. Interestingly, the ease and order with which cultures have become aware of these levels of abstraction in history and exploited them as units of writing is mirrored in the ease and order with which children become aware of them developmentally.... Awareness of clauses or propositions develops earlier and more easily than awareness of words. Awareness of words develops earlier and more easily than awareness of syllables. And awareness of syllables develops earlier and more easily than awareness of phonemes.

Adams was aware of the research findings that appeared between 1974 and 1990 showing that phoneme awareness was highly correlated to reading skill and that syllable and word awareness were not. But this was dismissed as a fluke of correlational statistics, in which "ceiling effects" (too many children getting all the answers right) created too little variance for correlational statistics to work properly.

For those misguided people who rely on good data for affirmation or disaffirmation of The Dogma, she had this advice: "To the statistically uninitiated, they [the results] almost beg the conclusion that phonemic awareness is the single most important skill to develop among prereaders.... It might be reasoned ... why waste time on any but the one that relates most strongly to reading?" (p. 295).

Why indeed? The reason is because these null results don't fit The Dogma. As Adams explains:

The lower correlations between reading achievement and measures of word and syllable awareness do not negate their importance.... The relative magnitudes of the correlations between children's reading acquisition and their awareness of spoken phonemes, syllables, and words are consistent with the evidence that each is more difficult and attained later in development than the next. They are uninterpretable with respect to the relative importance of these skills to reading. In fact, each is critically important. (p. 296)

That the correlational values are questionable due to ceiling and floor effects is certainly possible, but assuming that the same questionable data can support any theory is *impossible*. This is having your cake and eating it too.

The Dogma remains hale and hearty at the turn of the century. Brady (1997), Liberman's former student, added some nuances to an otherwise unchanged version. The locus of poor readers' problems is at the level of speech perception. A failure here will influence the form or clarity with which words are stored in memory: "If speech perception abilities indeed play an underlying role in the development of phoneme awareness, one would anticipate that the quality of a poor reader's phonological representations for words somehow differs from that of a good reader's." (Brady 1997, 38).

Brady proposed two hypotheses about poor readers' difficulties:

First, the child's phonological system may initially represent lexical items in terms of more global phonological attributes (i.e., gestures) that extend through the word. Shifting to a fully phonemic representation for words may be a gradual process that takes place over a number of years.... The emergence of phoneme awareness may be constrained for some children ... by a poor fit between the phonemic targets and a child's internal phonological representations. (p. 38)

The second argument is that the phonological representations of poor readers are "faulty or impoverished." ... According to this position, the phonemic structure is essentially the same for poor readers, but the robustness of the phonemic details differs. (p. 39)

In other words, what is stored in the lexicon (jargon for verbal long-term memory) is either "global" (*imprecise*), or perceptual processing is "impaired," so that stored representations of words are "fuzzy" (*imprecise*). There isn't much difference between the two hypotheses, except that one seems to imply a developmental lag and the other an impairment.

Brady's colleague Fowler (1991) put more of an emphasis on the "gestural theory" of speech perception of A. M. Liberman, and went further, suggesting that infants and young children aren't sensitive to phonemes in the first place:

It is not phonemes, but features or articulatory gestures, that are the fundamental units of perception and production. [This] … makes it possible to move smoothly from infant abilities to first words without having to invoke phoneme representations at some intermediate point. What may be changing over the course of phonological development is the ability of the child to coordinate gestures that initially extend the full length of the syllable into integrated subsyllabic routines. (p. 102)

As these gestures become more precise, and the subsyllable units narrower, phonemic processing finally materializes:

The important question pertains to when in early childhood the phoneme level of organization is sufficiently well developed to allow for the isolation, labeling, and manipulation of these segments…. The little evidence we have available suggests that the scope of gestures continues to become increasingly phonemic between 3 and 7 years of age, inviting comparison with phoneme awareness abilities over the same period. (p. 103)

Finally, officials in control of research funding at the highest level are guided by the principles of The Dogma. The head of the division at the National Institute of Child Health and Development that funds most of the scientific research on reading in the United States wrote:

Research from several disciplines converges in identifying the aspects of phonological processing that cause reading disability, including deficits in phoneme awareness, phonological recoding in short-term memory, and visual naming speed.... Weaknesses in phonological processing, in turn, limit the acquisition of sight-word reading and the automatic associations to large units of print that are necessary for reading words by analogy. (Lyons and Moats 1997, 578–579)[3]

Altogether, these statements make strong predictions about the development of speech perception, tying this to a slow emergence of phoneme awareness, and then to reading success or failure. Is it true that poor readers owe all their difficulties to impoverished phonological representations? Does phoneme awareness become more conscious with time, or is it there from the beginning and becomes less conscious with time?

Using the limited, analogical reasoning on which The Dogma is based, reading researchers believed they could set aside or bypass important issues and critical controls that are essential in science. If we can assume that phonological awareness derives from speech perception, we don't have to prove it. If we can assume that speech perception develops in a specific sequence, we don't have to prove this either. If we can assume that phoneme-processing skill is something the child brings to the table, we don't have to pay too much attention to how reading is taught, or to whether any relevant skills were *already taught* (by mothers or teachers) before a child enters a study.

Reading researchers needed much more than analogies and assumptions; they needed norms for language-related tasks across the age span, preferably using large populations of children. They needed good language tasks to measure developmental shifts from a time well before children were taught to read, across the beginning reading phase, and into the more advanced phase. Without such tasks, language development can't be disentangled from the impact of being taught to read an alphabetic writing system. Reading researchers needed a road map for natural language development. I am strongly in favor of maps before theories.

---

3. The evidence is overwhelming that no one can read words "by sight" and that reading by analogy is far inferior to phonemic decoding. See *Early Reading Instruction*.

The importance of valid tests with proper norms for natural language development is a not a lesson we learned with hindsight, but a logical consequence of the initial research questions: Does explicit phonological awareness emerge as part of natural language development in the following sequence: word, syllable, phoneme? Does phonological awareness have a causal connection to reading, and if so how, when, and why?

The precise developmental aspects of phonological sensitivity or speech discrimination have not been a priority for scientists in the field of reading, but they have been a priority for scientists studying the natural development of receptive language, and it is these studies that provide a true test of the theories.

Basic Premises of the Phonological-Development Theory

The phonological-development theory is complex, and it's hard to keep track of its twists and turns. Here is a list of the basic premises of the theory. The first premise has already been shown to be false—writing systems do not evolve. We'll see whether any of the remaining premises hold up as we review the evidence presented in the next five chapters.

1. Phonological development follows the order of the evolution of writing systems.
2. Infants have implicit sensitivity to phonemic units in words and syllables.
3. Explicit awareness of phonological units develops over childhood from larger to smaller units: words, syllables, onsets and rimes, phonemes.
4. Explicit phonological awareness develops slowly, and phoneme awareness emerges at age 6 or later.
5. If phonological awareness fails to develop in the sequence and time frame set out in the theory, this indicates some type of impairment. (There is no room for natural variation in this model.)
6. Phonological processing is a strong causal agent in reading skill.
7. There is no way to segment consonant phonemes due to coarticulation. This makes it difficult to teach an alphabetic writing system. Unless children develop phoneme awareness, they will have trouble learning to read.

8. Training in phonological awareness of syllables, onsets and rimes, improves phoneme awareness and reading skill.

9. Speech perception may appear normal in poor readers, but this masks subtle deficits in perception of acoustic cues for speech and nonspeech.

10. Phonological processing is the integrating principle that unifies all research on language-related correlates of reading skill.

DEVELOPMENT OF RECEPTIVE LANGUAGE IN THE FIRST YEAR OF LIFE

At this point I turn from the reading research to the research on language development carried out by psycholinguists, psychophysicists, and developmental psychologists. This work sheds considerable light on the questions raised in the previous chapter concerning the nature of speech development, and what young children can hear, compare, and remember. This chapter addresses the issue of *implicit sensitivities*, those features of the speech signal that infants and toddlers process and discriminate without any apparent analytic or cognitive capacity to reflect on them.

I want to temporarily set aside the minitheories in the phonological-development model outlined in the last chapter and focus exclusively on what the data reveal. This way we can formulate an accurate and un-cluttered picture of infants' capacities for processing speech, and then compare this picture to the theories.

Doing Developmental Research

Before presenting an analysis of the research on receptive language development, I want to share the trials and tribulations of researchers in this field. Measuring development across the age span is a formidable and, some say, impossible task. It begins with the assumption that there is some coherent or even universal domain, defined as "what most children do." Developmental milestones are reflected in average scores on some particular task or aptitude for a particular age.

Darwin discovered that there is biological variation for just about anything you care to measure. Without this variation, natural selection can't work, because species wouldn't adapt to adverse circumstances and survive. Thus, besides the garden-variety average 3-year-old, there is an average *normal variation* of 3-year-olds. This is one problem. The second problem is worse, because developmental variation has two dimensions. The first dimension is lateral extension, the variability across "all 36-month-old children" for a given task.

The second dimension is temporal, normal variation over time. A child's first word can appear anywhere from 10 to 18 months, and "this is completely normal," say all the parent books. Lateral and temporal variation aren't independent, and because of this, they are confused and confounded all the time. When pediatricians tell Jimmy's mom that he is ahead of norms on motor coordination but behind norms for talking, they're referring to temporal and not lateral variation. They're using *ahead* and *behind* as time words to point out that Jimmy is either exceeding or lagging behind the norm for 3-year-olds. They're not saying that Jimmy is 1 standard deviation above or below the mean for all American 3-year-olds at this moment. They're saying, in essence, that for a 3-year-old, Jimmy is more like he should have been 6 months ago, or more like he should be in 6 months, than he actually is now. And this, of course, is "completely normal."

Scientists doing research on children's language face another difficulty. Language isn't all of a piece. Receptive language always precedes productive language, a technical way of saying that children understand a lot more words than they can say. Studying spoken language alone is insufficient without knowledge of the size of the receptive vocabulary, and of how well the children comprehend other aspects of spoken language, such as syntax, pronoun reference, relative clauses, and so forth. This means that there are two time lines—natural temporal variation in receptive language and natural temporal variation in productive language—as well as the relationship between them.

Other difficulties remain that I will touch on as we go along, but one final problem is central to all research on children. This is the problem of designing tasks that measure what you think they measure, tasks children can carry out to their highest possible level. Edifices built from carefully collected data can collapse like a house of cards when someone discovers that children couldn't do a task simply because of the way it was presented. We have already seen one example of this in the last chapter, and there are many more to come.

Having said this, the scientific study of children's early language development is one of the great success stories of the late twentieth century.

Why Speech Doesn't Play Fair

Research on speech perception, and especially speech perception in young children, is a recent area of investigation. The field was launched by the scientists at the Haskins Laboratory in a brilliant paper describing the research on adults and what it implied (A. M. Liberman et al. 1967). This paper laid the foundation for the modern study of speech perception and has also strongly influenced reading research, for reasons that have already become apparent.

Two major discoveries were reported in the paper. The first was *coarticulation*. Speech sounds are coarticulated to such an extent that an initial consonant in a word is produced in tandem with the following vowel, which, in turn, is coarticulated with what comes next, and so on. Coarticulation dramatically speeds up speech production and speech recognition.

Coarticulation posed a serious problem for speech scientists. It was the first time in the 100-year history of psychophysics that "physics" didn't map systematically to "psycho"-logical experience. Instead, the perceiver hears something that has no physical referent in the acoustic signal (at least as measured so far). There is no way a word can be cut up (by tape or electronically) into isolated consonants and vowels and remain speechlike. It matters not a whit whether the consonant is voiced or unvoiced. In the word *pig*, /p/ is an "unvoiced plosive." In the word *big*, /b/ is a "voiced plosive." Both consonants are made in the identical fashion (lips compressed and popped apart) and differ only in terms of the onset of voicing (the point where the vocal cords begin to vibrate). It would seem like a simple matter to chop the unvoiced /p/ in *pig* neatly off the vowel, but this doesn't work. Consonants sliced off vowels sound like whistles, clicks, hisses, and squeaks, and whether they are voiced or unvoiced makes no difference. People can make a perfectly adequate unvoiced /p/ in isolation, but the instant we decide attach it to a word (*pig*, *pot*, *pan*, *pun*, *peek*, *paint*, *pool*, *point*, and so on), the mere thought of uttering the word will modify how /p/ is produced, and hence its acoustics. In physical terms, every /p/ is different depending on what it sits next to in a word. Yet, despite the great variety of /p/'s the speech spectogram reveals, human listeners have no trouble hearing /p/ no matter where it comes in a word. And this problem happens in reverse. Two sounds that look identical on an acoustic profile may be heard by the listener as completely different phonemes in different vowel contexts.

From the point of view of the speech scientist, phonemes are an impossibility. They don't have any physical reality. Yet for the ordinary speaker, something phonemelike has two very real types of existence. The first is perceptual. There is an instant awareness that *pig* and *big* are different words. We notice the difference immediately, though we may not know consciously where the difference is. And we can match either one in speech without a moment's reflection. If, on the other hand, we listen more intently, we can pinpoint the difference as residing in the initial consonant, and observe that one of the consonants is voiced and the other is not (one is "buzzy" and the other "fuzzy").

The second reality is motoric—speech production. We have an implicit sense that /p/ and /b/ are made with the same articulatory gesture, and that the second one is "buzzy." We can also become aware of speech patterns explicitly. Phonemes are elements in a voluntary behavior (speaking), and voluntary behaviors are accessible to consciousness in a way that involuntary behaviors (reflexes) are not. Explicit awareness of articulatory gestures can come about through simple observation: we hear an error in our own speech via auditory feedback, correct it, and observe what we did. Young children self-correct speech errors all the time. We can be made even more aware of articulatory gestures through training, something people find relatively simple to learn. What we can't be aware of is the exact timing in milliseconds of the patterns of coarticulation, or even *that* our speech is coarticulated. The speed and complexity lie outside the realm of our perceptual abilities and run on automatic pilot. But we can get some sense of it in slow motion. This is what trained singers learn to do, and this is what a good speech therapist teaches. This is also what beginning readers need to learn to do.

The other major discovery reported in the paper was *categorical perception*—"categorical" because the brain insists on filing speech sounds in separate bins or categories. The brain files something remotely like a *ba* in the **ba** slot in brain space, and something remotely like a *pa* in the **pa** slot, no matter whether it is spoken by a man, woman, or child, in a foreign accent, and (within reason) no matter how sloppily it is produced. This "sloppy tuning device" is a type of *perceptual invariance*. Our speech-perception system tolerates all sorts of variations in the signal and reacts as if they didn't exist. We can understand Walter the Weatherman even though his speech is seriously deficient.

The classic experiment goes like this: A speech synthesizer produces a perfect *ba* and a perfect *pa*. They differ in a single acoustic cue called *voice-onset time* (VOT). Vocal cords vibrate immediately for *ba* (zero delay) and 40 milliseconds later for *pa*. Next, VOT is gradually delayed by 5-millisecond increments (0 to 40 ms), slowly turning *ba* into *pa*. This is what happens electronically. But human listeners hear none of these transitions. They hear *only* perfectly respectable *ba*'s and perfectly respectable *pa*'s. When the transitional forms are presented in progression, listeners hear a series of consecutive *ba*'s that suddenly flip into *pa*'s. Vowels don't produce a categorical effect in isolation, and the effect is more modest when they are embedded in words.

It was on the basis of this research that A. M. Liberman et al. (1967, 441) concluded that the primary unit of speech perception is the *syllable* and not the phoneme: "Articulatory gestures corresponding to successive phonemes, or more precisely, their subphonemic features, are overlapped, or shingled, one onto another.... If phonemes are encoded syllabically in the sound stream, they must be recovered in perception by an appropriate decoder."

The implications for learning an alphabetic writing system are profound. If phonemes are tightly woven into syllables, perceptually and motorically, how can they form the basis for a writing system?

The authors did not speculate on how categorical perception came about. One would imagine that categorical perception is a consequence of an increasing familiarity with the language. As infants hear more and more speech, an awareness of phonetic contrasts increases until each phonetic element begins to act as an "attractor," pulling anything similar to it into the same neural network. This would undoubtedly be a slow developmental process, and categorical perception would sharpen over time.

Speech Perception in Infancy

The Whiz Kids

In 1971, Eimas and his colleagues published a paper in *Science* that flipped the theory in the last paragraph on its head. (Beware of theories that appear logically consistent with the data but have no proof.) Infants at 1 and 4 months of age exhibited categorical perception for CV contrasts just like adults. Furthermore, they did this almost instantly and needed no training.

This remarkable discovery was made possible by new testing techniques. Babies have no way to signal "Yes, I heard that as *ba* this time," but they can control simple behaviors that reflect what they hear and pay attention to. Babies will increase their sucking rate on a dummy nipple for something they notice and want to hear more of. This was the technique used by Eimas et al. (Babies can also learn to turn their heads to signal the same thing.) Responses to repetition will *habituate*—fail to hold attention. Listening to a repeated series of *ba*'s ultimately leads to boredom. When babies become bored, the game slows to a halt, and sucking declines to zero. If there is a change to something different or new (a *pa*, for instance), the baby signals that the game has become interesting again by sucking faster. Differential sucking rates show whether the infant noticed a difference, and whether they perceive categorically (i.e., can't tell different *ba*'s apart).

These results prompted an avalanche of studies on infant speech perception that have been expertly reviewed by Jusczyk (1998). Babies have nearly adult proficiency in discrimination and categorical perception for all consonant contrasts in their native language. When they are tested on alien sounds in a foreign language they have never heard before, they do just fine on these too. It seems that babies come into the world primed to discriminate every phonetic pattern in all the languages of the world. Questions have been raised about whether this sensitivity is due to some special language module in the brain or part of general auditory processing. The fact that animals have been shown to have categorical perception, and that infants and adults respond categorically to certain *nonspeech* sounds, has muddied the waters. There are several methodological issues that need to be sorted out with respect to the infant and animal studies. For example, animals need extensive training and infants do not.

Once scientists realized that some kind of capacity for speech analysis seemed "preprogrammed" or "primed" by the brain, they wondered what else infants could do and when they could do it. Several extraordinary discoveries followed. The fetus hears fairly well from the sixth month of gestation on. Infants can recognize auditory patterns at birth that they had heard repeatedly in the womb, such as the prosody of the mother's voice (pitch, inflection, pace), or a rhythm of a particular Dr. Seuss story (De-Casper and Fifer 1980; DeCasper and Spence 1986).

From birth onward, speech analysis progresses as a cascade of overlapping skills, each added to the one before it, until many skills are working in tandem, rather like a carpenter with ten arms. These skills are at the interface of a nature-nurture continuum promoted by brain operations that selectively respond to language input. The language systems of the brain do not operate in a vacuum, but tune themselves to a particular language (or languages, in the case of bilingual speakers). Sensitivities unfold in a top-down and bottom-up fashion at the same time. In the first few days of life (Mehler et al. 1988), infants show that they can recognize the difference between the prosody of their own language (syllable stress, inflection, rhythm) and that of a foreign language. Yet, at the same time, infants use their keen perception of phonetic segments to begin serious word work.

Mothers don't teach their infants to speak by uttering one word over and over again. Infants learn what a word is from hearing it in various contexts: "Daddy made some juice from the oranges. I'll bet this juice is good. Mommy is going to have some juice. Do you want some juice too?" How does the child learn that *juice* is a word, and not *somejuice* or *juicetoo* or *havesomejuice*? Jusczyk and his colleagues began a series of studies to investigate how and when infants learned to extract words from the speech stream (Jusczyk, Cutler, and Redganz 1993; Jusczyk, Luce, and Charles-Luce 1994; Jusczyk and Aslin 1995; Jusczyk, Houston, and Newsome 1999). The studies showed that at around 6 to 9 months, infants are hard at work isolating words from phrases using three lines of attack: attention to pauses, common stress patterns in words (strong/weak syllables), and analysis of phonotactic structure (legal versus illegal phoneme sequences). In common English words, stress is mainly on the first syllable in multisyllable words (*ba-by*). In French, stress is on the final syllable.

Consonant sequences or clusters provide three sources of information for locating word boundaries in English. Of the seventy-six legal clusters in English, all but three appear only in word-initial *or* in word-final position (McGuinness 1997a, 1997b). Not only this, but adjacent consonants at word boundaries (final + initial consonants) are usually illegal in the language or rare. Mattys et al. (1999) discovered that 9-month-old infants can differentiate between the legal consonant sequences most likely to occur *within* words from those most likely to occur *between* words. They created two-syllable nonsense words (CVC-CVC) with two types of syllable stress (strong-weak, weak-strong) and the two types of adjacent consonants. They measured the time infants looked at a loudspeaker playing these words. Results showed that the infants were sensitive to syllable stress and to phonotactic probability, showing a greater preference for strong-weak syllable patterns, with consonant sequences more likely to appear within words.

At the same time, infants come to understand that the word work they are doing has a purpose. They observe that specific patterns of speech noises (words) have reference and meaning. Until recently, the evidence suggested that infants begin to comprehend words sometime between 9 and 11 months. In 1999, Tincoff and Jusczyk pushed the clock back 3 months. They discovered that 6-month-olds will look preferentially at a video of their mother when they hear the word *mommy*, and at a video of their father when they heard the word *daddy*. They don't behave this way if they see pictures of an unknown man and woman. Mandel, Jusczyk, and Pisoni (1995) discovered that $4\frac{1}{2}$-month-old infants prefer listening to their own name above all other words or names, though this doesn't prove that the child knows this is a *name* and refers to her. Tincoff and Jusczyk's (1999) study, on the other hand, proved that by 6 months, most infants understand that words refer to something in the world.

In 1998, Aslin, Saffran, and Newport added a remarkable feat to the list. They showed that 8-month-old infants process the transitional probabilities of phonetic sequences, and not the number of times particular syllables are heard (frequency of occurrence). The infants heard 4 three-syllable nonsense words (CVCVCV) repeating in random order in an endless chain:

pabiku/tibudo/golatu/pabiku/daropi/golatu/tibudo/tibudo/pabiku/golatu/daropi/

The infants were able to code (remember) the sequential probabilities of these four words in about *2 minutes* of listening time, even though the words were spoken in a continuous stream without any inflection or pauses.

Furthermore, listening time was not influenced by how often a particular syllable appeared in the chain, but by how often the words appeared. The brain was coding absolute sequential patterns of *words*, and had already accorded them a better-than-zero rating within a few minutes of listening time, even though these words didn't fit English syllable patterns at all and had no meaning. The authors concluded that infants' brains have a "rapid statistical learning mechanism" for remembering recurring patterns among items in a set, as opposed to remembering the frequency of occurrence of the individual items (syllables). This is strong evidence for words being primary or dominant over syllables—even when the syllable structure is simple and obvious.

How much do babies understand? Mothers have long been aware that their babies understand far more words than most people believe, but until recently we had no idea how many. The MacArthur Foundation funded a study to find out, using hundreds of mothers and their infants (see Golinkoff and Hirsh-Pasek 1999). At 10 months of age, the average infant understood about 40 words. Natural variation was plainly in evidence, and receptive vocabulary ranged from 11 to 154 words. At 16 months, the average receptive vocabulary was 169 words with a range of 92 to 321 words. These numbers highlight the complexity created by lateral and temporal variation. Infants in the slow group had learned 81 more words. The average infant learned 129 more, and the fast group 164 more. If the gap for the haves and have-nots continued to widen, it could be very far apart indeed in a few years. But probably the truest statement one can make about early language development is that it is highly unpredictable.

An Unsolved Mystery
I have just presented a Yellow Brick Road model of speech-perception development. The infant arrives on the scene primed for speech analysis, proceeds at a breakneck pace to do complex word work, and ends up at the Wizard's castle comprehending speech in no time at all. According to this scenario, newborns are off and running on day one and get better and better as time goes by. But science is full of surprises, and one sticky fact could not be ignored. If infants get better and better, then schoolchildren should be better still, and adults best of all. But when Strange and Jenkins (1978) and Werker et al. (1981) tested adults on their ability to hear alien phonetic contrasts, the adults failed dismally. Werker and her colleagues devoted several years to pinning down when the "universal phonetic discriminator" began to falter (Werker and Tees 1983, 1984a, 1984b; Werker and Logan 1985; Werker and Lalonde 1988; Polka and Werker 1994).

They compared native speakers of Hindi and of Nathlakampx (an Indian language of the Pacific Northwest) with English-speaking adults, children, and infants, working forward and backward across the age span. They found that the ability to discriminate between alien phonetic contrasts starts to disappear between 8 and 10 months of age, and by 12 months it is pretty well zero. When they compared adults, 12-year-olds, 8-year-olds, and 4-year-olds, none had any success, and, if anything, 4-year-olds were worse than infants.

Tees and Werker (1984) also looked at the impact of early language exposure. They studied college students learning Hindi. Beginning students who had heard Hindi spoken before age 2, but not since, were able to discriminate two sets of Hindi contrasts almost perfectly after only 1 or 2 weeks of classes. They did as well or better than students with 5 years' training. Other beginning students tended to do poorly, and their discrimination did not improve after 1 year's training. This amazing finding shows that these consonant phonemes had been coded (recorded in memory) in infancy, and were still accessible despite their lack of use.

Here is a puzzle that, so far, no one has solved. The most obvious difficulty is how to explain that infants lose their aptitude for hearing alien speech sounds at 12 months, yet children up to around the age of 8 can learn a second language without a trace of an accent, while most older children and adults cannot. This aptitude, plus the ability to recover sounds of a language not heard since age 2, means that no easy answer is going to be found to explain these results. The simple fact is that, although 1-year-olds fail the tests, the universal phonetic discriminator doesn't self-destruct. Instead, it appears to get lost somewhere in brain space. Apparently, if it gets lost too soon and for too long, the brain can't find it again. By "lost in brain space," I mean that neural networks (dendritic connections) are strengthened to handle relevant input and gain in priority, while other connections weaken or become difficult to access.

Various theories have been proposed to explain these peculiar results, but none are satisfactory. One common form is the "No Room at the Inn" theory. In one version of this idea, children become so focused on ferreting out the phonetic structure of their own language that all attentional resources are used up, and none are left for processing alien sounds, which would create unnecessary interference. In another version, alien speech sounds get "pulled" toward the nearest-sounding phoneme in the native language and get co-opted by greedy "prototype" brain cells. However, current theories (including my minitheory above) are nothing more than "stories." After all, there is no cost to the brain to maintain this early aptitude, no reason why this would interfere with maintaining attention to learning a native language. Infants are unlikely to be bombarded with alien phonemes, but if they are, they seem to have no trouble whatsoever learning two languages. In any case, the infants who passed the alien-phoneme tests were certainly not aware of them before they took the test.

As scientists began to explore speech perception in older children, another puzzling factoid emerged that didn't fit either the Yellow Brick Road model or the No Room at the Inn model. If children focus so much attention on the sounds of their language, why did they seem to be getting worse rather than better? Not all 3- and 4-year-olds, alas, have perfect discrimination for every sound in their own language. For example, they may not be able to tell *suit* and *shoot* apart, or *wing* and *ring* apart. How could newborns be such whizzes at discriminating speech sounds they've never heard before, but preschoolers do so badly on the very sounds they have been listening to intently all that time?

Do Infants Hear Phonemes?

From our knowledge of how the brain codes auditory signals, and the skills exhibited by young infants and children, it is possible to speculate about the brain operations that are essential to isolate words in the speech stream and to assign meaning to these words.

There is considerable disagreement, even within the phonological-awareness development camp, over how to characterize what the child is actually doing in a categorical-perception task (and nothing gets much simpler than this). I. Y. Liberman et al. (1974) argued that categorical perception is evidence of phoneme analysis. Fowler (1991) suggested it was not. To Fowler (and to A. M. Liberman), speech analysis is global in nature and linked to coarticulated speech gestures. Jusczyk (1998, 113–115) also expressed some reservations about whether the phoneme was the unit of analysis in this task. Perhaps, he argued, infants may only hear a difference "somewhere." But this begs the question of what "somewhere" means.

It goes without saying that something akin to "phonemes" is being processed or registered by the brain—because the main distinction between similar-sounding CV syllables like *ba* and *pa* lies in their phonemic structure. It is also obvious that infants are sufficiently aware of these phonemelike sensitivities to be able to overtly respond to them. This is quite unlike sensory processing that goes on well below the level of consciousness. Some brain processes spin by so fast we can never be aware of them, even when we're told exactly what is going on. Categorical perception and coarticulation are prime examples. People can't tell minor variations in *ba*'s apart, and they aren't aware of the subtle differences in acoustics due to coarticulation effects.

I want to take a closer look at what infants' observable behavior shows us beyond mindless noticing. All sensory systems are activated by some form of energy (mechanical energy in the case of the auditory system). Energy propagates from a source in a highly predictable way, and the brain processes three properties of this oscillating energy: frequency, amplitude, and phase. *Frequency* is the number of oscillations per unit time, *amplitude* is the power of the oscillations, and *phase* refers to how each frequency relates to every other frequency. In hearing, frequency (cycles per second) translates to "pitch," amplitude to "loudness," and phase to "coherence" (timbre, harmonic structure, and so forth). It should be noted that, in nature, all sounds are complex sounds, which means every sound contains a full harmonic spectrum.

The brain keeps track to the microsecond of these constantly changing multiple frequencies, different amplitude variations for each frequency, and the phase relationships of their components. Frequencies and amplitudes never merge into some kind of unified "wudge" like colors mixed on a palette, but keep their identities. We can recognize the timbre (quality) of different musical instruments in an orchestra even when they are playing in unison (same pitch). No one knows how the brain keeps these qualities separate, but whatever it does, it does it *effortlessly*. Nor do we hear sounds as raw signals cranked into some dim form by an effort of will; instead we have immediate sensations of *that* person speaking, *this* bird singing, *those* violins playing, and *that* machine making that noise. This is a gift of the way the brain works.

Sensory systems learn by permanently registering recurring invariances in the input. The auditory system codes patterns on a mammoth scale, across a wide spectrum of the input, over long periods of time. The system works like a probability matching device, carefully keeping track of which patterns of signals are identical or similar, which patterns are most and least likely, and in which contexts. As time goes by, "most likely" patterns sharpen in awareness (discrimination improves) and need less effort and attention to be perceived (Pribram and McGuinness 1975).

Given that brain "wetware" is there in abundance to handle all aspects of the speech signal, what then does the infant *hear?* Perhaps we can think about speech perception in a slightly different way to explain the data from the infant research.

The infant arrives in the world able to distinguish recurring patterns of her native language that she heard in the womb. These include patterns of syllable stress (recurring variations in amplitude) and melodic contour (recurring variations in pitch). She can discriminate vowels and CV syllable contrasts in any language in the world. But which cues allow her to do this, phoneme cues or global CV syllable cues?

The argument of the "global-perception" proponents is that because /b/ + /ah/ in *ba* overlap acoustically (coarticulation), the phoneme is not an identifiable segment in its own right. This view is bolstered by the formidable problem of designing efficient computer speech-recognition and speech-production devices like Walter the Weatherman. So far, engineers can't build speech-recognition devices based on phoneme sequences. Instead, they rely on CV and VC units.

Perhaps the brain knows something the engineers do not. Phoneme-like segments may be identifiable by the auditory system in a way the engineers don't understand but the brain does. For example, the general view is that information on *phase* is irrelevant in speech-recognition devices, as Denes and Pinson (1993, 197) point out in their famous book: "Fortunately, for speech and most acoustic processing, phase is usually of little importance to how the acoustic signal is perceived as sound. Therefore, when we talk about a spectrum we will mean just the amplitude spectrum and will ignore phase completely."

This may not be such a good idea.

The problem is that if *ba* is processed by the brain as a global coarticulated unit, this would mean that instead of infants being equipped with an innate capacity to discriminate every phoneme contrast in the world, they would have the capacity to discriminate *all the vowels and the CV, VC, and CVC combinations in all possible languages in the world.* The brain could certainly manage this (after all, it has 10^{10} million neurons), but this doesn't seem like something an efficient, well-evolved brain would do, and here are some facts that suggest it does not.

During the first 6 to 8 months of life, the brain sets up a probability structure for native speech sounds. These are ratcheted up in the probability matrix, and alien sounds get values of zero (nonoccurrence). Meanwhile, the conscious infant and her brain continue to monitor syllable stress patterns, inflection, pauses, and duration to begin to isolate words from the speech stream. In natural speech, words run together without pauses. There are no gaps of silence between words like the spaces between words in print:

Wuddjusay? Icanthearwhatchersayin!

A major cue in isolating words from the speech stream are the transitional probabilities of phonetic sequences inside words, as Aslin's study has shown. Sometime between 6 and 9 months, the infant can notice words (the phonotactic patterns of legal/illegal phoneme sequences the brain is storing), including their probability structure (most to least likely). It's hard to see how this could work unless the phoneme had an acoustic profile that is identifiable by the listener.

English abounds in phonotactic clues for isolating words, as noted above. Words are more likely to begin and end with consonants than with vowels. Hundreds of common English words take the form CVC. Consonants vary acoustically according to whether they come in initial or final position in the word. Initial /b/'s (*bat*) are considerably more bombastic that final /b/'s (*cab*). The position of consonants varies in absolute terms and in probabilistic terms. Some phonemes never start a word (/ng/) or end a word (/h/ /w/). The sounds /n/ and /z/ are more likely to come at the end of words than at the beginning. The sounds /b/ and /g/ are more likely to appear at the beginning of words than at the end.

As we saw earlier, by far the most formidable cue in isolating words from a stream of speech is the consonant cluster. Of the seventy-six legal consonant clusters in English (not counting plurals), only three can come in both initial and final positions in a word: sp st sk. Plus there is a striking tendency for illegal clusters to form "word walls" between consonants that end and begin words. Here are the adjacent final/initial consonants from the first three sentences in this paragraph: *rth, stf, lc, sth, ntcl, vth, xl, lcl, shn, tc, ngpl, nb, df, lp, ngt, lcl, zt, mw, dw, zb, nc, ntsth, db, nw.* Only three are legal in English, and these are rare (*lk, lp, dw,* as in *milk, help, dwarf*).

Friederici and Wessels (1993) have shown that 9-month-old infants can tell legal and illegal consonant sequences apart, listening longer to words and syllables with legal sequences. Mattys et al. (1999) found that they can do even more. They can tell the difference between legal consonant sequences that are more or less likely to appear in the middle of words or between words.

If infants use consonant sequences and other phonotactic cues to discriminate between legal and illegal words, and to separate words from each other, these cues must be represented by the brain along with their probability structures. Unless phonemes had some status in the input, the brain would code these sequences as one phonetic unit. The brain would need one probability structure for legal clusters *inside* words and another probability structure for illegal clusters *between* words, representing every possible consonant combination of phonemes (of which the brain is supposedly unaware), and it would need to have this legal/illegal sorting device in place for every language of the world past, present, or future, *before the infant heard any words!*

But even this bizarre scenario wouldn't work, because the illegal clusters say: "*Split us!* We don't belong together." In other words, to know where a word ends, you must know where a phoneme ends—when it doesn't join to the next phoneme. If an infant couldn't hear individual phonemes, there is no way to use consonant sequences to split words from each other. And if infants "know" these cues (recognize and use words on the basis of these cues), then their brain must know them too. How could the brain know that illegal consonant sequences are splittable if it didn't code consonants as splittable phonemic units?

These results show that infants' sensitivity to vocal inflection, syllable stress, phonotactic cues, and transitional probabilities for phonetic sequences in words, calls on at least seven auditory/linguistic skills:

Monitoring temporal variation. Lengthening vowels mark phrase boundaries.
Monitoring changes in pitch. Pitch falls at the end of sentences, rising on a question.

Monitoring amplitude variation (rhythm). This marks recurring stress patterns.
Discriminating relevant speech units: phonemes, phonetic segments, words.
Segmenting (separating) phoneme units from each other.
Keeping tracking of the sequence of phonetic units over time (real time).
Registering these occurrences in memory as probabilities that are continuously updated.

These processing abilities, plus sensitivity to voice quality, are processed "in parallel," simultaneously. We know this because any one of these aptitudes can be demonstrated at any time in the behavior of infants. Infants do not shed one sensitivity for another. When young children learn to walk, they don't abandon balance for motion, and motion for direction, and direction for speed. Not only this, but these sensitivities endure, as Tees and Werker (1984) have shown.

So far, the research provides support for one part of I. Y. Liberman et al.'s theory at least—that infants are implicitly sensitive to phonemes, in the same way toddlers have an implicit sense that a certain stance and muscle tension keep them upright when they are learning to walk, and a certain stride length keeps them in motion instead of toppling over. It is only later that children can reflect on these things and test them out. (Can I stand on one leg? For how long?)

So far the data point to this developmental sequence of intrinsic sensitivities to these phonological units: *phonemes*, then *words*. Based on Aslin's findings, words are dominant over the CV syllables embedded in them. Fox and Routh (1975) found that ordinary syllables have no real integrity in the sense that words consistently split at noticeable or predictable syllable boundaries.

It will not be lost on people familiar with phonological-awareness research that the same skills involved in analyzing a native language are needed to do a phoneme-awareness task: discrimination (identification/ isolation), segmentation, sequencing. Does an infant's ability to process phonemes increase or decrease over time? When, or if, does a more "cognitive" or explicit awareness occur? These are the questions I take up next.

SPEECH PERCEPTION AFTER 3

In the previous chapter, I pointed out that unless infants were aware of phonemelike units of speech, they would be unable to separate words from the speech stream, something they begin to do at around 6 months. This is an implicit sensitivity—a gift of the way the brain works. At the same time, we know the infants are actively paying attention to phonetic segments, because their overt behavior reflects what they hear. They stop sucking (habituation) when their interest wanes, and increase sucking (orienting) when they hear something new.

In chapter 1, we learned that young children are explicitly aware of phonemes starting around age 3 and can demonstrate this by being able to segment speech vocally. However, these studies don't tell us *how* this is done or whether developmental changes are taking place. There have been a number of innovative studies on speech perception in young children to discover what aspects of the speech signal they are sensitive to. These studies are at the frontier of our knowledge and present a number of challenges for the researchers. They are difficult technically, conceptually, and practically, in the sense of creating tasks that young children find interesting and that reflect their true capabilities. For this reason, studies on children younger than age 3 are rare. This chapter reviews what we know about speech perception in young children.

Listening to Canned Speech

A series of studies on speech perception in children has been carried out by Susan Nittrouer and her colleagues over the past two decades. In an early study, Nittrouer and Studdert-Kennedy (1987) investigated the development of categorical perception in children age 3, 4, 5, and 7, and compared them to adults. Recall that in a categorical-perception task, CV syllables like *ba* and *pa* are made more and more alike by altering the acoustic cue that makes them different. (There is 40 ms of initial voicing in *ba* and none in *pa*.) People don't hear these transitions, but report only a *ba* or a *pa*. At the midpoint or boundary between them (in the range 15–20 ms), performance drops to chance, and people report hearing *either* a *ba* or a *pa* about 50 percent of the time.

Nittrouer and Kennedy were looking for answers to how young children process speech signals, and whether these processing skills improve with age. They wanted to know the precise elements in spoken words that children were listening to in order to make their judgments. To do this, they designed a categorical-perception task and varied coarticulation patterns at the same time. This allowed them to make inferences about what children could hear on the basis of their performance.

The children were asked to play a game. They had to point to a picture when they heard one of four words: a *shoe*, a girl named *Sue*, a boy pointing (*see*), and a girl (*she*). If they did a good job, they got rewarded with colored stickers. The first methodological novelty was the switch from nonsense syllables to meaningful words.

Sophisticated techniques were used to manipulate the phonetic elements in the words.

Words were constructed in a series of steps. First, a speaker recorded the words: *shoe, Sue, see, she*. The words were chosen for a reason. The vowel /ee/ is made with the jaw up and with a smile; the vowel /o͞o/ is made with lips pursed in a tiny circle. The /sh/ is also made with lips pursed. When /s/ precedes /ee/, it is made with a smile. When /s/ precedes /o͞o/, it is rounded, making it sound more /sh/-like. (Try it.) It was predicted that the *shoe-Sue* contrast would be more ambiguous than the *she-see* contrast, pushing categorical boundaries in opposite directions.

To compose the words, the initial consonant was deleted electronically, leaving only the vowels. Due to coarticulation, *each vowel retained traces of the original consonant*. Next, they synthesized a perfect /sh/ and a perfect /s/ to be the poles or end points of a continuum, and turned the /sh/ into /s/ in nine equal steps. At this point there were four vowel sounds bearing traces of /s/ and /sh/, plus nine electronic variations of

/sh/–/s/. The marriage between these components produced thirty-six varieties of the original four words.[1]

Because traces of the consonant qualities were left behind in the vowels, this made transition cues ambiguous. The authors speculated that there were two ways the auditory system would process these words. First, if the child was sensitive to the acoustic variations caused by coarticulation effects (as adults were known to be), this would mean that they, like adults, use these transitional elements to "recover phonetic form"—*phonemes*. Second, if the younger children weren't sensitive to these cues but older children were, this would mean that early speech perception is more likely to be based on "the invariant aspects of the signal." In other words, speech would be processed more holistically or globally by younger children.

The children were trained to listen to the four words using natural speech until they could point to the correct picture 100 percent of the time. Next, they were trained on synthetic speech (using the widest contrasts) until they were 90 percent correct. Then they started the main task. Adults had no training trials. Table 3.1 shows the results for adults and 3-year-olds.[2]

The table provides a picture of what categorical perception looks like. If categorical perception is perfect, a person will hear *she* for the first four steps, *she* or *see* about equally at the category boundary, then *see* for the remaining four steps.

The /ee/ words produced a normal categorical-perception effect, as expected. The performance of the adults and the 3-year-olds are contrasted in the table to show how similar they are. Three-year-olds were less secure at the category boundary, but the crossover point was at step

---

1. The /s/–/sh/ contrast is not like the /b/–/p/ contrast described earlier. The two sounds are distinguished by a gross difference in pitch, nearly an octave apart. The nine transitions involve wide pitch changes (166 Hz), about a half tone on the musical scale. Category judgment here is not based on brief temporal cues or fine differences in pitch as it is for some speech contrasts.

2. The values were derived from graphs of functions (slopes) illustrated in the original paper, and the numerical values may not be absolutely correct.

Table 3.1a
Categorical perception in % responses /ee/ vowels

	Model	Vowel from *she*	Vowel from *see*
Adults			
Say *she*	1. 100	100	100
↓	2. 100	100	100
	3. 100	100	100
	4. 100	95	85
	5. 50/50	**65/35**	**50/50**
↑	6. 100	72	72
	7. 100	86	90
	8. 100	97	98
Say *see*	9. 100	98	98
Three-year-olds			
Say *she*	1. 100	90	90
↓	2. 100	87	95
	3. 100	95	85
	4. 100	77	**68**
	5. 50/50	**50/50**	**37/63**
↑	6. 100	**63**	79
	7. 100	72	88
	8. 100	90	93
Say *see*	9. 100	92	92

Note: Midpoint values—category boundaries—are in boldface. Values are based on least-squares means and s.d. for each age group at each point. Data modified from Nittrouer and Studdert-Kennedy 1987.

5, where it should be. Five- and 7-year-olds resembled the adults, and the 4-year-olds were just below them.

The /o͞o/ words told a different story. When the consonant was mated with the vowel colored by the same consonant, the category boundaries were pushed in opposite directions. When the vowel came from *shoe*, adults continued to say "shoe" more than they should. When the vowel came from *Sue*, they said "Sue" more than they should. The 7-year-olds performed more like adults, but 5-year-olds were unstable on judgments for the *shoe*-vowel words.

Three- and 4-year-olds had far more trouble. On *Sue*-vowel words, the category boundary spilled across several steps. Three-year-olds were

Table 3.1b

Categorical perception in % responses /o͞o/ vowel

	Model	Vowel from *shoe*	Vowel from *Sue*
Adults			
Say *shoe*	1. 100	100	95
	2. 100	100	92
	3. 100	100	80
	4. 100	100	**50/50**
	5. 50/50	**68/32**	80
	6. 100	**69/31**	96
	7. 100	85	99
	8. 100	90	99
Say *Sue*	9. 100	94	99
Three-year-olds			
Say *shoe*	1. 100	92	79
	2. 100	99	77
	3. 100	88	79
	4. 100	91	**66**
	5. 50/50	100	**50/50**
	6. 100	**24**	72
	7. 100	**40**	85
	8. 100	**58/42**	91
Say *Sue*	9. 100	**65**	95

Note: Midpoint values—category boundaries—are in boldface. Values are based on least-squares means and s.d. for each age group at each point. Data modified from Nittrouer and Studdert-Kennedy 1987.

not consistent across most of the range. It seems that the younger children were strongly affected by the ambiguous cues in the vowel (coarticulation effects), and the qualitative judgments of /s/ and /sh/ were not as secure.

But there was something else going on that the authors did not discuss. Four-year-olds had weak categorical perception for the *shoe*-vowel words, but they were handily outdone by the 3-year-olds, who persisted in hearing *shoe* nearly the whole the way through. Because the younger children did not show this extreme pattern for any other word, perhaps there's something unusual about the word *shoe*. *Shoe* is a common early word in spoken vocabulary. It has a special place in infants' hearts along with *Mommy*, *Daddy*, and *juice*. The *"shoe effect"* could be due to word salience—how important the word is to the child. If this is the case, then word salience dominates perception, and minor transitional clues go out the window. This is true *global* perception, but caused by "top-down" effects (word familiarity plus emotion), not by sensory effects. This has important implications for a developmental model of phonemic sensitivity, and certainly for how words are chosen to measure it.

To summarize, children 7 and older had similar responses to adults at the category boundary between /s/ and /sh/, and like adults they were susceptible to vowel-context effects, showing they were equally sensitive to fine acoustic cues in coarticulation. Five-year-olds did marginally worse. Three- and 4-year-olds were like the older children on /ee/ vowel words, though category boundaries were less precise. They had considerable difficulty with /$\overline{oo}$/-vowel words for three reasons: confusion created by ambiguous transition cues, less secure category boundary for /s/ and /sh/, and word salience.

Although Nittrouer and Kennedy (1987) had several suggestions for how to interpret the youngest children's responses, they concluded as follows: "Our results suggest ... that perceptual sensitivity to certain forms of coarticulation is present from a very early age, and therefore, may be intrinsic to the process of speech perception. The child does not use segments to discover coarticulation, but rather coarticulation to discover segments. The adult, though more skilled at segmental recovery than the child, may still do much the same" (p. 329).

Because coarticulation normally lies outside the bounds of ordinary speech perception (conscious awareness), this is a rather startling conclusion. What is clear is that basic speech perception is very similar between young children and adults, except when highly ambiguous transition cues are embedded in unnatural speech. The excellent performance of all of the children is surprising in view of the fact that these kinds of experiments are long and rather tedious. The results for *shoe* could indeed be a word-familiarity effect, having little to do with auditory sensitivity to subtle acoustical shifts. These results are also consistent with the notion that young children need more exposure to the language to make finer discriminations between subphonemic cues.

It is important to stress that these words did not sound in any way like natural speech. Only four of the thirty-six word varieties had any resemblance to what a child actually hears in spoken language. No child had any difficulty making these judgments with natural speech.[3]

Over the next decade, Nittrouer and her colleagues accumulated evidence suggesting that young children focus more on dynamic-spectral qualities of the acoustic signal than on static differences, and that this gradually changes over time. This would mean that children initially focus on large acoustic shifts (those produced mainly by jaw movements) and only later on finer shifts (those produced by the tongue, lips, soft palate). Practice producing speech would gradually alter auditory perception. In other words, children's speech attempts sharpen the perception of their own and other people's speech.

Nittrouer and Miller (1997) proposed a theory called the *developmental weighting shift*. If the brain "weights" the dynamic properties of speech (presumably this means more attention is paid), this enhances the perception of *syllables*. As vocabulary expands and words become more similar, speech production needs to be more accurate and there is a shift of attention to *intrasyllable* units, or phonemic structure. According to this theory, an increasing vocabulary size leads to greater phoneme awareness. This is a direct test of whether explicit phoneme awareness develops.

Nittrouer and Crowther (1998) and Nittrouer, Crowther, and Miller (1998) tested this theory in two studies. The first study included children age 5 and 7 as well as adults. In the second study, a group of 3-year-olds was included. Nittrouer and Crowther created pairs of complex speechlike tones. The child's task was to tell the difference between them. The tones differed in one small acoustic cue (variations in pitch in a single formant). In one tone, the pitch was *static* (constant) over time. In the other, it was *dynamic* (glided from one pitch to another). Nittrouer and Crowther also measured the children's ability to detect silent gaps in continuous noise.

According to the hypothesis, if a "global-to-phonemic" developmental theory was correct, children and adults would respond differently

---

3. It is worth noting that Nittrouer and Studdert-Kennedy (1987, 328) followed the crowd in misrepresenting Fox and Routh's data: "Preliterate children do not have access to the phonemic structure of speech." They then had to try to explain this away in view of the fact that their data did not support this conclusion.

to the two types of cues. Children would be more sensitive (more accurate) in the dynamic-cue condition (better than or equal to adults) and much worse in the static-cue condition. No such effects appeared. The children were far worse in the dynamic-cue condition than in the static-cue condition (opposite to prediction), and they were significantly worse than adults on *both* cues. Five- and 7-year-olds did not differ, so there was no evidence for any developmental shift. Five-year-olds were significantly worse in the gap test. The idea that recognition of certain types of speech patterns can identify global versus phonemic perceivers is not supported by these results.

In a study using real words (Nittrouer, Crowther, and Miller 1998), the same type of acoustic cues were used to alter the words. Now the children performed much more like adults. Comparing the two studies, Nittrouer, Crowther, and Miller found that the difference between telling real words apart and telling speechlike tones apart was so large that 3-year-olds were as accurate at detecting small acoustic differences on the *word task* as 5-year-olds were on the *tones task*. In discussing these results, they stated that listeners appear to treat speech signals differently from how they treat other acoustic signals. We will see shortly that they treat them very differently.

These results don't support a global-to-segmental phonological-development theory, nor a phoneme-awareness development theory. The most parsimonious interpretation of the data so far is that infants and young children have good phonemic perception, but have more trouble with fine-grained auditory analysis (discrimination) than adults do. It should be noted that this analysis is below the level of the phoneme. And when something is unfamiliar (complex speechlike sounds that aren't speech), they have even more trouble. They do worse across the board and not differentially worse, as if they had focused on one type of cue more than another.

For all the technical elegance involved in concocting sets of artificial sounds and words, it is conceivable that it may not be possible to ferret out precise ways of listening using this approach. And there is a second problem. Children's aptitude appears to be critically dependent on which particular sounds and words are chosen. For example, 5-year-olds were close to adult levels of performance on categorical judgments of /ee/ vowel contrasts (*she-see*) with *those particular consonants*, but worse than adults on /o͞o/ vowel contrasts (*shoe-Sue*) with *those particular consonants*. Does this mean we need developmental norms for every syllable contrast in English? (The English language contains over 55,000 phonotactically legal syllables!)

Data in support of differences in speech discrimination between children and adults has been reported in a series of studies on categorical perception carried out by Elliott and her colleagues. The children were older, and we jump to the 6-to-10 age range. Elliott et al. (1981) used the standard CV syllables from the early research. One set (*ba, pa*) varied in voice-onset time (VOT). The other varied in place of articulation (PA). Here, pitch changes distinguish *ba, da*, and *ga*. Unlike the /s/–/sh/ contrast, these changes are very small and brief.

Six-year-olds were significantly worse than 10-year-olds and adults in correctly labeling the syllables, showed greater variability at the crossover points (were less categorical), and needed larger acoustic differences (wider pitch separations) to tell the syllables apart. This was clear evidence that 6-year-olds couldn't discriminate as well as 10-year-olds and adults. Ten-year-olds had caught up to adults on most (but not all) comparisons.

Elliott et al. concluded that children improve in discrimination of speech contrasts as they get older, but they doubted this tells us much about the nature of phoneme awareness: "If the construct of 'phoneme frequency effect' [adults have better discrimination of phoneme boundaries due to experience] has validity, one must then question why adults were able to make within-category discriminations whereas children could not" (p. 675).

In other words, adults can hear the fine acoustic changes inside phoneme boundaries (subphonemically) better than children. The authors speculated that the adults' superior auditory discrimination could be due to maturation of the auditory system, experience, and/or higher cognitive skills in applying problem-solving strategies to the task.

Elliott (Elliott et al. 1981; Elliott 1986) found similar age effects on the *ba-pa* contrast with children age 6 to 8 years, 8 to 11 years, and adults. As noted earlier, *ba* and *pa* are distinguished by a 40 ms difference in VOT. The younger children were significantly less accurate at the midpoint where *ba* flips into *pa*. A measure of sensitivity (d') showed that adults had better discrimination, and a sharp sensitivity peak between 15 and 20 ms (the exact phoneme boundary). Children's sensitivity was greater here as well, but not nearly as sharply defined. Keep in mind that this is a level of analysis well below the normal phoneme boundaries in natural speech.

The studies by Elliott and her colleagues showed that there is a strong increase with age in the ability to discriminate *pitch* differences (formant transitions) and *temporal* differences (VOT) at category boundaries for similar CV contrasts. This fine-grained auditory discrimination keeps improving beyond the age of 10.

Elliott and associates provide another illustration of how children's performance is a function of what they are asked to listen to. Here they heard canned (electronic) nonsense syllables in which acoustic cues were very brief. In Nittrouer's studies they heard words (except in one case), and transitional acoustic cues were large and sustained. Children appeared far more developmentally mature in the Nittrouer studies than in the Elliott studies. This makes it difficult to discover how or whether children gradually develop a more precise segmental analysis of words.

Taken together, these studies show that explicit phoneme awareness is present in children across all ages tested. Children differ from adults in the precision of category boundaries, and in the discrimination of fine acoustic difference inside phoneme boundaries. These results don't support the sequence in the phonological-development theory. If something was developing here, it did so subphonemically. The boundary judgments vary with age from one study to the next, depending on the particular CV syllables, whether speech is natural or canned, and whether words are real or nonwords. The enormous age discrepancies with respect to the different types of speech sounds need to be addressed.

Real Talk

Matching Partial Cues

Walley, Smith, and Jusczyk (1986) cited a number of studies showing that young children have difficulty counting phonemes, making same-different judgments between them, and rearranging or deleting phoneme segments. They interpreted this (as everyone else did) as part and parcel of the development of speech perception, rather than something else, such as memory and cognitive constraints, which we now know to be the case (see McGuinness 1997b; D. McGuinness, C. McGuinness, and Donohue 1995). Their hypothesis was based on Liberman et al.'s (1974) theory that children can identify syllable segments before they can identify phonemes.

Walley, Smith, and Jusczyk approached this in a more realistic context, by using natural speech where nothing is difficult to tell apart (discrimination *between sounds* was not a factor). Like Nittrouer, they used a game to keep the children's attention. Twelve kindergartners and twelve second graders were introduced to two puppets who had a peculiar language problem. Each puppet had a one-word vocabulary. One puppet said *nooly* and the other said *bago*. The children's first job was to learn to associate each nonsense word with one of the puppets by patting the puppet's head when they heard each word.

Their next job was to listen to a variety of two-syllable words, decide whether each word was more like *nooly* or *bago*, and pat the appropriate puppet. Test words were constructed so that they shared the first sound (*–/n/*), *or* the first two sounds (*–noo*), *or* the first three sounds (*–nool*) with one of the puppet's special words. Control words did not contain any phonemes present in *nooly* or *bago*.

The second graders scored around 83 percent correct for all three types of cue. The kindergartners scored at chance (59 percent) when only the first sound matched, but did significantly better than chance with the CV cue, and did as well as the second graders on the CVC segment. Kindergartners either needed more phonetic information to do the task, or perhaps had less awareness of sounds in words, because they hadn't been taught to read.

A second experiment was carried out using different children and different words: *sona* and *luttoo*. The test words shared phonemes with these words in the following positions: CV–(*so–*), –CV (*–na*), C–V (*s–a*), and –VC– (*–on–*). Two of these phonetic segments share a syllable with the standard word, two do not. The kindergartners performed nearly as well as the second graders on initial CV–segments (84 and 92 percent correct). Kindergartners scored close to chance on everything else. Second graders did equally well on final syllables (–CV) and on initial plus final sounds (C–V). There is no evidence from either study that kindergartners or second graders have any special sensitivity to syllables. In fact, second graders did better (but not significantly) matching initial–final sounds (C–V) (97 percent correct) than matching final syllables (–CV) (86 percent correct).

These findings show that younger children are more aware of beginning sounds in words, and need more information to make accurate choices. There is no evidence from either study that the syllable has any special relevance for either age group, or that syllables are any easier than isolated phonemes (C–V) to match to another word.

The small numbers of children in these studies led to some inconsistencies in the results. In experiment 2, kindergartners performed as well as second graders on the CV segments, scoring 84 percent correct. Yet, in experiment 1, kindergartners barely scored above chance (68 percent) on the CV segments. This is a problem if the goal is to establish developmental patterns. Also, a major confound makes these results even more questionable. The age effect may be due to learning to read an alphabetic writing system rather than a consequence of development. Seven-year-olds will have been learning to read for a year or more.

Word Familiarity

In 1990, Walley and Metsala investigated word familiarity as a potential factor in speech recognition. Until this study, word familiarity had received surprisingly little attention in speech-perception research. Their hypothesis was that the more familiar the word, the more someone can recognize it on the basis of partial cues. This is similar to the "shoe effect" where word salience dominates perception.

Previous research had shown that a subjective measure of word familiarity was a better predictor of word knowledge than a standard vocabulary test or word-frequency counts (frequency in print). This measure is known as the *age of acquisition* (AOA). To calculate AOAs, lists of words are rated on a numerical scale according to the age at which people believe they learned the word. Walley and Metsala asked adults to make AOA ratings for concrete nouns and apply the age range 2 to 13 years. Words were selected from these ratings to fit specific criteria for the 5- and 8-year-olds in the study. There were three categories of words: *early* words (words learned at a younger age), *current* words (learned recently), and *late* words (words not acquired yet).

The task was to listen to these words and respond to any mispronounced words. Mispronunciations consisted of phoneme errors that appeared in either the initial or middle position in the word. Walley and Metsala predicted that children would do better detecting errors at the beginning of words than in the middle, be worse overall than adults, and do best on words acquired early.

Across all measures, the AOA effects were very strong for the children. Five-year-olds did nearly as well as 8-year-olds detecting a mispronounced phoneme in *early* AOA words, more poorly on *current* words, and extremely poorly on *late* words. Eight-year-olds performed close to adult levels on *early* words, did less well on *current* words, and fell well behind on *late* words (all age comparisons for current and late words were significant). Adults' detection scores were nearly perfect throughout. However, the position of the mispronounced phoneme (initial or middle) had no effect on performance at any age for any type of word (early, current, late).

In a second experiment, 5-year-olds, 8-year-olds, and adults once more listened for correctly or incorrectly pronounced words. This time the context of the sentence varied so that it either did or did not link the target word to some realm of meaning: "The hunters in the jungle went on a *safari*," versus "It can be dangerous to go on a *safari*." Words were chosen to reflect *early*, *current*, and *late* AOAs. As in experiment 1, accuracy and sensitivity were strongly affected by age and how long the children had known the words. No other manipulations (context constraint/nonconstraint, the position of the mispronounced phoneme, and so on) had any consistent effect.

There is no evidence from these studies that adults can hear inner phonetic segments better than young children. Children's accuracy in detecting mispronounced words is strongly affected by *when the word was first learned*, not by where an error appears in the word. If children gradually acquire the ability to hear individual phonemes in words, this method didn't detect it. Instead, this study showed that children have more trouble detecting a mismatch to a real word that is not firmly embedded in memory. This is no different from the trouble we have hearing a long, unfamiliar word. "Length of residence" in memory sharpens the acoustic trace or phonetic profile of a word, and this seems to be independent of the context in which the word appears. The major impact on the development of speech perception appears to be due to how many words you know, and how many times you have heard them. This, of course, is a consequence of *learning*, not of development per se.

The authors reasoned that if adults could make AOA judgments for the children perhaps children could make their own especially as they are closer to the source. Using the words from the previous study, Walley and Metsala (1992) asked preschoolers (age 4 and 5) and 8-year-olds to estimate the age when they learned each word, or, if the word was unknown, the age when they thought they would be learning it. The ratings for each word for younger and older children and the adults' ratings from the previous study were almost perfectly correlated. The children and adults had nearly identical age estimates for *early* words, while children estimated *current* and *late* words as being acquired 1 year earlier than the adults had.

Next, Walley and Metsala tested another group of 5-year-olds on the mispronunciation task as a check on the validity of the children's estimates. The results were the same as in the previous study: strong effects of age and AOA categories, and no effect of the location of the mispronounced phoneme. In fact, the children's AOA ratings were stronger predictors of performance on both the mispronunciation task and vocabulary tests than the adults' ratings were.[4]

The authors concluded that, at least by age 5, children have considerable explicit knowledge about which words are familiar and how long they think they have known these words. In other words, young children know *that* they know *what* they know about words in their vocabulary.

Walley and Metsala's research has shown that words are not alike, and that the type of words used in research is critical to the analysis of children's speech perception. The more familiar the word, the easier it is to hear (and notice phonemes). These studies confirm the continuing theme that is emerging from the work reviewed in this chapter. Speech analysis varies as a function of many factors: word familiarity, whether speech is artificial or natural, whether words are nonsense or real. There is no evidence that children become more and more aware of phonemes due to some global-to-segmental developmental process (words to syllables to phonemes).

---

4. In a multiple regression analysis, children's AOA ratings accounted for 47 percent of the variance on the mispronunciation task, 66 percent of the variance on an expressive vocabulary test, and 48 percent of the variance on a receptive (picture) vocabulary test. Word frequency (frequency in the language) was not a factor. No other test contributed further, including a test of visual imagery.

Does Vocabulary Growth Cause Phoneme Awareness?

In 1997, Metsala added another variable to the mix, and the following year Metsala and Walley published a theory based on this research and the studies reviewed above. It is easier to understand the 1997 study if the theory is spelled out ahead of time. The essence of the theory is that as language develops, the child's speech recognition becomes less global and more oriented to phonetic segments in words. So far, nothing new here. However, in this model, the engine behind the change toward greater phonemic awareness is *vocabulary growth*, not necessarily maturation per se (Liberman et al. 1974) or speech development (Fowler 1991), more in line with the ideas of Nittrouer and Miller 1997. The more words you know that sound alike, the more you need to become aware of phonemes. The theory also includes a prediction for reading:

Deficits in lexical restructuring play a causal role in reading-disabled children's difficulties with phonological processing, phoneme awareness, and reading ability. If lexical representations do not become segmentalized in a developmentally appropriate manner or time-frame, children should be unable to access phonemes and to learn the relation between phonemes and graphemes (i.e. decipher the alphabet code). (Metsala and Walley 1998, 102)

Thus, an ever-increasing vocabulary size forces the child to pay more attention to phonetic segments in words, which has a spinoff for reading. And though vocabulary and phonetic sensitivity might appear to have separate developmental paths, vocabulary acquisition is primary.

In addition, phonemic awareness will be enhanced by specific characteristics of the language. Some words have more "neighbors" in the sense of sharing common phonemes. Many words differ by just one phoneme (**string**: *strong, strip, sting*). Luce (1986) categorized words according to whether they reside in "dense" neighborhoods (many words that sound alike) or "sparse" neighborhoods (words with few neighbors).[5]

---

5. If this idea was correct, it ought to make different predictions for different languages. If neighborhood density was an important variable in promoting phonemic awareness, then languages with few phonemes and many neighbors, like Hawaiian, would promote greater phonemic awareness earlier

Metsala (1997, 48–49) provided this account of how the theory would predict the development of speech perception:

The theory is that words that have many similar-sounding neighbors will undergo, developmentally early, segmental restructuring. That is, these words need to be encoded phonemically at an early age in order to be discriminated from similar-sounding words in the listener's lexicon. Words with many neighbors should therefore be recognized on the basis of less bottom-up input than words that are stored relatively more holistically, or have undergone segmental restructuring more recently.

The strong prediction for the study is that "developmental differences would be most pronounced for words that had few similar-sounding neighbors and were not heard frequently, those words that would be chronologically latest to undergo segmental restructuring" (p. 49).

Metsala tested children in three age groups: first and second grade, third and fourth grade, fifth grade, plus adults. They used a "gating task" in which the child had to recognize a word as successive bits of it were heard. The first gate was the first 100 ms of the word. Additional 50 ms increments were added until the word was recognized. The score was the number of milliseconds (cumulative gates) it took to identify the word.

Words were chosen to meet very stringent criteria. There were high- and low-frequency words (frequency in print), which came from high- or low-density neighborhoods according to Luce's (1986) tables of 918 words. All words were one-syllable nouns acquired no later than age 7. There were four categories of words: high frequency/dense neighborhood, high frequency/sparse neighborhood, low frequency/dense neighborhood, low frequency/sparse neighborhood.

Several types of analyses were carried out on the data, but I will focus on the primary one. This was the "isolation point" or the number of milliseconds it took to recognize the word.

Table 3.2 shows the average millisecond values for all age groups in all conditions. I added estimates of significant age differences (greater

in development than languages with many phonemes and sparser neighborhoods (Polish). Cross-cultural studies would provide a simple test of the model.

Table 3.2
Time in milliseconds (gates) to recognize a word

Frequency/ neighborhood	Adults	11 years	9 years	7 years	$\overline{X}$	s.d.
High/sparse	200	234	256	274	241	38
High/dense	290	302	319	322	308	39
Low/sparse	338	345	380	390	363	38
Low/dense	390	386	426	426	407	38

Note: 34 ms difference is "significant" according to the author's report.
Source: Adapted from Metsala 1997.

than 33 ms), and summed standard deviations across all conditions. As can be seen, 7- and 9-year-olds performed identically throughout. The same was true for the 11-year-olds and adults, except for the high-frequency/ sparse-neighborhood condition, where 11-year-olds were 33.5 ms slower. The greatest age difference was between 9- and 11-year-olds. On the basis of these patterns, I combined the age groups into "young" and "old," and the results are illustrated in figure 3.1. This provides an uncluttered view of the interaction between age, frequency, and neighborhood type.

Word frequency had the strongest effect. High-frequency words were recognized much faster than low-frequency words regardless of neighborhood density. Younger children needed more input (more gates) than older children and adults in all comparisons except for the high-frequency/dense condition, where no age effects were found. Finally, there was a strong interaction between frequency and neighborhood. High-frequency words with sparse neighborhoods were easiest to recognize. Low-frequency words in sparse neighborhoods were the hardest to recognize.

The results support Metsala's prediction that age effects will be minimal or nonexistent in the high-frequency/dense condition. But they do not support anything else in the theory. They don't support the prediction that developmental effects should be *greatest* in the low-frequency/sparse condition. Instead, developmental effects were strongest in the high-frequency/sparse condition. Nor can the prediction explain why no developmental effects were seen between the second and fourth graders whose ages spanned nearly 4 years (6:4 to 10:0). Results don't support the

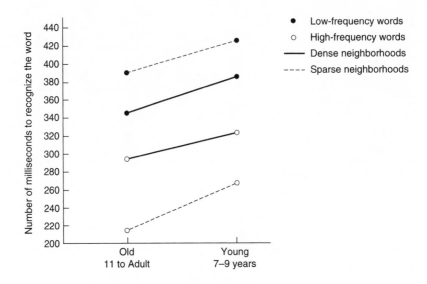

| Figure 3.1 |

Isolation point in milliseconds to identify words that differ in frequency in print and neighborhood size. Based on data from Metsala 1997.

prediction that words with many neighbors will be recognized faster (need less bottom-up input). Everyone was overwhelmingly better at recognizing high-frequency words in sparse neighborhoods. If children become automatic phonemic processors due to knowing more words from dense neighborhoods (predicting faster times), then why were they so much *faster* recognizing words in the high-frequency/sparse-neighborhood condition that is supposed to require only global processing? The same question applies to the adults.

On closer inspection, "neighborhoods" began springing leaks. According to Luce (1986), neighborhood density is calculated by the number of words that share all phonemes but one with the target word.[6]

---

6. Luce's tables were compiled by the following rules. (1) Change only *one phoneme* of the target word. (2) Do this in one of three ways: substitution, subtraction, addition. Thus, *cat* would reside in a neighborhood of *bat, fat, hat, mat, pat, rat, scat, cats,* plus *cut, cot, court, curt, cart,* plus *cab, cad, calf, can, cap, cash, cast, catch.*

Table 3.3
Mean neighborhood-density estimates for words on the list

	McGuinness	Luce	Sequential probability
High-frequency words			
Dense	23.3	14.9	5.7
Sparse	8.7	3.7	2.0
Low-frequency words			
Dense	19.1	12.6	6.4
Sparse	16.1	3.3	6.3

Because some of the neighborhood-density values looked suspiciously low, I reassessed the densities and compared them to the table values. In every case there were far more "neighbors" than appear in Luce's tables, nearly twice as many in most conditions and five times as many in the low-frequency/sparse group. In my analysis, three of the four categories of words had the same neighborhood densities (table 3.3).

Because Luce's estimates are incomplete, how does one explain the remarkably orderly results that vary systematically as a function of neighborhood density? I calculated sequential (linear) probabilities as a possible explanation, because this is what a gating task forces the listener to do (see table 3.3). I worked out the number of words that *could follow* the initial CV segments, for example *ca–cat, cab, can, can't, cap, cast, cash, catch, cats.*

These estimates perfectly mirror my neighborhood-density estimates. Therefore, a truly sparse neighborhood *or* a truly small sequential probability might explain the extremely fast recognition times that were observed for high-frequency words in sparse neighborhoods (a result opposite Metsala's prediction), but neither neighborhood size nor sequential probabilities can explain anything else. They can't explain why low-frequency/sparse-neighborhood words took so much longer to recognize than low-frequency/dense-neighborhood words, especially because the neighborhood densities and the sequential probabilities were identical in the two conditions.

In summary, the results are an artifact of something other than neighborhood densities. And while one result did fit Metsala's predictions, nothing else followed logically from that prediction. Truly "sparse" words with low sequential probabilities were responsible for the fastest recognition times for everyone, and this has nothing to do with phonemic or global processing. This is counter to prediction because it can't explain why words that were supposed to be processed phonemically (bottom up) took so much longer to recognize. Nor is there anything "developmental" here, especially because the age groups where one would expect to see large differences in phonemic awareness (7 and 9 years) were indistinguishable on every task.

Metsala (1997, 52) concluded differently:

My findings support the hypothesis that the development away from more holistic processing of spoken words is related to the sound-similarity relations and experienced frequency of individual lexical items. Developmental comparisons showed that with increasing age, less acoustic-phonetic information was needed to recognize high-frequency words in sparse neighborhoods, as well as low-frequency words in both sparse and dense neighborhoods.... The extent and developmental time course of lexical restructuring appears to be a function of a word's location (in terms of neighborhood structure) in the child's mental lexicon. The increasing shift from relatively holistic to more segmental processing, is, I suggest, the result of the increasing segmental structure of lexical representations.

There is no evidence for holistic processing, or otherwise, being involved in these judgments. In the high-frequency/sparse-neighborhood comparison, the two *youngest* age groups (age range 6–10 years) did not differ significantly on anything, precisely the ages one would predict will be most affected by "phonetic restructuring," if such a phenomenon exists. The results do not support the third conclusion that younger children need less phonetic information *proportionally* for low-frequency words. The data show they need more information for high-frequency/sparse words as well. The developmental time course cannot be a function of neighborhood structure, because neighborhood structure in this study is invalid.

What Does It All Mean?

The research on speech recognition in children illustrates science in action at the frontiers of knowledge. The results appear elusive because they are elusive. Outcomes can depend on the task, the type of stimulus, the measures used, and so forth. Studying human perception is not easy to do. How a perceiver perceives is invisible to the observer. And due to the phenomena of coarticulation and categorical perception, there is no sure way to force the listener to hear speech sounds in a particular way. As these clever and intriguing studies have shown, perception is influenced by word-familiarity effects, differences in syllable patterns, and "natural-ness" of speech signals, and it may not be possible to answer the question posed by these researchers: When and how do children develop an in-creasing awareness of the phonemic structure of language?

I submit the question is unanswerable because the underlying premise is false. There is no evidence whatsoever that children have any diffi-culty hearing phoneme contrasts in natural speech, especially for words acquired early in childhood. What the evidence does support is that young children have more difficulty than adults discriminating contrasts *below the level of the phoneme*. But even so, they do surprisingly well. The question is problematic as well because people don't need to be aware (explicitly) of phonemes as part of natural language development. They don't need this any more than they need to be aware of syllables (qua syllables). The only reason anyone would need to be explicitly aware of phonemes is if they have to learn an alphabetic writing system.

The studies in this chapter were presented in some depth because they represent the most promising approaches in the field. In every case, this is groundbreaking work, and these are truly innovative attempts to ac-cess the inner sanctum of how children hear and process speech. One thing is troubling. This field is as difficult as it is new. There is a tendency for some to conjure up deductive theories on the basis of a few studies. These theories can drive the research in a particular direction like a blin-kered horse, blocking out all other vistas. Deductive theories are especially seductive when they seem logically plausible. The very appealing theory of Metsala and Walley is reminiscent of the "very appealing theory" of Lib-erman et al. that sent us down the garden path in the first place.

While the theme of incremental phonetic sensitivity during the devel-opment of speech perception or vocabulary growth may sound reasonable and may be partly correct, none of these theories can be proven independ-ently of the particular sounds and words that are tested, and none of them may be *true*.

Nevertheless, we can see from these carefully crafted studies that even very young children are explicitly aware of phonemes in natural speech, and that this can be demonstrated at least by the age of 3. These results strongly confirm the findings of Fox and Routh that conscious manipulation of phoneme sequences is coming online between the ages of 3 and 4. They do not, however, support the claim of The Dogma that phoneme awareness materializes after the age of 6, if it materializes at all. Whether a 3-year-old would be able to apply this aptitude to the logic of an alphabetic writing system is another matter.

LINKS: AUDITORY ANALYSIS, SPEECH
PRODUCTION, AND PHONOLOGICAL AWARENESS

Phonological development has been implicated in two theories proposed by scientists outside the field of reading research. A. M. Liberman et al. (1967) proposed a motor or gestural theory of speech perception that accounted for their research on speech recognition. An update of this theory based on more recent data was published by A. M. Liberman and Mattingly in 1985. The link to the phonological-development model lies in the proposal that phonological awareness stems from motor programs in the brain that control speech gestures. These ideas were tied to reading in a subsequent paper by I. Y. Liberman and A. M. Liberman in 1989.

The second theory was proposed by Paula Tallal, an experimental psychologist who studies children with severe language problems. Because reading difficulties are common in these populations, the theory was extended to explain reading problems as well. The theory states that basic (nonverbal) auditory processing underpins speech perception, and that poor receptive language is due to auditory-processing problems.

The central question for us here is whether these new ideas shed any light on the central issue of how or whether phonological awareness develops and affects learning to read.

New Theoretical Perspectives

The Motor Theory of Speech Perception

A. M. Liberman and Mattingly (1985) proposed an inductive model of speech recognition that took into account the research over a 35-year period. I can't do justice to it here, because it is complex, abstract, and definitively argued. Instead, I will outline the major premises and focus on the relevance of the theory to the general topic of the connection between phonological awareness, speech production, and reading skill.

These researchers believe that an abnormal delay in speech-motor accuracy and clarity is a marker for reading difficulties.

The core of the theory is as follows. There is a speech-perception module in the brain that has different neural architecture and operates by different principles from the module for basic auditory processing. This explains how the listener is able to extract invariant phonetic patterns from coarticulated speech. There are no consistent acoustic signals, or specific, identifiable cues in the speech stream that yield the same perception. Everything depends on phonetic sequences, on what sits next to what within a word. For this reason, listening to speech must involve implicit perception of the *overlapping gestures* produced by the speaker, because only these gestures have any reality. An infant literally "hears" coarticulated speech gestures and not specific combinations of acoustic cues: "The objects of speech perception are the *intended phonetic gestures* of the speaker, represented in the brain as invariant motor commands that call for movements of the articulators through certain linguistically significant configurations. [These gestural commands] ... are the elementary events of speech production and perception" (Liberman and Mattingly 1985, 2; emphasis mine).

To frame the thinking behind this abstract proposal, I will briefly highlight the main points in the model:

1. The objects of perception (what is represented) are the intended gestures of the speaker.
2. If speech perception and production share the same gestures, they must be intimately linked. This link will be innately specified and automatic. In other words, this is not a learned skill.
3. The theory is based on the fact that these gestural movements overlap in time. The sensory system must keep track of the overlapping gestures to yield a percept, one that is peculiar to speech and unlike any other type of auditory perception.
4. There must be lawful dependencies among gestures, articulatory movements, vocal-tract shapes, and the signal being processed.
5. The model, therefore, must assert that productive language takes precedence in evolution, that perceptual systems develop as a consequence, and that both develop in tandem after this.

6. In ordinary perception the "distal object" is out there in the world (we localize sounds *in space*; we see in three dimensions *in space*). With speech, the distal object is a phonetic gesture, or more accurately, a "neural command" for the gesture, which puts the distal object inside the head. These are "neuromuscular processes" that are internal to the speaker.

7. The evidence for two modules comes from research on the competition between them. Acoustic signals, identical in every way, can be ordered in such a fashion (by a shift in sequence, or by splitting the input to each ear) that they are perceived by the listener as either speech or acoustic noise.

8. Not all cues have to be present to perceive a speechlike signal. Many acoustic cues are redundant, and can "trade" in identifying a word. The bottom line is that no particular cue is essential to the percept. Furthermore, there is no way one could ever make an exhaustive laundry list of all the acoustic cues in all possible speech gestures.

However, the theory leaves us with an unsolved problem. Liberman and Mattingly raise the question of how human listeners can hear linear strings of phonetic categories (phonemes) when phonemes "do not exist" acoustically. Based on the overlapping speech gestures we actually hear, we should only be aware of words or syllables. They have no answer, and their theory cannot provide an explanation.

Instead, they offer this suggestion. According to their theory coarticulation serves the purpose of dramatically increasing efficiency (speeding communication). If the process was reversed, and the gestures unraveled, we would get back to the original units of speech. In other words, if there is a mechanism that allows us to comprehend these overlapping speech gestures, there should be an equally efficient process for recovering discrete gestures from speech patterns.

Liberman and Mattingly's theory has been a hard sell, because it is not easy to understand, and it is short on analogies to make it understandable. There is a brain module *but no mechanism*. "Module" is simply jargon for the "boxes-in-the-head" flowcharts so beloved by cognitive psychologists. This sidesteps the problem of defining a mechanism by dumping a process into the brain without specifying exactly where it is or how it works. I'll come back to this problem below.

A major problem with the theory is that there is no known biological process where the perceptual component is up and running at birth but its behavioral counterpart takes several years to catch up. Speech-motor accuracy, monitored over childhood, keeps improving until age 18. If the analytic wetware for speech gestures is wired into a brain module so speech can be perceived instantaneously by infants, why can't these gestures be *produced* instantly as well?

Reviewing the evidence for the model, one gets the sense that it suffers from the very technology that led to such intriguing findings. Liberman and Mattingly devote a good deal of attention to the problem that auditory cues (those revealed by speech spectograms) don't combine in sufficiently consistent ways to positively identify the acoustic code or template for a word, syllable, or phoneme. In this type of bottom-up logic, individual cues are the building blocks of perception. Liberman and Mattingly reached an impasse following this path, and their model is the result.

The problems with speech-recognition technology were discussed in chapter 2. The electronic analysis fails to match the way sensory input is processed by brain. For most sensory systems, the brain codes three properties of the signal: *frequency*, *amplitude*, and *phase*. It also keeps track of time. The unifying glue that binds signals over time is phase. *Phase angle* is the technical or mathematical term for the measure of the relationships between the sine waves in the signal (the harmonic spectrum) over time. By contrast, electronic analysis represents only frequency, amplitude, and time. *Information on phase is missing* (Denes and Pinson 1993).[1]

The technology of speech synthesizers limits the number of variables available to interpret the data, and recovering phonemic structure is impossible within these limits. Yet it may be completely possible within the limits of what the brain can do. This could explain Liberman and Mattingly's fundamental dilemma, set out above. Suggesting that "gestures" are units of perception appears to be a fallback argument (a theory by default) due to incomplete evidence on how sensory signals are processed. If the

---

1. For a comprehensive account of how sensory systems use phase to transform incoming signals, and the mathematics that underpins this process, see Pribram 1991.

answer can't be individual acoustic cues, it must be motor gestures instantiated in the brain.

A simpler argument is that bottom-up, acoustic-cue models are wrong, because the language systems of the brain don't process sensory signals in this manner. We know from animal research that the auditory cortex carries out an analysis/synthesis (known as a Fourier transform) on the total harmonic structure of the input simultaneously and continuously (Pribram 1991; Sekular and Blake 1994). This processing occurs in parallel with a variety of other inputs.[2]

Quite apart from mechanism, the fundamental question is the one that Liberman and Mattingly don't address: Why does it take so long to learn to use these preprogrammed speech gestures? If there are indeed motor templates for gestures, why aren't they instantly accessible to the speech-motor articulators? Answering this question is central to a newer version of the phonological-development theory proposed by the Libermans that links speech perception and speech production to each other and to reading skill (I. Y. Liberman and A. M. Liberman 1989).

The expanded version goes as follows: speech perception is connected to speech production via brain modules that process speech gestures. Because perception and articulation are linked by the same type of operators (the modules), problems with articulation will correspond to problems with speech perception. *Here's the leap*: problems with speech perception will impede the development of phoneme awareness, which, in turn, leads to reading difficulties. As they put it:

That some children have particular difficulty in developing phonological awareness (and in learning to read) is apparently to be attributed to a general deficiency in the phonological component of their natural capacity for language. Thus, these children are also relatively poor in short-term memory for verbal information, in perceiving speech in noise, *in producing complex speech*

---

2. Liberman and Mattingly report several studies showing that mouth postures will dominate when they are in conflict with the actual auditory input. This is the only direct evidence in support of a gestural theory. But it still doesn't prove it.

patterns, and in finding the words that name objects. (from the abstract, p. 1; emphasis mine)

Once the reader has the phonological form of the word, the appropriate phonetic structure and its associated *articulatory movements* are automatically available to him for use in working memory, or for reading aloud. (p. 7; emphasis mine)

If the ability to hear speech arises from perception of speech gestures, and awareness of phonetic sequences (phonological structure) is the hallmark of a good reader, speech-motor problems should predict reading problems. Indeed, I. Y. Liberman and Shankweiler (1985) made precisely this argument in an earlier paper, stating that speech errors are a product of perceptual errors, and speech-motor difficulties are due to deficits in perceiving, storing, and retrieving "phonological structures"—the same problem that makes learning an alphabetic writing system difficult.

Because everything is linked in this developmental model, articulation problems ought to be a red flag for reading problems. But we know this isn't true from the longitudinal studies reviewed in part II. Poor articulation, on its own, does not predict reading problems. One unanswered question is whether articulation or receptive language is connected to subtle auditory-processing abilities that aren't picked up by the standard tests. Perhaps sophisticated speech-recognition techniques like those described in chapter 2 can provide more precise answers. The key question is whether these subtle perceptual problems affect phoneme awareness and reading.

The Nonverbal Auditory-Processing Theory
For Tallal, speech perception obeys the laws of basic auditory processing and doesn't require special neural architecture, except that the left hemisphere of the brain is specialized to process brief, rapidly changing acoustic signals. There is no "language module" for speech perception that operates by different rules. These auditory skills have an impact on *receptive language* and ultimately phoneme awareness, in just the same way, however. The theory does not specify any connection between speech perception and speech production. It links to reading in the proposition that auditory perception underpins receptive language (perception

of speech and vocabulary), which makes it possible to hear phoneme sequences in words: "The ability to process non-verbal auditory stimuli rapidly and the capacity to discriminate phonemes develops with age, reaching an asymptote ... by the age of $8\frac{1}{2}$ years" (Tallal and Piercy 1974, 92).

When this development is abnormal it can lead to an impairment, causing difficulties in receptive language as a whole.

Preliminary Ideas about Cause

Before moving on to studies that enlighten us about the validity of these theories, I want to remind the reader of important facts and present some new ones. Categorical perception and discrimination of phonemes are on "go" at birth and need no exposure whatsoever. Children show adult levels of phonetic analysis much earlier when they listen to natural rather than artificial speech, and to real words rather than nonsense words, especially highly familiar words. What is not known is whether individual differences in these skills provide any information about language delays, language impairment, or reading difficulties, or whether receptive language links to productive language or to phonological awareness.

From the research on language development we know that comprehension of natural speech far outstrips speech production during development. Speech analysis begins in the womb, and basic language skills are close to adult levels by age 3 or 4. Speech production marches to a different drummer. Learning to talk means learning how to map what you hear (so well) to what you can say (so imperfectly) until the two match precisely. This is a long trial-and-error process, prone to setbacks. It begins around 6 months, and reaching adult levels means *adult status*, a process that may take over 18 years to perfect (Hull et al. 1971).

We know that auditory feedback from the child's own speech plays a role in fine-tuning articulation. An early clue to this connection came from observations of reduplicative or "echoic" babbling: "da-da-da-da-da." This seemed to show that infants were practicing speaking, and listening to how it was going. Stronger support came from the discovery that deaf children's babbling phase is very late and extremely short lived (see Eliot 1999). It seems that in the absence of auditory feedback, speech production shuts down.

Vihman (1993) proposed that auditory feedback allows speech perception to sharpen in tandem with speech production, creating an "articulatory filter." The filter, in turn, makes the sounds favored by the infant equally salient when *spoken by others*, a possibility also entertained by Nittrouer. So far, this is more speculation than fact. Vihman's own research shows that proving the existence of an articulatory filter isn't easy. Some infants focus intensely on producing a few phonetic patterns (practice makes perfect), while others like to link phonetic patterns to related patterns (variations on a theme). Recordings of mother-infant interactions do not show that the infant necessarily imitates words or sounds the mother is producing or emphasizing at the time.

There are thus at least four points of view about the interaction between speech perception and speech production. The common view is that speech perception is primary and underpins (causes) accuracy in speech production and general language. Another view is A. M. Liberman and Mattingly's proposal that speech-motor gestures are primary and provide the neural templates for analyzing other people's speech. The third view is Tallal's position that the critical variable for speech perception, receptive language, and ultimately phonemic analysis, is nonverbal auditory processing of temporally brief cues. Connections to speech production are not part of the theory. In fact, Tallal and Newcombe (1978) reported a dissociation between speech production and speech perception in a study on brain-damaged patients. The fourth view is more in line with Vihman's idea presented above, and with my notion of "reciprocal causality" which will be discussed in part II. According to this view, while perceptual skills are online first, perceptual and motor systems act synergistically to "bootstrap" their way to increasing efficiency, and there is no way to pry this apart to find a cause. There isn't much evidence to support any of these positions, but considerable evidence that one of them is wrong.

Evidence for Links between Speech Perception and Production

Perception and production of individual consonants (natural language) have been linked in behavioral studies. In Holland, Raaymakers and Crul (1988) found that children who had difficulty producing a particular consonant sequence (/ts/) had equal difficulty hearing the difference between it and /t/ and /s/ alone. In a more direct attack on the problem, Jamieson and Rvachew (1992), and Rvachew and Jamieson (1989) reported that training children to discriminate between consonants they can't produce accurately led to a considerable improvement in speech production of those consonants. This shows that perception can lead production, but would training speech directly also have an impact on perception?

Research on Language-Delayed/Language-Impaired Children
For some reason, good research on the speech-perception/speech-production link is scarce. The earliest work was a series of studies by Stark, Tallal, and Curtiss (Stark, Tallal, and Curtiss 1975; Tallal, Stark, and Curtiss 1976; Stark and Tallal 1979) on language-impaired children. I report on the paper by Stark and Tallal (1979), the most comprehensive of the three. They tested twelve aphasic children attending a special school in England on their ability to hear vowel and syllable contrasts and on speech production. (The language problems of these children were severe and idiosyncratic and are outlined in appendix 1.) The children were between 7 and $9\frac{1}{2}$ years old, had superior nonverbal intelligence, and had no auditory or neurological problems. They were matched in age, sex, and nonverbal IQ to a group of normal children.

The aphasic children were able to discriminate between vowels as well as the normal children, and five aphasic children performed normally on judging a *ba-da* contrast. However, seven did not. The aphasic children were divided into "perceptually normal" and "perceptually impaired" groups and given tests of speech production. They were asked to say several words aloud, and these were tape-recorded and reproduced as speech spectograms on a paper printout. Two listeners judged that the aphasic children (all twelve) made more consonant speech errors than normal children.

Visual inspection of the spectograms provided measures of voicing cues. Voice-onset time, vowel duration, and vowel offset were measured in fourteen different words starting or ending with stop consonants (/b/ /p/ /d/ /t/ /g/ /k/). The vocal timing patterns of the aphasic children with good speech perception did not differ from their age-matched controls. The perceptually impaired group were noticeably different. They didn't begin voicing at a stable boundary. They were unable to clearly contrast voiced and unvoiced consonants. In some cases the voicing was delayed by more than 300 ms. Vowel duration preceding a final consonant was abnormally long. The difference between the two aphasic groups was so great that their scores did not overlap. Overall, the perceptually impaired children's speech could be described as slow and highly variable, and resembled the speech of much younger children.

Stark and Tallal concluded that speech-production problems were likely to be the consequence of perceptual problems in discriminating brief auditory cues and rapidly changing auditory signals. But they also suggested the process could go both ways: "It seems probable that the speech perception and speech production difficulties of the dysphasic children will interact with one another in a number of ways" (p. 1711). They postulated a "pervasive deficit of the central nervous system ... [that] affects both the acceptance of high-rate input in speech perception and the programming and timing of high-rate output in speech production" (p. 1711).

Stark and Tallal relied on human observers listening to tapes and visually inspecting a paper printout of a speech spectogram.

Edwards et al. (1999) appear to be the first researchers to compare precisely controlled electronic measures of both speech recognition and speech production. They tested 4-year-olds with poor articulation and delayed speech, but normal receptive vocabulary. They were matched to normal children in age and sex. Adults provided a model of accurate speech production. Although the authors described this as a pilot study, it provides an extensive analysis of each child's patterns of articulation and how this relates to speech recognition.

Speech perception was measured by a "gating task" similar to the one described in chapter 3. (Gates chop off successive parts of a word.) The gates were placed at various points of transition between consonants and vowels in CVC words. Another perceptual task was a "noise-center" task, in which the midpoint of the vowel was replaced by varying proportions of speechlike noise (0 to 70 percent). Children heard real words—*Pete, peep, peak, cap, keep, cup, bad, bead, bed, bird*—and had to point to the correct picture. (Lots of training was provided.) For the production task, the children repeated the phrases "baby dog," "good baby," and "Timmy picked up kitty." These were analyzed for frequency, rate, and components of the speech spectogram.

Normal children were extremely consistent in their performance on the gating task. They performed at around 40 percent correct for the first two gates, then close to 100 percent at the next three gates, which were as follows: final consonant release, the whole word (electronic), and a live voice saying the word. The children with articulation problems had the same difficulty at the first two gates, but were only marginally better at the next two, including the electronic version of the whole word. All scored 100 percent success with the live-voice presentation. These children were extremely variable across all the gates.

In the noise-center task, normal children were barely affected by how much of the vowel was usurped by noise. The children with articulation problems were profoundly affected. Most were unable to identify the vowel unless 70 percent of the vowel was intact.

Speech output was recorded, digitized, and analyzed by computer.[3] Individual records were created for each person saying the words *good*, *baby*, *dog*, set out here in the *true* order of short-, medium-, and long-duration vowels measured in milliseconds. (Note that the phoneticians' *accurate* assessment of vowel length bears no relationship to how the terms *long* and *short* vowels are used in the classroom where /ae/ in 'baby' is "long" and the /o/ in dog is "short.") Adults' speech profiles looked remarkably alike, whether measured as repetitions from the same person, or in comparisons between all six people. Both groups of children had slower speech (longer vowel duration) and were much more variable than adults.

The children with articulation problems were different from the normal children on a number of measures. They were unable to control their speaking rate (fast/slow) when asked to do so. They did not alter vowel length proportionally (short, medium, long) on the three vowels listed above. They executed the consonant leading to the vowel too quickly, relying on ballistic-type movements. They had equal difficulty linking the vowel and final consonant to such an extent that they often produced the wrong consonant: /t/ for /k/ and /d/ for /g/. These are gross errors, moving the place of articulation from the back to the front of the mouth. The analysis of the production patterns for the consonants /t/ and /k/ (*Timmy*,

---

3. Measures were overall vowel duration and transition duration, slope and starting frequency of second formant transitions, and first and second spectral moments or "center of gravity" and "skewness."

kitty) showed that many children couldn't vary their articulation suffi-ciently to distinguish them, whereas the speech profiles were quite distinct for the adults and normal children.

Edwards et al. concluded from their analysis of timing patterns that the cause of the problem was the child's inability to execute jaw move-ments and tongue movements independently of each other. This led to difficulties in timing speech gestures, sometimes starting the vowel too early, omitting final consonants, or substituting another one.

Nevertheless, children with speech-motor problems recognized and understood live-voice speech perfectly. Their perceptual difficulties were revealed only when speech was degraded or artificially produced, suggest-ing that their perceptions were woolly or more imprecise than those of the normal children. In brain terms, this is a signal-to-noise problem; the auditory system needs a stronger signal (louder, clearer, more acousti-cally complete) to discriminate it from the background noise of the brain (Conrad and Hull 1964; McGuinness 1985).

Edwards et al. will be continuing this work using a larger group of children, and felt that this new approach had been extremely productive. They commented on the remarkable link between speech perception and production:

The children with phonological disorders as a group clearly differ from their age peers in all three of these aspects of phonological competence: perception, production, and the inverse mapping between perception and production. These patterns suggest that at least part of the knowledge deficit that consti-tutes a "phonological disorder" for some children is a weak cognitive repre-sentation of the redundant perceptual cues for speech sounds or the motor control structures necessary for producing and coordinating gestures. These results are consistent with the view that phonological contrast is a cognitive property that emerges from the *incremental acquisition* of robust representa-tions of phonological knowledge *at many different levels*—not just at the level of categorical lexical contrast. (Edwards et al. 1999, 184; emphasis mine)

This is a clear statement of systems interaction or "reciprocal causality," where perception *and* motor gestures are both intimately involved in ex-pressive language.

Links |

Evidence from Normal Children

In a series of developmental studies on normal children by Nittrouer and her colleagues, electronic measures were made of both speech perception and speech production in children age 3, 4, 5, and 7. Nittrouer, Studdert-Kennedy, and McGowan (1989) measured the speech production of *shoe*, *Sue*, *she*, *see*, the words from the perception experiment reviewed in chapter 3 (Nittrouer and Studdert-Kennedy 1987). The children were asked to repeat word couplets (*shoe-shoe*). These were recorded and the output analyzed similarly to the previous study.[4]

The results showed that younger children (3, 4, and 5 years) spoke more slowly than 7-year-olds and adults. Vowels were contrasted well across all ages, but consonants were not. Three- and 4-year-olds had trouble producing distinct articulatory patterns for /s/ and /sh/. They had even more difficulty timing speech gestures and rushed coarticulation with the vowel. These patterns are similar to those found in the older speech-impaired children in the previous study. This confirms a growing body of evidence that speech-impaired children speak like much younger, normal children, and that speech problems are more likely to be due to a delay than to an impairment.

In subsequent studies, Nittrouer focused on timing and coarticulation (Nittrouer 1993, 1995; Nittrouer, Studdert-Kennedy, and Neely 1996). Children age 3, 5, and 7 years were compared to adults. Nittrouer's theoretical position shares features with Liberman and Mattingly in that specific *speech gestures* form the invariant and fundamental units of speech production. The long, slow progress of speech production has to do with the timing and integration of these gestures. In these studies, children were asked to produce word-pair repetitions or short sentences with the target word embedded in it ("It's a *shoe* Bob"). Speech patterns between and within syllables were compared.

There were significant differences between adults and children, but none between the younger age groups. All the children focused most on the vowel, and differentiated vowel production more than adults did. For example, children produced the vowel /ee/ with a higher pitch than vowels

---

4. Measures were relative amplitude/frequency, centroids, and contrast ratios for both vowels and second formant transitions for consonants.

/o͞o/ /ah/ /uh/. Adults did not produce this contrast. In children's speech, the high-pitched /ee/ vowel acted back on the preceding consonant (/s/ or /sh/) to raise its pitch as well, evidence of coarticulation.

The timing of children's speech gestures *between* syllable or word units was similar to that of the adults. Goodell and Studdert-Kennedy (1993) reported that 22-month-old children were noticeably different in this respect. A developmental shift seems to take place during the third year that leads to the production of clear syllable (or word) boundaries. By age 3, differences between children's and adults' speech lie *within the syllable*. Children initiate the vowel gesture earlier, sustain the vowel longer, and contrast different vowels to a greater extent than adults. Production of consonants is less precise.

Nittrouer et al. pointed out that children's vowel gestures are actually more "distinct spatially than those of adults," showing that children are not just "sloppy" talkers. However, children's speech gestures within syllables are more mechanically coupled and have greater temporal overlap. Their speech looks most adultlike when sequences of consonants and vowels are produced by articulators that are least anatomically related. Thus children's difficulties in developing adult-level speaking skills aren't due to problems with coarticulation, but in mastering the relative timing of speech gestures within syllables, and this is most difficult when the sequences involve adjacent articulators. Adults have the same trouble shifting between similar articulators in tongue twisters like *She sells seashells by the seashore.*

Although the goal of Nittrouer's studies was to document developmental patterns in speech perception and speech production, not to compare them directly, she and her colleagues came to the same conclusion as Edwards: "A child's phonology is grounded in both perceptual and motoric constraints. Certainly, perceptual capacity is logically prior to and must lead productive capacity, but perhaps the two are never far apart" (Nittrouer, Studdert-Kennedy, and McGowan 1989, 131).

The evidence is clear that difficulties in speech discrimination run in tandem with difficulties in articulation. If so, then fine-grained speech recognition (what Edwards et al. called "redundant perceptual cues") is yet another marker of normal temporal variation and tightly linked to speech production. There is certainly support for theories that link speech perception and production (Liberman and Mattingly 1985; Vihman 1993), but no proof that they are correct and no evidence for mechanism. Although Tallal's model makes no specific predictions about this link, her research with Stark shows the connection is strong. So far, most researchers are in agreement that speech perception leads speech production, contrary to Liberman and Mattingly's model.

Links between Nonverbal Auditory Perception and Language Development

There is little research on the connection between basic auditory (nonverbal) perception and language except for the studies carried out by Tallal and her colleagues. However, one team of researchers investigated this connection in a very unusual way, testing infants for their auditory sensitivity, then measuring language skills later in time.

Infants

Auditory perception was found to be linked to subsequent language development in a remarkable longitudinal study by Trehub, Schneider, and Henderson (1995) and Trehub and Henderson (1996). Infants $6\frac{1}{2}$ and 12 months old were trained in a head-turn procedure to signal if they heard a gap of silence in a brief tone. The silent gaps varied in duration, and could last 8, 12, 16, 20, 28, or 40 ms, very short intervals indeed. The $6\frac{1}{2}$-month-old infants detected the gaps from 12 ms on up significantly above chance, and the 12-month-olds could easily hear even the 8 ms gap, evidence for a development shift.

One hundred and twenty-eight children were followed up at 16 and 30 months of age. Parents filled out the MacArthur Communicative Development Inventory or CDI (Fenson et al. 1993), a measure of a range of expressive language capabilities: productive vocabulary, use of irregular verbs, sentence complexity, and mean length of utterance (MLU). The children were divided into two groups on the basis of their error rates on the gap test. The children in the group with higher error rates scored significantly lower on all measures of the CDI.

Trehub and Henderson urged caution in interpreting these results, commenting that an infant's aptitude for detecting a gap in a tone is just as likely to be determined by developmental status as by some inherent advantage in auditory-processing skill. Nevertheless, they were surprised to find such a consistent effect over this extended period of time.

Trehub and Henderson made the point that their results were based on normal children and in no way imply any type of impairment in the children with lower gap scores. They also made it clear that the results

have no bearing on the controversy surrounding temporal processing and language impairment (e.g., Studdert-Kennedy and Mody 1995; Tallal et al. 1993).... There are no suggestions ... that the level of temporal resolution exhibited by infants performing below the median ... is insufficient to support normal language acquisition.

It is also unclear whether the findings reflect factors specific to temporal resolution and language. What remains to be determined is whether infants with better temporal resolution than their age-mates are simply more attentive or developmentally advanced, or whether their superior performance is domain-specific. (p. 1319)

Trehub and Henderson continued to stress developmental status as critical to the association between auditory temporal processing and general language. There are, in fact, important neurological changes that occur in the auditory system during development. Sensory pathways take several years to become fully myelinated (Kolb and Wishaw 1990). (Myelin is a fatty sheath that grows around nerve fibers and rapidly speeds up neural transmission.) If a child's myelinization rate is slower, signals will take longer to propagate and may tend to be less precise temporally. This would make it harder to tell signals apart (discriminate among them) or notice very small gaps of silence.

It's important to understand what the brain is doing in the gap test. The auditory system has an amazing capacity to discriminate changes in signals within signals within signals. There are three auditory relays or processing stages in the brain stem (cochlear nucleus, superior olive, inferior colliculus). These systems can detect differences in the time of arrival of a signal to the left and right ears on the order of microseconds, a primary cue in sound localization (a microsecond is a thousandth of a millisecond). It's these brain-stem systems (not the auditory cortex) that function as "gap detectors." All the brain has to do in this task is register a brief period of silence. It doesn't have to compare signals or make judgments about them, tasks where the auditory cortex is critical. The fact that these brain-stem systems are hard wired (primitive and universal in mam-

mals) suggests that an explanation based on developmental status is likely
to be correct.

Auditory Processing in Children with Language Impairments
Most of the research in this section is based on the work of Tallal and
her associates. Tallal's theory has been highly influential in fashioning remedial programs for children with severe speech-production and speech-
perception problems. The theory, and the remedial programs, have been
extended to children with reading problems as well (Tallal 1980; Merzenich et al. 1993). My goal here is to look at the empirical support for her
theory of language development that is purported to explain reading acquisition. Tallal's research on children with reading problems is reviewed
in part III.

Tallal's theory is based on a set of assumed connections between auditory processing, speech perception, and language development that ultimately have an impact on reading. This is The Dogma with a twist:

Longitudinal studies have demonstrated that the vast majority of developmental dysphasic children have inordinate difficulty learning to read.... A
broad body of research now suggests that phonological awareness and coding
deficits may be at the heart of developmental reading disorders.... There
may be a continuum between developmental language disorders and the types
of reading disorders, which are characterized by deficits in phonological
awareness.... Deficits in *basic temporal processing* may interfere with phoneme
analysis leading to initial speech perception and/or language deficits, and subsequent deficits in phonological awareness and reading development. (Tallal,
Sainberg, and Jernigan 1991, 369, 370; emphasis mine)

According to Tallal et al., this is a genetically determined biological
deficit: "The physiological basis of phoneme awareness deficits in dyslexia
may be basic temporal integration and serial memory deficits, and ... it
may be these deficits which are transmitted genetically" (p. 370).

The central question for this section is whether these conclusions
(apart from the initial premise) are supported by the data. The origins
of Tallal's theory can be traced to the 1960s. Researchers had suggested
that severe language delays or "developmental aphasia" might be due to
a processing dysfunction in sequencing auditory input (Eisenson 1968;

Benton 1964; Stark 1967). Efron (1963) discovered that adult aphasics had difficulty telling two rapidly sequenced tones apart. He proposed that the left hemisphere of the brain, along with its other linguistic functions, is specialized for rapid temporal analysis of auditory signals. Lowe and Campbell (1965) used Efron's tones task to test children with language impairments; they found that these children had more difficulty on this task than normal children.

Tallal's doctoral thesis was based on this work. She and her colleague Piercy expanded Efron's test in a number of ways, and carried out a series of experiments on severely aphasic children (Tallal and Piercy 1973a, 1973b, 1974, 1975). These children had particular trouble processing rapid, brief, auditory signals. Because they had similar problems with tones and with CV syllables, it was concluded that the deficit was not specific to language, and that a nonspecific auditory deficit would play a causal role in creating a receptive language impairment.

This was (and is) the model that Tallal favored, even though there were other explanations for her results. Tallal herself suggested one in her thesis after analyzing the children's individual test scores. This was paraphrased in the 1974 paper:

The ability to process non-verbal auditory stimuli rapidly and the capacity to discriminate phonemes, develops with age, reaching an asymptote on the tests ... by the age of $8\frac{1}{2}$ years. A high proportion of dysphasic children eventually attain near-normal language proficiency and this was the case with two members of our dysphasic group who performed best on our tests. Accordingly, the possibility exists that developmental dysphasia results, not from a permanent deficit, but from *delayed development* of rapid auditory processing. (Tallal and Piercy 1974, 92; emphasis mine)

This is the first and last time a developmental delay was considered by Tallal.

In 1978, the final component of the model was put in place in a study on brain-damaged adults (Tallal and Newcombe 1978). In the opening section of this study, the "impairment" theme is prominent: "The results of these studies [meaning Tallal's previous studies] support the hypothesis that some developmental language disorders may result from a primary impairment in auditory temporal analysis" (p. 13).

On the basis of the brain-damaged patients' performance on Tallal's nonverbal tasks, Tallal and Newcombe argued that because many of the patients had marked *expressive* language difficulties, yet performed normally on the auditory tasks, an auditory-processing deficit is not necessarily related to speech production. However, it is intimately related to receptive language. And, because only the patients with left-hemisphere damage had problems with these auditory tests, the deficit must be related to a left-hemisphere function, as Efron had suggested.

It's a fallacy to compare brain-damaged adults to children with developmental language delays. A delay or deficit is not brain damage. There is also the problem that Tallal and Newcombe failed to report the precise locus of the brain lesions in these patients. There is no way to know *why* these patients had trouble with auditory processing (perception? memory? attention? motivation?), or what brain systems had to be affected for this to occur.

Superficially, Tallal's model seemed logical and persuasive to many people in the field. But a closer look at the children in the studies, the auditory tasks themselves, the way data were handled, and a variety of other methodological issues calls most of this research into question. Due to the highly technical nature of these problems, I put the complete analysis in appendix 1. Readers may want to consult this appendix for a more convincing proof of the following brief summary.

The Children Tallal's theory is based on the performance of the *same* twelve severely aphasic children, all attending a special school in England. This was an idiosyncratic group with extremely high nonverbal IQs and a myriad of language problems (see table 4.1). Despite this, the children were treated as a group and compared to a control group of normal children. One should not base a theory on children this unusual and generalize to all children with language delays or impairments. There is no way to know which language problem predicts which difficulty with Tallal's tasks. And this key issue remains a problem to the present day.

The Tasks Four tasks were designed to measure nonverbal and verbal auditory-processing skills. All tasks measured the ability to discriminate between two sounds and press one or two panels in response. Children must first learn to identify (*identification* task) two contrasting tones, and

Table 4.1

Profiles of twelve aphasic children based on Tallal and Piercy (1973 b)

Age	Receptive Language		Expressive Language		Schonell		Read/Spell
Yrs./ mos.	PPVT	Reynell	Reynell	Renfrew articu- lation	Read	Spell	Yrs. below age
8-4	3-1	3-1	3-6	<3	8-1	7-8	0
8-10	3-7	3-9	0	—	6-6	6-2	−2
8-7	—	4-6	6-0	4-6	7-5	7-5	−1
8-4	4-3	3-6	3-11	<3	8-2	7-9	0
8-8	6-2	4-8	4-8	4-4	7-3	7-7	−1
9-2	6-10	5-6	4-5	4-1	8-0	8-3	−1
9-2	7-7	>6	—	4-6	7-2	7-7	−2
7-9	5-1	>6	3-1	<3	6-5	7-0	−1
9-3	8-2	—	>6	3-6	7-3	7-3	−2
7-3	6-3	6-0	6-0	—	6-4	5-9	−1
6-9	5-10	>6	0	0	5-5	5-2	−1
9-1	12-1	—	—	4-7	8-5	8-3	−8 mos

Note: >6 ceiling (perfect score), — missing data. The language development scores are represented as years-months, set out in order of severity of the receptive language scores.

press panel 1 or 2. In a *same-different* judgment task, children press one panel if two tones are the same, and the other panel if they are different. In a sequencing task (*repetition* test), they hear two sounds in one of four orders (1–1, 1–2, 2–1, 2–2) and press the two panels accordingly. These sounds can vary in duration (long/short) and in presentation rate (slow/ fast). In the *memory* task, children press panels to indicate the order of extended tone sequences: 1–1–2–1–2.

Here are the problems:

1. The repetition test is not a valid psychophysical test. First, there aren't enough trials (only four) at each presentation rate/duration to produce reliable data. Second, this test measures the limits of auditory discrimination, technically known as a *difference threshold* (a just noticeable difference). People are deaf to signals below their sensory thresholds, and their only option is to guess. For this reason, data on responses to signals

below threshold must be discarded. This was not done here. Instead, all data were included in the statistical analyses.

2. None of the tasks meet requirements for a valid psychological test. There are no norms. The tasks are highly subject to guessing (press one of two panels, press two panels in sequence), and the nature of the tasks (long and tedious) increases this likelihood even further. The scores for each individual must be corrected for guessing by binomial test, and this was not done. No measures of performance consistency (split-half or test-retest reliabilities) were used.

As a result of points 1 and 2 above, the tasks won't measure what they purport to measure. This means they lack "construct validity"—there is no way to know if they are valid measures of auditory perception.

Data Analysis Corrections for guessing (by binomial test) needed to be carried out on all tests for each child individually, and this was not done. The wrong statistical tests were often used.

Due to these difficulties (plus others set out in appendix 1), I can report only general trends in the data. Three types of synthesized sounds were used in the early studies on which Tallal based her theory: (1) two complex "speechlike tones" in which one element (a formant) varied in pitch (100 versus 300 Hz); (2) two synthesized vowels, /e/ (*bet*) and /a/ (*bat*); and (3) two synthesized CV syllables, *ba* and *da*. The results were published in four separate papers, and I will take up each briefly.

To participate in the main tasks, the child first had to score twenty out of twenty-four trials on the identification test. The data for "speech-like tones" on the same-different task and the repetition test were reported in Tallal and Piercy 1973a. The control group performed nearly perfectly on these tasks for all signal durations at all presentation rates. From the figures, it appears that the majority of the aphasic children scored at chance on "brief" tones presented at rates of 150 ms or faster (see appendix 1). There was no information on which aphasic children scored above or below chance, because chance wasn't measured.

In a second report on the same data (Tallal and Piercy 1973b), the wrong statistical test was used, and this will not be considered further. This paper also included the *memory* task. Very few of the aphasic children were able to reach criterion at three, four, or five elements when the tones were brief (75 ms), but most succeeded when the tones were long (250 ms). Aphasic children were consistently worse than the normal children on sequences with four and five elements, indicating possible short-term memory problems.

The results on tasks using electronic speech (vowels and CV syllables) were reported in Tallal and Piercy 1974. The aphasic children had no problems with vowels at any duration or rate, with the exception of the five-element sequence in the memory task. The most striking difference between the groups was on the synthesized syllables: *ba* and *da*. Only five of the aphasic children reached criterion on the initial identification training, and only two were able to carry out the remaining tasks with any degree of success. These syllables are distinguished by initial patterns of voicing cues occurring within the first 40 ms. Overall, the results showed that aphasic children had more difficulty hearing and comparing *brief* acoustic cues.

Tallal and Piercy (1975) investigated whether it was the "brevity" or the *nature* of the sounds (tones or speech) that created the problems for the aphasic children. A pair of vowels was contrasted by shrinking the main acoustic cue to 43 ms. Consonants in the *ba/da* syllables were "stretched" so the critical cues lasted 95 ms. Now the results were reversed. Nearly half of the aphasic children failed to reach criterion on the vowels, and all but two of them failed most of the remaining tests. With consonant transitions prolonged, the aphasic children performed as well as the normal children. The results showed that signal duration was the important cue for accurate performance on these tasks. Children with severe language impairments had more trouble comparing sounds that are contrasted by brief acoustic signals.

Tallal and Piercy (1974, 91) interpreted the aphasics' difficulty as a discrimination problem for "rate of processing." However, *rate* could mean the pace of the signals or the brevity of the signals (or components of them). They opted for the brevity explanation, arguing that "it is the duration of the formant transition which results in the dysphasic children being unable to discriminate the consonant stimuli."

In 1975, they reaffirmed this conclusion: "The two experiments reported here strongly suggest that it is the brevity not the transitional character of this component of synthesized consonants which results in the impaired perception of our dysphasic children." They believed the deficit was not linguistic but due to "an impaired rate of processing auditory information" (p. 73).

What really caused these results? Did the children who struggled on these tasks have low verbal IQs? Were they younger? Were they less willing to pay attention during these long, tedious tasks? There is no explanation or information in any report on the apparent fact that some aphasic children did well and others did badly. What kind of language impairment predicted problems with these tasks?

An additional set of studies (Tallal and Stark 1981; Stark and Tallal 1981) was carried out on thirty-five children who fit the more typical clinical pattern of "specific language impairment" (SLI). These are children with normal (not superior) nonverbal IQ scores and poor language skills. The children ranged in age from 5 to $8\frac{1}{2}$ years, and were at least 1 year below norms on expressive and receptive language tests. Children with articulation problems were screened out to test Tallal's theory that auditory perceptual problems mainly have an impact on *receptive language* skills. A group of normal children (controls) were similar in age, performance IQ, and socioeconomic status.

The children were tested on six synthetic speech contrasts: /e/–/a/, *ba-da*, *da-ta*, *dob-dab*, *sa-sta*, and *sa-sha*. Vowels lasted 40 ms, syllables at least 250 ms, and neither varied in duration or rate of presentation. The children had to judge each pair of speech contrasts and were trained to a criterion of twelve out of sixteen consecutive trials correct. If they were not successful, they were considered to have failed the task.

The data consisted of trials to criterion and total errors. Because the SLI group needed more training trials, error scores were confounded by the number of trials. The error data were also unreliable. Because of these problems, I will limit my remarks to trials to criterion only.[5]

The SLI children took from one to ten trials longer to reach criterion on each of the six tasks, thirty-eight more trials altogether. They needed the most trials (ten) to master the *ba-da* contrast, and even then thirteen

---

5. Standard deviations were larger than the means on every task for both groups (nonnormally distributed). This is a telltale sign that the children were highly unstable in their performance and that the task is unreliable.

SLI children failed to meet the criterion of twelve out of sixteen, in contrast to two controls. On the *sa-sta* contrast twelve of the SLI group failed, versus four controls, and on the *sa-sha* contrast nine SLI failed versus three controls. There were no group differences for the remaining sounds.

This is one way to look at the data. But there's another way. The *success* rate was good in meeting the stringent criterion of twelve out of sixteen trials correct for the SLI children, as shown by the percent who succeeded.

Task	% successful
dab–dob	91
da–ta	89
/e/–/a/	89
sa–sha	74
sa–sta	66
ba–da	63

Well over half met criterion on all six tasks, and nearly everyone on three. The SLI children may take a few more trials to get there, but not much more: twenty-two versus seventeen trials on average. Thus, a fair interpretation of the results is that speech-recognition skills for most of these language-impaired children were essentially normal. Furthermore, several children in the control group had problems similar to those of the SLI children.

Findings from earlier studies were not replicated. The SLI group had no trouble with the very short (40 ms) vowels, though in the study by Tallal and Piercy (1975) the aphasic children had considerable trouble. There was no group difference on the *sa-sta* contrast, whereas Tallal and Stark 1978 had found one earlier. This could be due to a number of things: different degrees of severity between the groups, different ages between the children who failed or succeeded, invalid tests, incorrect data handling, wrong statistical tests, or highly unstable performance. Or it could simply be because groups of language-impaired children are too heterogeneous to provide consistent results.

This phase of the research culminated with a multiple regression analysis on data from twenty-six developmentally dysphasic children age 5 to 9 years (Tallal, Stark, and Mellits 1985). Upward of 200 different scores for each child were entered into the analysis.[6]

A multiple regression analysis is a highly unstable form of correlational statistics. Because of this, there are limits to how many tests can be entered into the analysis as a function of the number of people in the study. The least conservative criterion is $N/10 - 2$ (Biddle and Martin 1987), and even this wouldn't permit *one test* in a study with only twenty-six children ($26/10 - 2 = .6$), let alone up to 200 tests. This explains the anomalous result in which three measures of the *ba-da* contrast cumulatively predicted 61 percent of the variance in receptive language! (This statistical problem is taken up in chapter 11.)

Tallal, Stark, and Mellits drew far-reaching conclusions from these invalid results: "Of all the perceptual, motor, and demographic variables that were assessed in this study, including auditory, visual, tactile, and cross-modal sensory and perceptual functions, the only variables entering the multiple regression equation predicting levels of receptive language in dysphasic children, were acoustic perceptual variables." This was said to support earlier findings that "initially led us to hypothesize a direct relationship between deficits in *rapid temporal analysis* and disordered language development" (p. 530; emphasis mine).

There was further speculation on which areas of the brain might be involved in this type of auditory processing, and Tallal, Stark, and Mellits believed the results provided "strong anatomical support for our hypothesis concerning a precise timing mechanism underlying hemisphere specialization—for a deficient timing mechanism which may underlie the receptive language deficits of developmentally dysphasic children" (p. 533). This is a lot to pin on a correlational analysis even if the results had been valid.

---

6. Data were obtained on the six sound contrasts used in the study above, plus discrimination tests described as "auditory, visual, and cross modal," plus "a series of computer synthesized minimal pair speech sounds," requiring "detection, association, discrimination, sequencing, rate processing, and serial memory," and that are "presented in increasingly longer series at various rates of presentations." Also included were various receptive and expressive language tests; tests for motor control and coordination, balance, and tactile perception; and a test of laterality (Tallal, Stark, and Mellits 1985, 529).

Although the language-impaired children had more problems with these tests than normal children did, this group of studies does not explain why. Apart from the methodological concerns, what was needed were longitudinal studies that tracked individual children over time. The key question remains: Are children with these difficulties truly impaired or do they have a developmental delay?

Developmental Changes in Language-Impaired Children's Speech Perception
Elliott and Hammer (1988) are Elliott, Hammer, and Scholl (1989) carried out a longitudinal study on 6- to 9-year-olds predicted to be at risk for language problems and placed in special classes at school. They used the standard categorical-perception task in which consonant contrasts (*ba-da-ga, ba-pa*) slowly turn into one another. Children were followed for 3 years. They were well matched to a control group on IQ, so this was not a factor. The only significant result appeared in the first year of the study when the at-risk group had more trouble discriminating a *ba-da* contrast. They had no greater problems than the normal children on other contrasts (*ga-da, ba-pa*). By the second year of the study, there were no differences between the groups on any contrast.

Bernstein and Stark (1985) reported that auditory/speech-discrimination problems evaporated over time for language-impaired children who had done badly on Tallal's repetition test at age 6. At follow-up 4 years later, they were no different from the control group on any task. Nor did Lincoln et al. (1992) find any differences between normal and language-impaired adolescents and young adults, except on sequences that extended to six or seven elements (memory problems). Thus, discriminating artificial speech contrasts, especially *ba-da* (and not much else), improves with age for everyone, but at a slower rate for children identified as language impaired. These children reach normal levels sometime between the ages of 7 and 10 years, suggesting they are on the far-left side of the curve of normal temporal variation in speech perception. This does not mean, necessarily, that they don't have other language problems.

The Fate of Tallal's Theory
Tallal's theory was put to a definitive test in a study on twins (Bishop, Bishop et al. 1999; Tallal was a coauthor). This study included some of the important controls that had been missing in the earlier work. Tallal's

theory had changed little, despite the data from the longitudinal studies that pointed to a developmental explanation. Key assumptions included the following:

1. A nonverbal auditory-perception problem affects receptive language.
2. This perceptual problem is due to a *global temporal-processing deficit*; it is not specifically related to speech production.
3. This is a consequence of some malfunction of the left hemisphere that is hypothesized to have specialized neurons/circuits for processing rapidly changing signals.
4. Auditory temporal processing is critically involved in the development of phoneme awareness and is one of the major causes of reading skill.
5. In addition, Tallal predicted that her tests would be a strong marker for heritability of a language impairment.

Bishop et al. tried to accommodate Tallal's requirement for a receptive language problem in selecting the children for the study, but this only showed how difficult (nay impossible) it is to find children with only a receptive language disorder. The actual criteria had to be more inclusive. These were nonverbal IQ (Raven's matrices) above the 10th percentile (above 80), and scoring at or below the 10th percentile on two or more language measures, one of which had to be a receptive language test. Plus, there had to be no history of speech therapy (to rule out preexisting articulation problems).

Bishop et al. tested fifty-five twins (71 percent male) who met the criteria above, plus seventy-six normal children (42 percent male). The age range was 7 to 13 years. The groups differed in sex ratios, age (language impaired 1 year older), and nonverbal IQ. For this reason, sex, age, and nonverbal IQ were controlled in all statistical analyses.[7]

---

7. Bishop, Bishop, et al. (1999) supplied descriptive data for this study. The language-impaired group scored at 75 standard score (25 points below the controls) on three of the four language measures, which included verbal comprehension from the WISC. The least discrepant score (86) was on the TROG, a measure of receptive grammar.

In addition to taking language tests, the children were given a non-word repetition test (the child hears a nonsense word and has to repeat it), the "speechlike tones" version of Tallal's repetition test (two elements), and the sequencing test (three to seven elements). Tones were presented at either a leisurely pace (500 ms apart) or fast pace (10 ms or 70 ms). The data from the slow and fast rates were analyzed separately, but combined across *all sequence lengths* (three through seven elements). This meant that simple auditory discrimination (two or three elements) was confounded with short-term memory (four to seven elements). Also, these data should have been corrected for guessing but were not. These oversights may have affected the results.

With age, sex, and nonverbal IQ statistically controlled, the SLI children were significantly less accurate ($p < .004$) on Tallal's tests. However, there was no difference in accuracy due to presentation rate (fast or slow). In other words, there was no evidence that the SLI children were differentially worse processing "rapid temporal sequences" than slow ones. This led Bishop et al. to conclude that there was no evidence for a "global temporal-processing deficit" in these children: "Rather than providing an index of specific rate processing problems, the Repetition Test gave us an overall measure that reflected how well the child could discriminate and remember nonverbal auditory sequences" (p. 165).

A series of correlations on the four language tests showed that Tallal's repetition test had far less connection to the language tests than the non-word repetition test did. When age, sex, IQ, and nonword repetition scores were entered first into a multiple regression analysis, Tallal's test made no further contribution. When the order was reversed, nonword repetition continued to make a strong contribution. Bishop et al. had expected Tallal's repetition test to be highly correlated to the nonword test (both require good auditory processing), but this was not the case. These results suggest whatever it is that makes SLI children perform worse on Tallal's tasks may have *little or nothing to do with language!* This is especially problematic for Tallal's theory in view of the fact that the SLI children were chosen to fit a language profile predicted by her theory.

Nor did performance on Tallal's tasks have any hereditary connection to language skills. Bishop et al. compared monozygotic (identical) and dizygotic (fraternal) twins using three different formulaes to estimate heritability. The patterns of correlations between the two types of twin pairs showed no evidence for any genetic (biological) link between performance on Tallal's test and language status. By contrast, performance on the nonword repetition test was highly heritable.

In the same year, Bishop and her colleagues (Bishop, Carlyon et al. 1999) published a study on a subset of the twins that again failed to confirm Tallal's theory of an auditory temporal deficit in language-impaired children. This time children with language impairments and normal children were matched for nonverbal IQ, sex, and age. No differences were found between these groups on a variety of nonverbal auditory tasks that measured thresholds for various brief signals. These included detecting a 20 ms tone in a noise burst, pitch discrimination, and discrimination of frequency-modulated signals (wobble).

The most interesting result emerged from an analysis of the individual data. Children were tested five times on three different occasions to look at test-retest stability. The first surprise was that the children's hearing improved noticeably from the first to the second or third testing. In one task, they found a very large drop (−20 decibels) in hearing threshold (better hearing) from the first to the third testing. A second finding was proof of the boredom/fatigue factor suggested earlier. They found enormous variability in individual children's scores both within and between test sessions, showing that attention and motivation wandered excessively.

The boredom factor had been neatly pinned down by Hurford et al. (1994) in a longitudinal study using Tallal's repetition test. The children's complaints and their obvious frustration with this test led Hurford to break the data into trial blocks: early, middle, late. They did this for four test sessions beginning at early first grade to late second grade. I carried out a binomial test to determine significance above chance, with the following results. During the first session (early first grade) the children didn't score significantly above chance on any of the trial blocks. For the next 2 years, a consistent pattern appeared. On the first trial block (twelve trials), performance was significantly above chance; for the middle trial block, average scores were barely above chance, and for the final trial block, scores were no better than chance. Hurford et al. reported that the differences between the three trials blocks were highly significant ($p < .0001$), with children getting progressively worse over trials.

This is further evidence that Tallal's tests measure something that is unrelated to language, such as the child's ability or willingness to perform optimally on a tedious, difficult task. In view of the methodological problems with this work, there is no way to know what these tests are measuring. Furthermore, the studies on twins show that performance on these tasks doesn't fulfill the primary predictions of Tallal's theory: that the auditory deficit is due to an inherent flaw in left-hemisphere processing, that it is biological, and that it has genetic roots.

We will return to Tallal's theory once more in part III in the discussion of the controversy that has blown up over the alleged connection between reading skill and rapid temporal processing of auditory signals.

Summary

Tallal's theory can't be maintained in view of the serious methodological problems in this work, and the negative results from the better controlled studies. So far, one set of findings is of potential importance—the strong link between the development of speech perception and speech production (articulation). But this research does not tell us which of the three remaining hypotheses (if any) are correct. Do speech gestures form the template for speech recognition? Or does speech recognition (implicit sensitivity to phonetic structure) set up a platform or framework for the development of speech production? Or do they develop in some type of reciprocal interaction? There seems to be more support for the last two hypotheses than for the first.

The research by Stark and Tallal (1979), Edwards et al. (1999), and Nittrouer and her group (1989, 1995, 1996) shows that if speech gestures are the templates for speech recognition, *they are very poor templates indeed.* Accuracy, placement, and timing are so imprecise in young children or children with language delays that these speech patterns are highly unlikely to derive from innate gestural templates for speech perception. This argument is supported by the fact that perception of natural speech is essentially normal in these children. Furthermore, the gestural theory can't explain why speech perception is so strongly affected by receptive vocabulary.

Meanwhile, the last word on the connection between speech perception, speech production, and phonological awareness must go to Chaney (1992), whose outstanding research is reviewed in the following chapter.

YOUNG CHILDREN'S ANALYSIS OF LANGUAGE

Research on the link between speech perception and speech production outlined in the preceding chapter involved artificial, highly controlled tasks where the child had to engage in equally artificial types of behavior, such as repeating odd phrases: "It's a shoe Bob." These kinds of studies are extremely important because of their precision and the high degree of control over all variables. However, they don't measure what young children can do in more realistic situations, where tasks require normal, spontaneous behavior.

In this chapter we explore children's aptitude for processing and analyzing natural language. We will be looking at two things: first, whether the links between speech perception and speech production are reflected in normal behavioral responses in natural language tasks, and second, whether there is any evidence that *explicit awareness* of phonology proceeds from words to syllables to phonemes, or whether this awareness follows the time lines reported by I. Y. Liberman et al. (1974) or by Fox and Routh (1975). The single study in this chapter is a direct test of the validity of the tasks used in these two studies (see chapter 2).

When scientists embark on the study of a new domain of interest, such as whether children are "explicitly" aware of phonological units or whether this awareness develops in a particular sequence, the first step is to map the "domain of inquiry." The tried-and-true method is descriptive and correlational. Tests are devised to measure children's performance on all possible phonological units (words, syllables, rhyming endings, and phonemes), using all possible linguistic categories (semantic, syntactic, and morphemic). Furthermore, this should be done with strict objectivity, unconstrained by theoretical baggage. A remarkable study by Carol

Chaney fulfills all these requirements, one of the few studies to do so. It is also noteworthy for its excellent methodology.

Chaney (1992) set out to investigate the "metalinguistic" skills of normal 3-year-olds, and the subsequent impact of these skills on the process of learning to read. Metalinguistic ("above or beyond language") skills involve an explicit awareness of one's own speech attempts. There is considerable debate about whether metalinguistic awareness is part of general cognitive development—not specific to language per se—or whether it arises through competence in individual language skills. The "general cognitive" argument has been used to explain why 5- and 6-year olds have problems with complex phoneme-awareness tests. In this view, it's not the test that's the problem, *the child's developmental level is the problem*.

The alternative idea is that any metalevel skill develops in tandem with a particular domain and emerges as a function of competence in that domain. When basic-level skills become proficient and nearly automatic, there is more spare capacity to reflect on what you are doing while you are doing it. According to Chaney, metalinguistic abilities change as children go through stages of acquisition. From this perspective, *the tests are the problem*, not the child's developmental level.

Chaney defined metalinguistic awareness as "the ability to think explicitly about language; to manipulate structural features of language such as phonemes (speech sounds), words, and sentences; and to focus on the forms of language separately from the meanings." This includes "an ability to comprehend and produce language in a communicative way [plus] an ability to *separate language structure from communicative intent*" (p. 485; emphasis mine).

Metalinguistic ability is revealed by aptitudes like being able to segment sentences into words, segment words into syllables and phonemes, detect structural ambiguities, judge syntactic appropriateness of sentences, and so forth.

One of the difficulties in determining whether a child is metalinguistically aware has been the nature of the data up to this point, a central problem in all the research on phoneme awareness. By and large, the general cognitive theory is based on tasks that require mastery and are often abstract, drawing on multiple skills. The children have to hold and retrieve information from memory and perform several operations at once. It's common for the tasks to be explained to them using abstract language.

On the other hand, the evidence for children's spontaneous metalinguistic productions is anecdotal or observational and impossible to replicate. There are scores of idiosyncratic examples of 2- and 3-year-olds' metalinguistic-type utterances in the literature. Chaney provides several examples: word play ("cancake, pancake"), rhymes ("boodle, noodle—that matches"), alliteration ("deanut dutter danwich"), plus children fixing their own and other peoples' speech errors while making comments about them: "*Nafan* is hard to say. It has a /th/ in it."

Chaney's solution was to design tests that would allow children to show whether they were able to exhibit these more spontaneous behaviors in a controlled situation. She based her tasks on previous research (Smith and Tager-Flusberg 1982), as well as on the literature documenting children's spontaneous utterances. She was able to elicit some surprising linguistic feats from very young children. This requires cleverly designed tasks plus a good deal of skill putting young children at ease. She relied heavily on the use of puppets that had various difficulties with English, sometimes due to place of origin (Mars), and sometimes due to personal idiosyncrasies. The tasks, where possible, were set up in pairs. The child first had to listen for the puppet's mistakes (speech perception) and then help the puppet fix them (speech production). This made it possible to measure receptive and productive language on the same type of task.

Altogether Chaney invented (or adapted) twenty-one tasks. Descriptions of the tasks are provided in box 5.1.

Chaney also administered the following tests:

• The *Primary Language test* (Zimmerman, Steiner, and Evatt-Pond 1979), a measure of general knowledge, concepts (number, color), and language skills.
• *Receptive vocabulary* (PPVT-R).
• *Phonetic discrimination and speech articulation* (Wallach et al. 1977). In the discrimination tasks, the child sees three pictures of objects with phonologically confusing names: *goat-boat-ball*. The child names each picture, then points to the picture named by the examiner. Articulation is checked as the child names the pictures.
• *Sentence structure test.* This was designed by Chaney to measure receptive and productive syntax. Phrases were adapted from young children's speech. The child hears a phrase, has to repeat it, then act it out with

Box 5.1
Description of the metalinguistic tasks

New names Select an unusual object from a grab bag, explore its function, and give it a name. (10)

Phoneme synthesis Child hears three segmented phonemes (/k/ /a/ /t/) and has to "join the sounds" and point to one of three pictures that shows that word. (10)

Phoneme judgment Puppet says a series of words. Some are mispronounced by one phoneme. Child says "right" or "wrong." (14)
Phoneme correction Child has to fix any phoneme errors made by the puppet. (8)

Morpheme judgment Puppet says a series of phrases. Sometimes there are morpheme errors (of plurals, or using /er/ to mean person: *batter*). Child says "right" or "wrong." (10)
Morpheme correction Child has to fix any morpheme errors made by the puppet. (8)
Morpheme cloze Child has to finish a sentence left incomplete by the puppet. (16)

Say five words Child is asked to say any five words of his or her choice. (5)

Syntax A. Judgment Child hears a phrase spoken by the examiner. This phrase is repeated by the puppet, which does or does not violate word order. Child must judge "right" or "wrong." (*teeth brush your.*) (8)
Syntax A. Correction Child must correct any errors the puppet made. (4)
Syntax B. Judgment Same as Syntax A, except the first step is missing. (8)
Syntax B. Correction Same as Syntax A, except child never hears phrase spoken correctly first. (4)

Word play Child is encouraged to alter words in nursery rhymes to make a "joke." ("Mary had a little cow.") (10)

Real vs. nonword judgment Child judges whether the puppet said a real word or not. (10)

Box 5.1
(continued)

Word referent—Relabeling The Martian puppet teaches the child a Martian word for a common object (not present). The child answers questions about the object, referenced in "Martian." ("Is a *gok* orange?") (12)

Word segmenting Child hears two to three words per set, all run together, and has to separate them and say them clearly for the puppet. (*balloontreeshirt*.) (12)

Phonological play Child is encouraged to "play" by substituting wrong words in compound words. The examiner starts the game, and the child keeps going: *pancake, cancake, mancake.* (Example uses "rhymes," but rhyming was not a requirement of the test.) (7)

Rhyme judgment Puppet "Jed" likes words that rhyme with (sound like) his name. Child listens to words and says whether they sound like "Jed" or not. (10)

Rhyme production Puppet "Hi" also likes words that rhyme with (sound like) his name. Child is asked to say some words that Hi will like.

Initial phoneme judgment Puppet Max likes words that start with the first sound in his name, /mmm/. Child listens to words to see if they start with the /mmm/ sound. (10)

Initial phoneme production Puppet Sue likes words that start /sssss/. Child is asked to say some words that Sue will like.

Note: Number in brackets = number of items in the test.
Source: Based on Chaney 1992.

---

toys ("Mommy pats the baby, and Daddy pats puppy"). Children's knowledge about print and books was also measured. *ABC concepts* is the ability to identify and name letters, numbers, and shapes. *Book concepts* measures understanding of sequence (order of pages, lines, direction of print, letters in words) and reference (which units are letters and words, the connection between print and words, and so forth).

There were 43 three-year-olds in the study, ranging in age from 33 to 50 months (average age 44 months); the majority were white and 38 percent were African-American. The children were normal in every way, with no language impairments or speech delays. Two measures were reported for every task. The first score was the percent of children performing significantly above chance (percent at or above a criterion set at $p = .03$, binomial test). The second score was the overall (average) percent correct. To interpret these scores, the reader should keep in mind that almost all the receptive language tasks (except phoneme synthesis) have only two choices (right/wrong), and the chance of getting a right answer is 50 percent. Interrater reliabilities for all tasks were above 90 percent.

The results are presented in table 5.1. The tasks are set out according to the proportion of children meeting criterion (significantly above chance), ordering tasks from easy to hard. Criterion values for each task and overall percent correct are provided. "Percent correct" doesn't take guessing into account, and this isn't necessary when answers are open-ended. The letters P and R stand for "productive language" and "receptive language" tasks respectively.

The easiest thing for a 3-year-old to do is invent new words for unusual objects, and 95 percent of the children met the criterion for scoring above chance. The big surprise among the easy tasks was the phoneme-synthesis test. The child heard three segmented phonemes, saw three pictures, had to blend the phonemes into a word, and had to point to the correct picture (93 percent met criterion, 88 percent correct). (This outcome contradicts Liberman and Shankweiler's (1985) contention that words can't be segmented into phonemes without gross distortion.) Phoneme judgment (noticing a word containing a mispronounced phoneme) and phoneme correction (saying it the right way) were nearly as easy, with 91 percent and 88 percent of the children meeting criterion and achieving overall scores of 91 percent and 86 percent correct. Ninety-one percent could "say five words" of their own choosing, showing they had no trouble understanding what a "word" is (contrary to what some researchers claim).

The 3-year-olds found it easy to detect missing or mispronounced morphemes (word segments that alter meaning), which in all cases were phonemes as well (plurals: /s/ (*cats*) or /z/ (*dogs*); *person*: /er/ mister), and 91 percent met criterion. They were far less proficient at helping the puppet fix its mistake, and only 65 percent met criterion. This is the first pair of tasks where receptive and productive language part company. This

Table 5.1

Metalinguistic tasks ranked by order of difficulty

Task	Rank	Criterion	% Met criterion	% Correct overall	Language category
New names	1	8/10	95		P
Phoneme synthesis	2	6/10	93	88	R
Phoneme judgment	3	10/14	91	91	R
Morpheme judgment	4	6/10	91	91	R
Say five words	5	4/5	91		P
Phoneme correction	6	6/8	88	86	P
Syntax A. Judgment	7	6/8	79	87	R
Syntax A. Correction	8	3/4	70	70	P
Word play	9	7/10	70	72	P
Morpheme correction	10	5/8	65	66	P
Real vs. nonword judgment	11	8/10	60	78	R
Morpheme cloze	12	12/16	60	77	P
Word referent	13	9/12	53	72	P
Word segmenting	14	7/12	53	49	P
Syntax B. Judgment	15	6/8	37	69	R
Phonological play (syllables)	16	3/7	37	37	P
Rhyme production	17	1/1	35	42	P
Initial phoneme production	18	1/1	28	30	P
Rhyme judgment	19	8/10	26	61	R
Initial phoneme judgment	20	8/10	14	58	R
Syntax B. Correction	21	3/4	7	18	P

Note: P = productive language, R = receptive language. "Criterion" = significantly above chance $p = .03$. "% correct" is uncorrected for chance.
Source: Data based on Chaney 1992.

result shows that noticing a morpheme error in a short phrase is easy, but locating the error and fixing it are not.

Syntactic errors were somewhat harder for the children to detect. On Syntax A, 79 percent reached criterion on the detection phase, and 70 percent succeeded on the correction phase. Syntax A differed from Syntax B in one important respect. On Syntax A, the examiner said the phrase correctly for the puppet. The puppet tried to repeat it, and the child had to judge how well it did. On Syntax B, the first step was omitted. Otherwise, the two tasks were the same. The puppet might say the phrase correctly ("brush your teeth") or incorrectly ("teeth brush your"). The child had to say "right" or "wrong," and correct the puppet's mistakes. Hearing the phrase spoken correctly beforehand was obviously very helpful in being able to perform this task, because the majority of children passed Syntax A, while nearly everyone failed Syntax B.

Looking over the tasks in which 60 percent or more of the children met criterion, it can be seen that the majority of 3-year-olds can monitor, produce, and manipulate words, morphemes, phonemes, and syntax. Half can relabel a familiar object (not visible) with a "Martian" word (word-referent task) and answer questions about it: "Is a *bok* green?"

However, while linguists and developmental psychologists might stumble onto precocious 2- and 3-year-olds playing with words and rhymes, this is not something the average 3-year-old can pull out of a hat, even with lots of examples. Sixty-five percent of the children could not produce even one rhyming word immediately after hearing a puppet say eight out of ten words that rhymed with its name. Only 26 percent of the children reached criterion in monitoring the puppet's mistakes. Thinking of a word that "starts /m/" was harder, and 72 percent failed to make one correct attempt. Monitoring a puppet trying to say words that started with the same sound as its name (/s/ in *Sue*) was harder still, and 86 percent failed the criterion for this task.

These results show that children can carry out metalinguistic analyses when what they are asked to do involves natural language. They have a much harder time with tasks that require doing something unnatural, like splitting words at unusual boundaries, or being asked to listen for speech patterns that "sound like" other words or word fragments. It is clear that the phoneme is a more natural unit of speech than a rhyme. These results contradict The Dogma that phonological awareness develops from larger to smaller phonetic units.

The second phase of this work was correlational. Chaney combined the scores for the receptive and productive components of the same task ("judgment" + "correction") where possible, creating "domains" or constructs. The "phonological-awareness" domain included all the phoneme and rhyming tasks. The "word-awareness" domain included all the tasks involving words (inventing, naming, segmenting, reference, and so on), and the morpheme and syntax tests constituted a "structural-awareness" domain. However, domains can't be constituted simply on the basis of linguistic or semantic similarity. At the least, tasks in a domain should be correlated to one another. That was definitely not the case here. The patterns of correlations within domains are shown in table 5.2. The only domain that can be defended is "structural awareness."

Because the domains appear to be hollow vessels, I report instead on the patterns of first-order correlations using those that were significant at $p = .01$ or higher ($r = .37$). Correlations were age corrected (age partialed out). Age effects were very large indeed, and nearly all the variance shared

Table 5.2
Domain correlations

Phonological awareness				
1. Phoneme ID	2	3	4	5
2. Phoneme synthesis	.00	.11	.14	.21
3. Initial consonant		.10	−.15	.23
4. Rhyme			.31	.27
5. Phonological play				.37
Word awareness				
1. Word segment	2	3	4	5
2. Word play	.15	.17	.29	−.33
3. Real vs. nonword		.07	.12	.15
4. Word referent			.39	−.01
5. New names				−.23
Structural awareness				
Morpheme and syntax	.56			

Note: Age controlled in these correlations. $r > .37 = p < .01$; $>.49 = p < .001$.

between receptive vocabulary and other language skills disappeared when age was controlled. This is a consequence of the extremely rapid rate of vocabulary growth across the 33- to 50-month age span.

"Phoneme ID" (the combined judgment plus correction scores) was correlated to only one other measure ("morpheme ID") at $r = .48$, perhaps because morphemes were phonemes as well in these tasks (/s/ /z/ /er/). In both tasks, the child has to notice an error somewhere. Phoneme errors were much easier to fix than morpheme (grammatical) errors (88 percent versus 65 percent correct), which explains why the correlation between the two tasks isn't higher. It's interesting that the two types of phoneme tasks were not correlated to each other. This suggests that it's the operations required by the tasks, as well as the particular phonological units, that are at issue.

"Phoneme synthesis" (blending three segmented phonemes into a word) was strongly correlated to three other tasks (see table 5.3). The common links between these tasks are the ability to discriminate phonological units and keep track of sequence. Thus phoneme synthesis (phoneme discrimination and sequence) was highly correlated to Wallach's discrimination task (phoneme discrimination and sequence), to word

Table 5.3
Correlations between individual phonological tasks

Phoneme synthesis CVC	
Auditory discrimination	.55
Word segmenting	.47
Syntax	.46
Real vs. nonword	.36
PLS	.39
Phoneme ID	
Morphemes	.48
Rhyme	
Phonological play	.37
PLS	.40
Phonological play	
Rhyme	.37
PLS	.51

Note: Age controlled in these correlations. $r > .37 = p. < .01$; $> .50 = p < .001$.

segmenting (word discrimination and word order), and to syntax (word order). Correlations were weaker to real vs. nonword and PLS.

Tasks in which children have to identify, locate, compare, segment, and combine, definitely require conscious manipulation or explicit awareness. Skills involving perception and production of phonemes and words, plus the ability to segment words from sentences, and master syntax, are among the most fundamental language skills. These results support Chaney's view that metalinguistic awareness is more likely to emerge in tandem with well-honed language skills.

"Morpheme ID" and "syntax" were highly correlated ($r = .56$), though they tapped rather different linguistic skills, as seen in table 5.4. Morpheme ID was correlated not only to phoneme ID but to word segmenting and word reference (learning Martian words for common objects). Syntax was also correlated to word segmenting, to judging real/nonsense words, and to phoneme synthesis. "Sentence structure" (Chaney's in-house syntax test) didn't seem to be measuring syntax or much else.

Table 5.5 sets out the possible profiles of the standardized language test, the Primary Language Test (PLT), along with the tests that correlated to ABC concepts and book concepts. The PLT is set up here as

Table 5.4
Correlations between grammar tasks

Morpheme			
Syntax	.56		
Word segmenting	.51		
Phoneme ID	.48		
Word referent	.38		
PLS	.54		
Syntax		**Sentence structure ("syntax")**	
Morphemes	.56	Word referent	.50
Real vs. nonword	.59	Word play	.45
Word segmenting	.57	Syntax	.32
Phoneme synthesis	.46	PLS	.48
Sentence structure	.32		
PLS	.39		

Note: Age controlled in these correlations. $r > .37 = p < .01$; $>.50 = p < .001$.

Table 5.5

General language and cultural tasks

Correlates of the primary language test

Culture/general knowledge		Natural language	
ABC concepts	.56	Morphemes	.54
Book concepts	.52	PPVT vocabulary	.47
Phonological play	.51	Auditory discrimination	.42
Rhyme	.40	Word segmentation	.40
		Syntax	.39
		Phoneme synthesis	.39

Correlates of the cultural tasks

ABC concepts		Book concepts	
Phonological play	.63	Morpheme	.55
Initial sounds	.43	Phoneme synthesis	.52
Rhymes	.40	PPVT vocabulary	.47
		Real vs. nonword	.44
		Auditory discrimination	.41
		Syntax	.40
PLS	.56	PLS	.52

Note: Age controlled in these correlations. $r > .39 = p < .01; >.50 = p < .001.$

two arbitrary factors reflecting the content of the items. One group of items is related to concept formation (categorizing) and the other to natural language. The correlates of ABC concepts are quite fascinating, because this group of tests is clearly *cultural*, and reflects what parents teach in the home. The book-concepts group (which measures knowledge about print, and the logical grasp of sequence and reference) was highly correlated to a variety of basic language skills, including phoneme synthesis, which is a very interesting finding, and could reflect what is taught at home.

Drawing inferences from patterns of simple correlations is, of course, highly speculative. Nevertheless, this analysis does provide some new ways to think about language. For example, what "goes together" developmentally at age 3 is certainly not based solely on standard linguistic-phonological categories like phonemes, syllables, and words.

Chaney (1998) followed up forty-one of these children at the end of first grade. They were given a phoneme-segmenting task and a phoneme-deletion task, plus three subtests from the Woodcock Reading Mastery tests: word recognition, word attack, and passage comprehension. Children's test scores measured at age 3 were correlated with the reading and phoneme-awareness test scores at age 7. Unfortunately, the 3-year-olds' data consisted mainly of domain scores, which as we saw earlier, are invalid.

The phoneme-deletion test measured at age 7 was the strongest correlate for all three reading tests (average $r = .75$). Several measures taken at age 3 were also solid predictors:

1. "Print awareness" or ABC + book concepts ($r = .57$)
2. The Primary Language Test ($r = .54$)
3. The "structural-domain" score (syntax + morphemes), which correlated to word recognition ($r = .51$), comprehension ($r = .42$), and word attack ($r = .39$)
4. The "phonological-domain" score (phoneme ID, phoneme synthesis, rhyme, initial sound, word play), which correlated to all reading tests equally ($r = .48$) and to the phoneme-deletion test ($r = .44$)

I used Chaney's table of first-order correlations to tease apart the impact of the individual tests in the phonological-domain group. Three sets of scores were provided in the table: phonological domain (combined scores), rhyme only, and initial sound only. (Rhyme and initial sound were analyzed separately to test the popular theory that an aptitude for rhyming and alliteration enhances learning to read.) However, neither "rhyme" nor "initial sound" correlated significantly to any reading test (rhyme $r = .18$, alliteration $r = .29$). This means a substantial portion of the correlation between reading and the phonological-domain score ($r = .48$) is attributable to the remaining tests: phoneme ID, phoneme synthesis, and phonological play. Phonological play can also be ruled out, because it is significantly correlated to the rhyme test, and not to phoneme awareness. It seems fair to conclude that phoneme awareness at age 3 has some power to predict reading skill at age 7. The same type of analysis applies to the correlation ($r = .44$) between the phonological-domain score and the phoneme-deletion test measured at age 7, which was also high ($r = .44$). Rhyme and alliteration made no contribution here either ($r = .10, .17$).

A reasonable interpretation of this pattern of results is that phoneme analysis, plus knowledge of the syntactic and morphemic structure of language, contributes to subsequent skill in reading. In other words, basic language skills are more likely to be related to early reading than are culturally acquired skills like playing word games and learning about rhyme and alliteration. However, *this conclusion is extremely tentative.* IQ was not statistically subtracted in these analyses. The Primary Language Test (which overlaps with verbal IQ) was correlated to almost every test in the battery at age 3 and at age 7 as well, and the contribution of this test to all other tests was not controlled here.

Summary

Chaney has demonstrated that it is possible to design tasks that reveal a high degree of phonological and linguistic skill in 3-year-old children. Several of these tasks show that children can think about phonetic elements of language and operate on them. Children had most success when the tasks were related to what they naturally do and least success when they were asked to do unnatural types of analyses ("does it sound like?").

One of the most important findings is that "language" doesn't split neatly into the categories set up by linguists. Nor were tasks easy or hard as a function of the size of the phonetic unit. Three-year-olds seem to be able to think analytically at the level of the word and the phoneme equally well. They had much more trouble listening for phonological units that fall at phonetic boundaries between phonemes and words, and for tasks that require comparisons of phonological patterns.

Chaney provides irrefutable evidence that explicit phoneme awareness is online by age 3 for nearly all children, supporting the findings of Fox and Routh. There is also some tentative support, based on the patterns of correlations, that phoneme-analysis skills at age 3, plus knowledge and aptitude for monitoring syntactic and morphological elements in words and sentences, play a role in reading skills at age 7. However, this connection could be an IQ effect or due to something taught at home, and we have to be cautious in interpreting correlations. Finally, there is no evidence here, and much to the contrary, that phonological development proceeds from larger to smaller units.

Juxtaposing tasks that make demands on both receptive and productive language was informative. The "judgment" and "correction" scores were similar for the phoneme tasks and for Syntax A. But while judging morpheme and judging phoneme errors were equally easy (91 percent met criterion), morpheme production was much more difficult (65 percent met criterion). This suggests that young children have more difficulty pinpointing the location of grammatical errors than phoneme errors. The same split occurred in the Syntax B tasks, the version where children *didn't* hear the sentence before the puppet said it. Chaney pointed out that some tasks were more difficult due to memory load. For example, children made mistakes on the word-segmenting task (*balloontreeshirt*) not because they couldn't segment the words, but because they couldn't remember them.

WHAT IS PHONEME AWARENESS AND DOES IT MATTER?

Speech flows through time. It moves at such a rapid pace that the articulatory gestures used to produce it cause phonemes to overlap or anticipate each other. For children learning to read an alphabetic writing system, phoneme awareness has a specific connotation and function. It refers to the ability to slow down time, to stretch speech to the point where the individual sounds shake free, yet remain in the right order. Phoneme awareness has less to do with auditory or speech discrimination than with *unraveling*.

So far, we have seen that the research does not support The Dogma, either in terms of the sound units involved or the sequence in which these units are supposed to appear in language development. Instead, the research illustrates young children's phenomenal ability to make highly refined perceptual judgments and to participate in complex tasks. Nittrouer has shown that 3-year-olds can discriminate well at minimal phoneme boundaries and maintain attention to the task. Nittrouer, as well as Walley and Metsala, in particular, discovered that speech discrimination gets easier (better) the more familiar the words. Familiarity plays a major role in how much "effort" (metabolic energy used) it takes to keep one's conscious attention on a task (Pribram and McGuinness 1975).

Chaney found that 3-year-olds can easily detect a phoneme error in a word (phoneme ID) and fix the error by saying the word correctly. And nearly everyone met criterion (significantly above chance) for blending isolated phonemes into words. Phoneme synthesis has all the hallmarks of a high-level skill involving explicit awareness, the ability to hold phoneme sequences in mind (verbal memory), the ability to synthesize them mentally, and the ability to then match the final product to a picture. Yet this task was so easy that 93 percent of the children scored well above chance, scoring an average of 88 percent correct.

Chaney discovered that very few children could judge whether words rhymed, or produce words that matched in rhyming or initial sounds. Yet these are the very aptitudes that so many reading researchers claim naturally appear early in development and are so important for learning an alphabetic writing system. There's obviously something wrong with their notions of what is easy and hard for young children to do, and with their understanding of how this developmental path unfolds.

Doubts have been raised that children even need normal intelligence to have enough awareness of phonemes to be able to learn an alphabetic writing system. Cossu, Rossini, and Marshall (1993) studied ten Down's syndrome children in Italy, all of whom could read (decode) at close to a third-grade level, yet couldn't pass any of four basic phoneme-awareness tests (counting, deletion, segmenting, blending). The average IQ (WISC) of the Down's children was 44. They were being compared to a group of normal, reading-matched children (IQ 111, average age 7:3). The standardized reading test was well beyond anything an English-speaking second grader could cope with. It consisted of thirty regular, six- to nine-letter words, like *sbagliare*, thirty words with abnormal stress patterns, like *funebre*, and forty nonsense words. The Down's syndrome children scored 92 percent correct on the first set, 81 percent correct on the second set, and 88 percent on the nonsense words. Yet their average score on the four phoneme tasks was a miserable 17 percent correct.

The Italian alphabet is "transparent" with a nearly one-to-one correspondence between phoneme and symbol. Teaching the Italian alphabet code to severely mentally disabled children can be done by simple matching, sequencing, and repetition. As Cossu and his colleagues remarked (134),

The children do use normal implicit segmentation skills. What they apparently cannot do is access those abilities metalinguistically. We conclude, then, that all causal hypotheses relating PA to the acquisition of reading (or vice versa) are false if the connection is taken as a necessary one.... It is neither the case that lack of phonological awareness has prevented learning to read, nor that learning to read has developed phonological awareness.[1]

The same effect can be shown in another way. Wimmer, Mayringer, and Landerl (2000) reported on two cohorts of children in Salzburg, Austria. In Austria, children must be 6 or older to enter first grade, where they are first taught to read. At the start of school, cohort 1 (530 boys) was given a test of segmenting onsets and rimes (initial sounds/rhymes, and cohort 2 (300 boys and girls) was given a test of phoneme segmenting and a test of naming speed (letters and digits). A battery of reading tests was given at the end of grade 3. Did early onset-rime, phoneme-segmenting, or naming-speed scores predict subsequent reading success? The answer was no.

Next, the cohorts were divided into groups based on their initial success on these tasks. When children who scored more than 1 standard deviation below the mean on any task were compared to children who scored in the normal range, *no significant differences were found between them on any subsequent tests of reading accuracy*. Similar results were found on a spelling test with predictable (regular) spellings (the vast majority of German words are spelled regularly).

As noted earlier, the German alphabet code is not only "transparent," but teaching practice is appropriate in Salzburg. Reading and spelling are integrated so that the code nature of a writing system is revealed, and the logic is clear. Children learn to segment and blend phonemes in the context of learning to read and spell. Learning letter names and memorizing words by sight are actively discouraged.

The inescapable conclusion is that whether or not children develop the capacity for explicit phoneme awareness makes *no difference* to learning a transparent alphabetic writing system that is properly taught. Neither initial phonological skill nor naming speed had any impact on a child's ability to profit from classroom teaching, and everyone learned to read and spell successfully at very high levels of skill. Reading fluency was another story. About 7 percent of these young readers did not read fluently

---

1. Needless to say, Cossu, Rossini, and Marshall were severely attacked by proponents of The Dogma (see whole issue of Cognition, 1993, 48).

even though they could decode perfectly. (The studies on fluency are reviewed in chapters 15 and 16.)

Thinking Outside the Box

We can finesse the issue about whether phoneme awareness develops and "causes" reading with a little logic, and by asking a different question. To use an alphabetic writing system, the learner must access the phonemic level of the word. The phoneme is the sound unit that alphabetic writing systems employ. If children can be taught to access the phoneme level of their speech and connect phonemes to letter symbols, would any of these research questions matter?

1. Does speech perception correlate to reading?
2. Is auditory discrimination the forerunner of phoneme awareness?
3. Is speech perception the forerunner of phoneme awareness?
4. Does phonological awareness develop from larger to smaller units?
5. Does phoneme-awareness development predict reading skill?
6. Is phoneme awareness caused by parental input or training?
7. Is phoneme awareness caused by learning to read an alphabetic writing system?
8. Do children have to have an explicit awareness of phonemes to be able to learn an alphabetic writing system?

Because the answer to the original question—"Can children be taught to be aware of phonemes and connect them to symbols?"—is a resounding yes (see my review of the National Reading Panel results in *Early Reading Instruction*), trying to answer these questions is not only a waste of time but counterproductive. It merely confuses the issue. I won't abandon this topic just yet, because it's important to get some sense of the complexities and anomalies that arise from trying to answer questions like those listed above.

Research reviewed previously and the studies that follow in part II are devoted to a similar type of question that isn't among the questions listed above: What is the relationship between speech perception, speech production, and general language development? Answering this question has involved an enormous research effort on the part of scholars and scientists in at least six disciplines: phonetics, linguistics, speech and hearing sciences, psycholinguistics, developmental psychology, and psychophysics. This is a valid and important question about the development of a species-specific, biological process.

If learning to read was a biological process, it would make sense to study it in the same depth and with the same energy and intensity. But a writing system is an invention, and people must be taught to use inventions. It isn't part of our biological equipment to know how to use them. Children who aren't aware that phonemes are the basis for our writing system need to be made aware of them. They need to be taught the correspondences between the forty or more phonemes and their most common spelling (initially), connect this to meaning as soon as possible (read real words), and learn to sequence and order phonemes and graphemes appropriately. The only question relevant to the topic of this chapter is the following: What type of phoneme analysis is easiest to teach and most beneficial to learning to read?

Measuring Phoneme and Phonological Awareness

There is an unresolved issue, despite Cossu's assurance that phoneme awareness doesn't matter. This has to do with the fact that performance on phoneme-awareness tests is highly correlated to subsequent reading skill in normal children in English-speaking countries, even if it isn't in Italy or Austria. We saw this in Chaney's longitudinal study, and this is supported by countless other studies. Because a high correlation means that children vary in a similar fashion on both the phoneme and the reading tests, the relevant question is, what causes them to vary in phoneme awareness? (Of course, this is one of the questions that led us down that garden path.)

Why do some children "get it"—that phonemes are what we use for decoding our writing system—and sail away at reading and spelling, yet other children don't, despite the same inappropriate teaching? (I don't refer here to what goes on in classrooms where children are taught correctly.) There could be various reasons:

1. Children may have different degrees of talent for hearing phonemes and phoneme sequences.
2. Some children were taught phonemes or "letter sounds" by mom.
3. Some children figured out by chance that phonemes matter, but other children didn't.

4. Some children are so misled by their reading instruction, despite a talent for hearing phonemes, that they never knew this was relevant.[2]

The first task in trying to solve this puzzle is to find out which type of phoneme-analysis skill matters in learning to read and which does not. How to measure phoneme awareness has been a long-standing debate. The phoneme-discrimination tests available in the 1950s and 1960s were far too easy. All the child had to do was listen to two spoken phonemes and answer yes if they were the same, or no if they were different. The first real test of phoneme awareness, the word-analysis test, was designed by D. J. Bruce in the United Kingdom in 1964. His goal was to establish a developmental sequence for phoneme analysis. However, Bruce never used his test to predict reading ability, and he found that it did not predict oral spelling on a homemade test, the only reading activity measured.

In the word-analysis test the child has to repeat a word, delete a phoneme from the word, close up the remaining phonemes, and say the word that is left. After the phoneme is deleted and the remaining sounds elided, the outcome is another real word. The first item on the test is *stand*. The child is told to remove the "middle sound /t/" and report the result: *sand*.

Children were carefully trained on how to take the test. They had to repeat spoken words and phonemes, then master the concepts—first, middle, and last—using pictures and numbers. When this was accomplished (or if it was accomplished) the child was given the test. For each item in the test, the child was told the phoneme to be deleted (/f/) and its location (first, middle, last).

This is a considerable leap from a simple yes/no discrimination task in which all the child has to do is notice there's a difference "somewhere." In Bruce's deletion/elision test, the child must understand that words have individual phonemes and that they come in a sequence (temporal order). Next, the child must operate on the word in three ways: by *locating* the position of the phoneme, by pulling it out of the word (*manipulation*), and by closing the gap through *blending* the remaining sounds together.

---

2. For a variety of true stories about these kinds of children, see McGuinness 1997b, 1998.

Bruce tested children age 5 to $7\frac{1}{2}$ who were identified by their mental ages on an IQ test and not by chronological age. Unfortunately, this makes it impossible to interpret the results. For example, children with a mental age of 7 scored 33 percent correct, yet bright 5- and 6-year-olds with a mental age of 9 years or higher scored nearly perfectly. Whether test scores are due to IQ, chronological age, the number of years at school, talent for the task, or all the above, is unknown.

In 1971, Rosner and Simon published a similar test in the United States. The rationale behind this effort stemmed from the same issues raised above—that the discrimination tests were inadequate and that tests with yes/no answers are not good tests. Rosner and Simon were developing a reading curriculum and needed a test to measure what they believed was a critical skill in using an alphabetic writing system: the ability to "sort, order, and synthesize" phonemes in words.

The test they developed, the Auditory Analysis Test (AAT), is identical to Bruce's test in terms of the operations involved. The child has to isolate a phoneme in a word, remove the phoneme, close up the remaining phonemes, and recite the word that is left. In other respects the test is different. First-level words (items 1–20) are easy, and consist of two compound words and eighteen CVC words. In the compound-word task, the child is asked to remove one of the words: "say *cowboy* without the *cow*." The second level (items 21–40) is much more difficult. This level contains one-syllable words with consonant clusters, as well as multisyllable words where the child is asked to remove a syllable: "say *carpenter* without the *pen*," and report what remains: *carter*.

While the test itself is a remarkable look-alike to Bruce's test, the research was in an entirely different class. The AAT was tested on 284 children in kindergarten to sixth grade. Scores on the test were correlated to the Stanford reading test, as well as to the Otis-Lennon mental-abilities test (IQ). IQ was found to correlate both to the AAT and to the Stanford tests at high levels across the age span. For this reason, partial correlations were carried out to control for IQ. Both the original (untransformed) and the transformed correlations are presented in table 6.1.

Kindergartners don't appear in this table, because they couldn't do the test. Nine children couldn't pass the demonstration training and had to be eliminated. Of the remaining kindergartners, 66 percent fell by the wayside by item 10. There was a noticeable shift at first grade, and first

Table 6.1

Correlations between the AAT and Stanford Reading Tests with and without IQ controlled

Grade	Original	IQ controlled
1	.53	.40
2	.62	.52
3	.84	.64
4	.72	.60
5	.75	.50
6	.59	.10

Note: Data based on Rosner and Simon (1971).

and second graders scored similarly on the test. More than 90 percent made it through the first twenty items, and 38 percent to item 30. The average score was 18.5 correct. At age 8, there was another jump and from this age forward, the scores on the test fell into a normal distribution. The Rosner test is on its way to becoming a good test, but it needs to be normed on a much larger sample. It needs more easy items for younger children. It lacks reliability estimates. So far, none of these problems have been remedied.

Table 6.1 shows that unless IQ is statistically controlled, the AAT does not measure what it purports to measure. If one relied on the untransformed scores at sixth grade, one would conclude that the AAT score predicts some level of reading success, when it doesn't at all, but IQ does. Rosner and Simon speculated on the causes behind the correlations, and concluded that learning to read would be just as likely to cause phoneme-analysis skill, as phoneme-analysis skill was likely to cause reading. In other words, there's no way to determine the direction of causality in correlations.

One other phoneme-analysis test appeared during this time. The test was designed by Pat and Charles Lindamood and is called the Lindamood Auditory Conceptualization (LAC) Test (C. H. Lindamood and P. C. Lindamood 1971). It was designed originally to identify speech-discrimination problems in children with severe speech disorders. The test is similarly demanding to the tests described above, except that no verbal response is required. The test has two parts. In part I, the child matches a sequence of phonemes using a row of colored blocks. The tester says "Show me /b/ /b/," and two blocks of the same color (any color) are put out in left-to-right sequence. Another item might be "Show me /t/ /v/ /t/." Here, the child must place the same color in positions 1 and 3, and a different color in the middle.

In part II of the test, the child is directed to add, subtract, or substitute colored blocks in response to hearing pairs of nonsense words in a sequence or chain. The tester puts out a block and says, "If that says /i/ show me *ip*." The child must add a different-colored block on the right. The test continues: "If that is *ip* show me *pip*" (the color for both /p/'s must match); "if that is *pip* show me *pib*," and so forth. As the chain proceeds, the words get longer and the exchanges more difficult. If the child makes a mistake, an alternative chain is begun and testing continues. Testing ends when the child can do neither the original nor the alternative test item.

To do this task, the child must hold the temporal sequence of the old and transformed words in mind (if that is *pip* show me *pib*), isolate what is different between them, then mentally remove, exchange, or add a sound, match this mental operation to an overt act by changing, adding, inserting, or deleting a colored block, while ensuring that the colors are appropriate and checking to see whether the sequence is correct. The test requires a considerable degree of logic and memory in addition to phoneme analysis.

The LAC test was normed on 660 children in kindergarten through twelfth grade, and scores were compared to the reading and spelling subtests of the Wide Range Achievement Test (WRAT) (Calfee, P. C. Lindamood, and C. H. Lindamood 1973). Every kindergartner and 91 percent of first graders failed the higher-level part of the test. This problem didn't go away. The split between part I (easy) and part II (difficult) created a bimodal distribution at every age. Table values showed that 60 percent of the oldest children could do part II quite successfully, but 40 percent could barely do it at all.

The authors correlated the LAC test scores to reading tests on the WRAT and got results similar to those initially found by Rosner and Simon. However, they did not control IQ, a serious omission, and this test is compromised by the fact that the scores are bimodally distributed.

Thus, by the early 1970s, there were two main types of phoneme-awareness tests: those that were too easy and those that were too hard, at least for beginning readers, the children most likely to be of interest to reading researchers. The tasks designed for the Liberman et al. and for the Fox and Routh training studies described in chapter 1 (tapping tasks, and "say a little bit of_____") were never developed as properly normed tests (though they are often used in research anyway).

In the 1980s, Bradley and Bryant (1983, 1985) claimed that skill in alliteration (initial sounds match: *cat, cup, car*) and rhyme (*boat, coat, note*) represents an intermediate step in natural language development, and is a predictor of phoneme awareness and reading success. They developed the sound-categorization test, one of the best-known tests in the field. Their reasoning was as follows: children use word play and invent rhyming patterns and poems at very young ages. Word play involves analysis below the level of the word, for both rhyme and alliteration. Alphabets likewise require an analysis below the level of the word: "There are ... two good reasons for making a connection between a child's preschool experiences with rhyme and alliteration and his eventual success at learning to read and write. The first is that both activities depend on breaking words and syllables into phonological segments" (Bradley and Bryant 1985, 5).

Other reasons cited were that both word play and learning to read require explicit awareness, both are categorical in nature, and both involve the analysis of "like kind." Spontaneous rhyming patterns in children's utterances, and phonics "word families," were cited in support of this argument. Thus, their reasoning is by analogy between word play, rhyme, and an alphabetic writing system. But analogies do not a theory make. In the first place, alphabets don't work at the level of the rhyme. An aptitude for rhyming has no direct connection to being able to use a phonemic code, as Morais' research on illiterate poets has shown (Morais 1991).

The second problem is the assumption behind the analogy, that most children spontaneously use alliteration and rhyme. After citing examples of word play, and a little poem allegedly composed by a 2-year-old, Bradley and Bryant (1985, 4) wrote: "Here is a dramatic example of the importance of rhyme to young children. Not only do they recognize rhyme and produce rhyming sentences with ease, they also change the very form of words that they know to suit the rules of rhyme. It is quite plain that these children know a great deal about categorizing words by their sounds."

This is an old claim, yet Chaney found that idiosyncratic reports of children's word play don't prove that most children spontaneously generate word play and can do so at will. Her results showed fairly conclusively that they do not. Bradley and Bryant generalized these youthful efforts to all children, and then designed a test to prove it.

The sound-categorization test was intended to be suitable for pre-schoolers. The task is to listen and identify the odd one out in a set of CVC words. Each set contains ten word lists (lists are three words long for younger children, and four words for older children). The "odd one" differs in either initial, middle, or final phoneme. In the set for initial sound (alliteration), the CV units match in two cases, and the "odd one" does not. (*pot*, *dog*, *doll*).

In the middle and final phoneme judgment tasks, there is a strong emphasis on rhyme. Two-thirds of the items rhyme. The initial training focuses heavily on rhyme, priming the child to listen to *two* sounds. It's probably not surprising that all children found the middle and final sound sets far easier than the initial sound sets. Does this mean that children did better on the rhyming contrasts because they are more sensitive to rhyme, because they were primed to listen to rhymes, because two sounds provide more phonetic information than initial consonants, or all of the above?

There were 104 nursery school children (age 5), and 264 primary school children (age $5\frac{1}{2}$) in the study. All were nonreaders. No information was provided about the children's knowledge of letter names or letter-sound correspondences. The main research question was whether performance on these tasks will be correlated to reading tests measured 3 years later. Children were followed up at age 7 and given reading, spelling, and math tests. Age, WISC full-scale IQ, English Picture Vocabulary Test, and memory span were controlled in a multiple regression analysis. The goal was to find out whether performance on the alliteration/rhyme tasks would account for any additional variance in reading skill (have predictive power) with all these factors controlled.

Although this was a beautifully executed study on a very large group of children, there are problems with the test in terms of what it was intended to measure. The tasks offer limited choices and so are susceptible to guessing. I carried out the binomial test to see if children scored significantly better than chance. The alliteration task was too hard for the nursery school children, with over half performing at chance. Any interpretation based on the relative importance of rhyme or alliteration to reading would be confounded with task difficulty.

The older children scored well above chance, and results are likely to be valid. With age, IQ, vocabulary, and memory span controlled, the combined rhyming tasks (middle, final sound match) accounted for only 1 to

3 percent additional variance. Though some values were "significant," they have little practical relevance. The alliteration score accounted for a greater amount of variance on the reading and spelling tests (range 4 to 8 percent). However, the alliteration task predicted 9 percent of the variance on a standardized *mathematics* test as well. Perhaps the alliteration task is measuring learning rate, or logic; otherwise why would it predict mathematics and reading equally?

This study was a textbook example of good correlational research. If there had been no control for a nonreading task, this curious result would never have surfaced. The superior research design revealed the following facts. The strongest predictor for early reading success was receptive vocabulary. The ability to find the odd one out in rhyming words was unrelated to reading with age, IQ, vocabulary, and memory controlled. The ability to find the odd one out for initial sounds did have some predictive power for reading measured 3 years later, but it predicted math ability even better. Whatever this test is measuring, it isn't specific to reading. In other words, performance on the sound-categorization test is not a valid predictor of reading and spelling.

Now comes a sad lesson on the dangers of deductive theories in science. Bradley and Bryant (1985) expressed concern about these anomalies: the fact that the data went in the opposite direction for nursery and primary school children, the fact that the alliteration task predicted more of the variance on a mathematics test than on the reading and spelling tests, and the fact that rhyme tasks were much worse predictors of reading than alliteration, scarcely predicting reading at all. But none of this mattered in view of where they began:

Our longitudinal prediction was that a child's score in our tests of rhyme and alliteration would be closely related to his subsequent progress in reading and spelling, quite independently of his general verbal and intellectual skills.... We think that we have *established a causal link* between a very specific preschool skill and a particular educational achievement. This specificity is to us one of the most exciting things about our hypothesis and our results. (p. 116; emphasis mine)

Our proposal is that word games in general and those games that involve rhyme and alliteration in particular give children experience in breaking words up into phonetic segments, and also of grouping together words that are very different from each other but that do have phonetic segments in common. (p. 117)

We cannot know from our data anything about the role of parents. All we know is that a child's skill in tests of sound categorization at the time that he goes to school plays an important part in his learning to read and to spell. (p. 119)

They went on to outline the practical implications for using these new discoveries for children with reading problems and for early reading instruction. This work was followed up by Goswami and Bryant (1990), who changed the terminology to "onset" and "rime," where "onset" can include consonant clusters: *t-ake*, *br-eak*, *st-ake*. Indeed, the current mandated guidelines for early reading instruction in the United Kingdom (National Literacy Strategy) incorporate most of Goswami and Bryant's ideas, if not all of them. Many early reading programs in the United States have followed suit, and this practice is encouraged by comments like the following from leading American researchers:

In general, prereaders can perform tasks that require segmentation of words into syllables but not tasks that require segmentation into phonemes; their performance on tasks that are based on the intrasyllabic units of onset—and rime—falls in between. Through a yet-to-be understood transformation, experienced readers are able to perform phoneme-based tasks and perform at ceiling on most syllable-based tasks. (Wagner et al. 1993, 83)

It turns out that the sound-categorization test is not even a valid predictor of phonological awareness, let alone reading. In a comprehensive analysis of the performance of 945 children (kindergarten through grade 2) on various phonological tasks, Schatschneider et al. (1999) reported that the sound-categorization test was decidedly the odd one out to most phoneme-analysis tasks, as well as to a task of blending onsets and rimes. First, task difficulty varied enormously as a function of where the target word (the odd one) was located in each list (*bun, sun, **rug**, fun, vs. **rug**, bun, sun, fun*). There was a 2.6-standard-deviation gap between scores on the easy versus hard list locations. Second, the test is highly susceptible to guessing. Third, the test had the lowest discriminatory power of any test to measure the construct in question. This led the authors to conclude that the sound-categorization test was inferior to all other tests in measuring phonological awareness.

By contrast, they found that phoneme blending and onset-rime blending were the most discriminating tests, with phoneme blending being the most accurate measure of phonological ability across the entire age span. It is interesting that blending onsets and rimes was one of the easiest tasks and phoneme blending one of the hardest, yet performance on these two tests correlated almost perfectly ($r = .88$). However, the important question is not whether children can blend onsets and rimes, but whether this has anything to do with subsequent reading skill.

Goswami and Bryant (1990, 146) believe that it does, going so far as to say that there is a causal connection between them: "Our theory concentrates on causal connections: only these, we think, can explain the course of reading and spelling, why some children make quicker progress than others, and why there might be qualitative differences in the way that children read."

Their theory is based on some strange assumptions about speech development:

Children are sensitive to the sounds in words long before they learn to read, and they also categorize words by their sounds. But these sounds are not phonemes.... The important phonological units for young children are onset and rime.... Children who are taught about rhyme eventually do much better at reading ... and those who are given this training about rhyme are more successful at reading than those who are not given this training.... There is precious little evidence that young children use grapheme-phoneme relations when they read words. But it is another matter when we come to onsets and rimes. (p. 147)

These statements follow a short review of studies insufficiently rigorous to support either these comments or their conclusion: "So our first causal link begins with events that take place some time before children begin to learn to read. They hear, and produce, rhyme. They become adept at recognizing when words have common rimes or common onsets" (p. 147).

We have already seen from Chaney's study that children absolutely do not do any of these things. Nor have the better controlled studies provided any evidence that awareness of onsets and rimes affects the process of learning to read. For example, Nation and Hulme (1997) gave a test battery to seventy-five children age 6 to 9 (in grades 1, 3, and 4). They found that with age and memory controlled, performance on an onset-rime segmenting test was not connected to skill in reading or spelling. Phoneme segmenting, on the other hand, was highly predictive of both reading and spelling skill.

Moving out of the shadowy realm of correlational statistics to the experimental research on training studies, the National Reading Panel (2000) reported that onset-rime training and "analogy" teaching methods (*s-ick*, *tr-ick*, *st-ick*) are extremely unsuccessful. Children with this type of training do no better on reading tests than children in the control groups (basal readers or whole language). This is a dramatic contrast to reading programs that focus on phoneme-letter correspondences *at the outset*. Programs of this type produce gains (on average) of 1 year above control groups and 1 year above national norms, gains that are maintained over time (see *Early Reading Instruction* for a full analysis). This is real evidence for causality.

Research continues to show little support for the notion that early facility or training in clapping out syllable beats, or playing rhyming and alliteration games, help children learn to read and spell. Research support is, and always was, much stronger for the connection between phoneme-segmenting and phoneme-blending skills and reading and spelling. But there are still problems with this research, because experimenters don't control what the children have been taught about letters, sounds, letter-sound associations, and simple decoding, *prior to coming to school*. Unless these controls are in place, studies of phoneme awareness in young children have no validity. The same can be said about Bradley and Bryant's research, a problem they commented on but ignored in the design of their study.

Phoneme Tests That Matter

Meanwhile, the saga of building a better phoneme-awareness test continues. Helfgott (1976) was among the first to study simple segmenting and blending systematically. She tested kindergartners on Elkonin's

(1963, 1973) CVC segmenting task. The test uses pictures to help the children keep the word in mind, together with a row of empty squares. The child looks at the picture, says each phoneme separately, and moves a counter for each phoneme into a square. This was modified to include training for segmenting larger units, CV–C and C–VC. The children were also given a blending version of these three tasks.

Segmenting was more difficult than blending, and the CVC version of either task was more difficult than segmenting by larger units. CV–C was much easier to *blend* than C–VC (70 versus 58 percent correct), evidence against the onset-rime theory. Children did equally poorly on the segmenting version of this test (59 versus 54 percent). The highest correlation to the WRAT reading test measured 1 year later was the CVC segmenting task ($r = .72$). Helfgott reported that mental age (test not specified) correlated to reading at .41. This means that about 16 percent of the variance shared by reading and segmenting is due to IQ, indicating that about 36 percent of the variance is due to segmenting plus anything else not measured. Age was not controlled and nothing was known about prior reading skill or other factors that might have influenced these results.

As phoneme-awareness tests began to proliferate, Yopp (1988) performed a useful service by testing the overlap between these tests and their power to predict reading scores. Over 100 kindergartners (age 5:4 to 6:8) were given a total of eleven tests (not all at the same time), which are as follows:

1. Sound-to-word matching: Is there an /f/ in *calf*? (Yes/No auditory discrimination)
2. Sound-to-sound matching: Do *pen* and *pipe* begin with the same sound? (Yes/No)
3. Recognition or production of rhyme: Does *sun* rhyme with *run*? (Yes/No)
4. Phoneme identification: say the first sound in *rose*.
5. Phoneme segmentation: Say each sound in *hot*.
6. Phoneme counting: How many sounds do you hear in *cake*?
7. Phoneme blending: Put these sounds together to make a word: /k/ /a/ /t/.
8. Phoneme deletion: Say the word *stand* without the /t/.
9. Specify deleted phonemes: What sound in *meat* is missing in *eat*?
10. Phoneme reversal: Say the sounds *oz* backward.
11. Invented spellings: Write the word *monster*.

The tests were designed by Yopp and by other authors: blending (Roswell-Chall 1959), phoneme segmentation (Goldstein 1974), phoneme counting (Liberman et al. 1974), phoneme deletion (Bruce 1964), and phoneme deletion (Rosner and Simon 1971). Means, standard deviations, and test reliabilities were provided. Only one test (Yopp's word-to-word matching test) had an unacceptable reliability (.58). Most reliabilities were around .80 or higher. The two most reliable tests were the Roswell-Chall blending test and the Yopp-Singer phoneme-segmenting test (.96 and .95).

Three tests were subject to guessing (yes/no responses), and the data will be invalid because there was no correction for guessing. These were the rhyme test, word-to-word matching (both designed by Yopp), and the Wepman auditory-discrimination test. Two tests (Bruce, Rosner) were excessively difficult.

The test scores were submitted to a factor analysis to find out which tests overlap (are measuring the same thing). A factor analysis sorts tests into related groups on the strength of their similarity, providing "factor scores" or "loadings." Factor loadings should be around .80 or higher to be meaningful, especially with 11 tests and only 104 children.

Factor I included several tests with high factor loadings. These were in order: *segmenting* (Yopp-Singer, .89; Goldstein, .86); *blending* (Roswell-Chall, .84); *phoneme counting* (Liberman, .80); and *sound isolation* (Yopp, .76). Factor II included only one test, the *Rosner* (.94). The remaining tests did not load on any factor, showing they were unrelated to any other test and to each other.

As part of this project, Yopp trained children to learn to use the alphabet principle. Next, she correlated the scores on each of the tests above to the time it took the child to learn to read novel words. The tests most highly correlated (best predictors) were "phoneme isolation" (similar to the Fox and Routh task), phoneme segmenting, and blending. Test scores for auditory discrimination and alliteration/rhyming were unrelated to learning rate.

For the most part, Yopp's study and others like it (Stanovich, Cunningham, and Cramer 1984; Wagner et al. 1993; Wagner, Torgesen, and Rashotte 1994; Vandervelden and Siegel 1995; Nation and Hulme 1997; Schatschneider et al. 1999) show that tests measuring some aspect of isolating, segmenting, and blending phonemes are highly redundant.

The differences between these tasks largely have to do with task difficulty ("cognitive load") plus issues of test construction. These summary studies indicate that phoneme awareness is strongly correlated to reading and spelling, whereas performance on rhyme or syllable tasks is not.

Silent Partners: What Parents Teach at Home

Despite the proliferation of phoneme-awareness tasks, and numerous correlational studies on "teasing out causality" by measuring phoneme awareness at time 1 and reading at time 2, few researchers have controlled or studied what goes on at home prior to the child being tested at school or preschool. Chaney (1994; 1998) reported that many parents had taught alphabet letters, names, and sounds by age 3. Blachman (1984) found that half the kindergartners in her study knew letter names or sounds or both, and half knew none. Stuart (1995) looked at home environment and social class in the United Kingdom, interviewing parents and children. She found that the strongest predictor of early reading success was being taught letter-sound correspondences (not letter names) at home.

Letter names and letter-sound correspondences have to be taught. They aren't aptitudes that emerge without direct instruction. By contrast, phoneme-awareness skills are not taught. They are indirect measures of either some basic talent, or the consequence of something else that *was* taught (like "letter sounds"). A longitudinal study by Wagner, Torgesen, and Rashotte (1994) provides information on home or preschool instruction by measuring kindergartners' knowledge of letter names and letter sounds shortly after they arrived at school, and again over the next 2 years. Phoneme awareness, naming speed, and memory were also measured. Correlations were carried out between letter-name and letter-sound knowledge and the other tests plus two reading tests (Woodcock word ID and word attack). All the tests were administered each year. Table 6.2 provides the correlations between the children's letter-name and letter-sound knowledge from the start of kindergarten through first and second grade, and their ability to perform the tasks.

In view of the fact that neither age nor IQ was controlled in this study, the important details in the table are the *differences* in the size of the correlations for the letter-name/letter-sound scores and the other tests. As can be seen, letter-sound knowledge (something taught) was strongly related to skill on the phoneme-awareness tasks (something not taught),

Table 6.2

First-order correlations between letter-name/letter-sound knowledge, phoneme awareness, and reading

	Rosner	Odd one out	1st sound	Blending			Word ID	Word attack
				Onset rime	Words	Nonwords		
Kindergarten								
Letter names	.32	.26	.42	.36	.30	.27	.17	.10
Letter sounds	.53	.27	.52	.59	.53	.51	.30	.24
First grade								
Letter names	.27	.30	.38	.33	.34	.27	.26	.18
Letter sounds	.52	.36	.54	.62	.62	.53	.49	.42
Second grade								
Letter sounds	.48	.25	.45	.46	.54	.49	.47	.43

Note: Second graders' knowledge of letter names was essentially perfect and correlations will be invalid due to ceiling effects.

Source: Data from Wagner, Torgesen, and Rashotte 1994.

as well as the reading tests, while letter-name knowledge was not. Neither was strongly related to performance on the sound-categorization test (odd one out).

It is obvious from these consistent findings that phoneme segmenting and blending are important skills in learning an alphabetic writing system, that they are easy to teach, and that they should be taught in conjunction with letters and print for the best effect—nothing that wasn't known by many teachers in the nineteenth century (Dale 1898). What matters is how and when these skills should be trained and used in reading instruction. Answers to these questions can be found in *Early Reading Instruction*.

Conclusions to Part I

In a sense, the emphasis on phonological development and reading skill, while important initially to redirect the focus away from visual models of reading, is like a genie that escaped from the bottle, went out of control, and gobbled up the reading landscape. The central platform of the theory—that awareness phonological units "develops" and becomes "explicit" in a specific sequence and time—is not supported by the data. To examine the fate of the individual tenets of the theory, we'll return to the summary chart at the end of chapter 1 and see how each premise holds up in light of the evidence to this point.

The Phonological-Development Theory Scorecard
1. Phonological development follows the order of the evolution of writing systems.
Gelb's evolutionary model was not supported by evidence from paleography on the comparative analysis of writing systems. There is no way that writing systems mimic the order of phonological development, because this order doesn't exist. The form and substance of a writing system is highly constrained by a *particular* language and how the human mind works. All writing systems are designed to fit the phonotactic structure of the language using two main principles: (1) choose the largest (most audible) unit that (2) does not overload memory. Memory overloads at around 2,000 sound-symbol pairs. (For a detailed analysis of how this works and the evidence to support it, see *Early Reading Instruction*.)

2. Infants have implicit sensitivity to phonemic units in words and syllables.
Today the evidence is even stronger than when Liberman et al. com-

mented on the infant studies in 1974. It is definitely the case that infants must be sensitive to something phonemelike to be able to wrench words out of the speech stream. Phonemic sensitivity is online at birth, and word recognition follows several months later. While these new findings were acknowledged by Liberman et al., this was never really part of the theory so much as a concession to facts in evidence. These facts are actually contradictory to the logic of the "larger-to-smaller" sequence proposed for explicit phonological awareness.

3. Explicit awareness of phonological units develops over childhood from larger to smaller units: words, syllables, onset rimes, phonemes.   The well-controlled studies on children 3 years old and older, by Nittrouer, Elliott, Walley and Metsala, Chaney, and others, show that 3-year-olds can explicitly listen to, judge, manipulate, and sequence phonemes. Not only this, they show this facility in speech production by being able to blend three phonemes into a word. If there is a developmental shift in these aptitudes, this shift is *subphonemic*, as shown by the increasing precision of phoneme category boundaries with age. There is no evidence that the syllable is a stable or definable phonological unit during early language acquisition. Nor is there any evidence that children can spontaneously analyze words at the level of the rhyme. The salient units of speech for young children are exactly as they were in infancy: phonemes and words.

4. Explicit phonological awareness develops slowly, and phoneme awareness emerges at age 6 or later.   This statement is not supported by the facts outlined above. If phoneme awareness improves sharply at age 6 or 7, this is the result of being taught an alphabetic writing system. If this wasn't the case, one would have to argue that speech perception develops in a particular order and manner solely for the purpose of learning an alphabetic writing system!

5. If phonological awareness fails to develop in the sequence and time frame set out in the theory, this indicates some type of impairment. (There is no room for natural variation in this model.)   Because the true pattern of phonological development does not support the theory, this premise cannot be maintained. To specify normal sequences and time lines, we need evidence from longitudinal studies, evidence that Liberman and her colleagues never collected. We will be looking at time lines for natural development of receptive and productive language in part II.

6. Phonological processing is a strong causal agent in reading skill. So far, we have nothing but speculation and no direct evidence on whether the natural development of speech perception or speech production plays a causal role in reading skill. The fact that children with Down's syndrome can master a transparent alphabet by simple matching and repetition suggests it does not. The definitive evidence that this statement is not true is reported in parts II and III.

7. There is no way to segment consonant phonemes due to coarticulation. This makes it difficult to teach an alphabetic writing system. Unless children develop phoneme awareness, they will have trouble learning to read. Chaney's 3-year-olds could listen to isolated phonemes, repeat them in order, blend them into a word, and choose that word from among a set of pictures. Ninety-three percent scored above chance and the overall accuracy was 88 percent correct. In Fox and Routh's study, 4-year-olds scored 63 percent correct on a test where they had to identify, isolate, and produce initial phonemes in words. If 3- and 4-year-olds can blend and isolate phonemes, there is no reason teachers should find this difficult.

8. Training in phonological awareness of syllables, onsets, and rimes improves phoneme awareness and reading skill. Studies of this type were touched on briefly in this chapter. An extensive analysis of this literature is provided in *Early Reading Instruction*. In essence, training in syllable and rhyme awareness is, at best, a waste of time, and, at worst, a practice that can seriously mislead children about the nature of our writing system. The National Reading Panel reported that reading programs based on rhyme-analogy strategies have no more success than whole-language or other whole-word methods.

9. Speech perception may appear normal in poor readers, but this masks subtle deficits in perception of acoustic cues for speech and nonspeech. So far, there is no support for the notion that the analysis of nonspeech signals is in any way related to speech perception. However, the "subtle-deficit" hypothesis has not been explored as a function of reader status. Research that ties this premise to reading directly is reported in chapter 10.

10. Phonological processing is the integrating principle that unifies all research on language-related correlates of reading skill. Bacon's Idols of the Cave are alive and well in the twentieth-first century ("It feigns and supposes all other things to be somehow similar to those few things by which it is surrounded"). This particular Idol will meet its Maker in parts II and III. As we will see, individual variation in phonological awareness has little to do with the development of higher language functions such as verbal memory and syntactic and semantic ability—or with learning to read.

What Do We Know for Sure?

So far, the research on early language development shows that speech perception outdistances speech production early on, and the two run hand in hand developmentally until around age 3 or 4. Accurate speech production takes much longer. In younger children, serious problems with speech production are often mirrored by speech-perception problems, particularly when speech is degraded or electronically produced. But these are not long-term problems, as we will see in parts II and III. The general message from the studies in this section is that receptive language (accurate perception of speech sounds) and articulation (accurate production of speech sounds) are the most buffered biologically of all language functions.

We turn now to studies that map language development from early childhood to the late teens. These findings refute the phonological-development model as well, but they demonstrate other important connections that have, so far, not been reported in the literature. Thus there is a tantalizing link between general language development and reading skill of a much more mysterious and important kind.

II

EXPRESSIVE LANGUAGE, READING, AND ACADEMIC SKILLS

THE DEVELOPMENT OF EXPRESSIVE LANGUAGE

In part I, we explored one of two biological explanations for a language-literacy connection, the theory that phonological analysis develops in a particular manner and sequence, plus the inference that this has an impact on the process of learning to read. The evidence does not support the developmental sequence nor most of the assumptions about the aptitudes of young children. The primary aspect of reading skill addressed by this model was decoding, the ability to master the mechanics of reading—the phoneme-grapheme correspondences in our spelling system and how these are ordered in words.

Part II addresses a second possible biological basis for a language-literacy connection. Here, the parameters are different. This is "language" with a broad palette, and "reading" defined by a range of aptitudes. While the first biological explanation was more theoretical than factual, this explanation is the reverse. Instead, the search for a language-literacy connection is based on descriptive and exploratory research. This field is relatively free of presumptive theories. The key question is simply: Do individual differences in general language development affect reading skill and academic success? These studies have laid the foundation for a new awareness of the natural variation in general language, as well as of how or whether specific language skills have an impact on reading success in all its forms.

In this and the following chapter, I will be tracing the development of natural language from its beginnings, into the school system, and beyond. Research in this area has several goals. The first is to provide a road map of the path of normal language development over time. A second, related goal is to chart the degree and nature of lateral and temporal variation. The third goal is practical, to use this information to determine how to distinguish the children who are merely slow from those who have a language impairment (diagnosis and prognosis). The fourth goal is about implications, such as how or whether language delays affect academic skills.

Research on these important issues comes from a variety of disciplines, including phonetics, developmental psychology, and the speech and hearing sciences. Because this book is concerned with how specific language skills influence success in learning to read, the focus will be on the impact of language delays on reading skill across the age span. This becomes an issue of specifying a time line. How long does it take for temporal variation to run its course, and does this vary with each language skill? This is not a simple or straightforward story, because the developmental path of expressive language—unlike that of receptive language— is lengthy and unpredictable. And even though scientists have something more tangible to work with than those who study speech recognition, this doesn't make it any easier.

Rigorous steps to purse the goals listed above were a long time in coming, and this is a fairly recent area of research. For decades, the reigning language experts (mainly linguists) decreed that there were biological universals for speech development that determined which sounds in the language were produced in which sequence at which age. The most influential theory was proposed by Jakobsen ([1941] 1968). According to him, language development has two main stages, a prelinguistic babbling stage followed by a true linguistic stage. The babbling stage is not influenced by a child's native language and might include any sound in any language. The babbling stage ends abruptly, to be followed by the linguistic stage. Other universals operate at this stage. Phonemes will appear in a certain sequence as a function of a particular language, according to Jakobsen's "laws of irreversible solidarity." These laws govern such things as the order in which nasal consonants and vowels appear, and specify features like "optimal vowels" (/ah/) and "optimal consonants" (/p/). There were no data to support this theory, and Jakobsen did no research to test it.

Jakobsen's theory was given a boost when Lenneberg (1967) published a book largely sympathetic to his ideas. Lenneberg took the universal (biological) model one step further. Because babbling was supposed to be unrelated to the native language, he proposed that deaf and hearing children alike would babble on cue to a developmental clock. It was only at the "linguistic" stage that deaf children would begin to falter.

As knowledge slowly accumulated, these theories became unsustainable. During the 1970s a minor rebellion took place that had a major impact as newly fledged graduate students began to take a long, serious look at speech development. Linguists and phoneticians took on the "universal phoneme production machine" model of infant speech development. They made detailed phonetic transcriptions of individual children's utterances, hour by hour, day by day, over weeks and months. Developmental psychologists began studying language structure and the mental operations involved.

People in the speech and hearing sciences were faced with applied problems that couldn't be solved without good tests and solid norms. One key question was how much of a delay in talking had to occur, how many mispronounced phonemes had to exist, and how mangled syntax had to be, for this to constitute a language disorder, something the child is unlikely to outgrow with time. A second question was whether all language difficulties were cut from the same cloth. Was language a conglomerate of interlocking skills, or a group of loosely connected aptitudes that follow different developmental paths? To answer these enormous questions meant tackling temporal variation head on, and a lot more besides.

In this chapter, I chart the wild, unpredictable ride of early speech development. To keep this analysis relevant to research on reading, I will focus mainly on children who get off to a bumpy start. The central question here is this: Do early language delays and other problems predict subsequent language skills, and, if so, does this affect success in learning to read?

Early Speech

Nobody Is a Copycat

Even severely mentally disabled people can talk and carry on a conversation, though it may not always make sense. The language systems of the brain are insistent task masters and rarely give up. Yet, despite the fact that spoken language is a universal human trait, the route to fluent adult discourse is a messy business. Infant speakers exhibit some universal patterns, some native language patterns, and some idiosyncratic patterns all at the same time. The outcome is a tower of phonetic babble that linguists enter at their peril. Menn (1971) was one of the first to document (in great phonetic detail) the highly idiosyncratic path of her own infant's progression from babble to words.

A child's earliest linguistic efforts kick-start the language acquisition process, and signal patterns of extreme variation in speech development that may have a ripple effect later on. For this reason, I will briefly review the relevant facts about early speech production.

Three things happen together when the infant starts babbling at around 6 to 9 months, and they continue to influence speech production long after the infant has decided to say something meaningful. First, there are anatomical constraints on speech production. These have to do with the ease or complexity of the articulatory gestures used in speech. It is these gestures that lead to the "look-alike/sound-alike" universals that tend to be common to all beginning speakers. Infants can flap their jaw up and down, lips closing and opening, push out some air at the same time (with or without vocal cords closing), and lo and behold, bilabial stops or their approximations (nasal /mmmm/'s) get attached to a vowel, and out comes *ba*, *pa*, or *ma*. On other occasions, infants might wiggle the tip of their tongue up and down (jaw movement optional) and produce the dentals *ta* or *da*. Vihman and her colleagues (Vihman, Ferguson, and Elbert 1986; Vihman 1993), studying children learning to speak English, French, Swedish, and Japanese, found that labial and dental ("place") consonants as well as stop ("manner") consonants were by far the most common for beginning speakers across all four languages. I need to stress that no infant babbles in consonant phonemes. Early babbles consist mainly of CV syllables and isolated vowels.

Despite the universal tendencies noted above, the native language has an influence too. Work from the same team showed that even at the babbling stage, vowel and consonant production is influenced by the native language (Boysson-Bardies et al. 1989; Boysson-Bardies and Vihman 1991). French infants are more likely to produce nasal sounds than infants learning other languages. When infants were followed up at the fifty-word stage, the impact of the native language was more noticeable, especially in the types of syllables the child uttered. At the pure babbling stage (zero words), there was a fifty-fifty split between single-syllable and multisyllable utterances for nearly every infant (universal). But by the fifty-word stage, monosyllables had diminished to around 30 percent in all languages except English. English has a large corpus of common one-syllable words, especially of the CVC variety. Levitt et al. (1992) found that English infants favor CVC patterns, whereas French infants do not.

The third element in early speech production is the enormous individual variation, which is largely due to chance. Vihman (1993) has documented this variation not only at time 1 (zero words) and time 2 (fifty words) but in the *transition* from time 1 to time 2. One child (Emily) began her speaking career using the jaw-flap/lip-squeeze method described above. At time 1, 90 percent of Emily's consonants were labial consonants (half stop and half nasal). At time 2, these had dropped to 33 percent, and she was busily practicing dentals, /t/ /d/ (47 percent), which had zero occurrence at time 1. Although the variation between the children remained large at time 2, it was diminishing in the aggregate, as shown by shrinking standard deviations for almost every measure. In other words, as time went by, the children in a language group grew more similar to each other as they inched their way toward becoming native speakers.

The idiosyncrasies of children's early speech also reflect what the child wants to talk about, and what is meaningful to her. As noted previously, *shoe* and *juice* are common early words, even though the consonants are among the hardest for infants to say. The early *shoe* and *juice* attempts are far off the mark: *soo* for *shoe*, and *ooce* or *doo* for *juice*. Nelson (1998) discovered, contrary to popular belief, that first words aren't necessarily concrete nouns. Instead, the most common words are "event" words, words having to do with meals, bathtime, playtime, arrival, and departure.

What a child chooses to talk about can be a wild card in the foundation of a phonetic repertoire. A child's first words may be linked to a particular phoneme through something as simple as the first consonant in his or her name. A child named Lawrence might say /l/ words earlier and more often than other children. This phoneme usually appears late in speech acquisition.

Individual variation in speech production is so great during the first 2 years of life that even identical twins don't follow the same path. In a study by Leonard, Newhoff, and Mesalam (1980), twins were compared to ten unrelated children at the early stages of speech production. The twins had no more speech patterns in common with each other than they did with the unrelated children. And individual variation is so great that some children don't speak at all.

Lateral and Temporal Variation

There is considerable controversy over when speech production begins to settle into something like a normal pattern sufficient to predict a child's language development over the next few years. Some believe that this special moment arrives between 24 and 36 months. Others think it comes much later. The early estimate derives, in part, from the fact that vocabulary norms collected by different researchers are remarkably consistent.

Stoel-Gammon (1991) reports that the average size of productive vocabulary across the age range 18 to 36 months is 110 words at 18 months, 300 words at 24 months, 550 words at 30 months, and in excess of 1,000 words at 36 months. The norms for receptive vocabulary from the MacArthur Foundation study reported earlier were 40 words at 10 months and 169 words at 16 months. This represents about a two-to-one ratio between receptive and expressive vocabulary, at least for this age range.

The consonant repertoire in spontaneous speech for 50 percent of 2-year-olds is ten to twelve initial consonants (/b/ /t/ /d/ /g/ /k/ /m/ /n/ /h/ /w/ /f/ /s/) and six final consonants (/p/ /t/ /k/ /n/ /s/ /r/) (Stoel-Gammon 1985). The proportion of children able to produce particular syllable patterns at 24 months was as follows:

CV, V, CVC	97%
CVCV	79%
CVCVC	65%
CCV	58%
CVCC	48%

This doesn't mean that the syllable patterns were produced frequently, only that they occurred. Preisser, Hodson, and Paden (1988) reported that at 22–25 months, the most common errors were deleting a consonant in a cluster and deleting a liquid (/l/ /r/) in any position. By 26–29 months, speech errors reduce sharply, while the number of consonant phonemes increases. The most difficult consonants, and last in the sequence, are the group known as "stridents": /f/ /s/ /z/ /sh/ /ch/ /j/. Vowels are produced more accurately.

Despite a fair amount of consistency in these numbers, individual variation remains high. Stoel-Gammon (1985, 1989a, 1989b) found that the range of consonants produced at age 2 was three to sixteen for initial consonants and zero to eleven for final consonants. More important, the variation of the consonant repertoire predicted productive vocabulary size. Correlations were high between the number of initial and final consonants produced ($r = .74$), and between initial and final consonants and vocabulary size ($r = .79$, $r = .85$). The obvious conclusion is that productive vocabulary growth is dependent on the size of the phonetic speech inventory, but it is also likely that receptive vocabulary drives the phonetic inventory. It should be noted that the relationship between final consonants and vocabulary size is language specific. In some languages, the range of final consonants is extremely limited: /n/ and /ng/ (Chinese), /n/ (Japanese).

One consistent finding in this research is that lateral variation shrinks with age. This has been shown for the phonetic repertoire as well as for productive vocabulary size. Fenson et al. (1993) reported normative data that illustrates this effect. At 18 months the standard deviation was higher than the mean. In other words, vocabulary size was so variable that it did not fit a normal distribution. By 30 months it did.

Age (months)	Vocabulary size	Standard deviation
18	109.7	111.4
24	312	176.3
30	546	97.0

Stoel-Gammon (1991) used the analogy of traveling down a road to describe natural variation in language development. The width of the road represents lateral variation (with most children on the crown and some "in the ditch"). The rate down the road represents temporal variation (some children go quickly, some slowly). However, this doesn't account for the fact that the child "in the ditch" is miles behind *at the same time*. I designed a composite version that combines these two developmental paths.

Figure 7.1 shows an imaginary road moving in a clockwise spiral. Children start the journey at the open end of the spiral. Children of the same age march in a row, older children ahead and younger children behind. Most children are bunched together near the crown of the road. The rest are spread out. Slower children are close to the ditch on the

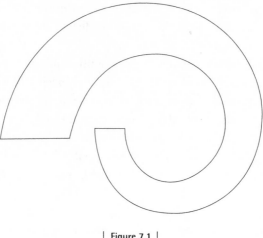

| **Figure 7.1** |
Spiral road.

left, and faster children are far from the ditch on the right. As the road bends, the children on the left side of the road line up with the younger children on the crown of the road *behind* them. The children on the right side of the road line up with the older children on the crown of the road *ahead* of them.

The road begins wide (large lateral variation) and gets increasingly narrow (lateral variation shrinks). As the road reaches the apex of the spiral, the rows get closer together until they merge into one row. Temporal variation has vanished, and only lateral variation remains. This signals the end of language development. It is this complexity that researchers have to be aware of and account for.

What happens to the children in the ditch on the far left, those with extreme delays? Do they remain there, and if not, when and how do they move toward the center? Stoel-Gammon suggested that on the basis of current norms, it's possible to identify atypical children by age 2. They tend to exhibit one or more "red flags" that, if persistent, predict serious language problems later on. These red flags are the absence of CV syllables, fewer than fifty words, numerous errors in vowel production, the absence of final consonants in CVC words, plus idiosyncratic patterns, such as final consonants appearing before initial consonants, and consonants coming into the repertoire in an atypical order.

The longitudinal research to test these predictions didn't get underway until the 1990s. This work revealed a group children who became known as "late talkers." The research reviewed in the following section is directed to answering a number of questions about these children. What is their incidence in the population? Do these dawdlers catch up and if so, when? What are the linguistic characteristics of late talkers, and do they predict subsequent development? Do late talkers have a normal phonetic repertoire but just refuse to talk? (Many people have heard a story of someone who "never said a word until he was 4, when out of the blue, he asked for a bacon and egg sandwich with lots of mayonnaise.")

Late Talkers

One of the most fascinating studies on late talkers happened by accident. Weismer, Murray-Branch, and Miller (1994) were investigating language development in twenty-three children in a longitudinal study. The study began when the children were 13 months old. They were normal in every respect, in onset of babbling, receptive vocabulary, and hearing. They were tested every 3 months until they were 25 months old. Receptive and expressive vocabulary were measured by the MacArthur Communicative Development Inventory (Fenson et al. 1993), a parent checklist of words collected from young children's receptive and spoken vocabularies. Spontaneous vocalizations were recorded, transcribed, and coded for the quantity and accuracy of "phonological processing."

In the speech and hearing sciences, *phonological processing* refers to speech production and not to speech recognition. This term includes measures of speech accuracy, phonetic output, voicing, breath control, and prosody. In reading research, the same term means the ability to *hear* phonological segments in speech (words, syllables, and phonemes). To avoid confusion, I will use the term *articulation* to reflect the composite speech-production measures.

In the Weismer, study, it was obvious by the second or third visit that four of the children had fallen so far behind that they were a cause for concern. Although it was not the authors' intention to investigate late talkers, this was a unique opportunity, and they decided to track these children for an additional year. Up to this point, most studies on late talkers had been retrospective, relying on parent reports and questionnaires. Here was a chance to follow these children from the outset. The

Table 7.1

Expressive vocabulary in normally developing children and late talkers

Months:	13	16	19	22	25
Normal children	14	47	135	264	442
Late talkers	5	6	16	29	54

Table 7.2

Expressive vocabulary for four late talkers

Months:	13	16	19	22	25	28	31	34
A.	6	5	17	41	51	273	579	646
B.	5	16	34	43	87	107	122	369
C.	0	1	8	15	52	216	563	623
D.	3	4	6	18	25	214	542	542

extreme deviation between the late talkers and the other children can be seen in table 7.1.

It was obvious to everyone that by the age of 2, the late talkers were headed for trouble. Imagine their surprise when they saw what happened next. The vocabulary scores of each of the four late talkers are shown in table 7.2.

At final testing at 34 months, the late talkers' receptive vocabulary was above normal. Expressive vocabulary and IQ scores were in the normal range. The number of words in a spoken phrase, known as *mean length of utterance* or MLU, was the only measure that remained below normal. This would be expected in view of the fact that these children had fewer words to practice with for a long time.

Weismer, and her colleagues could find no reason for the delay. Speech accuracy was not the problem. The phonetic repertoire of these children was close to the 2-year-old norms, and speech intelligibility was high as well, ranging from 69 to 86 percent. Clearly, these children were not held back by problems with articulation. The authors concluded that

the relative patterns of early development by the late talkers were not predictive of their later patterns of development.... With regard to the issue of prediction of language outcomes in late talkers, the findings from this investigation add to the pool of contradictory results from previous studies.... There was also no clear relationship between early patterns of productive grammatical skills measured via MLU and later development. (pp. 861, 865)

The only predictor was the fact that two of the four late talkers had a family history of slow language development. Rescorla and Schwartz (1990) also reported that 50 percent of the late talkers they studied had a family history of language delays.

I want to emphasize Weismer, Murray-Branch, and Miller's warning about terminology and labeling. They urged people in the field to stop describing late talkers as delayed or impaired. In their view, late talkers are "late bloomers," part of a continuum of normal temporal variation.

Weismer and colleagues studied very few children and even fewer late talkers. Other research has focused on late talkers as a group, using much larger samples. Perhaps the children in this study were unusual.

Rescorla (1989) was among the first to provide normative data on a large demographic sample of children. She tested 351 two-year-olds (22–26 months) from an entire town with a complete range of socioeconomic groups (SES range I–V). Productive vocabulary was measured by a parent checklist of common early words, and the scores differed significantly between groups, ranging from an average of 128 words in SES V to 169 words in SES I (a neighborhood with 68 percent professional families). Sex differences were highly significant, with girls well ahead of boys (169 words to 132 words).

Rescorla looked at the proportion of children who met various criteria for late talkers across the five SES groups. Using the criterion "less than 50 words," 14 percent of the children in all SES groups qualified as late talkers. When this was broadened to include "less than 50 words *or* no word combinations," the only change occurred in the SES V group, where the proportion of late talkers swelled to 20 percent.

Using a stricter criterion, "less than 30 words *or* no word combinations," proportions of late talkers dropped to 10 percent for all groups except SES V, which again had more late talkers (16.5 percent). Finally, the criterion "less than 30 words *and* no word combinations" identified 7 percent of the children across all SES groups. These results show that social class has a greater effect on word combinations or the length of utterance (MLU) than on the size of spoken vocabulary.

Depending on the criteria and SES, 7 to 20 percent of these 2-year-olds could be classified as late talkers, a wide margin of error indeed. But whatever the cutoff, late talkers were a lot more common than anyone suspected. The norm for spoken language is fifty words by 18 months, and fewer than fifty words at 24 months is a definite red flag according to Stoel-Gammon. Yet by this criterion alone, 14 percent of all the 2-year-olds in this town didn't pass muster. This is 40 children in a sample of 350.

Apart from documenting the incidence of late talkers in the population, an important first step, scientists in this field have largely been interested in two issues: Why does a child talk late? What predicts which children catch up and which do not?

Paul, Looney, and Dahm (1991) screened for late talkers in a large group of children age 18–34 months using a parent checklist. In the age range 18–23 months, seven children said ten or fewer words, and in the age range 24–34 months, fourteen children said fewer than fifty words. This represented 7 percent of children in both age groups; 71 percent were boys. To study developmental progress, the late talkers were matched in age, sex, and SES to twenty-one normally developing children, given further tests, and followed over time.

Mothers were interviewed using the Vineland Behavior Scales, which provide information on expressive and receptive language, daily living, socialization, and motor skills. Both young and older groups of late talkers had significantly lower scores on expressive language (as expected), and on receptive language and socialization as well. Scores on daily living and motor performance were in the normal range. Late talkers' socialization skills remained below normal even when verbal items were omitted ("says *please*"), and the data reanalyzed for nonverbal behaviors only ("obeys requests").

The children were followed up 12–18 months later and the Vineland test was given again. The late talkers *as a group* still had significantly lower expressive language and socialization scores, but no differences were found for receptive language. However, there were extreme differences among the late talkers in rates of development. Over half now had normal receptive and expressive language, and socialization scores. Yet one-third of the late talkers still lagged far behind in receptive vocabulary. There didn't seem to be any pattern. That is, a child with a very low expressive language score did not necessarily have a low receptive language or socialization score.

To find out if any combination of factors predicted subsequent status, they classified the children into one of four categories:

1. Low expressive language, normal receptive language and socialization scores (33 percent of the sample)
2. Low expressive language and socialization scores, normal receptive language (38 percent)
3. Low receptive and expressive language, normal socialization scores (one child—4.8 percent)
4. Children delayed on all three (24 percent)

(It should be noted that 71 percent had a normal receptive vocabulary score, and a low expressive vocabulary. This means that the vast majority of late talkers understand speech perfectly well).

Paul and her colleagues predicted that having *more* problems would be a worse prognosis than having fewer problems, but when they compared category membership across time, there was no prediction whatsoever: "It is tempting to hypothesize, as we did, that children who showed these concomitant deficits would be at greater risk for chronic delay than those with circumscribed expressive lags. This does not appear to be the case in our data, however" (p. 864).

As they note, all one can say about these results is that if children in the age range 18–34 months are slow to talk, there is a 50 percent chance they will be in the normal range later on, and a 50 percent chance they won't. So much for red flags.

Paul and Jennings (1992) did a more detailed analysis of late talkers' language skills in the age ranges 18–24 months and 24–34 months. Once again, 71 percent of the late talkers were boys. They were matched to normal children on sex, age, and SES. The children were videotaped to get samples of their speech from unstructured play sessions with their mothers. Three measures were derived from a phonetic analysis of the tape: degree of syllable complexity, percent consonants produced correctly in real words, and the number of different types of consonants.

Although the late talkers and the normal children differed significantly on each measure, the late talkers' scores resembled a delay and not a disorder. All syllable types were represented in their speech; they just didn't appear very often. Words were more likely to have a simple syllable structure. The consonant repertoire of late talkers was like that of younger children in terms of number and proportions of consonant types. When the older group of late talkers was compared to the younger, normal children, they did not differ on any measure, suggesting that the late talkers were 6 to 12 months delayed in speech production (extreme temporal variation).

Paul and Jennings concluded that late talkers are on a normal path but taking an awfully long time about it. They felt it was impossible to speculate about the causes of this delay. These children might talk less because their phonetic repertoire is smaller, or the phonetic repertoire might be smaller because they don't talk enough. This, of course, does not explain *why* this occurs, because speech production is completely under voluntary control. For some reason, late talkers choose not to talk.

The theory that late talkers are more like younger children was tested directly by Thal, Oroz, and McCaw (1995). Although this was a small sample (seventeen late talkers) and a large age range (18–33 months), this study added an important control. Late talkers were matched for productive vocabulary size to two groups, one by chronological age (lateral variation), and one by expressive vocabulary (temporal variation)—younger children normal for their age. On every measure—intelligibility, number of consonants spoken, syllable structure level, productive syntax—the late talkers were indistinguishable from the younger, vocabulary-matched children. This criterion-matched design is fundamental for pinning down natural temporal variation.

The most detailed measures of language across the age span were provided in a longitudinal study by Rescorla and her colleagues (Rescorla and Ratner 1996; Roberts et al. 1998). There were thirty late talkers (twenty-eight boys) in the age range 24–31 months in the study. They were at least 6 months below norms on the Reynell Expressive Language Scale. A group of normal children was matched for age and sex. The productive vocabulary scores were extremely discrepant between the two groups, with normal children saying around 225 words, and late talkers only 23 words.

Children were videotaped in parent-child play sessions, and the child's utterances were transcribed and scored. Nearly all measures of verbal production showed extreme differences between the groups. The normal children produced an average of 115 vocalizations in the play session compared to 52 for the late talkers. Late talkers used, on average, 7.3 vowels and 8.6 consonants, compared to 12.4 vowels and 17.4 consonants for normal children. Measures of frequency counts of initial consonants did not differ. The most common consonants were /b/ /d/ /m/ /n/ /h/ /w/, and the next most common /t/ /k/ /g/, and this was true for both groups of children. The main difference appeared in the tally of final consonants. Normal children produced a variety of final consonants typical of English words—/p/ /t/ /k/ /m/ /n/ /s/—and produced them often. Final-consonant output was close to zero for late talkers, apart from the occasional /m/ /n/ /s/. The children differed in the number of syllable types they used. Nearly 30 percent of the sounds produced by late talkers were single-vowel utterances, as opposed to 11 percent for normal children. The most common syllable pattern for both groups was CV, but the normal children produced a much larger number of CVC and two-syllable words.

These figures reveal that late talkers were perfectly capable of talking if they wanted to. Rescorla and Ratner explored a number of reasons for late talkers' reticence to speak. One interesting idea, first proposed by Murphy et al. (1983), is that mothers may respond to their infant's vocalizations in a manner appropriate for the *vocalizations* rather than the infant's age. In this case, mothers would speak to their late talkers as if they were much younger, and fail to be aware of their good receptive language skills. However, supporting evidence for this theory is marginal, and research has produced mixed results. Mother-child interactions are identical for normal and late talkers in terms of declaratives, questions, imperatives, and requests (Rescorla and Fechnay 1996), and in the number of maternal initiations and utterances (Nova and Rescorla 1994). On the other hand, differences have been observed in the number of times mothers ask for labels ("What's this?") and in verbal imitations (Nova and Rescorla 1994). Murphy et al. (1983) also found differences in whether the mother treats her child's attempt as a real word.

Rescorla and Ratner concluded in much the same vein as Paul and Jennings, that the profiles of the two groups of children seem to reflect a delayed, rather than deviant, patterning of phonological development (*phonological* in this case meaning articulation).

The children were followed up when they were 36 months old (Roberts et al. 1998). Once again, they were videotaped in a play session with their mothers. Late talkers did not differ from normal children on the number of vocalizations or on articulation errors. However, they scored well below normal children on every other measure: verbalizations (any vocalizations containing one word), fully intelligible utterances, phonetic inventory of consonants, percent consonants correct, and mean length of utterance.

As in previous studies, not all late talkers were the same. Roberts et al. divided the late talkers into two groups on the basis of their "verbalization" score (split at 1 standard deviation below the mean). The children scoring below the cutoff were called the "continuing-delay" group. The children scoring above it were called the "late bloomers." When they compared the two groups, the continuing-delay group scored well below the late bloomers on every measure. The late bloomers were indistinguishable from the normal children on the amount of fully intelligible utterances, but fell in between the other two groups on phonetic inventory, percent consonants correct, and MLU. MLU scores were 1.85, 2.94, and 4.14 for the continuing-delay group, late bloomers, and normal children respectively.

Roberts et al. came to the same conclusions as the other scientists. The profile of late talkers resembles a *delay* rather than anything abnormal. The late talkers produced less of everything. Consonants came in more slowly, but there were no unusual patterns of acquisition. Thus, there seems to be little support for Stoel-Gammon's red flags for aberrant developmental sequences, such as words ending in final consonants appearing before words with initial consonants.

Summary

This work provides a remarkably consistent body of evidence on late talkers. Weismer, Murray-Branch, and Miller showed that late talkers can be identified quite early, at about 16 to 19 months. They constitute around 7 to 14 percent of the normal population, depending on the selection criteria and which language test is used. About 70 percent are boys. The typical profile of the late talker is a receptive language score in the normal range but depressed scores on all production measures. Late talkers don't talk much, reasons unknown. When they do talk, their speech follows a normal developmental path, but they look like a much younger child in terms of phonetic repertoire and syllable patterns. While there is little support for Stoel-Gammon's red flags of deviant sequential patterns, there is support for red flags of less than fifty words at age 2, plus a seriously impoverished phonetic repertoire. Added to the list is a smaller range of syllable types.

All studies point to about a fifty-fifty split at around age 3 between late talkers who show a sudden spurt (developmental compression) and become late bloomers, and those who continue to lag behind. There is a strong consensus that nothing in particular seems to predict which child will end up in which group. These effects are due to the impact of natural variation (both temporal and lateral). While children with continuing delays fall significantly below normal children on every measure, the late bloomers catch up first on volubility and intelligibility. They speak at a normal rate in clearly articulated words. At age 3, they still lag behind the average child on measures of phoneme count and syllable complexity. Undoubtedly they will catch up here as well. Perhaps the children in the continuing-delay group will begin a language spurt like the late bloomers did. Unfortunately, we don't know what happens next, because late talkers have not been followed up past the age of 3.

Something else emerged from the data that is not specific to the normal-versus-late-talker issue. The size of the spoken phonetic repertoire was found to be highly correlated to spoken vocabulary in the study by Stoel-Gammon (1989a). This raises interesting questions about the *origin* or direction of the correlation, because there is no necessary relationship between these two measures. A small corpus of consonants, especially those that universally come in early (/b/ /p/ /d/ /t/ /m/ /n/ /s/), plus a few vowels, can generate a very large number of English words. A child doesn't need a large phonetic repertoire to have a sizable productive vocabulary.

Nevertheless, a large phonetic repertoire *is* necessary to produce coherent utterances in English (MLU). Even the most common English words in the simplest phrases have a great deal of phonetic complexity. Here are four simple two- and three-word utterances any toddler would want to say:

bye-bye
please cookie
oh-oh, fall down
go potty mommy

These four phrases require a repertoire of twelve consonants and seven vowels, and the young speaker will fall way short of this requirement. A child who experiences too great a mismatch between what she wants to say and the phonetic repertoire to say it could be blocked from speaking, leading to a low expressive vocabulary and shorter MLU.

Also, the language itself is a strong determiner of what "normal" means on measures of phoneme complexity and syllable counts. A Japanese-speaking child, who has to master concatenations of CV syllables, would look abnormal compared to an English-speaking child, as would a child who learns a language with a small number of phonemes, like Hawaiian.

One possible explanation for the tight link between a spoken phonetic repertoire and vocabulary is that the former drives the latter and so is *causal*. The more phonemes that are added to a spoken repertoire, the greater the variety of words that can be produced, and the easier it becomes to string words together. The phonetic repertoire, in turn, derives from receptive vocabulary and articulatory skill—the ability to translate phonetic patterns into speech gestures. As children extract phonetic sequences from the words they understand and learn to produce, the rate at which they are able to do this determines their expressive vocabulary at a particular point in time in their development.

This causal argument is opposite the one proposed by Metsala and Walley (Metsala 1997; Metsala and Walley 1998) outlined in chapter 3. According to their theory, children's spoken vocabulary determines their phonetic sensitivity. The number of words the children choose to say, and the similarity between those words, causes their awareness of phoneme sequences to increase. According to this theory, during vocabulary acquisition, the children would have to be able to generate words ad lib *prior to* being able to hear their phonemic structure. A finer analysis of phoneme sequences is only required when there are too many "neighbors" in the mix, too many words that sound alike. It is word similarity that leads to phonemic sensitivity.

By this reasoning, languages with few phonemes—those that build words by combining the same small set of syllables (such as Pacific island languages)—ought to lead to greater phoneme awareness than languages with a complex syllable structure, like English, German, and Dutch. In that case, according to the theory, children from the Pacific islands should have far less trouble mastering an alphabetic writing system. The "vocabulary causes phoneme awareness" theory is favored by many reading researchers. Here, the causal link to reading would go as follows: expressive vocabulary—phoneme awareness—reading.

This theory is not supported by the data. Nor is it even convincing. It divorces productive vocabulary from speech recognition and receptive vocabulary. It doesn't explain where productive vocabulary comes from, or the fact that deaf children don't spontaneously generate words ad lib. I want to propose a third possibility, that of reciprocal causality that works by *positive feedback* (positive feedback leads to mutual escalation). Children process the phonetic sequence in a word they hear and wish to produce, and hold this in mind while they try to produce it. They immediately get auditory feedback on whether what they said maps to their *auditory image*. If it does not, they will try again. If there is some success, they will make more speech attempts, and these multiple attempts translate into an increasing productive vocabulary. Because they are saying more words (increasing vocabulary size), the auditory feedback increases and continues to refine their speech production, opening up options for more phonetic combinations. This loop thrives on saying lots of different words (not lots of the same-sounding words). In this type of model, causality resides in the entire loop and not in any part of it. That is, there is *no direction of causality*.

There are two reasons this feedback loop might malfunction or break down. The first involves perceptual and/or motor development. If the auditory feedback is not clearly perceived, or the auditory image held in mind is too imprecise or fragile, or the motor production during articulation is too uncoordinated, the system won't function efficiently and may slow down or grind to a halt.

The second reason is that a child may simply make a decision not to talk. His verbal attempts don't meet his expectations, and he doesn't seem to be able to alter them so they do. It has been documented many times in developmental research that children won't tolerate adults imitating their incorrect utterances, even though they themselves are incapable of correcting their own speech errors. Another inhibiting factor is the failure of speech attempts to produce the reactions the children are trying to solicit in the people around them. Research on mother-infant interactions shows that certain extreme parenting styles slow down or stop the child's speech attempts (see Golinkoff and Hirsh-Pasek 1999).

A third factor might be personality. A child may get by with grunting and pointing, and if parents put up with it, that's good enough for him. Any combination of these factors could be a profile of a late talker.

At this point, the trail of the late talkers starts to go cold, and we must pick up the trail at age 4, not knowing when or by how much these children had fallen by the wayside in the meantime. To keep a tally going, let's assume that there are roughly 14 percent of the population who are late talkers at age 2, and only half of this group remain at age 3 (7 percent of the population). If nothing changes from age 3 to 4, or 3 to 5, these 7 percent should be in trouble later on.

THE IMPACT OF GENERAL LANGUAGE SKILLS ON READING AND ACADEMIC SUCCESS

The evidence reviewed in the last chapter has shown that late talkers reflect the lower tail of normal temporal variation. These children are rarely tracked beyond the age of 36 months, and when the trail is picked up at age 4, the explanation for language delays shifts from one of normal temporal variation or developmental lag, to an "impairment." The reason is largely historical, a consequence of the clinical (remedial) tradition in the speech and hearing sciences. Because of this schism in outlook and approach, normal temporal variation has not been tracked into the school system until recently, and even then only incidentally, as part of studies on so-called language-impaired children.

And there are other concerns. It was (and still is) far more common for parents to seek help for their child's speech-motor problems than for general language problems. As a consequence, children whose speech is reasonably intelligible but who have difficulty producing sentences with correct syntactic and semantic structure remain unidentified. For most of the twentieth century, the focus of clinical research was on the outcome of remedial efforts to improve speech clarity. Follow-on surveys conducted in the early 1970s showed that most children referred for speech-motor problems tended to outgrow them (Morley 1972; Renfrew and Geary 1973). But these studies had serious methodological problems. Most failed to control IQ or to employ objective (standardized) language tests, and they were often based on retrospective data (clinical notes or parent interviews). Myers (1987, 41) pointed out that even though standardized language tests began to appear in the 1970s, they were based on unsubstantiated psycholinguistic theories and lacked content validity: "During this time, content validity was asserted by simply using face validity as evidence that psycholinguistic abilities were measured by a test. The extensive use of these tests means that the assessment process has become vested in a model that yields little in-depth information regarding a child's language abilities."

Beitchman et al. (1986), in their review of earlier work, noted that the research was so poor that the incidence of speech and language impairment in the general population ranged wildly from 5 to 35 percent depending on which paper you read. They cited a number of other problems, such as nonrepresentative samples, lack of diagnostic criteria, untrained or poorly trained testers and no interrater reliability measures, the failure to distinguish speech difficulties from other language problems, and vague reporting of procedures and protocols to such an extent that the study could not be replicated.

One exception, and a major contribution to the field, was the National Speech and Hearing Survey (Hull et al. 1971). This was a normative study using geographic partitioning and stratification techniques developed by the U.S. Bureau of the Census. There were 100 sampling points across the United States. Speech accuracy and hearing were measured in students in grades 1–12 (approximate ages 6–18 years). There were 19,835 boys and 18,733 girls in the survey. This provided the first true measure of the incidence of articulation and hearing problems in children.

All procedures were highly controlled. Speech pathologists were trained to test each child individually on a variety of measures. On the basis of the test scores, children were assigned to one of three categories: acceptable speech, moderate deviation, extreme deviation. Figure 8.1 (derived from table 6 in Hull et al. 1971) shows the percentage of boys and girls that fit each criterion at each age. The figure illustrates a trade-off. As children's speech improves with age, they ascend to swell the ranks of the group with acceptable speech.

There are several key findings in this assessment. Perhaps the most important is the evidence of a long, slow developmental path of speech accuracy and fluency. Speech development is continuous (few spurts) and doesn't begin to level out, even at 18 years (the highest age tested). Second, there is a sharp decline in the incidence of extreme deviations in the age range 6 to 8 years, dropping from 12 to 5 percent, especially for boys. By grade 6 (12 years), children with severe speech problems constitute about 1 percent of the population.

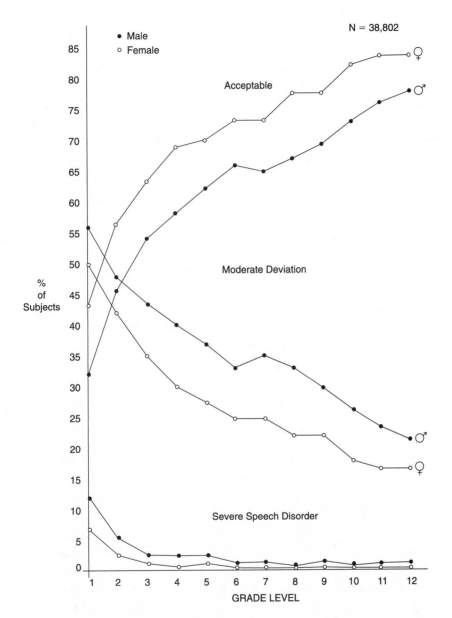

Language Skills and Reading and Academic Success |

| **Figure 8.1** |

Articulation development. Adopted from F. M. Hull et al. (1971).

The other striking result is that girls have an advantage from the outset and this only gets larger with time. Boys do not have a developmental lag they subsequently outgrow. At 6 and 7 years girls are 1 year ahead of boys in speech accuracy. By age 8, they are 2 years ahead. By age 11, they are 4 years ahead, and they maintain this advantage to at least age 18.

Sex differences did not appear on any of the hearing tests when the children were young, but by grades 6 and 7 (12 and 13 years), girls began to show an increasing sensitivity to high-frequency sounds. At the same age, boys' high-frequency sensitivity actually declined (gradual hearing loss). This pattern was not found for middle or low frequencies. Males' high-frequency hearing loss has been well documented in adults and becomes more severe with age (Corso 1959; McGuinness 1972, 1985). It is worth noting that high-frequency sensitivity is important for the perception of consonants characterized by high-frequency bursts (/f/ /j/ /k/ /s/ /t/ /z/ /sh/ /ch/).

Beginning in 1975, the first of several longitudinal studies appeared on the outcome of delays or deficits in receptive and expressive language skills, and their effect on academic success. These studies are at the heart of the issue of how or whether language development has an impact on reading skill.

Longitudinal Studies

Aram and Nation

The first longitudinal study to trace language development into the school, using a comprehensive battery of objective tests, was carried out by Aram and Nation and their colleagues (Wolpaw, Nation, and Aram 1976; Aram and Nation 1975, 1980; Aram, Ekelman, and Nation 1984). The children were diagnosed by speech-language pathologists as "language disordered" and were receiving language therapy at a speech and hearing clinic. Their ages ranged from 3:5 to 6:11 at the start of the study in 1971. They were given a battery of language tests, the Leiter nonverbal IQ test, and the Peabody Picture Vocabulary Test (PPVT). This is a test of receptive vocabulary in which the tester says a word and the child points to one of four pictures.

The children did extremely poorly on the language tests, confirming the diagnoses of the language specialists. Most of the children scored below the 10th percentile on both the receptive and expressive language subtests of the Northwestern Screening Test. Over half the children scored zero on the expressive language test.

The children were followed up at 5-year intervals. I report here on the 10-year follow up in 1984. Aram, Ekelman, and Nation were able to locate twenty of these children (80 percent boys). The children were given another battery of language and cognitive tests, plus the WISC IQ test, and the Wide Range Achievement Test (WRAT) for reading, spelling, and arithmetic. The results highlight some critical issues in research on children with limited language skills.

The first problem is what I call the *IQ problem*. This refers to the fact that a low verbal IQ is virtually synonymous with a "language impairment." This does not mean, however, that a language impairment is virtually synonymous with a low verbal IQ. Aram and Nation provided individual test scores for the twenty children—a rare practice that should be mandatory. At final testing, children now 13 to nearly 17 years of age were placed in four groups based on academic outcome. Group 1 was normal academically (no tutoring or grades repeated). Group 2 was in the main classroom, but had had tutoring or repeated a grade. Group 3 was in a special resource room for learning disabilities and were virtual nonreaders. Group 4 was diagnosed as educably mentally retarded (EMR). WISC verbal and performance subscales, as well as PPVT receptive vocabulary scores, showed marked differences between the groups. For example, full-scale IQ scores for groups 1 through 4 were 104, 92, 81, and 51, respectively. There were notable deviations from this pattern in groups 1–3, which I address below.

The potential for confounding low verbal IQ with expressive language delays is a particular problem with the WISC verbal IQ scale, because every subtest is based on a measure of *expressive* language, as shown below. A child with weak expressive language skills will be hard pressed to do well on these tests:

Vocabulary. The child is read a list of words by the examiner and must define each one orally to the examiner.

Information. The child is asked questions about general knowledge and must respond orally to the examiner.

Similarities.   The child is asked questions about ways two objects or two concepts are alike and must respond orally to the examiner.

Comprehension.   The child is given a series of different situations in which he or she must decide what should be done, or provide an explanation or rationale. Many of these situations deal with moral or social issues, rules, transgressions, and so on. The child does this orally to the examiner. (This measures socialization and commonsense reasoning.)

Sometime after Aram and Nation's work began, speech and hearing scientists created the diagnostic category: *specific language impairment* (SLI). Children are diagnosed SLI if they fall below certain cutoffs on language tests but have a normal or superior performance IQ. This separates SLI children from children who are educably mentally retarded (EMR) with low IQ scores across the board. The fact that *verbal IQ is not part of the SLI diagnosis* needs to be emphasized because it is rarely mentioned in the scientific reports on SLI children. The truth is that many SLI children have low verbal intelligence. This raises the fundamental question: What is verbal intelligence? Are verbal IQ subtests, like those listed above, a more valid measure of true "verbal IQ" than tests that measure natural language? So far, I have seen no attempt to address this problem.

Aram and Nation's individual data illustrate the idiosyncratic profiles of these children, and the difficulty of making a prognosis from a young child's language status. One child was nearly 6 when she was diagnosed with a language disorder. A late diagnosis ought to be more valid than an early one due to the lessening impact of temporal variation. If language problems predicted subsequent reading status, they should certainly do so here. But they did not. At age 16, this child had a most extraordinary profile. Her verbal IQ of 86 was surprisingly low in contrast to her performance IQ of 129 (the highest tested), and in contrast to her normal receptive vocabulary (PPVT = 103). Despite the low verbal IQ, her reading and spelling skills were phenomenal (87th and 94th percentile). This is a child of high intelligence whose problem is confined to expressive language. Yet 10 years earlier, she scored below the 10th percentile on *both* receptive and expressive language tests. This child was still "blooming" long after the age of 6.

Aram and Nation correlated the cognitive and language tests to reading and spelling scores measured in 1981.[1]

The strongest predictor from 1971 was the Leiter nonverbal IQ test. It correlated to WRAT reading in 1981 at $r = .49$, and to the WISC full-scale IQ in 1981 ($r = .84$), mainly through its connection to performance IQ ($r = .71$). The Leiter was uncorrelated to any verbal measure (WISC verbal IQ, $r = .05$; PPVT receptive vocabulary, $r = .27$). The same unusual pattern of correlations was found between tests given concurrently. Full-scale IQ was correlated to WRAT reading ($r = .78$) and to performance IQ ($r = .69$), but not to verbal IQ ($r = .22$).

This pattern of correlations is *not* typical of other findings in this field, nor in reading research, nor in normative studies on the WISC (Cooper 1995). A dissociation of this magnitude between verbal and performance IQ is rare, because these tests normally correlate at $r = .50$. This odd result may be due to the small sample size in combination with the extreme range of ability.

As a general conclusion, apart from the fact that performance IQ was a strong predictor of reading success in these children, there was no particular measure or set of measures that predicted outcomes for the majority of the children.

Bishop

A larger and more methodologically rigorous longitudinal study on general language development was reported by Bishop and her colleagues in England. The main goal of the study, apart from tracking language development over time, was to test three hypotheses about prognosis. One hypothesis was that an extremely uneven pattern of language development would predict a worse outcome than a uniform delay.

---

1. Because some test scores were nonnormally distributed, I recomputed the statistics using a more conservative estimate of the correlations between time 1 (1971) and time 2 (1981) test scores, and the concurrent test scores in 1981. Some of the data had too little variance (floor effects), and some were bimodally distributed. Spearman's rho was used to calculate the correlations for standardized tests where age is not a factor.

A second hypothesis was based on the idea that language is made up of several different processes, not necessarily related, each of which has a different developmental path. For example, children tend to outgrow articulation problems.

Bishop and Edmundson (1987) proposed a third hypothesis. They suggested that language was all of a piece, and that a specific language impairment (SLI) was as well. What language tests measure are different "vulnerabilities" of the elements of a total language system. According to this idea, the more elements that function at an abnormally low level, the worse the prognosis becomes, as a reflection of the severity of overall impairment. This is similar to the idea proposed by Paul, Looney, and Dahm (1991) that late talkers with the largest number of language difficulties would end up with the worst overall language skills, but their results did not support this.

The first report (Bishop and Edmundson 1987) was on 87 four-year-olds (3:9 to 4:2) at risk for language disorders. Seventy-two were boys (83 percent). These children had been identified by speech pathologists as having a variety of speech and language problems. Approximately 80 percent were receiving speech therapy. In the first phase of the study, the children were tested three times on the same test battery at ages 4, $4\frac{1}{2}$, and $5\frac{1}{2}$ years. A control group with normal language was matched for age and had the same proportion of boys. (Control groups were different at each testing, making this a "partial" longitudinal study, in which only the language-delayed group was followed over time.)

The children were screened on the Leiter nonverbal IQ test, and children who scored at least 2 standard deviations below the mean (< 70) were designated the *general-delay* group (22 percent). The children who passed this screening were divided further into two groups, one predicted to have a *good outcome* (34 percent) and one predicted to have a *poor outcome* (44 percent) on the basis of the number of cutoffs the child failed on the language tests. The word *outcome* is misleading because children were assigned to a group from the outset. To avoid confusion, I refer to these groups by prognosis, as *good*, *poor*, and *general delay*.

The test battery included tests of receptive vocabulary, speech production, volubility, intelligibility, percent consonants produced correctly, verbal comprehension, and several standardized tests of receptive and expressive syntax and semantics. Table 8.1 is a summary of the findings. The

Table 8.1
Mean scores for normal controls and two groups of language-delayed children

Test	Age 4			Age 4½			Age 5½		
	Control	Good	Poor	Control	Good	Poor	Control	Good	Poor
% unintelligible	6.4	15.0	26.7	2.3	12	19	2	2.7	8.5
% consonants correct	94	65	56		76	64		93	80
MLU	6.2	4.4	2.7	6.4	5.6	3.8	6.4	7.8	5.3
Naming vocabulary	75	69	55	82	76	64	90	86	75
Verbal comprehension	91	85	76	94	93	83	100	99	90
Picture information	23	19	14	25	25	19	26	27	24
Picture grammar	23	14	6	25	20	12	25	26	19
Bus story semantic memory	17	14	7	17	19	11	21	25	17
TROG receptive grammar centile scores		24	14		42	21		40	18
BPVS vocabulary centile scores		36	18		36	16		41	16

Note: Control groups were not given the TROG or the BPVS.
Source: Data based on Bishop and Edmundson 1987.

general-delay group is omitted from this table. Their scores were significantly below the poor group on every measure, with the exception of volubility.

At age 4, the good group scored significantly below the control group on only three tests: mean length of utterance (the child is asked to tell a story cued by pictures), Action Picture Grammar (a picture test of expressive grammar), and percent consonants produced correctly. By age $4\frac{1}{2}$, the good group no longer differed from the controls on any measure, showing that they had caught up. At age $5\frac{1}{2}$, they were even marginally superior on a test of expressive semantics and on percent consonants correct. The poor group scored significantly below the controls and below the good group on most measures at every age and was not beginning to catch up to either group by age $5\frac{1}{2}$. The data show that the poor group is delayed by about 1 year across the board. (Compare scores for the poor group at $5\frac{1}{2}$ to the good group at $4\frac{1}{2}$.) The poor group scored significantly higher than the general-delay group on most measures.

Correlations between all tests (all groups) were carried out, but the Leiter IQ score was not controlled and swamped the data. The Leiter was strongly correlated to PPVT receptive vocabulary ($r = .50$), whereas in Aram and Nation's study it was not. There were high test-retest correlations across the age span. The tests with the greatest consistency were mean length of utterance (MLU) and a test of expressive semantics (Bus Story), in which the child had to tell a story from a series of pictures.

To test their hypothesis that language skills are interconnected, Bishop and Edmundson categorized the children according to the cutoffs (pass/fail) on the various language tests. They set up a matrix of fifteen possible combinations of the four main types of language measures: speech/phonology, syntax, semantics, and verbal comprehension (receptive plus expressive vocabulary). Table 8.2 illustrates the number of children who fell below the cutoffs on these tests. Six patterns of language delays identified 90 percent of the children with normal performance IQs, and identified 93 percent of the children in the general-delay (low IQ) group. They are set out here in the order Bishop and Edmundson predicted would be most to least likely to lead to a good outcome.

As can be seen, the good group was concentrated in the categories where deficits were limited to speech and/or syntax problems. The poor

Table 8.2

The six most common categories of language-impairment. Incidence for 87 four-year-old children with language problems

Category	Normal IQ		Low IQ
	Good $N = 23$	Poor $N = 35$	$N = 17$
Articulation only	7	2	0
Syntax only	3	4	1
Articulation + syntax	9	7	0
Articulation + syntax + semantics	1	15	7
Syntax + semantics + comprehension	1	1	3
Articulation + syntax + semantics + comprehension	2	6	6

Source: Derived from Bishop and Edmundson 1987.

group was more heterogeneous, but the majority fit the following category: speech plus syntax plus semantics. The general-delay group was concentrated in the last three categories, two of which included verbal comprehension and appear to carry the heaviest penalty. This pattern supports Bishop and Edmundson's hypothesis, but it remains to be seen whether these classifications hold up over time.

The amount of language therapy was recorded to find out if this helped children recover from language difficulties. Because the worst-functioning children usually get the most therapy, hours of therapy is confounded with the severity of the language problem. This has been a consistent difficulty in these studies, leading to the awkward result that the more therapy children get, the worse off they are.

Eighty-two of the original 87 children were followed up at $8\frac{1}{2}$ years (Bishop and Adams 1990) and given a different battery of tests, which included reading tests. Results were compared to a different control group roughly matched in age and sex. The good group scored normally on almost every measure. They scored close to the norms on the British version of the PPVT (BPVS) and on WISC block design and picture completion. They were identical to the control group on MLU, expressive semantics, the Neale test of reading accuracy and comprehension, the Vernon spelling test, and tests of nonword reading and spelling. However, they scored significantly below the controls on receptive syntax (TROG) and on the WISC-R verbal comprehension test, a measure of knowledge of social norms and verbal reasoning.

By contrast, the poor group had started to slide. They now scored 84 on the BPVS vocabulary test, 78 on WISC verbal comprehension, and 91.5 on block design, significantly below normal (100) for the tests and well below the control group. They were also well below the controls on all other language and reading measures, with the exception of spelling. Not only this, but their IQ scores were beginning to resemble those of the general-delay group (WISC block design: 91.5 versus 87.5; WISC verbal comprehension: 78 versus 72.5; BPVS: 83.6 versus 76.1).

When IQ (WISC-R block design, picture completion, vocabulary) was statistically controlled in a covariance analysis, *no significant differences were found between any groups on reading accuracy*, though differences did remain for reading comprehension. The inescapable conclusion is that severe language problems are either synonymous with low IQ at the outset, or lead to low IQ as time goes by, and low IQ is highly predictive of reading problems.

To tease apart the patterns of relationships, I reassessed the results from a multiple regression analysis to look in more detail at how non-verbal IQ and receptive vocabulary affected the process of learning to read. Because not every child took all the tests, there were seventy-five children in the first analysis and eighty-one children in the second, and both are shown in table 8.3.[2]

Performance IQ plus receptive vocabulary accounted for between 15 and 20 percent of the variance in decoding skills, and 25 percent of the variance in reading comprehension. Added to this is the unique contribu-

---

2. The multiple regressions were carried out as follows. The variance due to the WISC performance IQ tests (block design and picture completion) and to receptive vocabulary (age $8\frac{1}{2}$ scores) was subtracted from each of the five reading tests. After this step, the other language tests given at ages $4\frac{1}{2}$ and $5\frac{1}{2}$ were free to vary (stepwise regression). I calculated the amount of shared variance (what the tests have in common) between the reading tests, WISC performance IQ, and the receptive vocabulary test, as well as the unique variance contributed by each independently.

Table 8.3

Summary of regression analyses for predicting reading and spelling at $8\frac{1}{2}$ years from PPVT and IQ at $8\frac{1}{2}$ and language scores at $4\frac{1}{2}$ and $5\frac{1}{2}$ years

Test scores at $8\frac{1}{2}$ $N = 75$	Shared variance PPVT + IQ	Unique variance PPVT	IQ	Total variance	Language at $4\frac{1}{2}$	% Explained variance
Neale reading	25%	5%	14%	44%	8%	52%
Neale reading comprehension	28	15	14	57	4	61
Vernon spelling	18	5	14	37	7	44
Nonword reading	24	7	13	44	5	49
Nonword spelling	21	4	13	38	5	43
Test scores at $8\frac{1}{2}$ $N = 81$					Language at $5\frac{1}{2}$	
Neale reading	16	9	14	39	9	48
Neale reading comprehension	22	19	13	54	19	73
Vernon spelling	13	7	13	33	7	40
Nonword reading	19	9	13	41	9	50
Nonword spelling	17	5	11	33	5	38

Note: Data are standard scores at $8\frac{1}{2}$ on the BPVS (British PPVT), WISC-R IQ subtests: block design, picture completion, verbal comprehension.

Source: Data based on Bishop and Adams 1990.

tion of receptive vocabulary to decoding (5 percent), spelling (9 percent), and reading comprehension (15–20 percent), as well as the unique contribution of performance IQ, which contributed 13–14 percent across the board.

Beyond this, there was a further contribution of MLU and percent consonants correct measured at age $4\frac{1}{2}$ and at age $5\frac{1}{2}$. Either test predicted 7–9 percent of the variance in decoding and spelling. MLU predicted 19 percent of the variance in reading comprehension.

The fact that the percent consonants correct and MLU measured years earlier predicted a significant proportion of the variance in reading skill suggests that slow language development (temporal variation) does have an impact on reading skill, and reading comprehension in particular.

This was not the end of the story. In 1998, Bishop's group (Stothard et al. 1998) reported a follow-on study when the children were $15\frac{1}{2}$ years old. There were seventy-one children from the original group of eighty-seven. The children were regrouped on the basis of their language scores at $5\frac{1}{2}$ years. Twenty-six children (36 percent) were considered "resolved" at age $5\frac{1}{2}$ (*good*); thirty children (42 percent) were "not resolved" (*poor*), and fifteen (21 percent) fell into the "general-delay" group. A control group was matched in age, SES, and proportion of boys. The children took the following tests: *receptive vocabulary* (BPVS), *IQ* (WISC-R subtests: vocabulary, comprehension, picture completion, block design), *reading and spelling* (WISC word tests), *expressive vocabulary* (picture naming), *sentence repetition* (CELF-R), and *receptive grammar* (TROG).[3]

Everything had changed. The good language group now performed significantly below the controls on every measure except for the WISC performance IQ and verbal comprehension. The poor group was so far below both the controls and the good group that they were indistinguish-

---

3. The authors restandardized the tests on the forty-nine children in the control group to fit with this population. But the sample size is too small, and the results must be interpreted with caution. Also troubling was the poor agreement between statements in the text and the notation in the tables about which results were significant. When there was a discrepancy, I relied on the means and standard deviations to report these results (greater than .5 standard deviation).

able from the general-delay group, and no comparisons between them were significant on any test.

The number of children who changed categories over the years reveals a startling degree of instability. Only 65 percent of the good group, considered resolved at age $5\frac{1}{2}$ and at age $8\frac{1}{2}$, remained "resolved." The other 35 percent shifted into the poor group, and one child fell into the general-delay group. Seventy percent of the poor group stayed put, 20 percent tumbled into the general-delay group due to declining IQ scores, and 10 percent graduated into the normal group. The strangest results were those of the general-delay (low-IQ) group. Only 47 percent remained in this group. Twenty percent scored in the normal range, and 33 percent moved up to the poor group, a total of 53 percent having shed their low-IQ status. This is like a game of musical chairs!

Two things may have produced this unusual outcome for the general-delay children. First, the children were assigned to this group at the outset of the study on the basis of their scores on the Leiter IQ test. This test measures categorizing and other types of visual and manual skills. It's possible that the test may be tapping developmental rate (temporal variation) in categorizing and visual discrimination in the same way that percent consonants correct taps developmental rate in speech production. While the Leiter test is highly predictive of performance IQ later in time, as shown by Aram and Nation's data, this may not be because it measures the same thing, but because it measures the time it takes for a child to acquire certain common skills. These are skills that, once acquired, don't tend to improve. Once you can produce every consonant in the language, there are no more consonants left to produce. Once you can sort colors and shapes into piles, you don't get any "better" at it.

A second and more important reason for the poor long-term predictability of certain tests may be the tradition of using cutoff scores to assign children to groups. This is a common clinical practice used in the speech and hearing sciences and elsewhere (with "dyslexia," for example). As Bishop and Adams observed, category boundaries are arbitrary and often separated by one or two points on a test. These results show that this is not the best methodology for research on language development, and that it is equally inadvisable clinically. There is a great danger in classifying young children as impaired or disabled before there is any understanding of whether this classification will change over time.

Table 8.4

IQ and reading for two ages (8 and 15) for controls and the three language-delayed groups

Test	Controls N = 49		Good N = 26		Poor N = 30		Low IQ N = 15	
	8	15	8	15	8	15	8	15
BPVS		101	97	93	84	78	77	76
WISC-comprehension		101	92	98	78	79	73	76
WISC-block design		102	105	96	92	85	88	73
WISC–picture completion		102	102	99	94	83	86	72
Neale reading	101		105		89		80	
Neale comprehension	98		102		84		73	
Vernon spelling	94		96		83		78	
WISC-WORD		100		89		71		65

Source: Data from Stothard et al. 1998.

Finally, table 8.4 summarizes the changes in test scores from age $8\frac{1}{2}$ to age 15. As can be seen, intelligence declined in every group. Only WISC comprehension (reasoning) remained stable, and actually improved in the good group. Reading test scores on the Neale and the Vernon tests given at age 8 were taken from the report by Bishop and Adams, and are compared to the reading tests on the WISC word given at age 15. The word test score reflects the same skills (word recognition, comprehension, spelling) tapped by the Neale and Vernon tests. The control groups scored similarly on these reading tests on both occasions. In contrast, reading scores slid precipitously for the language-delayed children. This could be due to differences in difficulty levels between the tests, or it could reflect a genuine decline. The latter explanation seems the most likely in view of the decline in general intelligence.

No correlations were provided in this report. There is no way to assess whether any of the language tests measured at this time or earlier predicted the outcome on the reading tests, a serious oversight.

Clearly, there is a great deal about language development that we don't understand, and a lot more about the interaction of IQ, language development, and reading skill that we don't grasp. Bishop and Adams (1990, 1037) commented on this complex relationship:

In the field of developmental reading disorders, there has been much debate not only over terminology (e.g. whether one should talk of "developmental dyslexia" or "specific reading retardation"), but also over defining criteria. We found that whether or not one finds continuity between specific language impairment and "developmental dyslexia" depends crucially on how the latter is defined. Our study ... suggests that only those reading-impaired children who still have measurable oral language deficits are characterized by a history of language delay. It is not the case that oral language problems disappear to be superseded by reading problems. Rather, some children have oral language problems that persist, but the focus of concern tends to shift to reading and spelling.... It follows that if one adopts a definition of developmental dyslexia that requires that the child has normal verbal and non-verbal intelligence in the face of a severe reading problem, then there will be little or no overlap between early SLI and later dyslexia. If, however, one requires only that non-verbal skills of dyslexic children be in the normal range, then some overlap between SLI and dyslexia will be found.

This also relates to the problem of overlap between SLI and low verbal IQ. Furthermore, a critical issue, ignored here, is whether difficulty with learning to read early on affects the subsequent development of language and cognitive skills and leads to declining IQ scores. In other words, poor reading may be a *causal factor* in this late decline. Genes may be another. These issues are taken up in more depth in chapter 12.

A critical piece of information was missing from this research. The children in this study had been referred for treatment by professionals who either specialized in treating language problems or referred to people who did. We don't know the proportion of children with language delays and language problems in the general population. They could be a minuscule fraction or a sizable number. The next study addressed this issue.

Beitchman

A comprehensive longitudinal study was carried by Beitchman and his colleagues in Toronto (Beitchman et al. 1986, 1989, 1994; Beitchman, Brownlie et al. 1996; Beitchman, Wilson et al. 1996; Johnson et al. 1999). The study lasted from 1982 to 1996. The children were drawn from a catchment population of 5,891 five-year-olds in the Ottawa-Carleton region of Ontario. Altogether, 1,655 children were individually screened for possible speech or language delays. A liberal cutoff was employed to avoid excluding children who might have language problems later on. Nineteen percent of the children, or 315, fell below the cutoff. Of this group, 61.6 percent were boys and 38.4 percent were girls. This represents a sex ratio of 1.6 boys to 1 girl, slightly more girls than are found in clinical populations.

The initial screening tests measured speech production for accuracy in producing consonants, stuttering, verbal comprehension, and measures of syntax and semantics, plus visual and auditory perception. Sex differences appeared on every test (more boys failing the cutoff) with the exception of verbal comprehension.

These children, plus a group of normal children, were given an additional battery of tests and were clinically evaluated by speech-language pathologists. Tests covered every aspect of language: articulation, fluency, expressive and receptive language, receptive vocabulary, and auditory memory. On the basis of these scores, the children were classified into two groups according to standard diagnostic protocols: speech impaired only (6.4 percent), and general language impaired with or without speech problems (12.6 percent). Permission was obtained from parents for 142 of the language-impaired children to participate in the longitudinal study, along with 142 normal children, matched for age, sex, and school.

Because the authors were interested in the clinical value of this work, they didn't exclude any children with secondary problems, such as hearing or vision difficulties, cleft palate, epilepsy, cerebral palsy, or low performance IQ. The goals were to study the stability of the diagnostic classification, the long-term prognosis for early problems in language development, and academic achievement. When Beitchman and his colleagues estimated the prevalence rates after excluding the 2.4 percent of children with secondary problems, 10.5 percent had general language problems, and 6.1 percent speech impairments only.

Of these children, 300 language impaired and 47 controls were also classified by the statistical technique of *cluster analysis*, which generates group profiles by computer. Four profiles emerged from the cluster analysis:

1. High on all language measures ($N = 30$)
2. Normal on most language measures, poor articulation ($N = 174$)

3. Below norms on most language measures, normal articulation ($N = 56$)
4. Below norms on both general language and articulation (87)

These groups will be referred to from now on as *normal, speech only, general language, both*. The four groups differed significantly on receptive vocabulary (PPVT), and scores fell out in the same order listed above as (1) 113, (2) 100, (3) 93, and (4) 79 (all comparisons differ significantly).

Patterns of language problems were found to vary with socioeconomic status. Fifty-three percent of the children with speech problems only were in the highest-SES group. Fifty-two percent of the children with both speech and general language problems came from the lowest-SES group. Low-SES children also had a higher incidence of additional problems. Twenty-five percent failed the audiometry screening, and 33 percent had birth abnormalities. By contrast, no one failed the audiometry screening and only 2 percent had birth abnormalities in the high-SES group.

Because the data were analyzed in two ways—by means of standard clinical measures and by computer classification—the results will be presented separately, first comparing the groups identified by the computer at ages 5 and 12, then comparing the groups identified by the clinical criteria at ages 5, 12, and 19.

The stability of the computer-generated profiles was measured by retesting 124 of the original 300 children at age 12, plus a control group. The average test scores based on the profile assigned at age 5 are presented in table 8.5 along with the scores for each group 7 years later. Data on the speech-only group are not reliable, because only 24 of the original 174 children in this group were retested. The other groups were reasonably intact.

At age 12, the computer profiles seem strongly determined by IQ. The children with both language deficits are established as a low-IQ group (WISC full-scale IQ = 86). The speech-only group scored just below the normal children (107 versus 115), and the general language group was just below them (102). The IQ scores are mirrored by the other standardized tests, including those for language and reading. This report provided no information on whether any children changed groups.

The clinical diagnostic process repeated at age 12 showed considerable instability from time 1 to time 2. The speech-only group was most

Table 8.5

Computer-derived profiles for normal and language-delayed children based on IQ and language pre- and post-test scores for ages 5 and 12 years

	Normal (30)	Articulation only (174)	General language impaired (56)	Articulation plus general language impaired (87)	
Post-WISC-R					
Full	115	106	102	86 ⎫	
Verbal	110	104	98	85 ⎬	$N = 121$
Performance	119	109	108	91 ⎭	
Receptive vocabulary					
Pre-PPVT-R	113	100	93	79	$N = 347$
Post-PPVT-R	117	107	98	82	$N = 123$
Memory					
Pre-GFW-content	63	59	57	44	$N = 347$
Post-GFW-content	52	50	48	43	$N = 119$
Pre-GFW-sequence	54	46	43	33	$N = 347$
Post-GFW-sequence	51	47	44	40	$N = 121$
Articulation (consonants)					
Pre-PAT % correct	76	11	62	23	$N = 347$
Post-PAT errors	1.5	3.6	.6	2.5	$N = 124$
Language					
Pre-STACL receptive	80	63	29	25 ⎫	$N = 347$
Pre-BLST expressive	88	72	49	16 ⎭	
Post-TOLD receptive	109	107	96	91 ⎫	
Post-TOLD expressive A	102	97	85	76 ⎪	
Post-TOLD expressive B	107	101	94	81 ⎬	$N = 123$
Post-CELF receptive	110	102	95	80 ⎪	
Post P&K pragmatic errors	1.9	2.0	5.1	5.1 ⎭	
Kaufman Reading—12 years					
Total	116	107	97	84	$N = 120$
Spelling	115	104	100	87	
Reading	117	107	99	86	
Math	114	108	97	85	

Table 8.5

(continued)

Note: PRE scores at age 5, POST scores at age 12.
Source: Data compiled from Beitchman et al. 1989, 1994; Beitchman, Wilson et al. 1996.
Terms:

WISC Wechsler Intelligence Scale for Children
PPVT-R Peabody Picture Vocabulary Test–Revised
GFW Goldman-Fristoe-Woodcock Auditory Memory Test
PAT Photo Articulation Test
STACL Screening Test for Auditory Comprehension of Language
BLST Bankson Language Screening Test
TOLD Test of Language Development
CELF Clinical Evaluation of Language Fundamentals
P&K Prutting and Kirchner Pragmatic Skills

resilient, far more likely to improve to normal status (65 percent), and only 9.3 percent exhibited a worsening of their status. The prognosis for children with general language impairment at age 5 was not good. Only 28 percent improved to normal levels on all measures. A further 14 percent had articulation problems only. Of the remaining 58 percent, over half were worse off and had fallen into the most severe category: both speech and language impaired. The most surprising finding was that 33 percent of the normal children did not stay "normal." Six percent had developed serious language problems, and the remaining 27 percent failed the articulation screening, though their problems were minor.

The clinical and computer classification schemes are quite a contrast in approach, prognosis, and outcome. One involves diagnostic criteria based on cutoff scores worked out over decades in applied research, and the other, abstract statistical categories based purely on the test scores. In only one case did the two classifications predict a similar outcome: children with speech problems alone are the most likely to recover. Otherwise, the two methods were completely at odds. The clinical diagnosis predicted rough times ahead for the 12-year-olds with a general language impairment. The computer-generated profiles, on the other hand, seemed to show that if a child has a normal IQ (three out of the four groups), everything else will be normal. What then happened next?

The final assessment (time 3) took place at age 19 (Johnson et al. 1999). So far, only the data from the clinical assessment have been reported. There were 114 of the language-impaired group and 128 controls (85 percent of the original sample) remaining in the study. Sixty-five percent were male. The three diagnostic groups were as before: normal, speech only, general language (with or without speech problems). The young men and women were given a hearing screening and a battery of tests, including the WAIS performance IQ, PPVT vocabulary, the TOAL test for receptive and productive vocabulary and grammar, the TAWF test of word finding, a pig Latin test (phoneme awareness), a test of articulation, plus various reading tests.

Individual clinical assessments showed that 50 percent of language-impaired groups had some articulation problems, as did 16 percent of the control group. However, these problems were minor and scarcely noticeable to untrained listeners.

A correlational analysis was carried out to measure the stability of test scores from time 1 (age 5) to time 3 (age 19). Time 1/time 3 correlations for the same tests were PPVT ($r = .71$), TOLD/TOAL ($r = .79$), and performance IQ ($r = .72$). These values show a 50 to 60 percent prediction rate across a 14-year age span. This is very impressive indeed and speaks to careful testing. Other findings are important. At age 19, performance IQ and PPVT vocabulary were highly correlated ($r = .62$). Not only that, but performance IQ *measured at age 5* correlated to PPVT at age 19 by the same amount ($r = .59$). These values are much more in line with the normative data on IQ reported by Cooper (1995) and are similar to Bishop's results. They do not support Aram and Nation's finding of a complete dissociation between performance IQ and verbal skills in language-disordered children.

IQ at age 12 is compared to IQ at age 19 in table 8.6. IQ scores tended to decline, but mainly for the control and the general language groups. Also, IQ scores were noticeably higher here than for the clinical populations used in the previous studies. SES levels were higher in the Toronto study as well.

Reading was measured on the Woodcock-Johnson Reading test battery and spelling on the Wide Range Achievement Test. Students were classified by their time 1 (age 5) language diagnosis and compared statistically. The controls and the speech-only group did not differ significantly on reading (average standard scores 113 and 108). The students in the general language group scored significantly lower, at 91. This pattern was

Table 8.6
Changes in PPTV-R and WPPSI/WAIS IQ from 12 to 19

	IQ at 12	IQ at 19
Controls		
PPVT-R	117	105
Full	115	108
Verbal	110	104
Performance	119	110
Speech impairment		
PPVT-R	107	101
Full	106	103
Verbal	104	100
Performance	109	105
Language impairment		
PPVT-R	90	80
Full	94	87
Verbal	92	85
Performance	100	92

Note: PPVT-R = Peabody Picture Vocabulary–Revised; WPPSI = Wechsler Preschool and Primary Scale of Intelligence; WAIS = Wechsler Adult Intelligence Scale.
Source: Johnson et al. 1999.

repeated for spelling: controls, 106; speech only, 104; general language, 92.

I was interested in the proportion of young adults as a whole who fit the profile of a general language impairment. Enough information was provided in figures and in the text to calculate these proportions as a function of the initial classification. Table 8.7 represents the estimated proportion of 19-year-olds in the population at large who are likely to fit the diagnosis of a general language impairment.

Nine percent of the control group, who began with no language or speech problems whatsoever, had developed serious language problems by age 19. A major contributing factor was a large decline in verbal IQ, causing them to fall below the cutoff of 80 standard score. The speech-only group resembled the normal students. As a group, they now represented only 1 percent of the total population. The children most at risk were those originally diagnosed with a general language impairment at

Table 8.7

Change in incidence of general language impairment over 14 years based on $N = 1,655$

	Age 5 % Impaired	Age 19		% Incidence in population
		% Impaired	% Normal	
Controls	0	11.7	88.3	9
Speech impairment only	0	13.9	86.1	1
General language impairment	12.6	73.1	26.9	9.2
Total of general language impairment in population*				19.2%

* Proportion of sample population converted to general population trend.
Source: Based on data from Johnson et al. 1999.

age 5. Only 28 percent of this group passed the screening for normal language function at age 19, and the remainder now constitute 9.2 percent of the general population, scoring low on language measures, reading, and academic tests.

Altogether, the percent of young adults with serious language difficulties is a whopping 19.2 percent. This is the same proportion found at age 5, except the composition of the groups had changed dramatically. This is nearly double the 10.7 percent functional illiteracy rate in Canada for the 16–25 years age group reported in an international study (Organization for Economic Cooperation and Development, 1995).

Now we have a problem. If there is any relationship between a general language impairment and literacy, it is a strange one. It is certainly the case that children diagnosed with a language impairment at age 5 are at high risk. But there is also the fact that half of the children with a general language impairment at age 19 had been completely normal at age 5. A major reason for their reclassification was a declining verbal IQ. Is it possible that borderline literacy skills contribute to or cause these declining scores in otherwise normal children? And if so, can the same explanation be applied to at least some of the children who begin with language problems?

This puzzle is increased by the fact that language and academic test scores start to tumble sometime after age 12. Bishop found a sharp drop between ages 8 and 15. Beitchman found a sharp drop between ages 12 and 19. Children who once were resolved turn out not to be resolved. Children who were normal to start with are no longer normal. Is the problem the school system, or does this sharp decline indicate some genetic effect, such as genes turning off? We'll come back to these questions in chapter 12.

One important fact has been obscured in this analysis. Clinical protocols (test-score cutoffs) were used to partition children into three groups: normal, speech only, and general language impaired—*with or without* a speech problem. The computer-generated profiles created a fourth group: deficits in both speech and general language. This "low-low" group represented 29 percent of all language-impaired children tested at age 5 (87 out of 300). This group scored 1 standard deviation below norms on verbal IQ at age 12 and 1.5 standard deviations below norms on the PPVT at age 5 and 12. No mention was made of this group in the time 3 follow-on study at age 19, so there is no estimate of how many of these children remain impaired. If we knew the answer to this, it would tell us whether a low verbal IQ at age 5 is a major risk factor for continuing language problems, along with reading and academic difficulties.

Studies like these are essentially a numbers game. The standardized tests are based on the normal curve. People scoring more than 1 standard deviation below the mean constitute 16 percent of the population. The fact that this population isn't constant tells us something about the tests (they may get harder as children get older), the school system, the child's genetic makeup, or all three. So far, we have no answers to this puzzle.

Language Impairment, Reading Problems, and Psychological Distress

The studies in this section document the overlap between language impairment and reading problems, and between language impairment and the risk of receiving a psychiatric diagnosis. It is clear, reviewing these studies, that how language impairment is diagnosed determines the amount of overlap between the diagnoses: "language impairment," "special reading disability," and a psychiatric diagnosis for emotional and behavioral problems. Two other factors appear to be critically involved in these diagnoses, the first having to do with whether IQ was part of the diagnosis, and the second, whether the child was a boy or a girl.

Learning Disabilities and SLI

As far as I am aware, there are only two studies where the authors looked at the language-reading connection in reverse: take a large group of poor readers and test them on a battery of speech and language tasks.

Gibbs and Cooper (1989) studied 242 children, age 8:6–12:6 (77 percent male), in Alabama. The children had been diagnosed as "learning disabled" by special-education personnel in the schools due to reading difficulties. Each child was assessed by a certified speech and language pathologist, a licensed audiologist, and trained graduate students in the speech and hearing sciences. They were given an IQ test, standardized achievement tests, and vision and hearing screenings. IQ scores ranged from 64 to 134 (average 93). Children who passed the vision and hearing screenings took several speech and language tests, including the TOLD— a standardized test on semantic and syntactic competence—plus tests for articulation, fluency, voicing (pitch, resonance, quality, and volume), along with more thorough tests of hearing and middle-ear function.

Altogether, 96 percent of the children with LD had some type of language problem by these criteria and failed one or more cutoffs for normal language function. The majority (91 percent) failed at least one of the TOLD subtests. Cutoff scores were liberal, however, and were defined simply as "below average." Some language problems were accompanied by speech abnormalities, and slight hearing loss was reported for 7 percent of the children, which is not excessive. Most surprising was the fact that these problems had gone virtually undetected in this largely middle-class population.

In Australia, McArthur et al. (2000) looked at the incidence of comorbidity in children diagnosed with a specific language impairment (SLI), and in children diagnosed with a specific reading disability (SRD). *Specific* in both cases refers to falling below test norms "despite normal intelligence." ("Intelligence" meant performance IQ for SLI but a variety of things for SRD.) McArthur et al. pointed to difficulties with these diagnoses, wondering whether a child with an SRD and impaired oral language could really be considered 'specifically' reading disabled when poor development of oral language has been found to precede reading disability.

Over 200 children in the age range 7–14 years, previously diagnosed SLI or SRD, were given a battery of language or reading-achievement tests. McArthur et al. found that 51 percent of the children with SLI fell

using these stringent cutoffs: below 2 standard deviations on at least one test, or below 1 standard deviation on at least two tests, out of ten standardized language tests. They discovered that 38 percent of the children had previously been diagnosed with a language problem by the school, yet 25 percent of the children had an equally severe language impairment that had not been diagnosed. Thus, 63 percent of all the children in this sample fit the profile of a general language impairment.

The chances of ending up at a psychiatric clinic and receiving a diagnosis was much more likely if you were a boy, and this had nothing to do with a language problem. The proportion of boys in the total sample was 67 percent irrespective of language status. The type of diagnosis the child received was highly determined by sex as well. Boys were about three times more likely to be diagnosed "ADHD," and girls were twice as likely to have an "emotional disorder."

The three groups of children (*previously diagnosed*, *undiagnosed*, and *normal*) were compared statistically on every test in the battery. The most important finding was that undiagnosed children fared much better academically than the children who had been diagnosed. This was despite the fact that these two groups were indistinguishable on every cognitive and language test: verbal and performance IQ, verbal memory, spatial ability, receptive and expressive vocabulary, syntax, sentence recall, and phoneme awareness. Both of the language-impaired groups scored significantly below the controls on every measure.

The undiagnosed children were also better readers on every reading test, including reading comprehension, scoring well within the normal range. For example, 54 percent of the children previously diagnosed scored 1.5 standard deviations or worse below norms on decoding skill (word attack) versus only 17 percent of the undiagnosed children. This was despite the fact that the two language impaired groups scored equally badly on the Rosner phoneme-awareness test, considered a major predictor of reading skill. It did not predict here, obviously.

To find out whether differences in reading skill between the two groups had to do with the severity of the language problems, Cohen et al. applied even stricter cutoffs for the language tests. When they compared these children, no differences between the two groups could be found on any language test.

In keeping with their greater academic skill, the undiagnosed children rated themselves high on "academic self-concept," while the diagnosed children rated themselves low. Otherwise, no other measure of self-concept distinguished between them. Nor did they differ on tests of social/emotional awareness. The undiagnosed children were far more likely to escape an ADHD diagnosis than the diagnosed children (36 versus 55 percent), and did not differ from the control group in this respect.

There appear to be only two explanations for these results, and neither is comforting. One possibility is that the reading problem led to the diagnosis. In this scenario, the child is referred by a teacher for special testing due to learning difficulties, and it is discovered that the child has a language impairment as well as a reading problem. Unfortunately, Cohen et al. don't provide information on *when* the diagnosis occurred. Most troubling is the finding that whatever remedial help was given had no impact on either language status or reading skill. The diagnosed children did not differ from the undiagnosed children on any language test (*despite remediation*) and fell far below them in reading (*despite remediation*).

The other possibility is that the language problem caused or contributed to the reading problem as a function of the diagnosis itself. In this scenario, most of the effort may go to fixing the language problem, while reading is neglected. The diagnosis may become an excuse for the parents, teachers, and child not to expect too much, and to believe that learning to read will be a challenge.

Bishop and Edmundson (1987, 156) noted that the dangers of the diagnosis itself represent a point of contention in the speech and hearing sciences: "The disorder might resolve naturally, and treatment could create more problems than it solves by producing low expectation in teachers, anxiety in parents, and self-consciousness in the child."

Conclusions to Part II

The course of language development "doth not run smooth." Unpredictability is the name of the game until around 5 years, when predictability improves to slightly better than marginal. From this age on, three findings stand out. First, articulation problems alone are rarely anything to worry about, perhaps because there is good speech therapy today, and/or because children outgrow them. Second, general language impairments are a cause for concern, as is low verbal or low performance IQ. Third, there is a pronounced slide in IQ and academic performance in the groups diagnosed with a general language impairment—a slide that starts late, sometime after the age of 12, even though children may seem to recover to normal language and reading levels prior to this.

For some unexplained reason, boys are uniformly penalized in this process, lagging years behind girls in speech clarity across the first 18 years of life. They constitute the bulk of the late talkers at age 2 and 3, and represent around 65 to 70 percent of the children with speech and language problems throughout the preschool and school years. It is perhaps not surprising, then, that boys tend to have more academic and reading difficulties than girls, and end up more often in psychiatric clinics.

Bishop and her group discovered that the most debilitating language problem is low receptive vocabulary and low verbal comprehension. In the absence of hearing difficulties, this will signal a deficit in other language functions: speech production, syntax, and semantics. Not one child out of the eighty-seven children in their study had a "pure" verbal-comprehension deficit. Of the twenty-three children with verbal-comprehension deficits, twenty-one were impaired in two or all three of the remaining language functions.

The idea proposed by I. Y. Liberman and A. M. Liberman (1989) that poor articulation is a consequence of weak or abnormal phonological development, and therefore a marker for reading problems, is not supported by these findings. Both Bishop's and Beitchman's studies show the opposite. Speech-motor problems alone, in the absence of other language difficulties, not only do not lead to low reading or spelling skills, they are a *negative predictor*. Children with poor articulation were as successful academically as normal children. This means either that articulation and phoneme awareness are relatively independent, or that an individual's spontaneous ability to access the phoneme level of speech *in the absence of suitable instruction* has little to do with learning to read. This is certainly supported by data from countries with a transparent writing system where reading is properly taught (Cossu, Rossini, and Marshall 1993; Wimmer et al. 1991).

The notion that phoneme awareness is the major causal agent for reading problems is also challenged by the findings of Cohen et al.

Whether children with severe language problems had or had not been diagnosed made no difference to their scores on a phoneme-awareness test, with both groups scoring extremely badly. Yet the children diagnosed had serious reading difficulties and the undiagnosed children did not. Obviously, something besides a lack of skill on phoneme awareness tests was causing the reading problems.

These and other findings presented in the last two chapters strongly refute premises 5, 6, and 10 of the phonological-development theory set out at the end of chapter 1. Briefly, these premises were as follows:

5. Phonological awareness develops in a specific manner, order, and time.
6. Abnormal development of phonological processing is the main cause of reading failure.
10. Phonological processing underpins and connects all other language skills.

The decline in verbal IQ to 1 or more standard deviations below the mean in about 75 percent of children with a general language impairment raises the issue of the overlap between verbal IQ and general language. While it seems reasonable to conclude that low verbal IQ leads to poorly developed language skills, it is equally likely that poorly developed language contributes to problems with learning to read, which, in turn, lead to *further declines in IQ*.

This raises a number of concerns about the nature and extent of language development over the age span. All the studies reported in this section identified children as language impaired because they fell below some cutoff on a normal curve of language test scores. Lateral variation of a species-specific biological function like language is normal. This normal variation also reflects temporal variation while development is ongoing, which for expressive language continues to at least 18 years.

Should we view the children "in the ditch" on the far left of the normal curve as impaired, delayed, or normal? The clinical-medical model, in which children are viewed dichotomously as normal or impaired, may be a practical short-term solution for standardizing intervention procedures, but this model doesn't work in the behavioral sciences. Measures of skilled behavior form a continuous (normal) distribution and not a dichotomy. The practice of using cutoff scores to assign children to groups, and then comparing the groups, makes it impossible to interpret results when children shift from one diagnosis to another over the course of the study.

The clinical model also has serious consequences for the children and their families if the children are diagnosed as impaired when they are merely delayed, as Bishop and Edmundson's study showed most clearly. It may be that the subsequent decline in children's academic skills among the children who appeared to be resolved (Stothard et al. 1998) was the result of a penalty they paid earlier for being diagnosed.

Cause or Effect?

So far, no one has addressed the following question: What role (if any) does *reading skill* play in producing a decline in IQ and other language functions? Most researchers assume that poor language skills and low IQ cause reading problems, a reasonable assumption from the evidence reviewed so far. But reading skill could be an amplifier. Weak or delayed language skills plus poor reading instruction would equal reading failure, which in turn would lead to poor academic skills and falling IQ scores. Conversely, good language skills and good reading instruction would equal reading success, leading in turn to good academic skills and rising IQ scores. A similar idea about reading and vocabulary development was presented by Stanovich (1986). He christened this the "Matthew effect": "To all those who have, more will be given—but from those who have nothing, even what they have will be taken away" (Matthew 13: 12).

The Matthew effect was put to the test on 400 children who were followed from first to fifth grade by Shaywitz et al. (1995). They found a Matthew effect for full-scale IQ, but not for a composite reading score (Woodcock-Johnson tests of decoding and passage comprehension), opposite to Stanovich's prediction. The Matthew effect appeared at the outer regions of the distribution. Children with IQs above 110 got "smarter." Children with IQs below 85 got "dumber." IQs in the middle range were stable over time. In contrast, reading test standard scores remained constant over time for every ability group. Using a more precise scaled score (Rasch scores) made no difference to this result, except that poor readers made slightly greater gains over time, opposite to what the Matthew effect would predict.

Yet reading and IQ are strongly correlated, as shown in the studies reviewed above and in studies presented later in the book. If IQ fans out as children get older, why don't reading scores as well? There are at least two possible explanations. The first has to do with the fact that the composite reading score was biased more toward decoding than toward reading comprehension. Decoding skill may vary differently from reading comprehension over time. According to the second explanation, the initial reading level may set the process in motion. The child's developmental status and knowledge of the alphabet code at the time reading instruction begins will determine the child's initial reading skill. The variation in reading skills at first grade is huge in English-speaking countries. When Shaywitz et al. sorted the first graders into eight ability groups, the average score for each these groups ranged from 70 to over 140 standard-score points!

The main analysis was based on "gain scores"—proportion gained over baseline each year. If every child improves in reading at about the same rate, as Shaywitz et al.'s data suggest, children's standing relative to their peers seems pretty well cast in concrete by age 6 or 7. Children off to a flying start, reading 5 or 6 years above grade level, are going to be reading quite different material from children who can scarcely read a word. Therefore, it is just as likely that the direction of the correlation goes from reading to IQ, as from IQ to reading; otherwise there would be no way to explain why there is a Matthew effect for IQ. Why should IQ get better or worse for no reason?

When the authors reported that the entire Matthew effect for IQ could be attributed to the mean IQ, without any additional effect for reading, they referred to the *cumulative* impact of reading, not to the *initial* position in the starting gate. The only way to resolve this complex question would be to break the cycle by some form of intervention. Finding a good method of reading instruction is far easier than trying to fix language impairment or change IQ. There are a number of highly successful classroom reading programs today (see *Early Reading Instruction*).

Finally, there's another problem no one has addressed. Countries with transparent alphabetic writing systems don't have the high illiteracy rates of English-speaking countries (Organization for Economic Cooperation and Development, 1995, 1997). In several European countries, there is no such thing as "dyslexia," because no child fails to learn to decode or spell (Wimmer 1993). If language development really played a causal role in learning to read, one would expect to find the same incidence of reading problems everywhere, because human language is a biological trait. It seems that whatever the language-reading connection might be, this must be qualified by the *specific writing system* the child has to learn. Unraveling this is not going to be easy.

We are left with a number of unanswered questions that need to be resolved in future research. Meanwhile, we move on to the study of which specific language skills predict reading success, which brings us to the heart of the mainstream research on reading. Four areas of interest have received enough attention to warrant a review of the findings: vocabulary, verbal memory, syntax, and naming speed. However, at this point, we encounter some serious methodological problems that need to be sorted out before we can proceed.

III

DIRECT TESTS OF THE LANGUAGE-READING RELATIONSHIP

AN INTRODUCTION TO READING RESEARCH:
SOME PITFALLS

The research presented in part II showed how scientists studying the natural development of expressive language stumbled onto a language-reading connection by asking open-ended (open-minded) questions and by good research design. This solid descriptive research is a textbook example of how to proceed when you are in complete ignorance of the facts. It is also virtually free of theoretical baggage. The kinds of questions that *should* guide the early stages of science are front and center and include the following. First, what is the normative process of natural language development? Second, what happens to children with language delays? Do they catch up, or do some have a permanent impairment? Third, what language systems or specific language skills are most vulnerable developmentally? Fourth, do language delays/impairments have an impact on academic performance? If so, when and how?

Part III brings us to reading research proper, the bread-and-butter studies that constitute about 90 percent of the research in the field. This "new-wave" research came into being after studies on instructional methods were discredited in the 1960s. The reasons for this historical shift are outlined in the introduction to this book. The new wave is oriented toward the investigation of reading predictors: what perceptual, linguistic, and cognitive skills predict success in learning to read? Topic areas overlap with those in previous chapters, but the nature of the studies, the rationale, and the methodology are different. Subject populations are chosen entirely on the basis of their reading test scores, and reading skill drives the research design.

Because reading research contrasts noticeably with the research reviewed so far, this raises a number of issues. I will be addressing two of the most important in this chapter. The first has to do with the implications of the research on language development for future studies on reading. Historically, reading researchers have paid little attention to the impact of *real* language development on reading skill, despite the fact that assumptions about this development underpin the major theories in the field. I would like to suggest ways to make research efforts more productive in light of what the language research has shown.

The second issue pertains to methodological problems, problems so serious that I was obliged to devote two chapters to this topic. This chapter focuses on a major breach in research design and what this implies for the use and interpretation of statistics. The second chapter on methodology (chapter 11) covers test construction and the nature and interpretation of correlations. These chapters are short, and I apologize that they have to be in this book at all. Readers well versed in research design and statistics may want to skim them, but please don't skip them entirely. Reading research is uninterpretable without this background knowledge.

Variables That Go Bump in the Night

Children's language development is ongoing when children enter school and is still subject to enormous lateral and temporal variation, variation that is completely normal. When lateral and temporal variation bump into a school system where children are sorted by age, some troubling things happen.

Beitchman's longitudinal study showed that 12.6 percent of children in Toronto enter school with delays or impairments in general language. They do not fare well. Seventy-three percent will ultimately fit the profile of a language-impaired child, have serious reading problems, remain below their peers in all academic subjects, and experience a sharp drop in IQ scores. An additional 6.4 percent with isolated speech-motor delays do well, and about 85 percent go on to do at least as well academically as children with normal language development. If these figures are representative of the population at large, this means that around 10 percent of children will have serious academic problems as a function of language delays or impairments.

Meanwhile, 9 percent of children with no language impairments and no language delays at age 5 subsequently fit the profile of a language-impaired child. They developed serious reading problems and gradually fell behind their peers in all academic subjects and in IQ. How could this happen? There must be something going on in the classroom that produces language-impaired children. Otherwise it would be the case that children develop normally for 5 years, then start developing abnormally. There is no other natural (biological) developmental process where this has been observed, and certainly not in 9 percent of the population. Something happens to these children at school. And children are much better off in Canada in this regard. Canada has the lowest functional illiteracy rate in the English-speaking world (Organization for Economic Cooperation and Development, 1997; also see McGuinness 1998).

These findings suggest that unless children with language problems are sorted from children with reading problems alone, the two will be confounded. Researchers need to consider developmental status and be aware that children with language delays are likely to be found in a group of poor readers. It would help to have a set of criteria that would make reading research more productive. One of the problems, as we will see in the following chapters, is the excessively wide age ranges used in many of the studies. Temporal variation in language is still extensive in the early grades. This should be kept to a minimum by studying children who are the same age, and by statistically controlling for age. IQ and sex are other correlates of language delays. About 70 percent of children with language delays are boys, and this needs to be taken into account. A standardized language test battery, like the TOLD, would be helpful in screening children before the study is conducted.

Home environment plays a critical role in promoting general language competency and reading as well. We will see the profound impact of parents' contribution to their children's vocabulary skills in chapter 12. Chaney (1998) reported that a strong early predictor of reading skill was a 3-year-old's familiarity with the alphabet and knowledge of how words are represented and ordered in books. This knowledge was predicted by family literacy practices. Stuart (1995) discovered that children who knew letter-sound correspondences (not letter names) when they started school had far more success in learning to read. This means we need to be careful to document what a child has been taught or has intuited about the phonetic basis of the alphabet code. Giving tests in a vacuum, and ignoring whether the children have been taught to "sound out" letters and learn to read, will prove nothing one way or the other about the role of phoneme awareness or anything else in learning to read.

The research on speech perception and general language has shown that the tasks are critical. They must measure what they were designed to measure and be free of ceiling and floor effects. For young children, in particular, they should be "child friendly" in terms of difficulty/length/boringness and be presented in an interesting way, so that children can show their true ability. Chaney's research on 3-year-olds proves the point raised by Fox and Routh (1975), that if tasks are well designed, children can *show* you what they know, even though they are unable to *talk* about what they know.

Keeping these issues in mind, we move on to an analysis of reading research methodology.

Reading Research Methodology

Basic research on reading is essentially correlational in nature, though judging by most research reports, one would never know this. Instead, the studies are often presented as "experiments," and employ the inferential statistical tests (t-tests, ANOVAs) designed for experimental research. As we will see, the vast majority of these studies use an invalid research design that nullifies the use of any statistics. This has major implications for the interpretation and validity of this research. More minor issues will be addressed as they arise in the context of individual studies. Here I take up the most serious breaches and discuss possible reasons for how and why reading research got into this parlous state.

What Is the Question?

Good science proceeds by asking the right questions. A question must be framed in such a way that it can be answered, and that tools (tasks, methods, research designs, statistics) are available to help the researcher answer it as rigorously as possible. What is the *real* question that researchers studying reading predictors are attempting to answer? Here is a stripped-down version of that question:

1. *What skills or aptitudes are correlated to success in learning to read?*

However, in the majority of studies, the same question is framed differently:

2. Are poor readers different from good readers on X?

(For *X*, substitute whatever seems relevant.)

There's a more fundamental question lurking beneath both of these questions. This is the question that researchers want to answer or think they are answering:

3. What causes children to become poor readers?

This is a much harder question to answer, because it means creating an effect by means of a *cause*, training groups of children in different ways. Correlational research, by contrast, allows the researcher to survey a variety of predictors in a single study, and find out what does or does not correlate to reading skill. As noted above, this is an optimum approach in any new science. It would be a waste of time, for example, to teach children to segment syllables, if syllable segmenting was unrelated to reading skill.

The obvious first step, then, is to answer question 1. Instead, most researchers have opted for question 2. This is very curious, because there are statistical tools to help answer question 1, and none to answer question 2. Not only that, but question 2 is a bad question. It only leads to more questions. How does one decide what *X* is in any particular study? How does one determine the potential universe of *X*'s? The answer so far has been to rely on opinion or logic, to or follow whatever hunch is playing best at the moment. Currently, it is fashionable for *X* to mean phonological processing, vocabulary, verbal memory, syntax, and naming speed.

But what about mean length of utterance, visual memory, eye-movement control, age of acquisition of the first fifty words, being a student in Mrs. Carter's class, number of books in the house, a mom who didn't teach the alphabet, low socioeconomic status, being born in Boston, Kyoto, or Stockholm, severity of middle-ear infections, type of reading strategy the child has adopted, and the list could go on.

The list goes on because question 2 makes no sense. This will become clearer if I insert the word *language* and revise the question slightly:

2. Do children with poor language differ from children with good language on X?

This question is a tautology because *X defines language*. Once you know what language is, you automatically know all the *X*'s. In a brief 30 years, linguists, phoneticians, speech and hearing scientists, and developmental psychologists have mapped out the components of language and have developed tests to measure them. They have studied individual differences and patterns of language development over time by sitting in people's homes, by noting down verbatim speech attempts, and by recording the interaction between mother and child. They have designed tests with norms and standard scores for all relevant types of *X*. This doesn't mean that everything has been pinned down, but pretty close. Of course, this task is easier. The options for *X* are limited by the fact that *language is a biological imperative*. Only the most extreme environments will hinder its development.

If you think about this for a while, it becomes obvious that reading researchers haven't even begun to face up to the most fundamental question of all: *What is reading?* What are all the things a child has to be able to do to be a good reader, and what are all the things that have to happen environmentally to make the child a good reader?

A Potted History of How We Got Here

Reading research contrasts sharply with research on language development, much of which is normative and descriptive. The goal in language research has been to "map" the developmental process, to take into consideration both lateral and temporal variation, and to ascertain the characteristics of children whose language skills fall outside normal parameters. Most of the work reviewed so far relies on frequency counts, averages, standard deviations, and, occasionally, correlational statistics. The tenor of the written reports is direct and relatively free of presumptive theories, and with rare exceptions, deductive theories don't drive research.

Research on reading is different in a number of ways. It is a hybrid of two different traditions that stretch back over a century. The first tradition is clinical and based on the medical model. In this model, people are viewed categorically as sick or well. The earliest attempts to understand why children failed to learn to read appeared as case reports written by clinical neurologists/pathologists and ophthalmologists (Richardson 1989). It was generally agreed by these experts that poor readers were "word blind" and suffered from some type of brain anomaly that runs in families. This put the problem in the child rather than the environment. But it did more than this. It ruled out the environment at the outset, so it was never an issue. This laid the foundation for the "dyslexia" model of reading failure. This model and its premise—*the problem is in the child*— has remained unchanged for over 100 years. The consequence of applying a quasi-neurological model to a learned skill was a crucial first step in getting reading research off track and into a methodological quagmire. It is this tradition that led to the poor-reader/good-reader research design.

The second tradition is developmental psychology, which began with Piaget in the early twentieth century. Piaget proposed a stage model of development in which children naturally progressed from one stage to another. Piaget's stage model was formulated to explain his data on the development of logical reasoning, but it was borrowed by other scientists for quite unrelated purposes. By the early 1970s, stage models of reading and spelling began to appear everywhere, and, unfortunately, they are still with us. A developmental model applied to the acquisition of a skill like reading translates into the notion that good readers are developing normally and poor readers are developing abnormally. I. Y. Liberman et al. (1974) *preferred* to explain the abrupt shift in phoneme awareness at age 6 or 7 as "developmental," rather than as a consequence of being taught to read.

The clinical and stage models reinforce each other, because they are both based on the same hidden assumption. This is that learning to read is directly or indirectly governed by a biological process in which the only requirement is exposure to an appropriate environment (a teacher teaching reading). There is little room in either approach for a consideration of the fact that reading is a learned skill. There is seldom any mention in these scientific reports that skills can be taught more or less successfully, depending on the method, how it is delivered, and when the learning process begins. Few people point out that ignorance or incompetence in teaching this skill can produce a very large number of children with severe reading problems, children who are indistinguishable from "dyslexics" who are thought to have bad reading genes. One of field's crisis moments occurred a few years ago when it was discovered that no objective tests could distinguish between children diagnosed as "dyslexic" on the basis of discrepant IQ scores and other measures, and plain-vanilla poor readers (Fletcher et al. 1992, 1994; Stanovich and Siegel 1994).

The methodological problems in reading research are a consequence of these traditions, not merely in the assumptions that lie behind them, but in how researchers working in these traditions are trained. The clinical medical model is descriptive, woolly, tends to rely on case studies, and divides the world into dichotomies: "well" and "sick." As noted above, this is not a scientific model for the study of complex, learned behaviors.

Developmental psychology is a branch of experimental psychology. This branch relies heavily on *experiments* (hence its name). This means *real* experiments and the inferential statistics (t-tests, ANOVAs) invented for the various experimental research designs. The goal in experimental psychology is to pin down causality by applying different treatments to people selected *randomly* from a normal population, who are then *randomly* assigned to the treatments.

Because the majority of scientists in mainstream reading research are either experimental psychologists by training, or educational psychologists with a similar background, they are most comfortable working within the methodological framework of experimental psychology, using the same research designs and statistical tools they learned in grad school and before.

The result has been a grotesque marriage between the sick/well (poor/good) model of clinical medicine and the experimental/statistical model of experimental psychology. The offspring of this marriage, and the most egregious methodological problem of all, is what I call the *isolated-groups design*. This research design has become so entrenched that it is difficult to recognize that it is even a problem. This will become clearer after a simple analysis of how statistics is supposed to work.

How Statistics Works

A statistical test is a measure of the likelihood that the mean and distribution of one set of data are either different or the same relative to another set of data with a probability greater than, or equal to, chance. Statistical tests used in the behavioral sciences can tell you only two things: the probability that two or more sets of scores taken from the same people are *alike* (correlations), and the probability that scores on a task from two or more groups of people treated differently are *different* (inferential statistics).

The great mathematical achievements of Francis Galton, Karl Pearson, William Gosset, and Ronald Fisher at the turn of the twentieth century were to create the statistical tests that allowed scientists to link a set of data to the mathematics of probability, mathematics worked out over a century earlier by De Moivre, Legendre, Laplace, and Gauss. The great benefit of statistics is that it dramatically reduces the number of times the experiment has to be replicated to ensure that the outcome is reliable. (Galileo reported that he ran each of his experiments 100 times.)

A statistical test is essentially a *mathematical transform* to get from runs of raw data to a probability estimate. As such it must obey the laws that obtain at the input side (the factors that determine the distribution of the raw data) and at the output side, the laws that govern the mathematics of probability. In solving this problem, Fisher in particular became acutely aware of how misleading a test statistic can be when all necessary assumptions aren't met. Because these assumptions are intimately bound up with the normal curve, I will introduce the normal curve in a very different way from how it is ordinarily presented in statistics textbooks.

What Is the Normal Curve?

The normal curve is a mathematical distribution (a probability calculus) with peculiar and important properties. It was discovered in 1738 by Abraham De Moivre, a Hugenot who fled religious persecution in France to live in London. He was trying to solve a problem posed by Bernoulli, the Swiss mathematician, on how many experiments a scientist should carry out to be certain to a degree greater than chance, that the experiment had succeeded. (This is an example of a binomial problem.) In working through the possible runs of "successes" and "failures" (think of successive heads or tails), De Moivre stumbled onto the normal curve, and with the help of his friend Newton's calculus, he discovered the standard deviation as well. He was able to prove that if you ran this "experiment" 100 times, you could be confident that it had either succeeded or failed at a probability of $p = .05$. This may not seem like much of an improvement on Galileo's method, but De Moivre had single-handedly invented the basis for modern statistics but didn't know it. Instead, he treated this as a mathematical challenge (a game) and was never aware of the significance of his accomplishment. De Moivre's work was largely forgotten until the late eighteenth century, when the normal curve began leaving its calling card in the most unlikely places.

In De Moivre's hands, the normal curve emerged as the binomial distribution (how many "successes" can occur in a row by chance?). In eighteenth-century astronomy and geodesics it was reborn as the "error law," the distribution of errors in runs of astronomical observations and measurements of the earth's surface. Laplace stumbled onto it while working on the erratic orbit of Jupiter. It described Darwinian natural variation and how this linked to heredity in Francis Galton's experiment on peas, which ultimately led to the discovery of regression and correlation.

The mathematical peculiarities of the shape and the properties of this curve were succinctly described by De Moivre (1738, 2nd ed. 236–237) who wrote this about the standard deviation (here called L) in *The Doctrine of Chances*: "The Interval denoted by 'L' is equal to the Boundaries or Limits of a central or middle Region. I also found that the Logarithm of the Ratio which the middle Term of a high Power has to any Term distant from it by an interval denoted by L, would be denoted by a very near approximation."

Fisher, writing 200 years later, said virtually the same thing. The normal distribution includes all values to infinity and works according to the mathematical law "that the logarithm of the frequency at any distance 'd' from the center of the distribution is less than the logarithm of the frequency at the center by a quantity proportional to d^2" (43). "Geometrically the standard deviation is the distance either side of the center of the points at which the slope is steepest, or the points of inflection of the curve" (Fisher, *Statistical Methods for Research Workers*, [1925] 1970, 44).

In short, the normal distribution looks like a bell, a bell that is slightly cinched at the waist. Its bell shape has the amazing property of bounding a distribution of the data (what De Moivre called an *interval* and what Pearson renamed a *standard deviation*) so that exactly 68.26 percent of the data fall within the points of inflection on either side of the mean (the top of the bell). This property makes the normal curve special, and it makes the standard deviation special, because it marks off the areas under the curve in a *constant* proportion to the height and width of the curve. This gives the normal distribution *the unusual property of being entirely described by two values: the mean and the standard deviation*. No other mathematical distribution has these properties.

Statistical Assumptions

Because the normal curve describes a series of outcomes in games of chance, identifies patterns of errors in astronomical measurement, marks the extent of biological variation, and has such simple and stable properties, nearly all statistical tests are based on it. But there is a price, and that price is a set of assumptions that must be met for the tests to be reliable. If any assumption is violated, this invalidates the test statistic and makes the probability value associated with it meaningless. I list the assumptions here:

Must be met by all statistical tests

1. Random selection of subjects from a given population must occur. Random selection means "independent selection," such that choosing one person doesn't affect or bias the selection of another person. (Fisher regarded this assumption as sacrosanct, far more important than whether the data were normally distributed.)

Must be met by parametric tests: Correlation coefficient, t-tests, ANOVA

2. Continuous distribution of interval or ratio data is necessary. The data must have equal intervals and be isomorphic to arithmetic (values remain in the same relationship when added, subtracted, divided, or multiplied).
3. Where possible, the sample is drawn from a population with normally distributed scores on the measure of interest.
4. The test scores of different groups (or different tests on the same groups) have equal variances (standard deviations squared).

Must be met for correlations and multivariate ANOVAs

5. The distributions of two or more sets of data must be linear combinations of their means across rows and columns. In other words, the data must be linear and additive.

The research design used in most reading research over the past 30 years violates all the assumptions of statistics. It's not that anything is necessarily wrong with this design, it's just that statistics can't be applied to it. This has the effect of plunging reading research back in time, back to the days where there were no statistical tests and results could only be reported as average scores.

Introducing the Isolated-Groups Design

In an isolated-groups design, the researcher decides to study good and poor readers to find out what subskills good readers have that poor readers lack. He or she begins by giving a large number of children a standardized reading test. The reading test scores are known to be normally distributed (standardized) in the population at each age (recorded in months). Based entirely on how they scored, children are assigned to two groups with an equal number of children in each group. One group scores below some arbitrary cutoff (85 standard score or worse). The other group scores above some arbitrary cutoff (105 standard score or better). The children who don't fit these profiles are excused from the study. The remaining children are given more tests (X, Y, Z), tests that the researcher believes might have something to do with reading. When testing is completed, the two groups are compared using either t-tests or F-tests. Probabilities are looked up in tables, and the researcher discovers that poor readers are worse than good readers ("significant at $p < .01$") and concludes that poor readers have a deficit in $X, Y,$ or Z.

A frequency distribution of real data using this type of design is shown in figure 9.1. The groups were selected on the basis of their reading-comprehension scores as well as on reading accuracy and speed.

Figure 9.1 shows why this design fails every assumption listed above. I have christened it the isolated-groups design for obvious reasons. No book on research methods or statistics includes any mention of such a design, because there are no statistics for it and none will ever be forthcoming. I will go through the assumptions one by one to show how they are violated.

It is clear that *by intention* (not accidentally or inadvertently), the first assumption is violated. That is, it was never *intended* for children to be randomly selected from a normal population of readers. As for assumption 2, the reading scores certainly could have been "continuous." They were continuous to start with. But the researcher has made them discontinuous by throwing out "average readers," so there is a big hole in the middle of the distribution. The selection process intentionally violates assumption 3,

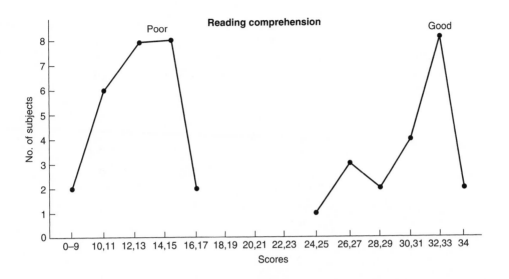

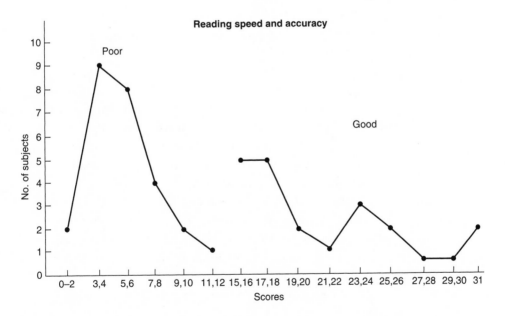

| Figure 9.1 |

Frequency polygraph for children selected as good and poor readers. Based on data from Vogel 1975.

because it would be impossible for groups selected this way to have even remotely normally distributed scores. Nor could the two groups possibly have equal variances (assumption 4), because the proportions of reader types (good/poor) don't reflect their true incidence in the normal population. Finally, if multivariate or correlational statistics were applied to these data (a common situation), there will be no linear (additive) relationship between them.

The isolated-groups design violates all five assumptions of statistics. Only *one* is sufficient to sink a study. I do not exaggerate this problem. I should also point out that if the children removed from the middle were put back, and groups split into halves (above/below average), this would still be an isolated-groups design.

And it gets worse. Because one group (the poor group) scores in an extreme region of the normal distribution (bottom far left of the curve), and the other group (the "controls") scores in the middle or to the right, this greatly enhances the chance of finding a significant result. This happens for several reasons. First, people who score at the bottom of the curve on *any* test are more likely to have other problems as well. Second, the number of poor readers in the study far exceeds their proportion in the normal population. Third, when the dependent variables (the measures used in the study) are highly correlated to the instrument used to screen people into the study, the chance of finding a significant difference between the groups is almost a foregone conclusion.

Studies that produce significant results are far more likely to get published. Behavioral scientists have particular difficulty publishing studies that fail to replicate or merely affirm the null hypothesis. This means that quite apart from the bias inherent in the isolated-groups design in generating significant results, publication rates grossly inflate this bias. The isolated-groups design has led to a curious state of affairs in which a nonsignificant result is more valid than one that is significant. If all the cards are stacked in favor of finding a significant result, *finding nothing is more improbable than finding something!*

One could argue that the same criticism could be leveled against language researchers who compare language-impaired children with children who have normal language development. But by and large, language researchers are far more cautious in how they interpret their data and how they apply statistics, if they use statistics at all. More importantly, language *develops*; it runs on a biological clock, no matter how complicated this clock turns out to be. There are norms for natural lateral and temporal variation that allow the scientist to track extreme groups such as late talkers.

Reading, on the other hand, definitely does not "develop." It isn't remotely biological or natural. Although some children might be at the bottom of the reading curve because of a biological clock, this is likely to be a *language* clock, not a reading clock. Other poor readers are at the bottom of the curve for reasons having nothing to do with language development. One reason is the writing system itself, and this is due to an accident of birth. Another reason is how well teachers are trained to teach the writing system, whatever it is. This is why children who learn transparent orthographies (like those in Spain, Italy, Germany, Austria, or Sweden) read so much better than English-speaking children, who learn an opaque orthography (Organization for Economic Cooperation and Development, 1995; Cossu 1993; Wimmer and Goswami 1994; Landerl, Wimmer, and Frith 1997).

It is not an exaggeration to say that much of the basic research on reading is invalid, because it relies on the isolated-groups design. By the strict standards of science, this book would be much shorter than it is. I have chosen, instead, to present a profile of this work to illuminate what the studies really showed. This is especially critical in view of the fact that, far too often, the most famous studies are the least reliable, while relatively unknown studies that make a major contribution to the field are ignored.

From this point forward, the reader must keep in mind that *all research using a good- versus poor-reader design is invalid*. The results from studies using an isolated-groups design will be limited to the descriptive data only (simple means) or to correlational data in those cases where combined group scores are likely to be normally distributed (overlapping or adjacent distributions). I will not present any statistical values or state that an outcome is "significant" unless I specify the reason for doing so.

I also need to say that not all this research is flawed. There are many excellent studies in the field, and the reader will be made aware of them.

AUDITORY AND SPEECH PERCEPTION AND READING

In this chapter, we return to research on auditory processing. In these studies, children are selected on the basis of their reading test scores. (It should be noted that all but one of the studies considered in this chapter use the invalid isolated-groups design. If you don't know what this means, you need to read the preceding chapter.) Earlier, I reviewed studies by Tallal and others on auditory-processing skills in children with severe language problems. Tallal's theory predicts that difficulties hearing brief auditory signals will have an impact on receptive language, plus the ad hoc assumptions that poor auditory sensitivity will affect phoneme awareness and, ultimately, reading skill. We have already seen that the research evidence does not support the first premise, and so cannot support the second and third.

Tallal (1980) tested the final step in her theory directly in a study on good and poor readers. This is one of the most frequently cited studies in the literature. It is mentioned every time someone wants to make the point that poor readers have auditory-processing problems, so it is important to look at what this study really showed. There were twenty poor readers in the study, all attending a school for learning disabilities. Ages ranged from 9 to 12 years, and 80 percent were boys. They scored at least 1 year below norms on the Metropolitan Reading Test. All had IQs in the normal range. Data from twelve normal readers ($8\frac{1}{2}$ years) tested in a previous study were used as the "control group." (Thus groups were not matched in number, age, sex, or IQ.) The children did Tallal's tasks described in chapter 4 (and see appendix 1), which were identification (identify each of two sounds), same-different judgment, and the repetition test. The sounds were "speechlike tones" lasting 75 ms, presented at varying rates (slow to fast).

All the children reached criterion on the identification task, and good readers performed almost perfectly on the remaining tasks. Poor readers weren't far behind, scoring 83 percent correct on the repetition test, and 88 percent correct on the same-different judgment task. Tallal reported that 60 percent of the poor readers performed like the normal children on all tasks, but 40 percent made errors. The main statistical analysis on which Tallal based her conclusions was a series of correlations between the errors on the auditory tasks and reading test scores. Unfortunately, correlations have no validity when these circumstances apply:

1. The research design violates the assumptions of statistics.
2. The data are nonnormally distributed due to ceiling effects (good readers) and bimodal distribution (poor readers).
3. The two groups aren't matched in any way.

This was Tallal's interpretation of the results:

There was no significant difference between the number of errors made by the reading-impaired group on the sequencing task ... and the discrimination task. It was only when stimuli were presented more rapidly that reading-impaired children's performance became significantly inferior.... [These] auditory perceptual deficits would be primarily related to difficulty in learning the sound-symbol relationships that are the basis of phonics rules. (p. 193)

This conclusion is not justified in light of the methodological problems with this study.

Other researchers have studied good and poor readers using the standard categorical-perception tasks using synthesized CV syllables: *ba-da*, *da-ga* (Brandt and Rosen 1980; Godfrey et al. 1981; Werker and Tees 1987; Reed 1989). Overall, there was a general trend for poor readers to be more variable at the category boundaries, but the outcomes of these studies were erratic, significant in some cases but not in others.

The most rigorous study in this group is the one by Reed (1989). This was a replication and extension of Tallal's study using better methodology—though, unfortunately, no improvement in research design. A group of poor readers (8 to 10 years) was matched by sex, age, and grade to normal readers. IQ was not controlled, a major oversight.

Children were tested on Tallal's repetition test using speechlike tones (75 ms long), vowels /a/ /e/ (50 ms), and CV syllables (*ba-da*) at various presentation rates. The children also did a categorical-perception task (*ba-da*), and were asked to discriminate words starting with similar-sounding consonants, like *top cop*. (I computed binomial tests and most scores were significantly above chance.)

Reed expanded the trials on the repetition test from 4 to 12 with the result that the auditory functions began to look respectable (linear). Good and poor readers alike made hardly any errors on the vowel contrast. Good readers scored nearly perfectly on the CV syllables, while poor readers made errors at all rates of presentation. Both groups had more trouble with tones than with speech. The poor readers did particularly badly at the fastest presentation rates, largely performing at chance.

Overall, poor readers did slightly worse on the speech-discrimination and categorical-perception tasks, but whether these differences were "significant" (as claimed) can't be known due to the research design. Reed commented that some poor readers did as well as the normal children, but no information was provided about these children.

In the second phase of the study, Reed selected ten children with the highest error rates on Tallal's repetition test, along with their matched controls. They were asked to discriminate between two vowels masked by noise, discriminate between visual patterns seen briefly, and repeat words with ambiguous initial consonants. The two reader groups performed similarly except on the words with ambiguous consonants.

Reed (1989, 285) summarized the findings as follows: "No evidence of deficient performance was found in the temporal order judgement tasks with either longer but difficult to discriminate cues (vowels in noise) or in briefly available visual cues.... [There was] a substantial degree of specificity to briefly available auditory cues."

Reed speculated that perhaps "this difficulty may also relate to differences in the sharpness of category boundaries and the ability to discriminate stop consonants in natural speech" (p. 286). Because phoneme discrimination is a problem for poor readers, and consonants are difficult to segment, Reed concluded that the ability to segment consonants or consonant clusters might be a consequence of perceptual difficulties that contribute to "inadequately defined phonological representations" (p. 289).

As to the source of "inadequately defined phonological representations," Reed suggested problems with general language. Language measures would certainly have been useful here, especially because Reed (like Tallal) remarks on the large individual differences among the poor readers. In general, it appears that the majority of poor readers in these studies scored in the normal range, and the remainder performed more like the language-delayed children. If this is the case, one would expect them to outgrow these minor auditory-discrimination problems with age, as occurred in the longitudinal studies reported in chapter 4.

Werker and Tees (1987) raised the issue of general language delays in their paper as well. But they didn't believe their study proved one way or the other that poor readers had a perceptual deficit, pointing out that "more research is required to determine whether this less stable phonological representation is caused by a primary perceptual deficit (cf Tallal, 1980) or is the result of other subtle language difficulties resulting in lack of boundary sharpening" (p. 82).

Despite the tempered caution in these quotes, the implication is clear that whatever the problem might be, it *exists in the child.* Yet there is no way that studies like these can determine whether the slight difficulties poor readers had in hearing brief auditory cues were due to some inherent flaw or to an environmental cause. They can't rule out the strong possibility that good readers have had far more opportunity to discriminate phonemes, causing auditory discrimination to improve. This is a reasonable explanation given the fact that children in these studies were 8 years old or older.

Dissenting Voices

By the late 1990s, several studies appeared that sounded the death knell for the theory that poor readers *as a group,* or *as a rule,* have subtle auditory or speech-perception impairments. Nittrouer (1999) set out to discover what it was, precisely, that poor readers couldn't hear, if anything. She measured phonological awareness *and* auditory processing *and* reading in a large group of normal children 8 to 10 years old. (This is a perfect recipe for a solid correlational study, but, alas, the isolated-groups design appeared instead.)

Children were divided into reading groups based on their scores on the Wide Range Achievement Test (WRAT). Poor readers ($N = 17$)

averaged 77 standard score (2 years below grade), and good readers ($N = 108$) scored above that. The groups didn't differ on the WISC block-design test or on an articulation test.

The children were given three phoneme-awareness tests, a memory test using rhyming and nonrhyming words, and a syntax test in which they had to act out sentences with toys. Tallal's repetition test was used to measure auditory/speech recognition. However, this time Nittrouer synthesized real tones (sine waves), rather than Tallal's "tones," which sound more like alien vowels. Tones were brief (75 ms), sequences were two, three, and four elements, and presentation rates ranged from slow to fast (320 to 20 ms).

Children also did a categorical-perception task that used four contrasting syllables: *ta-da*, *say-stay*, *sa-sha*, *Sue-shoe*. The *say-stay* continuum can be varied in two ways: by the length of the silent gap that separates /s/ from the following sound, and by a pitch change in one component (F1 formant transition). The two cues "trade," in the sense that only one cue is needed to tell *say* and *stay* apart. By manipulating the two cues, Nittrouer could determine which cue each child relied on to tell them apart.

Poor readers had little trouble on the auditory and speech-perception tasks. (I carried out binomial tests to make sure that guessing was not a factor in these results.) When all the data were combined for the repetition tests (fifteen conditions), poor readers did marginally worse. But when separate comparisons were made for each rate separately, they scored as well as the normal readers. Scores were identical for the two groups on the categorical-perception tasks for the *ta-da* and *say-stay* contrasts. Poor readers had less stable judgments at the category boundary for the /s/–/sh/ continuum.

In contrast, poor readers had considerable trouble on all the language tasks—phoneme analysis, verbal memory, and syntax—showing that poor phoneme awareness and low general language skills are much more likely to characterize a poor reader than basic auditory or speech-perception problems.

Nittrouer analyzed the error patterns to determine how the auditory judgments were made. There was no evidence from this analysis that poor readers' performance had anything to do an inability to process brief signals. As Nittrouer (1999) put it,

Contrary to predictions of the temporal processing hypothesis, children with demonstrated phonological processing problems *depended* on brief and transitional signal portions for speech perception. In fact, for decisions regarding syllable-initial fricatives, children with poor phonological awareness based their phonetic judgements more on formant transitions [brief cues] than the other children. At the same time, they failed to make as much use of the long, steady-state information provided by the fricative noises. (p. 937; italics mine)

Nittrouer pointed out that this pattern is characteristic of younger, normal children.

In other words, poor readers relied more on fleeting (brief) transitions than good readers did, and less on extended (nonbrief) sounds, as a function of what they were asked to listen to. Nittrouer surmised that the problem was a subtle perceptual difficulty, making it hard to discriminate between perceptually similar signals. She referred to this as a "deficit." But this is debatable. There are more clues about what it might be in the next study discussed here.

Mody, Studdert-Kennedy, and Brady (1997) were interested in two issues. First, do poor readers have a "global auditory processing deficit" as Tallal claims, or is the problem restricted to speech perception? And if so, what exactly is it (if anything) that poor readers can't hear? They answered these questions by comparing the performance of good and poor readers on Tallal's repetition test and a categorical-perception test, using speech and nonspeech contrasts.

Twenty poor readers and twenty good readers participated. Children were in second grade (age range 7:0 to 9:3). Poor readers were at least 5 months below norms on the word identification and word attack subtests of the Woodcock Reading Mastery series, with the group averaging 1 year below age norms. The normal and poor readers were matched in age, vocabulary (PPVT-R), and IQ (WISC-R).

Because the primary purpose of the study was to test Tallal's theory, they had to screen 220 children to find 20 poor readers who could *not* discriminate a *ba-da* contrast on Tallal's tests. This was to ensure that they had the same problem as the worst readers in Tallal's (1980) study. The main focus of the study was to pin down any perceptual difficulties with various types of tone or speech contrasts.

In the first test, children had to discriminate between the contrasts *ba-da*, *ba-sa*, and *da-sha*. The first contrast differs in only one acoustic feature (a brief pitch glide); the others differ in three features. The question was whether it was the number of features that made discrimination difficult for poor readers. (I computed the binomial test, and guessing was not a factor in these results.) The only difference appeared on the *ba-da* contrast. Poor readers made more errors during training and at fast presentation rates (100 ms or less). Good readers made zero errors at all rates. Mody, Studdert-Kennedy, and Brady (1997, 215–216) concluded that "poor readers judge temporal order accurately, even at rapid rates of presentation if they can identify the items to be ordered. Perhaps, then, their difficulties with ba-da are phonological."

Next, children were tested on a nonspeech contrast (tones) modeled on the *ba-da* spectral (acoustic) patterns. The "syllables" varied by one feature in the same way as *ba* and *da*. Both reader groups made more errors on this task, but now they didn't differ from each other. The data from the two studies were plotted in a single figure and reveal an interesting effect (figure 10.1).

Scores for the two groups are identical, with the exception that good readers were better at telling *ba* and *da* syllables apart. If good readers had better overall auditory discrimination for brief acoustic cues, they would be better on the tones version as well, but they were not. Mody and her colleagues expressed this another way: "Whatever difficulties were induced in the poor readers by increasingly rapid presentation of synthetic stop-vowel syllables were not similarly induced by the nonspeech control patterns. These results demonstrate that the poor readers' difficulties with ba-da discrimination were specific to speech, and cannot be attributed to a general auditory deficit" (pp. 218–219). This is true, but I believe it illustrates something quite different, which I will come back to shortly.

The last test in the series investigated discrimination of brief acoustic signals. Was it "briefness" that the poor readers had trouble with, or something else? As noted above, the words *say* and *stay* are contrasted by two redundant cues. In this study the silent gap was fixed. The variable cue was an onset-frequency rise (an upward shifting pitch) that was varied in nine equal steps from normal to extremely brief. Good and poor readers did not differ on any measure on this test.

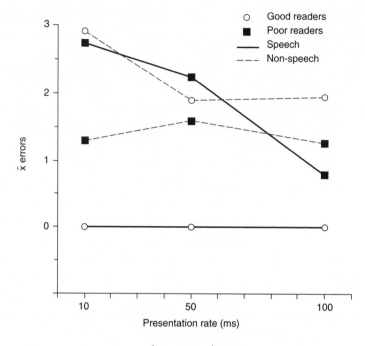

| Figure 10.1 |

Mean number of errors by good and poor readers as a function of ISI on speech (/ba/–/da/) and nonspeech discrimination. From Mody, Studdert-Kennedy, and Brady 1997.

Mody and her colleagues concluded poor readers had problems discriminating between speech sounds that differ by one acoustic feature, the same conclusion reached by Nittrouer. Poor readers had no difficulty with speech contrasts that varied on three features (*ba-sa* and *da-sha*) or had rapid and variable transitions (*say-stay*), or with nonspeech tones modeled to resemble *ba-da*. As they remarked, "The poor readers of this study ... clearly did not suffer either from the general auditory deficit posited by Tallal (1980) or from a corresponding domain-specific, phonetic deficit in the perception of brief formant transitions. Nor did they exhibit [a] developmental delay" (p. 223).

If it isn't temporal processing, or rapid transitions, or briefness that is causing the problem, why did the poor readers in this study (and in many other studies reviewed above) have more trouble with a one-feature phonetic contrast, like *ba-da*? Why did they also have trouble with the contrast /s/–/sh/ (Nittrouer 1999)? Mody, Studdert-Kennedy, and Brady didn't have a good answer. They suggested, like Reed, as well as Werker and Tees, that it might be a language problem—or perhaps "attention deficit disorder." The list could go on. But there is a simpler explanation if we stop viewing poor readers as "impaired."

The simple answer is that good readers' phoneme-discrimination skills are *superior* to those of poor readers. The last two studies provide the clearest evidence so far that it is just as likely that lack of knowledge about the existence of phonemes, and the corresponding lack of practice in listening for phonemes in words, leads to slightly poorer speech discrimination, as it is likely that poor speech discrimination "causes" poor phoneme awareness. The *deviant* children in this study were the good readers whose only triumph was being able to hear the difference between canned *ba* and *da* syllables at an ambiguous category boundary. They did nothing else any better than poor readers. *The important question isn't why poor readers had trouble with this discrimination, but why the good readers did not.*

The answer to this puzzle was already in the literature. Hurford and Sanders (1990) tested good and poor readers on another version of Tallal's tests. These poor readers were very poor indeed, scoring 40–50 percentile points below the good readers on the Woodcock-Johnson reading battery. The children were second and fourth graders, average age $8\frac{1}{2}$ and $10\frac{1}{2}$ years. All children had full-scale IQs above 90.

The children had to judge whether pairs of CV syllables (*bee, dee, ghee*) were the same or different when presented at various rates. Trials to criteria did not differ for either age groups or reading groups. There was no difference in error scores for the older children or for younger good readers (scores ranged from 87 to 95 percent correct). However, error scores for the younger, *poor* readers were not significantly above chance (78 percent correct) at any presentation rate.

These results show that speech-perception accuracy (at least for canned CV syllables starting /b/ /d/ or /g/) is a function of age and reading skill. Hurford and Sanders interpreted this as a development delay in phoneme-processing skill. But it could be interpreted as an environmental effect: poor readers not knowing that phonemic processing exists, or that it is relevant to anything.

Hurford and Sanders didn't stop there. They decided to fix the poor readers' speech-discrimination problem with some training. Children who scored below 84 percent on the discrimination test were identified and split into two groups. One was trained on speech sounds and the other on a pitch-discrimination task for nonspeech tones. The training took the form of a computer game. The children decided if two sounds were the same or different and pressed a key. When they got the right answer, they saw a smiley face on the monitor. As their performance improved, the rate of presentation was gradually speeded up.

The speech-training group began by listening to pairs of vowels. When they were able to tell the vowels apart at fast presentation rates, they moved on to easy CV syllable contrasts. When they succeeded at this, they heard the CV syllables from the original set. After 3 hours or less (over 3–4 days), the poor readers in the speech-sounds training group scored as well as the good readers on the original CV syllables. Not only this, but they did equally well when they had to transfer their new skill to a syllable contrast they hadn't heard before. By contrast, the poor readers trained on nonspeech tones did not improve. The fact that training on tones had no impact on discrimination of speech sounds is further evidence against Tallal's theory that language builds on basic auditory perception.

These results, like those of Mody, Studdert-Kennedy, and Brady, support the argument that the difficulty is just as likely to be due to not being aware of how to listen at the phonemic level of speech, as to a deficit or an impairment. The fact that this is so easy to train accords with scores of other studies (see McGuinness 1997b and *Early Reading Instruction*). Hurford's results suggest that the problem is more one of knowing how hard to listen and what to pay attention to.

Research has failed to demonstrate that there is anything wrong with poor readers' speech perception, certainly nothing that can't be fixed with a little training. The studies by Mody, Studdert-Kennedy, and Brady and by Nittrouer challenge the field and essentially topple 25 years of research. The results show that *every speech contrast* is different, only those with minimal acoustic cues are hard to tell apart, and only for a small portion of poor readers.

Furthermore, the CV syllables used in all these studies consisted of electronically contrived speech sounds that are quite unlike natural language. If poor readers have little difficulty discriminating between most of these contrasts, they are not likely to have *more* difficulty with natural speech.

And the Debate Goes On

As a footnote to this section, the feelings engendered by a deeply held deductive theory have led to emotionally charged attacks on research that disproves the theory. Denenberg (1999) took issue with the Mody study. His main complaints were methodological: "The Mody et al. article ... is so seriously flawed that it fails to address the controversies surrounding the Tallal hypothesis" (p. 379). He stated that their poor readers were not as impaired as those used by Tallal, which isn't true. He complained that the children were much younger, but that isn't true either. If it had been, their results would be even more convincing, because these minor auditory problems correct themselves with age. He criticized them for improper data handling and statistics, and for using the wrong test for bimodally distributed data (ceiling effects), violating the assumptions of ANOVA statistics, and so forth, all of which *is* true. But he did not see the central problem of the *invalid research design* that was used in nearly every study reviewed in this chapter, including Tallal's. He did not level any of the same criticisms (bimodal data, ceiling and floor effects, invalid use of statistical tests) at Tallal.

His final point was an interesting one, and referred to the problem of "proving the null hypothesis." That is, you should never argue from finding nothing (no significant effects) to something, unless you specify a minimal level of power ahead of time. As he pointed out, twenty children in each reader group is not enough power. And he went on to say that when power is low, as it was here, finding a significant result is much more *unlikely* than finding a nonsignificant result.

This may be true in real experimental research where subjects are chosen randomly from a normal distribution. But it is definitely not true here, where the experimental design (isolated groups) is invalid to start with, and *biased* in favor of producing a significant result. Given this critical fact, finding nothing is more valid and more informative than finding something, especially when the poor readers in Mody's study were carefully selected to have auditory perceptual problems in the first place. A methodological critique should be leveled at all research impartially.

Listening to Words in Noise

There is another way to stress auditory resources, and that is to embed words in noise. Brady, Shankweiler, and Mann (1983) were the first to test good and poor readers' ability to repeat words degraded by noise. They found that poor readers had a harder time hearing and repeating words masked by noise. These results were not replicated by Snowling et al. (1986), who found that noise had no differential effect on good and poor readers. Because these two studies used the identical word lists and noise masks, they provide a paradigmatic case for the kinds of problems created by the isolated-groups design.

I will be reporting "significant results" for these studies. The reader should keep in mind that statistics are off limits for an isolated-groups research design, and the statistics are for illustrative purposes only.

Brady, Shankweiler, and Mann tested good and poor readers, average age $8\frac{1}{2}$ years. PPVT-R vocabulary scores were within the range 90 to 120. All passed a hearing screening. Good readers scored, on average, three grade levels higher than poor readers on a reading test battery. The sex composition of the groups was not reported.

Common and rare words (high and low frequency in print), varying in complexity (CVC to CCVCC words), were recorded in a male voice. Noise masks were created for each word by a process known as *amplitude matching*.[1]

In a second part of the study, the children had to identify twenty-four common environmental sounds (birdsong, car door slamming, knocking) presented in noise or no-noise conditions.

The results showed that poor readers did worse when *words* (not environmental sounds) were masked by noise; otherwise they performed identically to the good readers. Common words (high frequency in print) were much easier to hear and repeat than rare words. This was true for both groups, and there was no difference between them as a function of word frequency. (See table 10.1.)

---

1. The signal-to-noise ratio (words/noise) was zero (equal volume). Words, or words plus noise, were presented at a moderately loud volume of 78 decibels, SPL.

Table 10.1
Word-repetition accuracy in good and poor readers for high- and low-frequency words played in high-noise or no-noise mode

	No noise			High noise		
	High-frequency words %	Low-frequency words %	Non-words %	High-frequency words %	Low-frequency words %	Non-words %
Brady						
Poor		98		71	42	
Good		97		83	58	
Snowling						
Dyslexics	95	97	77	90	76	61
RA	94	96	84	92	73	76
CA	99	95	92	96	84	80

Note: RA = reading age matched; CA = chronological age matched.

The majority of errors were made on the initial consonant, the next most on the final consonant, and the fewest on the vowel. The main "significant" difference between good and poor readers was on stop consonants in the initial position in a word. (/b/ and /d/ are stop consonants.)

Snowling et al. used the same words, recorded by a woman instead of a man. Noise masks were produced in the identical way (amplitude matching). In addition to providing common and rare words, they created a set of nonsense words by changing the initial phonemes of the real words (*knife-mife*). There were three noise conditions: no noise, low noise, and high noise. The high noise level was equivalent to the noise level used in the Brady study.

The poor readers in this study came from a school for dyslexics in London, and ranged in age from 9:0 to 12:8. There were two control groups. One was matched for chronological age (CA), with reading scores 2 to 3 years higher than the poor readers. The other group was matched in reading age (RA) and were 2 years younger (age range 7:6–10:2). The authors report that the control groups' vocabulary scores were "in the same range" as the dyslexics' full-scale IQ, but these aren't comparable tests, and this is not an adequate match. Children were not screened for hearing loss. The sex composition of the groups was not reported. The average scores are shown in table 10.1.

In the Brady study, good and poor readers were identical in their ability to repeat words in the no-noise condition, but poor readers made 10 percent more errors than good readers in the noise condition (group times noise interaction, $p < .001$). Noise had a strong effect on recognizing rare words for both groups to the same extent (group times word-frequency interaction was not significant).

In the Snowling study, the results were exactly the opposite. Noise had no differential effect on any reader group, in any noise condition. This was true even in studies 2 and 3 on word judgment.[2] All group times noise-level interactions were not significant. This result was so consistent that the authors concluded that whatever might be wrong with poor readers, it has nothing to do with auditory discrimination of speech. On the other hand, word frequency (common, rare, nonword) had a differential effect on the reader groups, with poor readers having a good deal more trouble hearing and repeating rare words and nonsense words (group times word-frequency interaction, $p < .05$).

Snowling et al. reported that on the nonword task, eight of the dyslexics (42 percent) scored as well as the older normal readers, and five of the young good readers (26 percent) did as badly as the poorest dyslexics. This highlights the fact that there is a lot going on that has not been controlled.

Table 10.1 illustrates the strange result in which the *dyslexics* in the Snowling study did better than the *good* readers in the Brady study. Perhaps some procedural variables might explain these contradictory and paradoxical results. Here are some possibilities:

1. The loudness level was higher in the Brady study, predicting that children would hear the words more clearly. But the results were opposite this prediction. Children in the Brady study did worse overall.

---

2. Snowling carried out three experiments in this paper. Study 1 was the replication of Brady, Shankweiler, and Mann 1983. Studies 2 and 3 involved a "lexical decision task" in which children decide if a common word, rare word, or pseudoword is a real word. I found, using the binomial test, that children were at chance across the board on rare words and pseudowords (just guessing). Therefore, results from studies 2 and 3 are invalid.

2. Words were recorded by a male (Brady) and a female (Snowling). It is possible that women's voices are harder to mask with noise. This might explain the group effects for noise but can't explain the word-frequency effect.

3. The children are much older in the Snowling study and should do better overall. This can't explain why Snowling's *younger good* readers (RA), who were the same age as Brady's *good* readers, did so much better in the noise condition.

4. Children were screened for hearing loss by Brady but not by Snowling. If Snowling's "dyslexics" had undetected hearing problems, they would have done worse. However, the children in the Snowling study did better than the children in the Brady study.

5. Perhaps there were different sex ratios in the good and poor groups in the two studies. This can't explain why the results go in opposite directions for noise and word frequency.

6. Snowling et al. mentioned this possibility: *order effects*. The children in the Brady study heard the same words in the same order, first in noise and then in no noise. In their study, word order was varied. They argued that "poor readers may have found the noise-masked stimuli relatively more difficult because of unfamiliarity per se. Furthermore, this fixed order of presentation may have contributed toward a ceiling effect in the data" (p. 498). With this, Brady's results were dismissed and not referred to again. Yet it is hard to imagine why order effects would selectively impair poor readers, or why the high scores in Brady's no-noise condition (ceiling effects) were any more remarkable than the ceiling effects in their own data.

I could continue with this exercise, but the fact is that there are no procedural explanations for these discrepant results. Results like these are a product of the isolated-groups design, which by its nature amplifies minor variations between extreme groups. Spurious significant results are amplified further by the small number of subjects. This is not to say that these studies were not carried out by responsible scientists, acting in good faith, and executing their research expertly and carefully. My point is different. It is that the isolated-groups design is likely to throw up these kinds of anomalous results because it is statistically (mathematically) invalid.

Despite these extraordinary discrepancies, Snowling et al. did not hesitate to draw far-reaching conclusions about what the results meant. Because they failed to find a noise effect but did find a word-frequency effect, they concluded that dyslexic children's somewhat greater difficulty in hearing and repeating rare words and nonsense words

will hamper the acquisition of new spoken words. If dyslexics take longer to learn new words, then, in comparison with mental-age matched normal readers, their vocabulary may be reduced.... If our hypothesis is correct, and dyslexics have impoverished knowledge of words, then they should have more difficulty than CA-matched controls when asked to decide between words and nonwords in an auditory lexical decision task. (p. 499)

Snowling et al. speculated that this might be due to their limited reading experience. But this idea was quickly set aside for a preferred theory: "Dyslexic readers suffer a developmental lag with respect to the rate at which they can acquire lexical knowledge.... They performed like younger children rather than at the level appropriate for their age and intelligence" (p. 499).

At this point the authors invented a new disorder called *nonlexical repetition deficit*. Their reasoning was that if dyslexic children have no more trouble than good readers hearing words in noise (at least not in *their* study), the problem can't be at the input stage of speech perception. Because none of these children had articulation problems (it was not stated how this was known), this deficit isn't due to a speech-output problem either. Hence, it is "most likely dyslexics have difficulty with speech analysis—a procedure which must involve phoneme segmentation.... Our results suggest that the dyslexics' difficulty may have developmental repercussions.... New word learning will be compromised. [They] will take longer to establish lexical representations for words which they encounter auditorily than age-matched normal readers" (p. 504). From their perspective, the word-judgment tasks revealed a phoneme-segmenting problem, and these results "throw light upon the developmental course of dyslexia" (p. 504).

Here is what Brady, Shankweiler, and Mann (1983) had to say. (There were no discrepancies that had to be explained away when they wrote this.)

This pattern of results suggest that the poor readers could process the speech signal adequately, but they required a higher quality signal for error-free performance than the good readers.... The poor readers require more complete stimulus information than good readers in order to apprehend the phonetic shape of spoken words.... Good and poor readers did not differ in the effect of word frequency on item identifiability. Therefore, the greater susceptibility of the poor readers to errors of identification apparently *does not arise from differences between good and poor readers in vocabulary level....* The poor readers' problems would seem to stem from failure to adequately internalize certain formal properties of language: in these instances, properties relating to the phonetic pattern. (p. 364; italics mine)

Now we see the power of The Dogma in action. *Completely contradictory results* from a nearly identical pair of studies must be interpreted in accordance with The Dogma. Whichever way the wind blows, however, the results turn out, despite the small number of children in the studies, and in the face of no supporting evidence, or even contradictory evidence, the interpretation can always be twisted to imply something about poor readers' weak phoneme awareness (something that was never tested). Notice that these are *strong causal arguments* and have no place in these descriptive studies, studies that don't even satisfy the minimum requirements to qualify as correlational research.

Summary

The results of these studies are straightforward. Some poor readers, possibly 40 percent, have trouble hearing a speech contrast (*ba-da*) that (1) is artificially (synthetically) constructed, (2) is not composed of legal English syllables, (3) occurs at an ambiguous category boundary, and (4) is contrasted with only one acoustic feature. With respect to all other auditory and speech contrasts, good and poor readers do not differ in their ability to tell them apart. Nor is there any evidence that poor readers are unable to attend to brief cues. Unless one wants to build a "speech-perception deficit" model on a single syllable contrast that doesn't even conform to any of the 55,000 legal syllables in English, the conclusion must be that *poor readers do not have auditory- or speech-discrimination problems.*

These studies directly contradict the 9th and 10th premises of The Dogma (see end of chapter 1):

9. Speech perception may appear normal in poor readers, but this masks subtle deficits in perception of acoustic cues for speech and nonspeech.
10. Phonological processing is the integrating principle that unifies all research on language-related correlates of reading skill.

As we saw in this chapter, almost anything will fit under a phonological-processing umbrella if you want it to, even including diametrically opposite results from two identical studies.

Instead, all the evidence points to a contrasting explanation. Poor readers are less likely to have learned or been taught how to listen at the right phonetic level to be able to master an alphabetic writing system and therefore have more difficulty with fine phonetic discriminations.

METHODOLOGICAL ISSUES IN RESEARCH ON GENERAL LANGUAGE AND READING

This is the second (and last) chapter on research methodology. Besides investigating phonological awareness and auditory analysis, reading researchers have targeted four other language domains: vocabulary, verbal memory, syntax, and naming speed. In some cases, the studies employ well-developed tests that are properly normed and standardized. But, for the most part, the tests are designed by the researchers themselves, even though well-designed, standardized tests are available. Most of these good language tests were described in chapter 8. When researchers design tests from scratch, questions about test construction, norms, reliability estimates, and so forth immediately become relevant. If a test is unreliable and doesn't measure what it purports to measure, the study will be invalid at the outset.

As a point of interest, none of the phoneme-awareness tests reviewed in chapter 6 were properly constructed tests. Only a few had norms. None were standardized. In the scheme of things this may not matter too much, because we know that phoneme awareness *doesn't* develop and cause reading, and we know it can easily be taught. But general language functions *do* develop, require extensive exposure, and aren't easily taught. Nor are language skills easy to define and segregate. Trying to tease apart which language skills matter for reading and which do not is a formidable task, and it's imperative that we have proper measures of these skills.

Another methodological issue has to do with correlational statistics. As noted in chapter 9, correlations provide the only valid method to study connections between tests, such as tests of language skills and tests of reading. However, scientists in the field expect far more from correlational statistics than these statistics can deliver. Correlations are a highly unstable form of analysis, especially when critical assumptions have not been met.

Apart from the pervasive problem of the isolated-groups design, the studies discussed in the remaining chapters stand or fall according to whether these additional methodological problems are handled appropriately.

What's in a Test?

Proper test construction is critical to the study of natural language, particularly in the analysis of how it affects a learned cognitive skill. In the speech and hearing sciences, standardized tests have been developed to measure every aspect of language, and most tests have solid norms and standard scores for children age 4 years and up. These tests are largely responsible for the excellent progress in the field, because they ensure that results from one study to the next are likely to mean the same thing.

In reading research, good psychometric tests are lacking, apart from tests measuring IQ, vocabulary, and reading itself. Rather than use the existing language tests, reading researchers are more likely to invent their own. The affection for in-house tests is, in large part, a consequence of training in experimental psychology, where a student's aptitude for creating ingenious tasks is highly regarded. This works well in experimental research but doesn't work well in correlational research, where the goal is different. Homemade tests have no place in *normative studies*, where researchers are trying to create a map of which perceptual, linguistic, and cognitive abilities "go together" and which of them correlate to higher-order skills like reading.

The problem of test construction is nothing new in psychology. In 1911, Woodworth and Wells were commissioned by the American Psychological Association to prepare a special report due to a growing concern about this issue. Their job was to review a variety of tests and testing conditions used in research and point out their shortcomings. They wrote this in the introduction to their report: "The methods have not been much subjected to the kind of experimental criticism which is here attempted. Usually the investigator has pressed forward to the solution of his problem, devising tests that seemed suitable to his purpose, and then abiding by them" (Woodworth and Wells 1911, 2).

Woodworth and Wells listed potential sources of error in behavioral research. Performance can be affected by the individual's background knowledge, shifts in mental alertness over time, and errors created by the test items themselves, due to ambiguity, lack of familiarity, and confounding. They provided useful guidelines for how to overcome these problems. These guidelines included retesting to guarantee low variability across time or over repeated trials, and to minimize fatigue due to practice effects. They also advised researchers to use the new statistical tool of correlation (Spearman's rho) to ensure reliability within a test and validity between similar tests. This solid advice was added to over the years, and we now have a wealth of knowledge about the number and importance of these problems, along with better statistical tools.

This knowledge has been passed down to students of psychology and educational psychology for decades. It is puzzling, therefore, why this important information is either unknown or not applied in much of the research on reading. We have already seen examples of badly constructed tests, tests so unreliable that they either measure nothing (pure guessing) or measure something different from what the researchers intended.

To put these issues in perspective and make it easier to evaluate the research that follows, I want to summarize the excellent review of language tests by McCauley and Swisher (1984). They outlined the critical psychometric factors that must be accounted for in tests designed for young children. This is a good starting point for an analysis of why solid test construction is essential in efforts to answer the following question: Which language skills (if any) predict success in learning to read? Their discussion is also instructive in view of the in-house tests presented so far. What is perhaps the most striking flaw is researchers' failure to attempt any type of validation, the first topic of McCauley and Swisher's report.

Psychometric Properties of Good Tests
This is a summary of the key points in McCauley and Swisher's review. Most of these points will be well known to anyone who has had a course on psychometrics. Readers familiar with these concepts may want to skim this section. However, certain aspects of this review are particularly relevant to reading research, and I would advise everyone to read the

subsection on norms and how various types of data conversion relate to lateral and temporal variation.

Validity   A good test must measure what it purports to measure. There are several types of validity. *Construct validity* refers to the degree to which the test does or does not measure a theoretical construct. For example, a test of syntax should measure syntax and be able to identify children who do or do not speak grammatically, or who do or do not use syntactic information to understand the meaning of spoken language. *Content validity* is the validity of all the items, singly and collectively, to provide a true measure of the construct. This includes the child's ability to perform to his or her appropriate level on each test item. *Face validity* refers to test items in terms of how they are experienced by the test taker. Is this a test the child wants to participate in? Is the language appropriate for the age group, or is it abstract and confusing? *Concurrent validity* refers to the agreement between the test score and some other measure of the same construct. This might be another test or a clinical evaluation. Finally, *predictive validity* refers to how well the test will predict an outcome on the same construct at a later date. Predictive validity is crucial for tracking temporal variation.

Reliability   This refers to the consistency with which a test measures the construct. A test should be consistent within itself and produce a similar score when taken some time later. Measures of reliability include *item analysis*, along with *split-half* and *test-retest reliability coefficients*. While validity can be hard to prove, especially when investigating something new, an unreliable test cannot be excused. This would show that there was no attempt to apply simple, basic checks on whether the test actually measured something consistently. Many things can go wrong with test construction. The difficulty level may increase too quickly or not at all. Items can be ambiguous and can lead to different responses on different occasions. The test may be too long, so that the performance on the first half is quite different from the performance on the last half.

   When test norms are not available, an important reliability check is an *interexaminer reliability* score. This is a measure of agreement between two different people who test the same children on the same test. Examiners can cause less-than-optimal performance for various reasons, such as having an intimidating manner, being ill at ease with children, or being in a rush. Because this can happen in all testing situations, a good test will provide careful descriptions of test procedures, and/or of what training might be required before giving it.

The Normative Sample and Scoring

Test norms are a requirement of a good test. Norms must include a large number of children at each precise age (years:months), be based on a range of socioeconomic levels, and for language tests, provide information on geographic region in case dialect may be a factor in children's performance.

The test manual should provide tables and/or methods for transforming raw scores into some type of norm-based score. I want to spend some time on this issue, because it is critical in correlational research. The failure to control or account for age is a major contributor to the unstable and contradictory results from one study to the next.

Correcting for age is important for two reasons. First, in a typical U.S. classroom, poor readers are held back (retained in grade), and good readers are pushed forward. Because it is not uncommon for a child to "fail" kindergarten because he or she "isn't ready" to move ahead, the age range within a grade begins to broaden quite early. Montessori schools, and other private schools where children move ahead at their own pace, favor large age ranges in a class. When the age range of the children in a study is too broad, especially in studies on the relationship between measures that vary developmentally, age alone can gobble up a large proportion of the variance on reading tests, leaving little variance for anything else.

The second reason to correct for age is mathematical. The main assumption behind a statistical test is that the sample is drawn from a normal population, and that it represents a subset of that population. Standardized tests reflect that population and provide a way for researchers to link their sample to a larger normative sample. Controlling for age can be achieved at this level by converting a raw score to a score that reflects either lateral or temporal variation, depending on what the data are for. Standardized tests are used for various reasons, including placement in grade, intervention/remediation, and research. The best age conversion is determined by what a test is used for.

Most standardized test manuals provide four types of data conversion. Only one is valid for scientific research.

Standard Scores   A standard score is a transform of an individual child's raw score on the basis of age norms (in months). This conversion controls (corrects) for age while maintaining the "lateral variation" reflected in the raw scores. That is, a child's standard score reflects his or her ability with respect to age peers in standard-deviation units. Converting raw scores to standard scores will fit the data to a normal distribution and eliminate outliers or skew. The data, now "normalized," are appropriate for statistical analysis (normally distributed, linear, and so on). *Standard scores preserve all the information in the data with very little distortion.* They have the added advantage of allowing researchers to compare the test scores to other standardized test scores directly. Unless there is some reason not to use standard scores (extremely nonnormal populations), they should always be used in statistical analysis.

Percentile Ranks   This is the another form of data conversion representing lateral variation. Percentile ranks are gross descriptive measures for comparing a particular child to norms or to classmates, and are useful for grade placement or for parents' night. (It makes more sense to be told that your child scored in the 91st percentile than that she scored "1 standard deviation above the mean.") Percentile ranks grossly distort the intervals between the original raw scores. Large differences between the scores at the extreme ends of the distribution are transformed into small ones, and the opposite happens in the middle of the distribution. *Percentile ranks should not be used in statistical analysis of the data.*

Age-Equivalent Scores   Age-equivalent scores transform the data on the basis of temporal variation. Each child's raw score is compared to that of the average child of a particular age. If an 8-year-old scored 48 on a reading test, and 48 was the average score for children age 10:8, the 8-year-old has an age-equivalent score of 10:8. It is common in reading research to refer to poor readers as being 1 or 2 years below age or grade norms, and equally common for researchers to use *reading-level matched* controls, in which poor readers are matched to much younger children scoring in the same range on a reading test.

There are serious problems with transforming data into a distribution based on temporal variation. In the example of the spiral road (see figure 7.1), temporal variation shrinks across the age span, until it disappears altogether. The rate of change in temporal variation is nonlinear—very fast at the beginning, slowing down, and then stopping. And this rate of change is different for different skills.

Nonlinear rates of change translate into a statistical problem. When a distribution (reading skill as a function of age) is curvilinear, it cannot, by definition, be linear. The units between the various reading ages cannot be equal. Nonlinear data with unequal units are off limits for common statistical tests. Transforming data into age-equivalent scores creates another problem in terms of what might be assumed about performance. What does it mean for 7-year-old children to have the "reading age of a 12-year-old" in terms of overall cognitive development? Should they also have the vocabulary, reading-comprehension level, and expertise in syntax of a 12-year-old? If they don't, then it makes no sense to correlate their reading score to tests of vocabulary, comprehension, and syntax.[1]

Grade-Equivalent Scores Grade-equivalent scores are a much cruder measure of temporal variation. If age-equivalent scores are problematic, grade-equivalent scores are much worse. A "grade" includes children who are held back, skipped ahead, or delayed due to illness or because the school advocates large age ranges in a classroom. Grade-equivalent scores should never be used in research. Nor should researchers identify their subjects by grade level and omit information on age.

Statistical Control of Age There is another valid way to control age apart from using standard scores. If the researcher feels the test norms are a problem for a particular group of children, age can be controlled after the fact, by partialing it out statistically (subtracting the variance age contributes to all measures). In first-order correlations, this would be done with partial correlations; in multiple regression analysis, it would be

---

1. I have tested many young children with excellent decoding skills who can read lots of words they don't understand, as revealed by unusual stress patterns. When you ask the children if they know the word, they will say "no."

handled by entering age as the first step in the regression; and in ANOVA statistics, it would be done by analysis of covariance.

Criteria for Good Tests

McCauley and Swisher set up a list of criteria or guidelines that they believed language tests ought to meet:

1. Clear description of the standardization sample, including information on age, geographic region, socioeconomic status, and groups of individuals who were excluded from the sample.
2. Information on sample size. An adequate sample size should be approximately 100 per subgroup for those items listed under criterion 1.
3. Information on item analysis, including the quantitative measures used.
4. Tables with means and standard deviations for the groups as a whole and for subgroups.
5. Evidence of concurrent validity based on comparisons with other methods.
6. Predictive validity. Comparison of subsequent performance on a comparable test.
7. Information on test-retest reliability, which should be .90 or better.
8. Information on interexaminer reliability, which should be .90 or better.
9. Test-administration procedures sufficient to administer, score, and interpret the test results.
10. Special qualifications required to administer the test.

McCauley and Swisher located thirty published tests that were designed to be used for language evaluation in preschool children and that were norm-referenced tests. They rated each test on the information provided in the test manuals. This method could not establish whether the criterion had been met but was omitted from the manual or had not been met. They were inclined to believe the latter.

Few tests passed muster. The clear winner was the Test of Language Development (TOLD) (Newcomer and Hammill 1977), which met eight of the ten criteria. The TOLD measures both receptive and productive language abilities using five subtests, and it is possible to derive standard scores for each subtest individually. The Peabody Picture Vocabulary Test (PPVT-R)—a test of receptive vocabulary (Dunn and Dunn

1982)—and the Illinois Test of Psycholinguistic Abilities (ITPA) (Kirk, McCarthy, and Kirk 1968) came next, meeting six and five criteria respectively. Most tests fulfilled criterion 9, and about half, criterion 10. Apart from this, the remaining tests fulfilled few other criteria. No test presented interexaminer reliability data or information about predictive validity. Only two (TOLD, PPVT-R) provided test-retest reliability coefficients, and only three (IPTA, PPVT-R, TOLD) provided descriptions of the normative sample. (I have corrected an author error in which the PPVT-R was not listed with tests providing information on test-retest results.)

There are other good language tests designed for older children that are not reviewed here, such as the Clinical Evaluation of Language Fundamentals–Revised (CELF-R), developed by Semel, Wiig, and Secord (1986). And there are several excellent tests that appeared after McCauley and Swisher's report was published. These include the Test for Reception of Grammar (TROG), developed by Bishop (1983), and two more versions of the TOLD, one for older children (TOLD–2) and one for adolescents and adults (TAAL-3), developed by Newcomer and Hammill (1988) and the TOAL by Hammill et al. (1994).

McCauley and Swisher's report was intended to alert language researchers and clinicians to potential dangers and to chasten test developers. But from the perspective of reading research, their report is light-years ahead of the curve. While reading researchers have relied on the excellent PPVT as a standardized measure of receptive vocabulary, they rarely avail themselves of the excellent language tests, tests that are psychometrically sound and honed through clinical experience. The ITPA was published in the late 1960s, and the outstanding TOLD in 1977. Instead, reading researchers have created their own tests. They have done this despite little or no training in linguistics, speech and language disorders, and, seemingly, in test construction.

If the tests are critical, so too are the statistical techniques that determine how and whether test performance predicts reading skills.

Correlational Research: Beware All Ye Who Enter Here

Reading researchers have employed two types of research designs in an attempt to discover which subskills (if any) predict reading ability. One is the infamous isolated-groups design (in reality a bogus correlational study). The second is a true correlational study, which is the appropriate and valid method of discovering reading predictors. But answers don't come easily. Fathoming the meaning of correlational values can be like "looking through a glass darkly," and valid correlational research is critically dependent on the sample size, the distribution of the data, and the quality of the tests used to plot the landmarks on the map.

Determining What Is Logically Prior

One of the most consistent findings in reading research over the past few decades is that everything correlates to everything, to the point where it is surprising when something *doesn't correlate* to anything else. This pattern was obvious in Bond and Dykstra's research in the 1960s, and continues to this day. Making sense of correlational patterns requires good judgment in combination with well-controlled multiple regression analyses. But even this is only speculative and preliminary. Causality will never be found in correlations, which merely point the way to appropriate training studies.

To make sense of the endlessly redundant, interlocking correlational patterns, one has to know which skills are required by the tasks. Skills that are "logically prior" develop naturally and have nothing to do with reading, but may critically affect learning to read, as opposed to skills that develop from learning to read. Skills or aptitudes can be sorted along a continuum ranging from fundamental to abstract, using the simple logic that primary (innate) behaviors precede complex, learned behaviors. A fundamental or basic-level language skill is one that comes in early, is most natural and automatic, requires little or no training, and operates with the least conscious analysis. Based on the developmental research, the top candidate for a linguistic fundamental is speech comprehension, specifically receptive vocabulary. At the other end of the continuum are language tasks requiring skills that are the most unnatural and least automatic, might never appear without training, and require a high degree of cognitive effort. Tasks in this category that come to mind are those like the Rosner and Simon phoneme-awareness test.

Moreover, Chaney's research has shown that metalinguistic analysis is not synonymous with "unnatural." Quite the contrary. Children can employ a "meta" level of analysis for tasks based on natural skills much more easily than for tasks based on unnatural skills. Clarity about what the tasks are actually measuring is the first half of the battle. The second half is understanding what correlational statistics imply.

A Potted Lesson on Correlational Statistics

Readers well versed in correlational statistics and the assumptions that must be met for statistical values to be reliable, might want to skip this section. When I started writing this book, I assumed *everyone* could skip this topic (and I could skip writing it), but the methodological problems in the correlational research are too ubiquitous to overlook and suggest that many readers may find this discussion helpful.

A correlation coefficient (*r*) is a mathematically determined value. By this I do not refer to cookbook computations, but to strong mathematical assumptions that make correlational statistics meaningful. No amount of massaging the data or fancy statistics software will make these assumptions go away.

McNemar (1949), who had one of the wisest and the clearest ways of thinking about these issues, wrote:

Intelligent use of the correlation coefficient and critical understanding of its use by others are impossible without knowledge of its properties. It is not sufficient that we be able merely to recognize r as a measure of relationship. *It is a peculiar kind of measure which permits certain interpretations provided certain assumptions are tenable and provided one considers possible disturbing factors.* (p. 99; italics mine)

The validity of a correlation coefficient is completely dependent on the type of data (interval or ratio) and on the distribution of the data (continuous) derived from two or more measures from the same or related people. The relationship between the two measures can be seen in a carefully prepared scatterplot, divided into cells. In figure 11.1, each cell is a tally of the number of points of intersection between two sets of scores from parents and their adult offspring. If you peer into this scatterplot—with normally distributed data from both sets of scores—across every row and down every column you will see numerical tallies that reveal miniature normal distributions over the face of a two-dimensional surface or plane. *The spread of these minidistributions, or arrays, conveys the magnitude of error.*

The "error" is the limit of the array described in terms of the standard deviation of the array distribution. Every array has a mean and a standard deviation all its own. The basic assumption of a correlation

Number of adult children of various statures born of 205 mid-parents of various statures. (All female heights have been multiplied by 1.08).

Heights of the mid-parents in inches	Heights of the adult children														Total number of		Medians
	Below	62.2	63.2	64.2	65.2	66.2	67.2	68.2	69.2	70.2	71.2	72.2	73.2	Above	Adult children	Mid-parents	
Above	—	—	—	—	—	—	—	—	—	—	—	1	3	—	4	5	—
72.5	—	—	—	—	—	—	—	1	2	1	2	7	2	4	19	6	72.2
71.5	—	—	—	—	1	3	4	3	5	10	4	9	2	2	43	11	69.9
70.5	1	—	1	—	1	1	3	12	18	14	7	4	3	3	68	22	69.5
69.5	—	—	1	16	4	17	27	20	33	25	20	11	4	5	183	41	68.9
68.5	1	—	7	11	16	25	31	34	48	21	18	4	3	—	219	49	68.2
67.5	—	3	5	14	15	36	38	28	38	19	11	4	—	—	211	33	67.6
66.5	—	3	3	5	2	17	17	14	13	4	—	—	—	—	78	20	67.2
65.5	1	—	9	5	7	11	11	7	7	5	2	1	—	—	66	12	66.7
64.5	1	1	4	4	1	5	5	—	2	—	—	—	—	—	23	5	65.8
Below	1	—	2	4	1	2	2	1	1	—	—	—	—	—	14	1	—
Totals	5	7	32	59	48	117	138	120	167	99	64	41	17	14	928	205	—
Medians	—	66.3	67.8	67.9	67.9	67.7	67.9	68.3	68.5	69.0	69.0	70.0	—	—	—	—	—

Note: In calculating the Medians, the entries have been taken as referring to the middle of the squares in which they stand. The reason why the headings run 62.2, 63.2, &c., instead of 62.5, 63.5, &c., is that the observations are unequally distributed between 62 and 63, 63 and 64, &c., there being a strong bias in favour of integral inches. After careful consideration, I concluded that the headings, as adopted, best satisfied the conditions. This inequality was not apparent in the case of the Mid-parents.

| Figure 11.1 |

From F. Galton. Family likeness in stature. *Proceedings of the Royal Society 40*, 42–72. [Table III, p. 68].

coefficient is that when you plot a line through the centers of these mini-arrays (the cells with the maximum tally marks), the line *should be straight.* In other words, the relationship must be linear. (It can't be curved. It can't have a big hole in it. It can't be bimodal.)

Here is the second mathematical assumption behind correlations: the distributions of all the miniarrays in the vertical and in the horizontal planes must be the same or very close throughout the plane. If this is the case, one measure of dispersion can be used for all vertical arrays, and one measure for all horizontal arrays. These measures are known as the *error of estimate,* usually computed as the *standard error of estimate,* which is the square root of $Y - Y/N$. This assumption, that the data are sufficiently normally distributed to contain multiple arrays of mininormal distributions, is known as *homoscedasticity.*

A correlational coefficient must meet the requirement of homoscedasticity to be valid. In a nutshell, the standard error of estimate is interpreted as a standard deviation, and this assumes that the array distributions are not only equal in dispersion, but also normally distributed (linear and with equal variances).

What does r mean? The final computational value in a correlation co-efficient is written r. This value describes the size of the error of estimate. If r is .00, then the error is 100 percent by the formula known as the *coefficient of alienation*: $1 - r$. Because the error reduces by the square root of $1 - r$, this means it is not related arithmetically to r. In other words, you can't assume that .60 is "twice as good" or "twice as meaningful" as .30. The size of the error actually reduces very slowly. A correlation of $r = .50$ has an error of estimate of 86.6 percent, $r = .70$ of 71.4 percent, and even when r reaches .90, the error of estimate has only fallen to 43.6 percent. This means that when researchers talk about "predicting" something from a correlation, they need to be aware of the degree of error in their prediction.

There is also an important issue concerning the term *accounts for significant variance,* common parlance in reading research. What does this mean? One way to interpret r is in terms of the common variance shared by two sets of data, computed by squaring r. This estimate of "shared variance" is quite reliable. You can safely say that $r = .60$ squared means that two test scores share 36 percent of something in common. Whatever this "something" is, it is a measure of the redundancy between the two sets of scores. From this you can say to a reasonable degree of certainty: If I give test A, I can predict test B with 36 percent accuracy. *And* you can say: This leaves 64 percent of the variance unexplained—that is, 64 percent of whatever it is that makes the two tests different. It does not mean that one variable *causes* 36 percent of something in another variable, because the overlap in variance doesn't tell you the direction of the relationship, and may be due to something that hasn't been measured.

McNemar used the word "disturbing," to refer to the fact that correlation coefficients are unstable when these assumptions have not been met. In other words, the correlational values cannot tell you whether these assumptions have been met, nor can tables of statistical probability. Correlational values can shift in unpredictable ways. A few years ago, I was analyzing the data for ninety-six first graders. We ran correlations for a large set of variables, then decided to eliminate the "little professor" as an outlier, because we felt his scores would bias the results. (The little professor was a 6-year-old with a reading age of 33 years!) When his data were pulled, to our amazement, *every correlation coefficient changed*. This shows what one wild card can do to correlational values for a population of nearly 100 children.

Meeting the basic assumptions for correlational statistics is the responsibility of the researcher, and fulfills another assumption held by the scientific community. This is that when a correlation coefficient appears in a scientific paper, the reader has the right to expect that the researcher has met all these assumptions. In other words, the onus is on the researcher (not the researcher's audience) to ensure that the data fulfilled the requirements of linearity and homoscedasticity before the correlational statistics were carried out and the results published. The reader should not have to imagine a scatterplot with gaping holes created by the data from an isolated-groups design, in order to second-guess the meaning of the values of r reported in the study. This is the responsibility of the scientist, not the responsibility of the reviewer or reader.

Multiple Regression Analysis

An estimate of variance assumes the linearity of each and every pair of measures. This has important consequences for multiple regression analysis, because the basic assumption in multiple regressions is that *every first-order correlation is linear.* Multiple regression is a technique whereby common variance shared between several measures can be statistically subtracted, and the process continued (iteratively) until all significant common variance shared by the measures is exhausted. For example, a variety of tests are found to be correlated to reading. Age is one of the measures. By entering age first in a multiple regression equation, the variance due to age that is shared by any of the measures is subtracted, and the amount of variance shared between this variable (age) and the criterion variable (reading) is provided. The correlations are then recomputed with age pulled out or "partialed out." However, if age was nonlinearly related to any measure, say because researchers pooled the data from children of contrasting age groups (4, 8, 12 years), a multiple regression analysis will be invalid.

The sequence of how the measures are entered in the analysis can (and should be) specified in advance, because this is determined by logic and not by mathematics. As McNemar (1949, 153) observed, "The relationship among variables is a logical problem which must be faced by the investigator as a logician rather than as a statistician." How to determine which measures are or are not "logically prior" was discussed above.

McNemar also addressed a paradoxical aspect of multiple regression analyses that is especially important in reading research: "It is possible to increase prediction by utilizing a variable which shows no, or low, correlation with the criterion, provided it correlates well with a variable which does correlate with the criterion" (p. 163).

Here is an example. In a hypothetical study, memory is found to be uncorrelated to reading (the criterion variable) but is correlated to a phoneme-awareness test. The phoneme-awareness test, however, is highly correlated to reading. The "paradox" refers to the fact that the predictive power increases if memory is included in the regression analysis, because it may have an effect on reading via another measure.

Another feature of multiple regression analysis (or other complex correlational statistics like factor analysis or path analysis) is its extreme instability. Complex correlational statistics requires very high power, otherwise the results will be utterly spurious. Power equates to the number of subjects in the study. For a multiple regression to yield valid results, the formula cited earlier is a reasonable rule of thumb: $N/10 - 2$. This means that if you tested 200 people, this is enough power to support a multiple regression analysis for 18 different measures ($200/10 - 2$) (Biddle and Martin 1987). More conservative statisticians recommend 20 subjects per measure, in which case only 8 measures would be allowed. Small samples are the norm in reading research, and most of these studies will not support a multiple regression analysis. Despite this, multiple regressions are used all the time. Even by the lenient formula above, researchers need 40 subjects for two dependent measures, 50 for three, and 60 for four.

Variance estimates can be powerful tools if used appropriately, but researchers can sometimes fall into the "variance trap." Variance estimates can weave a magic spell to the point where words like *predict* and *accounts for* are assumed to mean "prior to" and "causing." This is a slippery slope that leads to the tantalizing sensation that causality is almost within one's grasp. "Hierarchical multiple regressions" often induce this trancelike state. This is where the researcher, like the Wizard of Oz at his electric console, mixes and matches variables in every conceivable way to "prove" that a particular measure has greater predictive power (accounts for more variance) than any other, and that this power represents causality.

The fundamental problem with hierarchical multiple regressions is that researchers must be 100 percent certain that the tests that produced this particular result were not only *truly* measuring what they thought they did, but *only* what they thought they did.

Having said all this, here is a list of the critical factors likely to produce a reliable correlation coefficient, based on suggestions from McNemar:

1. The children in the study represent a random sampling of a defined population, and no selective factors have operated to increase or decrease r. (*No isolated groups.*)
2. The range of scores is reasonably wide.
3. There should be no skew in the data. Skew occurs when the test is too easy (ceiling effects) or too hard (floor effects). Or, if skew is not excessive, steps have been taken to eliminate it by one of several transforms (Fisher's z, for example).
4. The measures are reliable, so that if a child took the test again at a later time, her score would be nearly the same.
5. Care has been taken to avoid heterogeneity with respect to a third variable. This is where a correlation between measures is compromised by

something they share that was not measured, or where spurious correlations occur because something is ignored. An example is a school system with a grade-acceleration policy in which high-IQ children are passed up to higher grades. This would mean that the younger children in a class would be brighter on average than the older children. Here IQ is confounded with age, when it usually is not. (An IQ standard score is corrected for age.)

McNemar recommends that researchers include this information in all published reports:

1. Definition of the population sampled and a statement of the method used to draw the sample
2. A statement relative to the homogeneity of the sample with respect to potentially relevant variables such as age, sex, and race
3. The means and standard deviations of all measures being correlated
4. The reliability coefficients for the measures and the method of determining reliability

I would like to recommend an additional item:

5. In-house tests. There should be a description of test construction and evidence of pilot trials (numbers of subjects, data distribution, norms) for all in-house tests. The full test should be included in the published report.

At this point I take up the studies on the relationship between various language tasks and reading, and leave you with McNemar's (1949, 143) important warning: "The researcher who is cognizant of the assumptions requisite for a given interpretation of a correlation coefficient and who is also fully aware of the many factors which may affect its magnitude will not regard the correlational technique as an easy road to scientific discovery."

VOCABULARY AND READING

Parts I and II have given us a partial road map for which aspects of language development have an impact on subsequent reading and academic skills. We have unassailable evidence that speech perception and basic auditory processing play no direct causal role in learning to read. Similarly, despite the fact that expressive language and speech-motor development is so variable during early and middle childhood, there appears to no way to predict late bloomers, nor is there any obvious or direct connection between this development and reading skill. Children whose language problems are restricted entirely to articulation have no greater difficulties with academic pursuits than normal children.

Instead, higher-order language abilities, referred to as *general language skills*, do affect academic success. Equally important, this is a "late effect," being most pronounced when children are tested after the age of 12, which suggests that the reading difficulties are less likely to be due to decoding than to fluency and comprehension. Because this discovery is so new, we don't understand why the effect is late, which of the general language skills are critical, or what role the school system might play in this equation.

In the speech and hearing sciences, children are identified as "general language impaired" when they fall below some cutoff on tests that measure receptive and productive vocabulary, syntax, and semantics. The diagnostic category *specific language impairment* adds the proviso that performance IQ is normal. There is concern about the use of cutoff scores and about the global nature of these diagnostic categories, especially among the researchers in the speech and hearing sciences who have to rely on them. The idiosyncratic profiles of the language-impaired children provided by Tallal and Piercy (1973b, 1974, 1975), and by Aram and

Nation (1980) in their longitudinal study, illustrate this problem. These profiles provide a glimpse of the extraordinary complexity of a language system. There is evidence from both studies that a high performance IQ can compensate for extremely poor language skills, allowing some children to score in the normal range or higher on reading tests. In Aram and Nation's study, performance IQ was the only consistent predictor of reading skills on a battery of language tests.

In Bishop's longitudinal study (Bishop and Edmundson 1987; Bishop and Adams 1990; Stothard et al. 1998), children were split into three groups based on cutoff scores on a battery of language tests. These groups were unstable, and children shifted from one group to another over time. Bishop and Adams found that verbal IQ, measured by receptive vocabulary and the WISC verbal-comprehension test, was the strongest predictor of which group a child was in. A multiple regression analysis was used to measure the connection between the various language tests and reading when the children were 8 years old. Performance IQ and the PPVT receptive vocabulary test were the most highly correlated to all three reading skills: decoding, spelling, and reading comprehension. The only test that contributed significantly beyond these measures was the child's "mean length of utterance" at ages 4 and 5. Unfortunately, correlations between the language and reading tests were not carried out in the follow-up study when the children were 15 years old.

Assigning children to groups on the basis of composite scores was a feature of Beitchman's longitudinal studies as well. The clinical diagnostic categories were based on cutoff scores and produced two groups— speech-motor only and general language impairment. When test scores were used for computer-generated profiles, three language-impaired groups emerged: speech only, general language, and both general language and speech problems. The major markers for these categories (the most discrepant scores) were tests of verbal IQ (WISC verbal IQ, PPVT receptive vocabulary), plus expressive language tests that measured syntax and semantics. The power of these scores fell out in the order listed above. Performance IQ was one of the least discriminating tests (see table 8.5). Unfortunately, no first-order correlations or multiple regression analyses were carried out at any stage of this study.

Thus we are faced with the problem of knowing that general language is a strong predictor for subsequent difficulties with reading and other academic skills, but we don't know which general language skills matter most, or why.

Fortunately, reading research can partially fill this gap. A number of studies on language-related skills have been carried out over the past two decades that are correlational in nature that have focused on a variety of these skills. The vocabulary-reading link was shown in both Bishop's and Beitchman's research on language-impaired children. And this link is generally assumed by reading researchers. For this reason, vocabulary is controlled in most studies on reading predictors.

Paradoxically, the vocabulary-reading link is tenuous in studies using normal populations, and this link has been hard to pin down. This is despite the fact that the majority of studies are well-conducted, proper correlational studies involving normal children with a broad range of reading skills (no isolated groups here). And there is another problem. Results are far from consistent from one study to the next. There is no better illustration of the instability of correlational research than these studies, because both the reading and vocabulary tests are properly normed, standardized, and reliable. One would expect to find consistent correlations every time these tests are given. This has not been the case, and results can range from zero to .70.

The lack of stability appears to be due to several factors. The first is subject selection. Are the children in the sample representative of the population on which the test was normed? The second factor is the age range of the children. As noted in chapter 11, standard scores not only correct for age but produce normally distributed data, and should always be used in research. Failing this, age must be controlled statistically. The third factor is that receptive and expressive vocabulary are quite different phenomena and don't measure the same thing. A receptive vocabulary test requires recognition memory (memory prompted with pictures); an expressive test requires recall memory (spontaneous oral definitions). It is possible that one type of test is better than another in predicting reading skill.

Table 12.1 summarizes the major correlational studies using standardized measures of vocabulary and reading on large samples of children. The table sets out the correlational values plus information on what type of test was used, what type of data was employed (raw scores or standard scores), and whether age was controlled by converting each child's test score to a standard score.

Table 12.1

Correlations between vocabulary and reading test scores

Bond and Dykstra 1967 $N = 4,266$	6:0			
Stanford vocabulary				
Stanford word recognition	.51			
Stanford spelling	.40			
Stanford comprehension	.49			
Age controlled: unknown				
Share et al. 1984 $N =$ orig: 543		7:0 (525)	8:0 (479)	
PPVT vocabulary (age 5:3)				
Neale/Schonell composite (lag)		.41	.39	
Age controlled: NO				
Age correlation to reading at				
7 years .09 at 8 years .14				

	Gr. 1	Gr. 2			
Juel, Griffith, and Gough 1986					
$N = 129$	(129)	(80)			
WISC vocabulary					
WRAT word recognition	.31	.29			
spelling	.24	ns			
IOWA comprehension	.40	.40			
Bryant Decoding (range)	ns to .26	.24–.26			
Age controlled: NO					

	Gr. 1		Gr. 3	Gr. 5	Gr. 7
Stanovich et al. 1984, 1986, 1988					
$N = 288$					
PPVT (raw scores) Metropolitan					
comprehension					
Cohort 1	.34		.59	.58	
Cohort 2			.76	.64	
Cohort 3			.50	.51	.70
Lag: 3rd–5th 5th–7th				.74	.58
Age controlled: NO					
Metropolitan: Grade-equivalent scores					

Wagner et al. 1993 $N = 184$	5:11 (95)		8:1 (89)	
Stanford-Binet vocabulary				
Woodcock word ID	.35		.38	
Age controlled: NO				
Wagner, Torgesen, and Rashotte	5:8	6:8	7:8	
1994 $N = 244$				
Stanford-Binet vocabulary				
Woodcock word ID	.26	.36	.48	
Woodcock word attack	.24	.34	.47	
Age controlled: NO				

Table 12.1
(continued)

Hansen and Bowey 1994 $N = 68$	7:0	
PPVT standard score		
Woodcock word ID	.17	
Woodcock word attack	.23	
Woodcock comprehension	.29	
Age controlled: reading age-equivalent scores		
Hurford et al. 1994 $N = 171$		8:3
PPVT (5:8) time 1		
Woodcock word ID time 4		.40
Woodcock word attack time 4		.37
Age controlled: standard scores		
D. McGuinness, C. McGuinness, and Donohue 1995 $N = 94$	7:0	
PPVT standard score		
Woodcock word ID SS	.15	
Woodcock word attack SS	.01	
PPVT raw score		
Woodcock word ID raw score	.34	
Woodcock word attack raw score	.27	
Age controlled: standard scores		

Bond and Dykstra's (1967) analysis of the combined basal reader classes, included 4,000 children. The correlational values should be a benchmark against which all other studies can be compared. Unfortunately, Bond and Dykstra did not report what kind of data was used to calculate the correlations between the four Stanford Achievement Tests: vocabulary, reading, spelling, and comprehension. If standard scores weren't used, or age wasn't controlled in some other way, the correlations may simply mean that *older children have larger vocabularies and higher reading scores than younger children*. As a point of information, the Stanford test is a *receptive* vocabulary test, similar to the Peabody Picture Vocabulary Test (PPVT). The child hears a word, then selects a match from among several pictures.

Another large-scale study was carried out in Australia (Share et al. 1984; Jorm et al. 1986). There were 543 kindergartners tested in the fall, followed up at the end of the school year, and again tested at age 7.

Receptive vocabulary (PPVT) was measured at the start of kindergarten and correlated to reading scores at the end of kindergarten and first grade. These "lagged" correlations are shown in table 12.1. The values are similar to those found by Bond and Dykstra, but the same criticism applies. It isn't known whether the correlations reflect uncontrolled age effects.

There were other problems in this study. The reading test score was a composite of two tests, the Neale and Schonell, both normed and standardized in the United Kingdom on children who were taught to read 1 year earlier. The composite score included measures of word recognition, word attack, fluency, comprehension, and spelling. Composite scores are always problematic, especially when one of their tests had a test-retest reliability of only .41. A composite score is particularly problematic here, because there is no way a standard score could be derived from it.

As a rule, Australian children don't learn to read until age 6, and by the end of kindergarten most children are essentially nonreaders (Tunmer, Herriman, and Nesdale 1988; Hansen and Bowey 1994). Curiously, Share et al. reported that formal reading instruction commences in kindergarten in Australia. Perhaps reading instruction varies by district, but in any case, it is unlikely that the kindergartners could read well enough to score much above zero on the reading tests. For this reason, one would expect zero or low correlations between vocabulary and reading measured at the end of kindergarten and stronger correlations when reading was well underway at the end of first grade. This is not what was found. The correlations were virtually identical at both ages (.41 and .39). The authors reported that age was not correlated to their composite reading score at either grade, but they provided no information on whether age was correlated to *vocabulary*. Nor is there any information on whether the vocabulary scores were converted to standard scores. Due to these concerns, and the possibility that age was signficantly correlated to vocabulary, the results may not be reliable.

Juel, Griffith, and Gough (1986) tested 129 first graders, and 80 children were followed up in second grade. The children were given the WISC-R vocabulary test and several types of standardized reading tests, as shown in table 12.1. The WISC is an *expressive vocabulary* test, and children must orally define words. No information was provided on the age of the children in this study, nor was age controlled in any statistical analysis. A table of descriptive data revealed that standard scores were not used for any measure. Even so, the correlations were much lower than those in the previous studies—so low that had age been controlled, values might have been close to zero. There was no explanation for this.

Three studies were carried out by Stanovich and his colleagues to look at the relationship between vocabulary and reading comprehension in first, third, fifth, and seventh graders (see Stanovich, Nathan, and Vala-Rossi 1986; Stanovich, Nathan, and Zolmna 1988). No age ranges were provided. It appears that raw scores were used for the PPVT. Grade-equivalent scores were used for the reading test from the Metropolitan Achievement Tests, a group-administered test. There are several sources of error here. Neither raw scores nor grade-equivalent scores are valid for statistical analysis. Group testing produces less reliable data. The Metropolitan is not one of the better reading tests. There are three different tests for this age range: *Primary* for grade 1, *Elementary* for grade 3, and *Intermediate* for grades 5 and 7. Because of the narrow age ranges for each test, they are likely to produce both ceiling and floor effects.

The correlational values are the highest so far, but they are inconsistent between the classes in the *same* grade at the *same* school. This is also reflected in a sample of the longitudinal data. Fifth-grade reading was better predicted by third-grade vocabulary (.74) than by fifth-grade vocabulary (.51)! Inconsistent results like these are generally a consequence of weak tests and/or poor test administration.

Wagner and his colleagues carried out a cross-sectional study (Wagner et al. 1993) and a longitudinal study (Wagner, Torgesen, and Rashotte 1994) on kindergartners, first graders, and second graders. The authors raised a number of concerns about correlational research, such as the importance of controlling verbal ability (vocabulary), measurement error due to the tests, and the testing procedures. Nevertheless, they failed to account for a major source of error in their own studies by not controlling for age. Also raw scores were used in all cases. These controls are critical here, because of the 2-year age range.

The Stanford-Binet vocabulary test was used to control for verbal IQ; this measures both receptive and expressive vocabulary. Reading was measured by the Woodcock subtests: word ID (1993, 1994 studies) and word attack (1994 study only). The authors reported that kindergartners were nonreaders (floor effects), so the correlations between vocabulary and reading at this age are meaningless. However, correlations did increase from kindergarten to grade 1, and from grade 1 to grade 2. But did this increase reflect a growing connection between vocabulary and reading, or between vocabulary, reading, *and age*—with older children having higher vocabularies and being better readers?

There are a few studies in the literature where age was controlled. Hansen and Bowey (1994) tested 68 seven-year-olds from a broad SES background. One problem with this study was the use of age-equivalent reading scores instead of standard scores. In any event, there was little evidence that PPVT vocabulary and reading were correlated.

The studies by Hurford et al. (1994) and by D. McGuinness, C. McGuinness, and Donohue (1995) tell an interesting tale, all the more interesting because they used standard scores from the same tests: PPVT as well as the Woodcock word ID and word attack tests. Hurford et al. carried out a longitudinal study on 171 children. They were tested in early first grade and followed up three more times to the end of second grade. Lag correlations were carried out between the vocabulary test measured at time 1 and reading scores measured at the end of second grade (time 4 testing), as shown in table 12.1.

Children were divided into three reading groups to find out what measures predicted outcomes from time 1 to time 4. The cutoff for establishing groups was 1 standard deviation or more below the mean on the tests (85 standard score). Children scoring above the cutoff on both reading and vocabulary were classified as "normal" ($N = 145$). Children scoring below on reading but above on vocabulary were classified as "reading disabled" ($N = 16$). Children scoring below on both measures were classified as "garden-variety poor readers" ($N = 10$).

A discriminant analysis was carried out to identify (predict) which group a child would be in at time 4 on the basis of time 1 test scores. This test determines a coefficient or "estimate" of the power of each test to predict the assignment to a reading group. With all three groups included in the analysis, the PPVT vocabulary test had the greatest discriminatory power (coefficient of .85). But when the garden-variety poor readers were excluded from the analysis, the PPVT scores did not discriminate between the two remaining groups (coefficient dropped to .12). Yet other measures, like prior reading scores and phoneme awareness, continued to predict equally well. This is an important result. It means that the coefficient of .85 was largely due to a very low receptive vocabulary in only 6 percent of the children. If this result holds up, then the conclusion must be that *receptive vocabulary has no impact on learning to read* unless the standard score is below 80. The average PPVT score for this very low group was 74.

This finding was indirectly supported by D. McGuinness, C. McGuinness, and Donohue (1995), who tested ninety-four first graders on the same tests. Correlations were computed using both standard scores and raw scores. As shown in table 12.1, correlations were significant when raw scores were used and close to zero when standard scores were used. The same effect was shown another way. Age was found to be highly correlated to the PPVT raw scores (.52) but not to PPVT standard scores (.09), illustrating the strong impact of age on vocabulary within one school grade. Superficially, these results seem at odds with those of Hurford et al., who found significant correlations using standard scores, but there was an important difference between the two studies.

The children in the Hurford study represented a broad SES spectrum. The two private schools that participated in the McGuinness study catered mainly to upper-middle-class families. Only three of the 94 children had PPVT standard scores below 100 (50th percentile). Not one child would have fit Hurford's category of "garden-variety poor readers," yet many children had serious reading problems. The higher SES status and the distribution of the test scores may explain why, *when age was controlled*, receptive vocabulary and reading were not correlated.

The last three studies are compatible in showing the same effect, but in different ways. When age is controlled, receptive vocabulary has no relationship to reading skill unless scores are extremely low. Whether a 75–80 standard score is the true cutoff for *when* receptive vocabulary starts to matter remains to be seen.

In conclusion, correlations between vocabulary and reading in most of the research are likely to be inflated, due to the failure to control for age. There is some indication that reading comprehension is more strongly linked to vocabulary than to simple decoding, and that this connection is stronger in older children. (Bond and Dykstra found no such effect for 6-year-olds.) This is shown in the study by Juel, Griffith, and Gough, and may partly explain the higher values in Stanovich's studies where only comprehension was measured. It seems reasonable to conclude that, for 90 to 95 percent of schoolchildren, a child's receptive vocabulary will be perfectly adequate to support the acquisition of early reading skills. The jury is still out for expressive vocabulary, which has not received enough attention.

What Causes Vocabulary?

Vocabulary is one of the few basic language skills for which genetic and environmental effects have been determined. Hurford et al.'s discovery of a vocabulary-reading connection only for children scoring in the extreme low range on a receptive vocabulary test (about 6 percent of the children), and Beitchman et al.'s findings based on computer profiles that 5.5 percent of the population fall into a language-plus-speech-impaired group (with extremely low vocabulary and reading scores), are supported by studies on the heritability of vocabulary and verbal ability.

Genes

In his research on identical twins over 125 years ago, Francis Galton initiated the nature-nurture debate that continues to this day. No one would argue now about nature versus nurture as the source of individual differences in receptive or expressive vocabulary. Instead, current research is directed toward estimating genetic effects and two types of environmental effect: *shared environment* (whatever is going on in families that is shared by the offspring), and *nonshared environment*, which includes school, peer groups, random events, and measurement error (in short, any events that can't be accounted for by genes or by direct family influence).

Twin Studies   Plomin and his colleagues (see Plomin and Dale 2000) have carried out several large-scale studies on the heritability of verbal and other skills. Dale et al. (1998) in the United Kingdom studied over 2,000 monozygotic (identical) and dizygotic (fraternal) twin pairs. When the children were 2 years old, parents filled out the MacArthur Communicative Development Inventory (CDI), a checklist that measures the child's expressive vocabulary. This is a highly reliable test and correlates well with individually administered tests.

Dale et al. discovered that the bottom 5 percent of these children constituted a unique group. The concordance rates for vocabulary for this group were 81 percent for monozygotic (MZ) or identical twins and 42 percent for dizygotic (DZ) or fraternal twins. Discrepant concordance rates between MZ and DZ twins is strong evidence for heredity, because MZ twins share 100 percent of their genes but DZ twins share only 50 percent. When Dale et al. controlled for error and regression effects, the heritability estimate for this extreme group of children was 74 percent, and the estimate of "shared environment" was minimal at 18 percent. Not only this, but there was a large sex difference. Heritability was nearly perfect for boys (90 percent) but not for girls (40 percent). This may partly explain the preponderance of boys among children diagnosed with a general language impairment.

When the same analysis was applied to the remaining 95 percent of the twins, concordance rates for MZ and DZ twins were similar (93 versus 81 percent), revealing less impact of genetic factors on vocabulary. Final estimates showed that 25 percent was due to genetic effects, and a substantial 69 percent was due to shared environment.

If these results are connected in any way to those in the Hurford study, this would mean that children (mostly boys) with extremely low scores on a vocabulary test are at high risk for reading problems. This doesn't mean they necessarily *have* to have reading problems, but that given current practices in reading instruction, they are *likely* to have them. Also relevant is Bishop and Edmundson's (1987) finding that children with severe language delays rarely have an isolated vocabulary deficit. Low vocabulary scores are typically accompanied by difficulties with syntax and semantics.

Dale et al. experimented with different cutoffs to see if the heritability effect would hold. When they ran the same analysis on the bottom 10 percent of the children, this effect was sharply curtailed. The strong genetic effect appears to apply to an extremely limited range, for children scoring lower than 1.5 standard deviations below the mean (approximately 7 percent of the population). We know that the lower bound of this range is at least 5 percent, and the upper bound is less than 10 percent. Hurford's "vocabulary effect" on reading skill also held for 6 percent of the children he tested.

The numbers are beginning to add up:

• 5 percent but less than 10 percent of children have a hereditary vocabulary deficit (estimate at 7 percent, <1.5 s.d.).
• 6 percent of the children have vocabularies so low that it hinders reading acquisition.

• 5.5 percent of the 1,655 children in the Toronto sample were identified with both general language impairment and speech impairments, and had low vocabulary scores and poor reading and academic skills.

Adoption Studies   Estimates of the impact of shared environment on cognitive development have largely been based on adopted children compared to their adoptive and biological parents. In 1997, Plomin et al. published a 15-year longitudinal study on adopted children tracked from age 1 to 16 years. The study included a matched control group of children who grew up with their biological parents. It should be pointed out that what parents contribute to their child's cognitive ability in terms of shared environment can't be known by this methodology, because the only evidence is a set of test scores. Shared environment is determined by exclusion: what *isn't* due to heredity.

Plomin et al. measured verbal ability, spatial reasoning, perceptual speed, recognition memory, and IQ. Test were given throughout childhood to age 16, and to biological and adoptive parents as well. The results showed that adopted children didn't resemble their adoptive parents in cognitive ability (a composite of test scores) at any point in time, and correlations were zero across the age span. By contrast, both the adopted children and the control children came to resemble their biological parents more and more as time went by. The correlations for the adopted children and their biological parents were .12 at 3 and 4 years, .18 in middle childhood, .20 in early adolescence, and .38 in late adolescence. The values for the control group were nearly identical. The highest heritability coefficient was for verbal ability. The only test on which adopted children ever remotely resembled their adoptive parents was on full-scale IQ, and this was short lived, peaking at age 3 (.20) and falling to zero by age 8.

In studies of this type, correlational values reflect half the genetic heritability, because each parent contributes 50 percent of his or her genes to their offspring. True heritability is determined by doubling these values and correcting for assortative mating (people with similar abilities tend to marry each other). When this was done, the final estimate at age 16 was a 56 percent heritability for overall cognitive skills, with 54 percent for verbal ability alone. Spatial ability was moderately heritable (39 percent), and speed of processing and memory were less so (both 26 percent).

This result has no direct bearing on reading skill, because this wasn't measured. However, it might go some way toward explaining how children with early language problems may seem to recover in mid-childhood, then unexpectedly fail to progress at a normal rate during adolescence. This phenomenon was seen in both Bishop's and Beitchman's longitudinal studies. It could have something to do with the tests themselves and the cutoffs for diagnosis. Or it may be a consequence of limits set by genes that "switch off" or "switch down" sometime during adolescence. Whatever the cause, this affects about 54 percent of the developmental growth of verbal ability.

Plomin and his colleagues were quite emphatic that these results do not mean that parents have no influence on their children's cognitive abilities. It is, rather, that parents' performance on cognitive tests explains about half the variance in their biological children's performance on cognitive tests. And whatever adoptive parents do, this never makes their adopted children perform like them on cognitive tests. Nevertheless, adoptive parents could influence their children's cognitive development in a variety of other ways, which include parenting style and emotional support, along with intellectual, musical, and artistic stimulation. The other way to look at this result is that if there is a 54 percent genetic relatedness between 16-year-olds and their biological parents in verbal ability, this leaves 44 percent of this relationship unexplained, and much of this is due to shared environment.

Compatible findings were reported by Bishop (2001), in which two large cohorts of twins were tested on language, IQ, and a nonword reading test (word attack). One cohort consisted of children diagnosed SLI, and the other cohort was normal. Bishop found moderate evidence of a hereditary effect for reading with the language-impaired cohort when IQ was controlled (.40), but no hereditary effect and a high impact of shared environment (.82) for the normal children. When this was linked to socioeconomic status, the shared-environment effect held up even with IQ controlled. Bishop's argument is much like that presented in this book. Poor language status is heritable, and reading is "heritable" by association. Reading per se can't be directly heritable, because reading is not a biologically determined aptitude. In her concluding remarks, Bishop had this to say:

In effect, this is an argument about base rates. Suppose we adopt the over-simplifying hypothesis that there are two causes of poor reading, one environ-mental and one genetic. Further suppose that the environmental cause is much more common than the genetic cause, but the genetic cause leads to more se-vere and extensive problems, which are likely to attract parental and clinical concern.... In a sample selected on the basis of ... clinically significant lan-guage impairments, we will include a higher proportion of those with genetic impairments, and so raise the probability of finding significant heritability (p. 185).

Shared Environment

As far as I am aware, there has been only one attempt to identify specific factors of a shared environment that might affect language development and subsequent academic skills. In this remarkable study, Hart and Risley (1992, 1995) investigated the connection between parents' communicative and emotional style and their childrens' expressive vocabulary develop-ment. This was a formidable undertaking designed to find out how and why Head Start children fall so far behind middle-class children in verbal development.

Parent-child interactions were taped for 1 hour every month from the time each child was 9 months old until the age of 3. For the most part, the parent was the mother. Ultimately forty-two children and their families made it to the end of the study. Thirteen families were high SES (profes-sional), twenty-three were middle class, and six families were on wel-fare. All welfare families were African-American, and there were eleven African-American families equally divided between middle-class and pro-fessional groups. The remaining families were white. The focus was on the child's *expressive vocabulary* in terms of vocabulary size and rate of growth. IQ was measured at age 3, and various academic tests, including reading tests, were administered at a follow-up when the children were 9 years old.

Parents' communications to their children were scored for the number of words per hour; for frequency counts of nouns, adjectives, past-tense verbs, *wh*-questions; and for the use of imperatives, state-ments of approval and disapproval, positive and negative feedback, and so forth. These measures were subsequently categorized as follows: *lan-guage diversity* (number of different nouns and modifiers); *positive-feedback tone* (repetitions, extensions, expansions, confirmations, praise, approval); *negative-feedback tone* (imperatives, prohibitions, disconfirmations, criticisms, disparagements); *symbolic emphasis* (the degree to which parents made connections between things and events, as indicated by richness of nouns, modifiers, and number of past-tense verbs); *guidance style* (the number of invitations ("Shall we?") divided by the number of imperatives ("Stop it!")); and *responsiveness* (the number of responses to the child ("Oh, you want Mommy to take the ball") divided by the number of initiations to the child ("Why not play with your blocks?")).

There were enormous differences between the high-, middle-, and low-SES groups in terms of mothers' verbal output to their children. The average number of words per hour addressed to the child between the ages of 13 and 36 months was over 2,000 for the high-SES group, 1,250 for the middle-class group, and 616 for the welfare mothers. This happened even though the welfare mothers spent, overall, more time in the same room with the child. There were differences, as well, as a function of the child's age. High-SES mothers not only talked much more to their *babies* (1,500 words per hour at 9–12 months), but the number of words per hour increased linearly with the child's age, leveling off by 30 months at around 2,500 words per hour. The middle-class parents spoke less often overall, and their rate increased more modestly (1,000 to 1,500 words). The range for the welfare mothers was virtually nonexistent (600–750 words). Based on a cumulative frequency count, it was estimated that by age 3, a high-SES child would have heard 33 million words, a middle-class child 20 million, and a child of a welfare mother 9 million.

But this did not tell the whole story. Parents in the three SES groups differed noticeably in their communicative style. High-SES mothers used a richer vocabulary with greater symbolic reference. Their interactions were consistently affirmative, at twice the rate of middle-class mothers and five times the rate of welfare mothers. They rarely used negative feedback of any type. They were highly responsive and far less inclined to be directive. Middle-class parents could be described as "similar but less so" in terms of the positive measures. Welfare mothers had a very different style of verbal interaction with their children. Almost 80 percent of the feedback to the child was negative and prohibitive. They frequently discouraged or disparaged their youngsters, calling them "stupid" or "dumb." Encouragement was rare.

Because all the welfare mothers in the study were African-American, it isn't known if this profile is typical of welfare mothers in all racial groups. This seems likely, because middle- and professional-class African Americans were no different in their interactions with their children from their white counterparts. And when welfare mothers were excluded from the statistical analysis, race was not a factor on any measure for either parents or children.

Children's vocabulary development was strongly related to the sheer quantity of verbal input. At age 3, high-SES children had a true expressive vocabulary of 1,115 words (actual count), middle-class children could say 750 words, and children of welfare mothers, 525. Although the middle-class and welfare children were not that far apart, the differences in IQ between the social classes were huge. The average Stanford-Binet IQ scores measured at age 3, were 117, 107, and 79 for the three SES groups.

Now we are at the crux of the nature-nurture issue. Could Hart and Risley's data be an artifact of IQ and have nothing to do with shared environment? Perhaps all that's going on is that high-IQ mothers have larger vocabularies, are more verbal (talk a lot), and handle the interaction with their child more sensitively (more "intelligently"). There is certainly evidence for this interpretation. Parents' receptive vocabulary scores (PPVT) were highly correlated to their children's actual (recorded) expressive vocabulary ($r = .70$), as well as to their children's IQ (values ranging around $r = .77$). Because IQ varied with SES, this is support for the effect of heredity.

When each family's SES score (socioeconomic index value) was correlated to the child's vocabulary growth, vocabulary use, and IQ at age 3, and to their receptive vocabulary (PPVT) and expressive language (TOLD) at age 9, correlations ranged from .49 to .65, solid support for the effect of heredity. *Or is it?* When Hart and Risley excluded the extreme groups from this analysis and recomputed the correlations for the twenty-three middle-class families only, the correlations between SES scores and children's language development were no longer significant (ranging from $r = .15$ to .46). Heredity is there all right, but it appears to be influencing the *tails* of the distribution, much as we have seen in the heritability research, and in Shaywitz et al.'s study on the Matthew effect reported in chapter 8.

Did the quality of interaction matter? Hart and Risley created composite scores for the five categories of communicative style outlined above. For the total sample, correlations between the parent's communicative style and children's scores on vocabulary, IQ, and general language tests were extremely high (.77 to .82). They recomputed the data after excluding the extreme SES groups, expecting the correlations to collapse as they did for vocabulary, yet they remained unchanged (.74 to .80). Not only this, but these qualitative measures predicted children's language skills at age 9. Correlations between the parent's language style and her child's PPVT were $r = .78$ (all SES combined) and $r = .82$ (middle class only). Correlations between the parent's language style and the child's TOLD scores were $r = .78$ (all SES) and $r = .75$ (middle class).

Unfortunately, Hart and Risley did not take the important next step, which would be to statistically subtract each parent's vocabulary (PPVT) from the correlations and look at the residual effect of communicative style. Because this wasn't done, there is no answer to two important questions: How much is parenting style a function of parents' vocabulary and verbal IQ? How much do the qualitative factors contribute beyond this?

Nevertheless, we *can* know the answer to several other questions. First, the mother's verbal output (sheer quantity) predicted a child's vocabulary later in time. Second, qualitative measures of the mother-child interaction were much stronger predictors of the child's verbal development than SES (assuming SES as a rough proxy for IQ), and therefore likely to contribute beyond IQ. Third, several qualitative or "shared-environment" factors influencing language development were identified. The predictors of age 3 vocabulary and IQ, in order of size of correlations, were: guidance style (.67 to .73), symbolic emphasis (.69 to .72), feedback tone (.58 to .71), language diversity (.53 to .73), and responsiveness (.52 to .62). When the children were followed up at age 9, the best predictors of PPVT and TOLD followed the same pattern: guidance style (.77 and .71), symbolic emphasis (.64 and .70), feedback tone (.59 and .64), and language diversity (TOLD only, .59). Responsiveness was not significant.

Did the child's vocabulary or IQ measured at age 3 predict reading skill at age 9? Not at all. Correlations were not significant between the rate of growth of the child's vocabulary, absolute vocabulary score, or

IQ at age 3, and reading, writing, and arithmetic (Comprehensive Test of Basic Skills), spelling (WRAT), or comprehension (Otis-Lennon School Ability). These tests were properly administered on an individual basis. Nevertheless, the same early measures did predict age 9 vocabulary (PPVT) and expressive language (TOLD).

The results at age 9 could be an artifact of SES status in the final sample of Hart and Risley's study. There were only twenty-nine children in the follow-up, and they were, by chance, mainly middle class. Six of the thirteen high-SES families did not agree to more testing, and three out of the six welfare children could not be located. Not only were early-vocabulary and IQ scores uncorrelated to age 9 reading skills in this restricted sample, but IQ scores were *unrelated* to the SES scores. Yet IQ and SES rank were highly correlated when all forty-two children were included in the analysis. This means the absence of a vocabulary/IQ connection to subsequent reading and spelling ability is likely to be due to two things: the small sample size and the restricted variance in the test scores, which eliminated the tails of the distribution (very high and very low scores).

Hart and Risley's answer to their original question about how to boost the skills of Head Start children was not encouraging. They worked out how much additional help would be necessary to bring welfare children up to the level of the middle-class children:

A linear extrapolation from the averages in the observational data to a 100-hour week (given a 14-hour waking day) shows the average child in the professional families provided with 215,000 words of language experience, the average child in a working-class family provided with 125,000, and the average child in a welfare family provided with 62,000 words of language experience. In a 5,200-hour year, the amount would be 11 million words for a child in a professional family, 6 million words for a child in a working-class family, and 3 million words for a child in a welfare family. (p. 199)

Because the language experience is cumulative, building day by day, differences between the social groups grow increasingly wide. And the same is true for language style (amount of positive feedback, richness of vocabulary, and so forth). Hart and Risley estimated that getting welfare children up to the level of middle-class children would take 41 hours per week of intensive outside experience, experience *at least as rich as that found in professional families*. They also emphasized that the welfare families in this study were in good shape and were in no way dysfunctional, a situation that could create even greater barriers.

This does not mean that nothing can be done. Even a remote resemblance to a perfect plan is better than nothing. Nevertheless, studies presented in *Early Reading Instruction* show just how difficult it can be to teach vocabulary directly.

Summary

For the general population, vocabulary appears to play little role in learning how to decode, though a somewhat greater role in reading comprehension. Vocabulary begins to matter only for the bottom 5 to 6 percent of children, especially boys. Vocabulary is a major component of verbal IQ. Thus, the more general statement is that a very low verbal IQ is a major risk factor for learning an alphabet code, particularly when reading instruction is weak or misleading. Verbal IQ is one of the most heritable of the cognitive measures studied so far, and heritability accounts for over 50 percent of the variance in verbal IQ scores.

But genes are not the whole story, and "shared environment" plays a strong role in a child's verbal development. Hart and Risley's study pointed to several important parenting styles that either enhance or inhibit this development that, so far, seem to be independent of IQ. Whether this holds up in subsequent research remains to be seen.

VERBAL MEMORY AND READING

To ask if memory is related to a cognitive skill like reading is like asking whether oxygen is related to life. It goes without saying that memory is involved in mastering the alphabet code and in reading comprehension. But there are many types of memory and many modes of access (auditory, visual, kinesthetic), and too few studies to provide an in-depth assessment of this issue. For the most part, research has been primarily devoted to the relationship between verbal memory and reading skill. And while visual memory is clearly important, individual differences in reading skill have not been attributed to visual memory, or, at least, this has been very hard to prove (Jorm 1983).

Three topics are covered in this chapter. The first topic describes the various kinds of memory systems in the brain. These range from very-short-term buffer memories to the long-term memories that last a lifetime. Reading is a complex act and it's important to pin down which memory systems matter most.

The second topic has to do with important subject variables like age, sex, and IQ, which strongly affect memory skills. Memory improves noticeably over childhood. Females excel in verbal-memory tasks throughout the life span. Verbal memory is so integral to performance on verbal IQ tests that it is almost impossible to disentangle them.

The third topic relates to the research itself. Research linking memory to the acquisition of reading skills tends to be weak for all the reasons cited earlier. Few scientists have given much thought to which memory systems or memory skills are likely to be relevant to learning to read. There is no general plan of attack or set of empirical goals. By and large, the best research has focused on specific *types* of memory worked out over decades in mainstream research, but these studies are the least common.

The Anatomy of Memory

The study of memory is one of the oldest disciplines in experimental psychology and dates back to the pioneering research of Hermann Ebbinghaus in the nineteenth century (Ebbinghaus [1885] 1964; see McGuinness 1986). Ebbinghaus was the first to identify factors that influenced performance on psychological tests, like time of day, fatigue, presentation rate, the number of repetitions, and, above all, the *meaningfulness* of the words to be remembered. Meaning turned out to be so important that he forswore it altogether, basing his entire research program, and ultimately his "laws" of memory, on lists of nonsense words. He believed that this would erase the past experience of the subject (which was mainly himself), and make it possible to extract immutable laws of memory independent of a person's individual history.

There was a major flaw in this reasoning, because every one of Ebbinghaus's laws collapsed when scientists began to study memory for meaningful information. The "law" that people can only hold seven items in mind long enough to remember them isn't true if the items are words in meaningful sentences. The "law" that memory decays exponentially with time isn't true if the items to be remembered have meaning. Memories of surprising, novel occurrences, or events of high relevance, actually increase with time. Even memory for not-so-meaningful inputs, like random sequences of concrete nouns, improves with repeated recall trials, a phenomenon known as *hypermnesia* (Erdelyi, Buschke, and Finkelstein 1977; McGuinness, Olson, and Chaplin 1990).

Not only is the study of memory one of the oldest topics in experimental psychology, but it is the most heavily researched. This has made it possible to classify types of memory and to specify how to measure them behaviorally. Before moving on to the studies on memory and reading, I need to set out this classification briefly.

Types of Memory Systems

Buffer Memories   All sensory systems have buffer memories in which the neural activity outlasts the input, keeping a memory trace alive for a brief period of time. This is a physiological effect due to ongoing electrochemical activity in neurons, first discovered by Marshall, Talbot, and Ades (1943). In the psychological literature, buffer memories are variously known as *very-short-term memory, echoic memory* (auditory), and *iconic memory* (visual). Echoic memory makes it possible to hear a spoken sentence up to 10 seconds after it has been uttered. Iconic memory allows us to see movement from a sequence of static images (movies).

Short-Term Memory   Short-term memory, or memory span, represents the ability to remember a random sequence of items like a telephone number or lists of unrelated words. It is a measure of what the brain is capable of holding in mind when the input has no relevance. An early notion of short-term memory, which persisted throughout most of the 1970s, was that this was a limited-capacity system (a box in the head) through which all incoming signals had to pass and be rehearsed before entering long-term memory.

Working Memory   The idea of working memory developed out of dissatisfaction with the limits of the short-term memory concept. Working memory is conceived as a sort of place or space in the head, but imbued with a dynamic rather than a static quality, a place where operations are carried out on input from the outside world, or from pure thought, or both. Working memory is conceptually indistinguishable from "attention span" or "span of consciousness," in which we act as observers of our own experience. It represents our intuitive sense of the limits of what we can be aware of, contemplate, or analyze, at any moment in time. The contents of consciousness (working memory) are limited by the difficulty of the operations and by their compatibility. Because one's sense of limitation is tightly coupled to *expertise*, there is no support for the notion that working memory or attention span is a set of operations in a single place in the brain containing a fixed number of elements. Instead, it is the sum of the parallel neural processing in all parts of the brain relevant to the task that we are aware of at any one time (Pribram and McGuinness 1975; Pribram and McGuinness 1992).

Long-Term Memory   Long-term memory is like a library where what is important or memorable is permanently stored by the brain and can be accessed relatively easily. All inputs above sensory thresholds are registered by the nervous system, but only what is meaningful, relevant, or registered often (familiar) can be retrieved. Long-term memory is the repository of our vocabulary. The age when words are acquired plus their familiarity (how often they appear in daily conversations) act back on the input to bias perception. These "top-down" effects have been documented a number of times in this book, and even apply to nonsense words (Dollaghan, Biber, and Campbell 1995), the very words Ebbinghaus was so confident would be untainted by prior experience.

Modes of Operation

Performance on memory tasks has been found to vary significantly depending on the task and on how people are tested.

Recognition and Recall Recognition memory is remembering with a "prompt." The prompt can be a face, a spoken or printed word, a picture, a smell, or anything that brings an association or a complete experience to mind. Recognition memory is much easier to access than recall memory because it invokes associations and a "feeling of familiarity." Recall memory involves remembering *without* a prompt or any type of support. The difference between them can be illustrated by a receptive vocabulary test (recognition memory) and an expressive vocabulary test (recall memory), or by the difference between reading (recognition memory) and spelling (recall memory).

Type of Response Responses can be oral, written, or a simple key press. In a receptive vocabulary test, the child hears a word and points to a picture among a set of pictures. In an expressive vocabulary test, the child hears a word and has to define it orally. The mode of responding may or may not match the mode of perception. A child may be asked to look at a series of pictures and name them orally. Tasks that call on more than one mode of processing are known as *cross-modal tasks*. As a general rule, cross-modal tasks are more difficult than single-mode tasks (hear a word, say the word).

Order of Responding A short-term memory task typically requires verbatim recall, reproducing the input in the exact order. If the order requirement is relinquished and any order is allowed, people remember more items. This flies in the face of the early memory models in which words were thought to enter short-term memory impartially and accumulate like a stack of pancakes. One would imagine that if they went in a particular order, it would be easier to get them out in the same order, but this turns out not to be the case.

Intentional and Incidental Learning   The most common type of memory task is an intentional task, in which people are told ahead of time to remember what they hear or see. In an incidental task, people are asked to make judgments about a set of words or pictures, then are unexpectedly asked to recall them. For example, they may be asked to rate pictures on a 1-to-10 scale of how much they like them. When the judgments require meaningful processing, incidental learning produces much better memory performance than intentional learning, another example of the importance of meaning to memory, and a useful bit of information for the classroom.

Why Individual Differences Matter

Individual differences, like age, sex, and IQ, matter in all research on reading to some extent, but they play a dominant role in research on memory, and there is a wealth of data on this topic. Much of the research on reading and memory fails to control one or more of these factors, and their importance can't be emphasized enough.

Age

Dempster (1981) collated the data from over twenty studies on *digit span* for children age 2 to 12 years. This is a short-term memory test in which a series of numbers is recalled in the correct order. The average 5-year-old has a span of just over four digits. This increases to five digits at age 7, six digits at 9, six and a half at 12, and seven for adults. Digit span varies considerably *within* each age group, with an average spread of four digits (plus or minus two). A person's digit span is stable over repeated testing, one reason digit span is part of an IQ test.

The focus of much of the developmental research on memory has been on the putative causes of age differences in memory span. Dempster reviewed the evidence for and against ten possible sources of development differences. He was able to rule out, with minor reservations, differences in how the children approached the task. Adults use a variety of memory-boosting strategies but children do not. This means that memory-span differences in children are a truer measure of pure memory skill.

An early, popular theory was that children's memory *capacity* increased with age. This fit with the notion of a "box" or a "space" in the head that got bigger as the child got older. There is no support for this idea, and it has been abandoned. Capacity is a function of *efficiency*—how automatic, effortless, and skilled one is at the task (Pribram and McGuinness 1975; Pribram and McGuinness 1992). Memory is tied to experience and processing skill, and no memory task is ever pure.

The remaining causes of the age effects, those that received the most attention from researchers, were speed of *item identification* (the time it takes to begin to say a word, or "discrete naming speed") and *articulation rate* (time to say the whole word). These studies are also important for reading, because a major theory links reading skill to naming speed and fluency (see chapter 15). A series of studies by Case and others (Case and Kurland 1980; Case, Kurland, and Goldberg 1982) showed that when memory span was matched across different age groups, this equalized item-identification speed. Memory span was consistently correlated to identification speed at around $r = -.35$. When age was controlled statistically, the correlation between memory span and item-identification speed remained unchanged. Case and colleagues concluded that speed of item identification was a critical factor in performance on a memory-span task. They also found that word familiarity played a strong role.

The facility to mentally rehearse items in memory, including subvocal production time (*articulation rate*), was explored by Baddeley and Hitch (1974) and Baddeley, Thomson, and Buchanan (1975), whose research on reading and working memory is in the final section of this chapter. Baddeley and his group proposed that there was an "articulatory loop" linked to working memory, acting as an "output buffer." This idea connects to reading via the phonological-development theory. It is assumed that items are phonologically repeated or rehearsed, and that the capacity of the loop is limited by the time it takes to say the words. This is, in essence, a time-based "limited-capacity" system.

Dempster (1981) felt that Baddeley's results were problematic in two ways: first, because they can't always be replicated, and second, because they don't *prove* that a limited-capacity output buffer exists or is even necessary. For instance, the item-identification theory would fit Baddeley's data just as well. Support for the theory is problematic, too, because it was based on correlations between articulation speed, memory span, and reading speed in college students. Reading speed is confounded by decoding skill (item identification).

However, the articulation-rate hypothesis has received support in developmental studies by Hulme et al. (1984). They found a strong and consistent (linear) relationship across the age range between memory span and articulation speed, and this held for any word length ($r = .72$ for single-syllable words, and $r = .67$ for three-syllable words).

Both Case and Baddeley's theories were put to the test in a series of experiments by Henry and Millar (1991). Five- and 7-year-olds were matched for identification rate (discrete naming speed), or the time to say a whole word (duration time), or articulation rate (the time to repeat the same word three times). The words on the tests varied in familiarity (high, medium, low). The rationale for the study was that when children of different ages are either matched for item-identification speed, *or* speaking duration, *or* articulation rate, and then tested for recall on the same words, if either of the theories described above is correct, age differences in memory span should diminish or disappear. However, when children were matched on any one of these measures, significant differences in memory span between the two age groups did not go away. This means memory span isn't a simple function of speed in recognizing and reporting the words. Henry and Millar also reported that age differences were smaller for high-frequency words (familiar words) than for low-frequency words.

When memory span was correlated to measures of speed, they got values similar to those of Case and Baddeley. This shows that a correlation between memory span and identification speed or articulation rate does not provide evidence of *cause* of developmental changes in memory span. Much more is going on to produce the age differences. As Henry and Millar (1991, 477) put it, "The fact that age differences in span were found despite successful matching, and despite the fact that high correlations between articulation rate and memory span were demonstrated, is strong evidence that the two hypothesized factors are not, in fact, direct causal factors." Furthermore, word familiarity plays a strong role in naming speed: "Older children may be at an advantage because of their greater familiarity with words in other respects apart from articulation speed. This suggests that a role for longer term or semantic memory needs to be included in models of span development with age" (p. 481).

This work is important, because it complements the evidence presented earlier in the book showing that prior knowledge (vocabulary, word familiarity, age of acquisition) has a profound effect on speech recognition and on a variety of processing skills. Thus, it is not surprising that these factors strongly affect memory span and working memory.

The overall message for reading research is that to demonstrate any connection between memory and reading, age must be tightly controlled. Otherwise any variables influenced by age (speed of recognition or "item identification," articulation rate, word familiarity, and so forth) would have to be controlled instead.

IQ

One of the issues in studying the connection between memory and reading is whether the memory task is measuring memory, IQ, or both, and if both, then what precisely is specific to reading? This is a nontrivial problem because many subtests in an IQ battery engage memory systems of one type or another. The memory-loaded tests are highly correlated to full-scale IQ and to each other. Digit span correlates to full-scale IQ ($r = .43$), mainly through its connection to verbal IQ ($r = .42$) (Cooper 1995). It is a pure test of *verbal* short-term memory. Items are presented orally and the child responds orally in the correct sequence.

All subtests in the verbal-IQ scale make large memory demands. I list the main tests from the verbal-IQ subscale once more to illustrate this:

Vocabulary. The children are read a list of words by the examiner and must define each word orally to the examiner.
Information. The children are asked questions about general knowledge and must respond orally to the examiner.
Similarities. The children are asked questions about ways two objects or two concepts are alike and must respond orally to the examiner.
Comprehension. The children are told about a series of different situations in which they must decide what should be done, or provide an explanation or rationale. Many of these situations deal with moral or social issues, rules, and transgressions. The children do this orally to the examiner.

Another WISC subtest highly linked to reading skill has received virtually no attention from reading researchers. This is the *coding* subtest, which taps working memory, paired-associate learning (matching symbols), plus speed (Sattler 1992). On this task, the children see a list of symbols and must consult a chart of symbol pairs, find the correct match, and write the matching symbol beside each symbol in the list. The test has a time limit, and the children are encouraged to work quickly.

Coding is a not a strong measure of general intelligence like the digit-span test. It correlates weakly to full-scale IQ ($r = .33$), and even less well to verbal IQ ($r = .26$). It is one of the few tests in the battery to tap skills directly relevant to learning a writing system that is fairly independent of verbal IQ. Interestingly, sex differences in favor of girls (whose verbal skills are also stronger) are particularly notable on this test (Kaufman 1979; O'Donnell, Granier, and Dersh 1991).

Children with reading difficulties show a consistent pattern of performance on the WISC subtests. The easiest tasks for these children (ranks 1, 2, 3) are the nonverbal tasks: object assembly, picture completion, picture arrangement. The hardest tasks are coding, arithmetic, and information (ranks 8, 9, and 10) (Kaufman, Harrison, and Ittenback 1990). Digit span (an optional test in the IQ battery) ranks with arithmetic. None of the easy tests make much of a demand, if any, on memory, whereas all the difficult tests do.

Jorm (1983) has pointed to further confounding due to the problematic good- versus poor-reader research design. Poor readers are at a disadvantage on these particular subtests: "If such children are matched for overall IQ to a group of normal readers, they will necessarily have to perform better on the other subtests to gain the same IQ. In short, the problem is that the IQ test used for matching subjects may measure, in part, certain memory abilities which are to be investigated experimentally" (p. 313).

Sex Differences

In Maccoby and Jacklin's (1974) review of the research on sex differences in cognitive ability, three findings were consistently supported by the data: female superiority in verbal memory, and male superiority in visuospatial ability (three-dimensional imagery) and in higher mathematics. These conclusions have been confirmed in subsequent reviews of the literature (McGuinness and Pribram 1978; McGuinness 1985). The female superiority in verbal memory is remarkable in that it appears at all ages.

In an effort to pin down the nature and consistency of these differences, a series of five studies was carried out on 380 children in two age groups: 8 to 9 years and 16 to 18 years (McGuinness, Olson, and Chaplin 1990). Memory span was tested in two modes of presentation, using several types of tasks, and multiple-trial recall:

1. Children saw pictures or printed words representing the same common objects.
2. Children did an intentional- or incidental-learning task.
3. The incidental task was either meaningful or meaningless.
4. All children had to recall the same items several times (multiple-recall trials).[1]

The following results were consistent for both sexes: younger children found pictures easier to remember than words. A meaningful incidental task ("Look at each word/picture and write B or G if it reminds you more of a boy or a girl") produced higher recall scores (nearly twice as high) as a meaningless task ("Count the 'r's and 't's in these words"). The meaningful incidental task also produced significantly higher recall scores than intentional recall, where children are instructed to remember ahead of time. Finally, memory improved significantly over repeated recall trials.

Sex differences were ubiquitous. Girls had significantly higher memory scores in twenty out of twenty-six paired comparisons (by a conservative test). Boys were superior in none. The younger girls did better than the boys in both the picture and the word conditions. Adolescent girls were superior in all word conditions, but no sex differences were found on tasks using pictures. Memory scores improved more for girls over repeated recall trials. Adolescent girls remembered, on average, two more items than boys on the first recall trial, and three to five more items on the last recall trial, regardless of whether the input was verbal or visual.

---

1. This was a four-way $2 \times 2 \times 3 \times 3$ mixed design (sex × stimuli × task × recall trials) with random groups on three factors and repeated measures on recall trials. Data for the two age groups were analyzed independently.

The younger girls remembered one and a half to two more items across the board. In several conditions, boys did not show any memory enhancement over time. This was most noticeable in the intentional-learning task, the most common type of task in memory research. In every case, the studies in the following sections involve intentional-memory tasks.

McGuinness et al. interpreted the girls' memory advantage as due to more efficient memory consolidation over time. But this explanation leaves something to be desired. It would predict that girls had larger vocabularies than boys, yet this is one of the few verbal abilities where sex differences do not appear. Perhaps girls' superior verbal memory has an impact on efficiency in mastering new verbal tasks. Because the younger girls had better recall of both words and pictures, this would give them a speed advantage in mastering a writing system. I am unaware of any research that tests this hypothesis directly, although it is the case that more boys are at risk for language and reading problems (see chapters 7 and 8, as well as D. McGuinness, C. McGuinness, and Donohue 1995).

The evidence shows that unless age, verbal IQ, and sex are controlled in studies on memory and reading, the results will be uninterpretable, especially in cases where researchers use the isolated-groups design (true of most studies covered in this chapter). Not only is this design invalid for statistical purposes, but the poor reader group is more likely to consist of boys and to have lower verbal IQs.

Research on Verbal Memory and Reading

There are four areas where research has sufficient depth to warrant a review of the findings:

1. Short-term memory (digit span, letter span)
2. Paired-associate learning (similar to the coding subtest of the WISC)
3. Memory for acoustically confusing letters and words (thought to reflect phonological discrimination)
4. Nonword repetition tasks (thought to measure phonological processing in working memory)

The first two areas involve tasks refined over years in both memory and IQ research. The tasks in the remaining two areas are problematic, first, because the form of the task changes from one study to the next, and second, because the interpretation of what the tasks are measuring changes as well.

Verbal Short-Term Memory

Traditionally, short-term memory is measured by a verbal task. The subject hears or sees a list of items, then recalls them orally or in writing. Verbal short-term memory has been found to be consistently correlated to reading test scores. However, short-term memory is also correlated to vocabulary, and vocabulary is controlled for this reason. As we will see, it matters which type of vocabulary test is used. Another consideration is that the test content must be equivalent across the age span. Not all young children (below age 7) are equally familiar with the names of letters and digits, despite what most people believe (see chapter 15). For this reason, I won't consider research on children younger than 7 unless the children's knowledge has been verified.

In a study comparing good and poor readers age $7\frac{1}{2}$ to $8\frac{1}{2}$ years, Vogel (1975) found that with receptive vocabulary (PPVT) controlled, and reading groups individually matched for sex and age, poor readers scored lower on the WISC digit-span test than good readers did (5.5 versus 7.7 digits on average), a very large difference indeed. Poor readers also had lower word-span scores on the Detroit Test of Learning Aptitude (36.7 versus 42.2). Bowey, Cain, and Ryan (1992) replicated this result on fourth graders. Poor readers were compared to two control groups who were either age matched or reading matched (younger, normal readers). Sex ratios are unknown. With PPVT vocabulary controlled, digit span for the normal readers was 6.7. The poor readers and the younger good readers had digit-span scores of 5.2. This suggests that poor readers have developmental delays in short-term memory. However, this finding does not hold up in studies where reading scores are normally distributed.

In a study on second graders of all ability groups, Hansen and Bowey (1994) measured digit span, word span, and reading using a much narrower age range (7 to 8 years old), and an equal representation of boys and girls. They found that digit span and word span were correlated to PPVT vocabulary ($r = .39$) and to the TOLD test of expressive syntax ($r = .50$), but that neither memory-span task was correlated to reading. First-order correlations were close to zero.

A 2-year longitudinal study in Australia (Rohl and Pratt 1996) produced different results. Although the children were tested in early first grade, only the results from the end of first grade and 1 year later are reliable. I report here on a multiple regression analysis looking at the contribution of short-term memory (letter-span forward and backward) at the end of first grade, and reading test scores at the end of second grade. With age and receptive vocabulary (PPVT) controlled, letter-span forward accounted for 7 percent additional variance in decoding, 9 percent in reading accuracy, 7 percent in comprehension, and 10 percent in spelling on the Neale reading test battery. Letter-span backward contributed additional variance: 7 percent decoding, 9 percent accuracy, 5 percent comprehension, and 9 percent spelling.

Ackerman and Dykman (1993) tested 119 children (age range $7\frac{1}{2}$ to 12 years). They used the WISC digit-span test as a model to develop nineteen different memory-span tasks. These included auditory and visual presentations of digits, letters, and words. Age and full-scale IQ were statistically subtracted (covaried) from each memory test separately prior to comparing reader status. Due to the wide age range, age accounted for most of the variance, and IQ gobbled up the rest. With age and IQ controlled, and children with different reading skills compared, there was no difference between them on eighteen of the nineteen memory tests. These results may be due to the wide age range, or it may simply reflect the fact that digit span is an IQ subtest, and that the variance due to digit span was subtracted when full-scale IQ was controlled.

Finally, a study by Bowers, Steffy, and Tate (1988) (not to be confused with Bowey) illustrates the same effect. Canadian children ($8\frac{1}{2}$ to $10\frac{1}{2}$ years) were given a battery of tests, including the WISC digit span and the Detroit sentence-memory test. Digit span was correlated to the WISC verbal IQ (.34), and to the Woodcock-Johnson reading tests at .52 (word ID) and .45 (word attack). Similar values were found for the sentence-memory test.

Bowers, Steffy, and Tate carried out a series of stepwise regressions on the reading tests. Age was entered at step 1. Performance IQ was entered at step 2, and accounted for *no* additional variance in reading. When either digit span or sentence memory was entered next at step 3; it accounted for 16 percent of the variance on the word ID and word attack tests. By contrast, when verbal IQ was entered at step 2, it accounted for

27 percent of the variance in word ID and 18 percent in word attack, and neither digit span nor sentence memory contributed further.

These studies show that verbal IQ tests (expressive vocabulary plus verbal memory) engage short-term memory skills to such an extent that verbal IQ accounted for all the variance on reading tests. On the other hand, receptive vocabulary (PPVT) did not. Which of these tests really has something to do with reading? *These are very different tests.* Memory-span tasks, like digit span, measure verbatim recall in the short term (the immediate now). This test has no cognitive load, and requires only knowledge of ten number names. On the other hand, the WISC verbal IQ subtests make heavy demands on long-term memory and have a high cognitive load (reasoning, prior knowledge), while a receptive vocabulary test like the PPVT does not. The skill necessary for performance on verbal IQ subtests and digit span, not shared by the PPVT, is *recall memory.* Overall, the evidence from this group of studies suggests that recall memory plays a much more important role in reading and spelling than recognition memory does.

Much more research is needed on this topic, with larger samples of children. We need to compare the individual subtests from a verbal IQ test battery to the PPVT and to reading test scores to sort this out. So far, all we know is that when age, sex, and verbal IQ are controlled, there is no contribution of verbal short-term memory to reading. When verbal IQ is not controlled, and/or receptive vocabulary alone is controlled, short-term memory is found to be strongly correlated to reading.

Paired-Associate Learning

One task that might be expected to have a relationship to decoding accuracy and speed is the paired-associate learning task. This test is similar to the coding subtest in the WISC IQ battery. Paired-associate memory involves intermediate to long-term memory skill, because it is measured by the number of trials it takes to memorize associations between arbitrary pairs. These can be random words (*pie-read*), word plus symbol (*pie*-#), or a phoneme and its spelling (/b/–<u>B</u>). In the coding subtest of the WISC, each item on a list has to be matched to its respective pair by consulting a chart, and then recording it on an answer sheet. Speed is a critical part of the score. The coding test measures memorization on the fly as the test proceeds, because the items repeat randomly down the list. Paired-associate memory for codes like a number system or writing system involves long-term memory. Mastery of these codes ensures automaticity—instant recognition without conscious reflection.

The WISC coding test is one of the highest correlates of reading accuracy (decoding) in the IQ battery, and one might imagine that the relationship between reading and paired-associate learning has been studied for decades. This is not the case, and I was only able to locate three studies over a 40-year period that had merit and were methodologically sound.

Paired-associate memory as a function of reader status was first investigated by Otto (1961). Children in three age groups (grades 2, 4, and 6) were divided into three reading groups: good, average, poor. There were 108 children in the study, and IQ was restricted to the range 95–110. Sex was not controlled. The task was to memorize nonsense names of five geometric shapes. There were three learning conditions:

1. *Auditory + visual* 1. A picture of a shape appeared in a viewing frame, and its name was spoken by the examiner.
2. *Auditory + visual* 2. The same as condition 1, plus an external picture of the shape was shown as well.
3. *Auditory + visual + kinesthetic.* The same as 2, plus the children were asked to trace the shape with their finger.

The score was the number of trials to get 100 percent correct. In all cases, learning rate was a function of grade (age) and reader status. Older children and better readers learned faster. For example, it took grade 2 *good* readers slightly less time (10.6 trials) to master the tasks than grade 6 *poor* readers (11.3 trials), whereas the grade 6 *good* readers needed only 7 trials. The fact that IQ was so limited in range suggests that the difference between reader groups may have little to do with IQ. As noted earlier, paired-associate learning (coding speed) is not highly correlated to full-scale or verbal IQ in any case.

The impact of the type of training depended on the age of the child. The basic training (auditory + visual 1) was least effective for everyone. For the youngest children, adding some extra visual support didn't help much, but training was rapidly speeded up when they got tactile/kinesthetic feedback by tracing the pattern. The fourth- and sixth-grade children did equally well with either extra visual support or added tactile support. The moral of the story is this: to enhance paired-associate learning, (such as memorizing sound-letter relationships) use multimodal training and involve the tactile and kinesthetic senses, especially for younger children.

When children were retested 24 hours later and asked to recall the names of the geometric shapes, the rate of forgetting was not a function of grade or reader group. Everyone scored at around 60 percent of their original score. This means differences between the age groups and reader groups are in the *acquisition phase*, not in long-term memory storage or retrieval. The implications for reading instruction are obvious: engage the tactile and kinesthetic senses (*write* letters) to speed up learning. Ensure complete mastery of all forty phoneme-symbol pairs for *every* child before moving on. Reading programs that incorporate these features are, in fact, highly successful, and it has been proven repeatedly that writing letters (as opposed to seeing them, using letter tiles, or typing on a computer keyboard) is by far the best way to learn them. (Research demonstrating the power of these training techniques is reviewed in *Early Reading Instruction*.)

The 1970s saw a flurry of studies on "cross-modal" learning. This involves two sensory modalities (auditory-visual) in contrast to a single modality (visual-visual). Vellutino et al. (1975) studied good and poor readers learning either visual-auditory pairs or visual-visual pairs. The children were in the fourth through sixth grades, with sixty children in each condition. The auditory-visual task was similar to Otto's, but more complex. Geometric shapes were paired with nonsense syllables and combined into two-syllable nonsense words. For example, geometric shapes representing *heg* and *pid* were combined to form the word *hegpid*. Children were trained to memorize five pairs of these compound nonsense words. They were then tested on a transfer task where the geometric shapes were recombined to form new nonsense words (*pidheg*). The children had ten trials to learn to "read" the new words. The training regime was the same for the visual-visual condition, except the pairs consisted of matching two geometric shapes.

Good and poor readers did not differ on the visual-visual matching tasks (geometric shapes alone) either in the training phase or the transfer phase, and this type of task was much easier for everyone. In the visual-auditory task, with verbal IQ controlled, poor readers scored 30 percent lower overall. Their problem was limited to the initial training phase. Poor readers learned fewer pairs in the allotted trials, but once they had mastered them, it was just as easy for them to transfer this knowledge to new combinations as it was for the good readers. This confirms Otto's finding that the poor reader's problems are in the initial learning phase, not to problems in long-term memory or with memory retrieval. Vellutino et al.'s study also showed that poor readers don't lack the cognitive flexibility to be able to "decode" the new symbol-syllable combinations. Vellutino et al. believed the initial learning problem was phonological—with poor readers being less sensitive to the phonetic sequences in the nonsense words—and not due to any memory difficulties. However, the problem is just as likely to be due to poor instruction and a lack of practice mapping sounds to letter symbols.

The last study to be considered here (Mayringer and Wimmer 2000) was done in Austria with good and poor readers. All Austrian children read accurately, so a poor reader is defined as a "slow reader." (Wimmer's research will be covered in chapter 16.) These super-slow readers were in the bottom 7 percent in the city of Salzburg. They were matched to normally fast readers in age and sex, and given a battery of tests. A paired-associate task was one of the few tasks that discriminated between the two groups. The task was to match names to pictures of children or to drawings of fantasy animals. Slow readers had no problem learning to match *familiar* names to the pictures of children, but had considerable difficulty matching *rare* names or *pseudo*names to the pictures of children and fantasy animals.

Mayringer and Wimmer pointed out that the slow readers didn't have a problem with paired-associate learning per se, because their learning rate was normal with familiar names. Their problem was in committing novel or rare phonological forms to memory, conclusions similar to those reached by Vellutino et al. The critical difference between good and poor readers in both studies appeared at the initial learning stage and not in retrieval from long-term memory. It should be noted, however, that these slow readers had low verbal IQs, and IQ was not controlled.

Despite the fact that paired-associate learning has received so little attention in reading research, these are among the few studies reviewed in this chapter to produce consistent results. The reasons less skilled readers have trouble with these tasks should be explored further, because this type of task underpins decoding accuracy and, it appears, decoding *speed* as well. Training that helps speed up paired-associate learning (the initial foundation for the mastery of a writing system) is of the greatest importance.

Acoustic Confusion and Reading

In 1964, Conrad published his now-famous study on the impact of acoustically confusing letter names on short-term memory. Conrad was not interested in reading, but his task became linked to reading research via Baddeley's theory on the "phonological loop" and working memory reviewed earlier, as well as in a series of studies in the phonological-development framework of I. Y. Liberman and Shankweiler.

Previous research on acoustic confusion showed that if words are masked by noise, or sound too much alike, short-term memory is impaired. Conrad was interested in whether the confusion effect was perceptual (auditory processing) and/or whether it occurred during spontaneous *phonological recoding*, the mental translating of visual symbols into a phonological form (letter names) prior to recalling them.

Conrad compared two large groups of adults on a visual and a verbal version of the same task. One group (300 post-office workers) *heard* a sequence of letter names spoken over a faint background noise and had to write them down (verbal condition). A second group (387 telephone-operator trainees) *saw* rows of consonants flash on a screen and had to write them down (visual condition). Because the input was visual and the response was manual, the task didn't require verbal processing. But it was well known that people spontaneously recoded letters by their names. If phonological-confusion errors occurred in the visual-manual condition, this would be evidence of phonological recoding and rehearsal. And if the error patterns were similar in the two conditions, this would mean the phonological-recoding explanation for the confusion effect was correct.

The subjects saw letter sequences made up of a pool of letters: B C P T V F M N S X (bee, see, pee, tee, vee, and ef, em, en, ess, ex). The first set has different initial consonants and ends in the same vowel (rhyme), and the second set starts with the same vowel and ends in different consonants. As Conrad predicted, no differences in the patterns of errors were found between the performances on the auditory versus visual tasks, providing support for phonological recoding. Confusion errors (mistaking one letter name for another) were organized into a "confusion matrix," a tabulation of the number of times pairs of letter names were confused with each other. The ranks of the confusion errors in the two conditions (auditory versus visual) were strongly correlated (.64).[2]

The nasal letter names M (em) and N (en) were confused most often, ranking number 1 for highest substitution errors. The next most confusable letter names were the affricates F (ef), S (ess), and X (ex), consonants with high-pitched hissing sounds. Letter names ending in the same vowel (rhyming) came next (the B C P T V group). In the rankings for the least confusable letter names, nasals and affricates were less likely to be confused with each other. For example, X (ex) was almost never confused with a nonfricative sound and occupied pride of place in the least-confusing-pairs category.

In this study, acoustic or phonological confusion occurred for two reasons: first, when final consonants share similar acoustic features (nasality, friction), and second, when final vowels are identical (rhyme). And this is true regardless of whether the people hear the words spoken or see them in print, evidence that acoustic confusion occurs during recoding (transforming visual input to language) and holding items in short-term memory prior to writing them down.

From this, Conrad concluded: "One could argue that the more chance there is of acoustic confusion within the stimulus set, the poorer will recall be. It would follow that the memory span would be a function of the acoustic similarity of the members of a set. The span might depend not on the number of alternative items in the set, but on the number of acoustically similar items in the set" (p. 80).

Conrad favored Brown's (1959) explanation that memories decay as a function of the signal-to-noise ratio of the input, *noise* meaning neural background noise. To put this into slightly different language, the more optimal the phonological recoding, the higher the signal relative to the noise, the stronger the memory trace, and the more it endures. It follows that it is easier to hear similar-sounding words as distinct when phonological coding is precise.

---

2. This was a somewhat unusual statistical procedure, in which the pairs of letters become the "subjects" or "objects" in the study, and the people doing the tasks function as "judges" of what letter was seen or heard—similar to interrater reliability estimates.

In the late 1970s, Conrad's study inspired a program of research on good and poor readers carried out by I. Y. Liberman, Shankweiler, and their associates. Conrad's study was also followed up by Byrne and Shea (1979) in Australia. Shankweiler et al. (1979) reported that good and poor readers had different patterns of scores on a memory-span task depending on whether the letter names rhymed or didn't rhyme. Their theory (The Dogma) that the problems of poor readers are mainly due to phonological-processing deficits led them to interpret the data in a way that was compatible to the theory. They found that good readers remembered far more nonrhyming letter names (nonconfusing) than rhyming letter names, and christened this the *confusion effect*. Good readers are "confused," according to the theory, because they are "phonologically aware." This is diametrically opposite Conrad's interpretation of the data. We'll come back to these studies shortly.

Byrne and Shea (1979) had a different view of the evidence on acoustic confusion and reading skill. They argued that young children are biased toward meaning and not toward the structural properties of words, of which they are largely unaware. It is possible that good readers, more clued in to the alphabet principle, are sensitive to both meaning and phonetic structure, while poor readers focus mainly on meaning.

The prediction was that poor readers won't pay much attention to phonetic cues unless the task demands it. This was tested using real words (meaningful) and nonsense words (meaningless). The critical test was whether, in the absence of meaning, poor readers would be forced to rely on phonetic information to remember the nonsense words.

The task was a "running memory-span" test in which some words repeat at random intervals. The list is read aloud, and the children have to decide whether they have heard each word before (i.e., whether it is "old" or "new"), a test of *recognition memory*. Words in the lists of real words could be *unrelated*, *semantically related*, or *acoustically related* (rhyming).

The two reading groups didn't differ in overall error or false-positive rates (saying "old" to new items). But poor readers were more likely to say "old" to new items that were *semantically* related (semantic confusions) and less likely if they were *phonologically* related (three semantic errors versus .7 phonological errors). Errors for good readers' scores were about evenly split (2.1 versus 2.8 errors). This supports Byrne and Shea's hypothesis that if poor readers focused largely on meaning, synonyms would be more confused (*home, house*) than words that sound alike (*home, comb*). The main difference between the groups was that the false-negative rate was much higher for the poor readers—saying "new" to old items (good readers made 5.9 errors and poor readers, 9.5).

Byrne and Shea thought that the poor readers' failure to pay attention to phonological structure may be due to a lack of experience, either because it hadn't been revealed to them during reading instruction, or because they needed more time to learn it.

In a second study, nonsense words were used, one-third of which rhymed (*jome, vome*). The reader groups didn't differ on any measure, and both groups were penalized more by rhyming than by nonrhyming words. In fact, tests of significance within reader groups (which are valid in this case) showed that the discrepancy between rhyming and nonrhyming errors was statistically greater for poor readers ($t = 4.08$, $p < .01$) than for good readers ($t = 2.13$, $p < .05$). If anything, poor readers were more confused than good readers on the rhyming nonsense words, results opposite what Liberman and Shankweiler's theory would predict.

In their conclusions, Byrne and Shea explored several possible explanations, and came out in favor of this one: "It seems more parsimonious to conceptualize the two groups of children as adopting different strategies, the poor readers selecting a meaning-based code for storage and good readers equally at home with deep and surface aspects of the words" (p. 337).

Before moving on to an analysis of Liberman and Shankweiler's research and to more recent studies, I want to recap the three main hypotheses:

Conrad. Poor perception of the acoustic details of the input, and/or poor translation of these details into phonological memory, will create an impoverished representation, and a greater likelihood that words will be more liable to decay rapidly in short-term-memory. Extrapolating to poor readers, if they have phonological problems, memory for acoustically confusing items will be worse for them than for good readers.

Liberman and Shankweiler. Poor readers have poor phonological processing, affecting perception and the translation of phonetic information into memory. This leads to less acoustic confusion because they are unaware of phonetic detail. Less acoustic confusion translates into better memory for acoustically confusing input (letters/word) relative to nonconfusing input. In contrast, good readers will show much greater confusion for acoustically similar input than for nonconfusing input.

Byrne and Shea. Poor readers have poorer perception of the acoustic details of words because they are unaware of them, and because they focus mainly on meaning. On tests using real words, they will be less susceptible to acoustic confusion and more prone to semantic confusion. Good readers, on the other hand, with more skill in mastering a phonetic code, will do equally well on both. When poor readers are forced to focus on phonology, because no other cues (like meaning) are available, they perform very much like good readers. This is an attentional model; it factors what the child *is doing* into the equation. So far, this applies to recognition memory and not to recall. Byrne and Shea's data strongly support this interpretation.

With this background, we return to the study of Liberman and Shankweiler. A number of earlier studies were combined in a paper by Shankweiler et al. (1979), in which the same group of 8-year-olds saw or heard items presented simultaneously or in succession. The children were split into three reader groups: good, marginal, and poor. This is an isolated-groups design with a small sample size, in which age, IQ, and sex were not statistically controlled. This is the first problem.

The second problem is the task. The task had wandered far from Conrad's original version. Letters were drawn from one of two sets. The first set rhymed: B C D G P T V Z (bee, see, dee, gee, pee, tee, vee, zee). The second set did not: H K L Q R S W Y (aitch, kay, ell, cue, are, ess, double-you, why). These sets are in no way comparable. In one set, every item contains two phonemes. In the other set, items consist of one to six phonemes each. To complicate things, the children heard (or saw) eight *sets* of rhyming letters and eight *sets* of nonrhyming letters (five items per set) mixed randomly, and were expected to recall the items in the proper order.

Here is the problem. In each session the children heard a total of sixteen sequences of letter names. When the human brain is fed a barrage of similar-sounding, meaningless input, it goes into a tailspin and is unable to keep track of immediate time. This produces what is known as *proactive interference*, in which items from previous lists pop up during recall of the current list. Because the children had only 15 seconds' relief between each set, proactive interference is likely to be extremely high. Rhyming letters/words cause confusion within one trial, as everyone has shown.

This fact is verified by Shankweiler et al.'s analysis of error rates for each position in the list of rhyming letters. The first two items were recalled fairly well, but the remaining items in the list were not (the children averaged five to seven errors at each position). This pattern was similar for the two weaker reader groups on the nonrhyming names as well, though it was less severe. Good readers showed high accuracy on nonrhyming letter names at all serial positions.

A third point is instructive. These studies have nothing to do with rhyme per se. The final vowel /ee/ is redundant in rhyming letter names. The only way to distinguish and remember them is by the initial consonant, which requires phoneme analysis. The nonrhyming task is easier because no sounds repeat, and because the sounds themselves are more variable. This means there is a confound due to *task difficulty*, a confound that was not present in Conrad's study.

Results will be combined, because they were essentially the same for all three tasks. First, all reader groups did poorly on the lists of rhyming (confusable) letter names, and weaker readers did worse (were more "confused"). Second, all reader groups did better on the lists of nonrhyming letter names. And third, good readers did much better than the other reader groups on nonrhyming names. If statistics were valid here (which they are not), the main result is the superior performance of good readers on nonrhyming words. Of course, differences between the groups could also be a function of age, IQ, or sex, none of which were controlled.

Error scores on nonrhyming and rhyming letter names (a low score is good)

	Nonrhyming names	Rhyming names
Good readers	9.0	21.1
Marginal readers	20.0	25.9
Poor readers	23.3	30.5

The authors pointed out correctly that "it is apparent ... that the superior readers were more adversely affected by item confusability than the other groups" (p. 535). "They also noted that the recall performance of both the mildly backward readers and the severely backward readers was less penalized by phonetic confusability than that of the superior readers" (p. 541). This highlights the relative impact of acoustic similarity on the three groups.

But they interpreted the results like this:

The findings ... support the hypothesis that good and poor readers differ in their use of speech coding, whatever the route of access ... [and] individual variation in coding efficiency places limits on reading acquisition. (p. 541)

We suspect that the difficulties of poor readers are ... of a more general nature [and this] permits us to view the findings as related manifestations of a unitary underlying deficit both within the confines of our experimental task and in the reading process generally. (p. 541)

These conclusions are unwarranted by the data, even if the study had been valid and had no methodological problems.

This work was expanded in a series of studies by Mann, Liberman, and others to look at memory for rhyming and nonrhyming words and sentences. Mann, Liberman, and Shankweiler (1980) studied fifteen good and fifteen poor readers with nonoverlapping reading scores, average age 8 years old. IQ was controlled, but age and sex were not.

The children were asked to listen to meaningful or meaningless (anomalous) sentences containing words that did or did not rhyme. The task was to repeat the sentences verbatim. Scores consisted of errors of omission, substitution, and reversals. The error scores are reported in the accompanying table for the four types of sentence. (Low scores are good.)

Errors in sentence repetition

	Nonrhyming words	Rhyming words
Meaningful		
Good readers	2.2	4.9
Poor readers	5.0	5.6
Meaningless		
Good readers	5.2	6.9
Poor readers	7.5	7.1

Two patterns stand out. Everyone did better on meaningful sentences, especially when the words didn't rhyme. Good readers did better than poor readers when the words didn't rhyme, but not when they did. This effect was greater for meaningful sentences.

In a companion study, the same children were tested 6 weeks later on random lists of the words from the sentences, half rhyming words and half nonrhyming. Error scores are shown in the accompanying table.

Errors in word recall

	Nonrhyming	Rhyming
Good readers	1.4	2.4
Poor readers	2.2	2.3

Good readers got a boost when the words didn't rhyme, much as they did for sentences.

Two longitudinal studies were carried out using the same or similar lists (Liberman and Mann 1981; Mann 1984; Mann and Liberman 1984). The first study involved sixty-two children (equally balanced between the sexes) who began the study at the end of kindergarten. One year later they took the memory tests again along with reading tests, and were divided into good-, average-, and poor-reader groups. Sex ratios were not reported. The results shown in the accompanying table are for kindergartners and first graders as a function of reader status. Scores are errors.

Errors in word recall

	Nonrhyming	Rhyming
Kindergarten scores		
Good readers	8.1	13.4
Average readers	12.8	15.4
Poor readers	13.2	15.0
First-grade scores		
Good readers	5.5	12.1
Average readers	9.2	11.3
Poor readers	13.7	12.7

Here is the same effect again. Good readers did better remembering words that didn't rhyme. This was evident in kindergarten for good readers, and in first grade for good and average readers.

In a second longitudinal study (Mann 1984), forty-four kindergartners were tested at midyear and followed up the next year when they were divided into good, average, and poor readers on the basis of first-grade reading scores. Only nonrhyming word lists were used in this study. The accompanying table shows the kindergarten scores.

Errors in nonrhyming word recall

Good readers ($N = 10$)	5.2
Average readers ($N = 22$)	11.1
Poor readers ($N = 12$)	15.0

Assuming the tests were comparable from one study to the next, once more, good readers were the odd ones out with respect to average and poor readers.

In a preview of this work at a conference on sex differences in reading, Liberman and Mann (1981) reported that the sex composition of these groups was lopsided—with one and a half times more boys among poor readers and twice as many girls among good readers. They tested the boys and girls *within* each reader group, and finding no sex differences, concluded that sex was not a factor in their results. But the issue is the relative proportion of boys and girls *between* reader groups, not within groups. Boys and girls were artificially selected to be in these good and poor groups in the first place, so it's hardly surprising they didn't differ. In light of this revelation, the results in all the studies discussed above are just as likely to be due to sex differences as to reading status.

The straightforward interpretation of Mann and Liberman's research is that good readers (more girls) have better verbal memories, but do as badly as poor readers (more boys) when words are phonetically confusable due to proactive interference and task difficulty. This is not how the results were interpreted. Instead, because their theory requires that good readers be susceptible to acoustic (phonological) confusion and that poor readers not be, the interpretation of the data must reflect the differential performance between the groups on the confusing and nonconfusing tasks. And, because normal children are supposed to be proportionally worse on rhyming words, poor readers are deviant by default. Differential performance rates are a requirement of the theory, even though the two memory tasks (rhyme/nonrhyme) are unrelated to each other. That is, there is no necessary connection between them.

This rationale led to statements like "poor readers [are] markedly impaired by phonetic confusability" when there is no evidence from any study reviewed above that poor readers were more "markedly impaired." Scores for rhyming letter names, words, and sentences were nearly identical for all reader groups in these studies. The Dogma asserts that poor readers have a global phonological deficit, and so they will:

Since the same pattern of interaction with phonetic confusability has been found for three different classes of items-letters, words, and sentences, a common etiology is implicated. We follow Liberman et al. (1977) in suggesting that the poor readers' substandard recall of verbal material may be caused by failure to make effective use of phonetic decoding in working memory. (Mann, Liberman, and Shankweiler 1980, 333)

Future good readers were showing evidence of relying on phonetic representation, as seen in their particular difficulty with repeating strings of phonetically confusable words. The future poor readers, on the other hand, were relatively tolerant of our manipulations of phonetic confusability. (Mann and Liberman 1984, 596)

The data don't support these conclusions, and Hall et al. (1983) didn't believe they did either. They addressed two issues in a series of five studies. First, they pointed out that there is a difference between being a poor reader and being a poor achiever (doing badly in all academic areas), and so far, these studies had not controlled for this. Second, they noted that unless task difficulty is controlled, there is a risk of interpreting differential performance on these two tasks as due to a phonetic-confusion effect, when it is actually a *task-difficulty* effect. This is similar to the point I raised above about proactive interference due to limited phonetic cues in rhyming words.

Hall et al. set out to replicate the early studies and were unable to do so when math achievement scores were in the normal range and cognitive ability was controlled (Woodcock-Johnson Cognitive Scale). The children were followed up the next year, and, again, no differences were found between reader groups for recall of letter names or words.

In another experiment, a new group of children was added who scored well below norms in reading and mathematics and on the cognitive test. This "low-low" group performed more poorly on the memory tasks than the other two groups did. With the four-letter lists, the "low-low" group had a similar profile to the other two groups. With the five-letter lists, they replicated Liberman and Shankweiler's results. However, they didn't believe this proved anything about a differential effect of phonetic confusability: "Interpretation of the critical interaction is clouded by the fact that the low ability group performed much worse than the normal readers on the nonrhyming lists.... A group x list type interaction under such circumstances is meaningless, leaving unresolved the question of a possible deficit in phonetic encoding" (Hall et al. 1983, 523).

To investigate the impact of task difficulty independently of reader groups, they recruited college students (all good readers) to carry out the same type of memory task, this time using lists seven letters long. Half of the students did an interfering task prior to recall, increasing task difficulty, and half did not. This produced a significant interaction between task difficulty and rhyming/nonrhyming memory scores ($p < .001$). (Statistical tests are valid here.) The students who did the easy task exhibited the usual discrepancy in error scores for the two memory tasks, and the students who did the difficult task did not. Hall et al. concluded:

Our findings seem to argue quite strongly against certain possibilities, including the idea the children with deficits specific to reading are fundamentally less able than are normal readers to generate phonetic codes for visually or orally presented items.... Another possibility that seems to be ruled out is that their phonetic codes are fundamentally of a lower quality. If their codes were present but degraded in some way, one might expect that items that were similar phonemically would be often more difficult for them than for children with more distinctive phonetic representations. That is, one might expect a group x list interaction of just the opposite sort from that found by Shankweiler et al. (1979) if low readers' phonetic codes were lower in quality. (p. 526)

This statement is similar to the point I raised earlier with respect to the predictions based on Conrad's interpretation of the confusion effect, versus the interpretation proposed by Shankweiler et al.

Further research followed that strongly supported the rationale provided by Hall et al., even when the study was not originally designed to test this. Olson et al. (1984) tested 141 poor readers, each matched to a control child in age, sex, and SES (but not IQ). The age range was large: 7:8 to 16:8. The children participated in a running memory-span task similar to the one used by Byrne and Shea. The children had to report whether they had seen each word before. When Olson et al. examined false-positive errors (said "old" when the word was new), both reader groups made more rhyme-confusion errors than nonrhyme errors. However, on closer inspection, the phonetic-confusion effect was specific to the younger children.

When Olson et al. plotted scores across age, there was a systematic shift as a function of age, reader status, and whether or not the words rhymed. As poor readers got older, there was sharp decline in error scores for *nonrhyming words*, compared to a relatively static performance on rhyming words. The pattern for normal readers was the opposite—less change for nonrhyming words, and a sharp decline in phonetic-confusion errors. These results, coupled with the children's scores on a nonword reading test (word attack), led the authors to conclude that the shifting relationships between decoding and memory span across the age span complicated any interpretation of the data. Nevertheless, the results support a developmental lag in verbal memory span for poor readers, plus an effect of task difficulty.

A similar finding was reported by Johnston (1982) on 100 Scottish children. Poor readers were selected from three age groups (9, 12, and 14 years), and matched for either chronological age or reading age. The children had to remember lists of letters that did or did not rhyme. Recall was either immediate or delayed. Age, IQ, and sex were not controlled. This is a problem, because the poor readers had lower PPVT vocabulary scores.

The poor readers did worse overall than the chronologically age matched children, which was expected. But they performed remarkably like their reading-level matched controls in all respects, suggesting that task difficulty, not impaired phonological awareness, is the crucial factor in these memory-span tests. There were no differences between any age groups or between good versus poor readers in the *degree* of a "phonetic-confusion effect," which was consistently present in all cases. Johnson noted that these results did not support the theories of either Shankweiler et al. (1979) or Baddeley, Thomson, and Buchanan (1975), who stated that poor readers' memory difficulties stemmed from inadequate (phonological) rehearsal in an articulatory loop.

In a direct attack on the task-difficulty issue, Holligan and Johnston (1988) tested various groups of good and poor readers, average age $8\frac{1}{2}$ years old. Again, age, sex, and IQ were not controlled. By manipulating the length of the items in lists of letters and words that did or did not rhyme (four experiments), they found that when the task difficulty was too high, the poor readers' performance slipped noticeably on the *non-rhyming* items, causing performance to match that on rhyming words. When the task was easy, poor readers scored similarly to normal readers, doing equally well on nonconfusable words. The identical effect of task difficulty was seen for good readers.

Finally, Brady, Mann, and Schmidt (1987) examined the types of substitution errors that good and poor readers made in nonsense-word memory tasks. Poor readers made the same types of phonetic errors that good readers did; they just made more of them. PPVT vocabulary and age were covaried separately and did not alter these results. There was no evidence that poor readers had a qualitatively different way of listening to words.

Again, I must caution the reader that the majority of these studies are problematic. The isolated-groups design, plus small sample sizes, amplify spurious effects, especially when sex, age, and verbal IQ/vocabulary are not controlled. A review of subsequent research on this topic reveals that the situation has not improved, and I won't burden the reader further with this type of study. Taken as a whole, the studies represent a tempest in a teapot. Thousands of hours have been wasted to *disprove* a flawed theory based on faulty research. So far we have learned that good and poor readers are equally "confused" by phonological similarity, and that poor readers have smaller memory spans for nonconfusable items that they tend to grow out of. But having said this, even apart from the isolated-groups design, most of this research is confounded by task difficulty, sex, and IQ, and may be meaningless.

Two large-scale correlational studies call into question the notion that phonetic confusion has anything to do with reading, or at least they put an entirely new face on a worn-out topic. In their monumental study of 543 normal children followed from kindergarten through first grade, Share et al. (1984) found no support for a selective phonetic-confusability effect. In a subsample of good and poor readers at first grade, Jorm et al. (1986)

reported that memory for rhyming sentences was worse than memory for nonrhyming sentences for everyone, and that there was no difference between poor and good readers. In a follow-on study at second grade, the children's performance on rhyming sentences was greatly improved relative to their performance on nonrhyming sentences.

In a multiple regression analysis using all the children, the following tests accounted for 59 percent of the variance in reading scores at age 6: phoneme segmenting (39 percent), letter copying (8 percent), sex (5 percent), letter-name knowledge (4 percent), and memory for rhyming sentences (3 percent). Nothing else contributed significantly after this.

D. McGuinness, C. McGuinness, and Donohue (1995) reported similar findings for ninety-five first graders followed over one school year. All the children did better on a memory-span task of nonrhyming words than on rhyming words. When the data were analyzed separately for boys and girls, memory for *rhyming words* was a significant predictor for girls' reading skill, accounting for 10 percent of the variance in word ID and 11 percent of the variance in word attack, after the variance for age, PPVT vocabulary, and phoneme awareness (LAC test) had been accounted for. Memory for nonrhyming words was not as highly correlated to reading.

Neither memory task accounted for any of the variance in boys' reading test scores, and simple correlations between memory for rhyming words and reading tests were near zero. Instead, a visual (nonverbal) version of a digit-span task (the Probe test) was a much stronger predictor of reading for boys, and with age, vocabulary, and phoneme awareness controlled, the Probe test accounted for 8.6 percent additional variance in word attack. The Probe test was also highly correlated to word ID for the boys (not for girls).

A female superiority in verbal memory was noted earlier, and it appeared here also. Girls had higher scores on the standard memory task (nonrhyming words, $p < .01$) and did marginally better on the rhyming-word task ($p < .07$). The two memory tests were perfectly correlated for boys (.89) but not for girls (.69), suggesting that boys and girls approach these tasks differently. Girls also had significantly higher reading scores on the Woodcock Reading Mastery subtests: word identification and word attack.

These large-scale studies show that memory for *rhyming* words is a better predictor of reading skill than memory for nonrhyming words.

Nothing in Shankweiler et al.'s results, or in their theory, would have predicted this. That this is mainly true for girls adds to the puzzle. It suggests that girls are doing something quite different when they try to remember lists of rhyming words. Because these words can be distinguished only by their initial consonant(s), perhaps it's the ability to maintain these phonetic distinctions in short-term memory and focus attention on them that gives girls their advantage.

Overall, the results from the studies on acoustic or phonological confusion and reading show that good and poor readers alike suffer the same confusion effect. On the other hand, good readers have better verbal memory for nonconfusable items, and this is most noticeable on tasks that are not too difficult. Memory span is affected by age and sex and is also linked to verbal IQ. There was only one study (D. McGuinness, C. McGuinness, and Donohue 1995) where all three variables were controlled, and where an invalid research design did not preclude statistical tests. In this study, there was a significant correlation between reading skills and memory span for acoustically confusing words *for girls* but not for boys. This effect was independent of age and vocabulary, suggesting that girls have a strong verbal bias. The fact that boys' reading skill (and not girls') was correlated to *visual* memory span may also reflect a bias, with boys relying more on visual memory when learning to read.

Nonword Repetition: A Test for All Reasons

Several years ago, I designed a nonword or "nonsense-word" repetition test as a screening tool for phoneme-processing difficulties. My hunch was that this task would reflect speech-perception accuracy. I believed this would be a more natural test of phoneme sensitivity for younger children than the abstract phoneme-awareness tasks they routinely failed. The test was designed to be faithful to the phonotactically legal syllables in English. Words ranged in length from CVC words to complex multisyllable words up to five syllables long. The first step was to establish rudimentary age norms for children 3 years and up to see if the test scores were normally distributed for each age group.

A tally of 200 children was disappointing. It signaled two major roadblocks. First, the younger children's performance was extremely idiosyncratic. Some 3-year-olds were terrific on the test, but some couldn't do it at all. Nor did this necessarily depend on whether they were *old* 3-year-

Table 13.1

Percentage of children scoring correctly at five levels on a nonword repetition test

Age	Range of Scores				
	Below 25%	25–49%	50–74%	75–89%	90–100%
3	27%	27%	36%	9%	0%
4	0	29	51	15	5
5	0	0	38	50	12
6	0	3	17	45	35
7	0	0	16	37	47

Source: McGuinness, D. 1997. *Why Our Children Can't Read.* NY: Free Press.

olds or *young* 3-year-olds. Four-year-olds were nearly as variable. Large individual differences on a test designed to be age sensitive is bad news, because it means the test scores will be nonnormally distributed, standard deviations will be huge, and the test will be useless.

The second roadblock was that the test became too easy too quickly and topped out at age 7 when half of the children scored 90 percent correct or higher. This meant test items would either have to be expanded to words of six or seven syllables, or the test restricted to a narrow age range of 4:6 to 7:0. And for test norms to be valid, data would need to be collected for each age *in months* (not years, as is the rule for most standardized tests). There was no possibility of undertaking something on this scale, and the project was abandoned.

Not much could be done with the 200 scores, except to illustrate some developmental trends. These could only be seen by coarse blocking of the data, then tallying the proportion of children in each age group who fell into each block. This solution, shown in table 13.1, provides a picture of global developmental effects and the impression of the nonnormal distribution of test scores.

This firsthand experience with designing a diagnostic test was very enlightening. It showed how carefully a test like this needs to constructed, and how important it is to establish reliable norms before using the test in research. Another problem came to light during an item analysis. This revealed that what was complex in terms of syllable length was not necessarily the most difficult word to hear and repeat. It showed that I hadn't pinned down word structure sufficiently to know what was easy or hard for a child to hear.

The studies reported in this section are rather like this pilot study minus the attempt to establish norms, minus any item analysis, plus the assumption that the data could be analyzed as if the scores were normally distributed across the age range, plus the assumption that the test measured—not speech perception—but verbal working memory, plus the assumption that verbal working memory causes vocabulary. In the end, the issues all boil down to the validity of the nonword repetition test in predicting anything important about reading or about language.

A Nonword Repetition Test Is Born

There is nothing more disruptive of progress in the behavioral sciences than a test that consistently produces the same effects (is highly replicable) for all the wrong reasons. We have seen many tests like this, such as Tallal's repetition test and Liberman and Shankweiler's "rhyme-confusion" test. The nonword repetition test is another such test. Performance on this test correlates with a variety of different language skills and with reading, and the temptation has been to favor the particular language-reading relationship that fits the hypothesis. Every time the test produces the same effect, the belief in the hypothesis is strengthened, and the test begins to take on a life of its own.

Over time, the test itself becomes the object of investigation, and a flurry of studies appear to find out exactly what the test is measuring, if anything. We have just reached this point with the nonword repetition test. Could this have been avoided? Of course it could have. McCauley and Swisher pointed out all sorts of ways (see chapter 11).

In general, I would not bother to report this research, except for the fact that nonword repetition is used so often in reading research. The most frequently used test was designed by Gathercole and Baddeley (1989) in the United Kingdom. This test correlates highly to reading test scores. It was used by D. V. M. Bishop, S. J. Bishop, et al. (1999) in their study on hereditary factors in language (see chapter 8). They found that language-impaired children scored significantly lower on this test than children with normal language did. However, it did *not* predict scores on language tests when age, sex, and IQ were controlled. The big question is, what does this test measure? As Bishop and her colleagues observed, it was far from pure: "Poor performance could reflect difficulties in phonological segmentation, rapid decay in short-term memory, or problems in formulating an articulatory program. In addition, there could be top-down influences, whereby weak vocabulary knowledge or poor ability to use prosodic information leads children to encode incoming material in a suboptimal fashion" (D. V. M. Bishop, S. J. Bishop, et al. 1999, 166).

Thus, Bishop et al. identified five different subskills that might be tapped by this test, and I identified another: sensitivity to phonotactically legal syllable structure.

Gathercole and Baddeley (1989) had a different conception of the problem. According to Baddeley's theory of working memory described earlier, nonword repetition involves working memory and an "articulatory loop." The loop makes it possible to "keep items in mind," as verbal input is reviewed (refreshed) or actively rehearsed. As Gathercole and Baddeley remark in the introduction to the study, "The present study is part of a program of research investigating the function of the articulatory loop component of working memory in complex verbal skills." Two sentences later the wording changed, and they described the "importance of the phonological loop component of working memory in the acquisition of vocabulary" (p. 200).

At the outset the reader is confused about which operations in working memory—articulatory (motor), or phonological (perceptual)—they are referring to, and whether "vocabulary" and "complex verbal skills" mean the same thing. Later they used the expression "complex verbal skill" to refer to learning to read.

Baddeley's theory of vocabulary acquisition is controversial. Bishop, who is a leading expert on language acquisition, conceives of receptive vocabulary as logically prior to the ability to repeat a nonsense word, because the child's vocabulary will determine how well the nonsense word is perceived. This position has considerable support. Predictable syllable sequences, the child's age at acquisition of a word, and word frequency in the language strongly influence infants' and children's speech perception (see chapter 3). And there is direct support for this conclusion, as we will see shortly.

Gathercole and Baddeley conceived of "phonological working memory" (i.e., nonword repetition) as logically prior to vocabulary. It is extremely doubtful that correlational research can sort this out, but the 1989 study was a first attempt. This was a longitudinal study on 150 children ranging in age from 4:0 to 5:2. Children took a battery of tests, including the nonword repetition test, the British version of the PPVT, and the Raven's matrices nonverbal IQ test. They were followed up 1 year later and given the same tests again, plus a standardized reading test: the British Ability Scales (BAS). It is worth mentioning that children are taught to read at age 5 in the United Kingdom.

The nonword repetition test was not provided in this or subsequent papers of this period. Means and standard deviations were nowhere to be found. There was no mention of norms, or of prior work to establish the reliability of this test. There was no demonstration of how the scores were distributed by age. Means were reported for each of the standardized tests listed above, but standard deviations were not.

Most of the data analysis was in the form of correlations and multiple regressions, but it was highly selective (no table of first-order correlations appeared). However, Gathercole and Baddeley's data did show that the nonword repetition test was correlated to the PPVT vocabulary test at $r = .53$. Multiple regression analyses were carried out on vocabulary in the short term and at a 1-year delay. Age plus nonverbal IQ accounted for 18 percent of the variance on the PPVT at age 4, but for only 3 percent at age 5. Nonword repetition scores, entered next, accounted for an additional 13 percent of the variance on the PPVT at age 4 and for 21 percent at age 5. No other test contributed further. These unstable values are suspicious.[3]

They also looked at what predicted PPVT vocabulary scores 1 year later. Age and Raven's nonverbal IQ accounted for 10 percent of the variance in vocabulary. Vocabulary measured at age 4 accounted for another 30 percent, and the nonword repetition test for an additional 8 percent. The next step should have been to reverse this analysis to see if *vocabulary* would predict nonword repetition test scores above and beyond age 4

---

3. Correlational values were extremely unstable in this and other studies by this group. Particularly worrisome was the fact that test-retest correlations based on test scores at age 4 and 5, on the *same* standardized test, were much lower than is normally found. The test-retest correlation on the Raven's IQ was .43 (18.5 percent agreement). For the PPVT, it was .60 (36 percent agreement). This may be due to using age-equivalent scores instead of standard scores, or to poor test administration, or both.

nonword repetition scores. This would be the appropriate test of their theory. Instead, they skipped this important control, and concluded that "this indicates that phonological short-term memory (nonword repetition) continues to be important for further vocabulary acquisition during a child's first year at school" (p. 211). This *causal* argument assumes that age 4 phonological memory (nonword repetition) is a pure measure once age, IQ, and vocabulary are controlled. But various factors may contribute to performance on this test, as noted above. More importantly, it is equally likely that vocabulary will *cause* individuals to perform differently on a nonword repetition test, should the authors care to test this.

Only one measure correlated to the BAS reading test, and this was Raven's nonverbal IQ ($r = .56$). Since they did not report the correlation between the BAS and nonword repetition, one assumes it did not correlate to reading. Because nonword repetition correlates to reading in everyone's else's data, it may be that children weren't reading well enough (floor effects) to make this analysis valid.

Gathercole and Baddeley (1990, 439) carried out another study to "explore the possibility of a causal relationship between phonological memory and vocabulary acquisition." Phonological memory was measured by the nonword repetition test, and vocabulary acquisition by a paired-associate learning task, in which the children memorized the names of Monsters (as shown in pictures). 5- and 6-year-olds were divided into two extreme groups based on their scores on the nonword repetition test. This selection procedure (isolated groups) is invalid, and more so here, because the two groups differed in a number of other ways. For example, the average PPVT scores were 2 years apart. It is highly likely that the good "nonword repetitors" were better at memorizing the Monsters' names because of their superior vocabulary and larger digit span, than because of their performance on the nonword repetition test.

A multiple regression analysis was carried out to see what contributed to the paired-associate learning scores. All statistics are off limits with this research design, but these results provide an illuminating case of just how confusing invalid statistics can be, as well as the power of a theory to take precedence over the data. In the regression analysis, Raven's IQ and reading scores were entered first. PPVT vocabulary scores were entered next and accounted for no additional variance in the speed to memorize the Monsters' names. If this finding was real, it would mean that *vocabulary skills have nothing to do with vocabulary acquisition.* Yet Gathercole and Baddeley's theory states that phonological memory (nonword repetition) causes vocabulary, in which case why didn't vocabulary matter when

- Groups were selected with high or low scores on the nonword repetition test.
- The skills measured by the nonword repetition test are supposed to "cause" vocabulary.

In a different analysis of the same data, the two groups were compared for learning speed. With vocabulary controlled (covaried out of the data), no difference in learning speed between the groups was found. This means that vocabulary alone accounted for all of the variance in the two groups' ability to learn a paired-associate memory task.

Now we have a glaring contradiction in the data. On the one hand, vocabulary didn't matter at all (zero variance). On the other hand, it explained everything. To get around this problem, Gathercole and Baddeley explained away the results that contradicted their theory, and then ignored them. "These results ... seem entirely predictable on the basis of the shared links of vocabulary scores, reading scores, and non-name learning speed with non-word repetition skills, and in our view, do not present a serious challenge to the hypothesis that non-word repetition abilities play a role in learning unfamiliar phonological forms" (p. 449). This is a blatant example of a case where the data are subordinate to the theory.

Of course, these results are meaningless (spurious) due to the research design and other factors, but the authors didn't know this and continued to misrepresent what the statistics showed:

Although the two groups also differed on vocabulary and reading scores, neither of these two measures were [sic] significantly associated with learning speed after the variance associated with non-verbal intelligence had been taken into account. These findings suggest that non-word repetition ability, rather than either vocabulary or reading knowledge, are [sic] the basis for the different rates of learning in the two groups. (p. 450)

These results provide *experimental* support for the previous correlational evidence that non-word repetition skills contribute to vocabulary acquisition in unselected young children, ... and may play a critical role in the poor vocabulary development of language disordered children. The present *experimental demonstration* of a direct link between repetition abilities and the speed of learning names for novel objects lends considerable further weight to a *strong causal interpretation* of the relationship between repetition and vocabulary knowledge. (pp. 450–451; emphasis mine)

Training two nonrandomly selected groups on the same task is not "an experiment." These statements speak for themselves.

Gathercole, Willis, and Baddeley (1991, 387) referred to these earlier studies as providing "considerable evidence linking children's non-word repetition abilities with their vocabulary development." (And so myths are born.) In this study, children $4\frac{1}{2}$ and $5\frac{1}{2}$ were tested on the nonword repetition test, a digit-span test, the sound-categorization test, Raven's nonverbal IQ, and the PPVT. The goal was to find out the contributions made by nonword repetition and phonological awareness to reading skill.

Reading was measured by the British Abilities Scales (BAS), the France Primary Reading test, and an in-house word-recognition test. The France test involves matching a picture to one of four printed words. Chance is 25 percent correct, which is precisely how the 4-year-olds scored (four out of sixteen correct). Despite this, and the flood of zeros on the other reading tests, statistics were carried out nonetheless. This means that all data analyses using reading scores are invalid in this study. It's worth mentioning that the strongest correlation between nonword repetition and any test was to digit span (short-term memory) for both age groups ($r = .52, .67$), *and not to vocabulary* (.41, .42).

These invalid data were reanalyzed four different ways (with four statistical tests), producing highly unstable results that didn't tally with each other or with previous findings. In summarizing the results of an invalid factor analysis (too few subjects, nonexistent research design, reading scores of zero), Gathercole, Willis, and Baddeley concluded, once again, that an aptitude for nonword repetition (i.e., "phonological working memory") *causes* vocabulary: "In simple terms, if a child has difficulty in retaining the sound of a new word for a few seconds, it seems likely that the child will experience difficulty in retrieving that sound sequence from long-term memory at a later date" (p. 403).

They elaborated further on the ways phonological working memory would affect reading, first as a memory device for learning letter-sound correspondences, then in mediating the long-term retention of new words, and finally in providing a "buffer-storage" system for the sound segments that would be generated via an alphabetic strategy (i.e., while decoding). This is pure speculation.

There is an astonishing disconnect in these reports between the conflicting results from obviously unreliable data, and the authors' conclusions based on them. These results have shown essentially nothing, and so far, we have no idea what the nonword repetition test actually measures.

What Does a Nonword Repetition Test Measure?
In 1995, Gathercole began to look at this issue for the first time. By now, the test had changed and was published in a separate report (Gathercole et al. 1994). It was supplied in an appendix to the 1995 paper, and consisted of ten words each of two, three, four, and five syllables.

The study was intended to find out whether the "wordlikeness" of the nonwords affected performance, and if this had any relationship to vocabulary. This answers one of Bishop's concerns. Adults rated the nonwords by how much each one was "like a real word" on a scale of 1–5. Words were then divided into high and low wordlike words.

Seventy children were tested at age 4 to age 5. Once again, test-retest correlations on highly respected standardized tests were suspiciously low. The PPVT correlated to itself at a mere $r = .38$, evidence of inconsistent test administration. Children took a reading test developed by Bryant et al. (1989) for 4- and 5-year-olds. Whether there were norms or standard scores for this test is unknown. The most consistent finding was that performance on the low wordlike words was significantly correlated to reading test scores. Wordlikeness is a function of phonotactics and vocabulary. When nonwords aren't wordlike, children must rely more on phonetic analysis, as Byrne and Shea (1979) have shown. This might explain the connection to reading.

The correlational data were inconclusive. For 4-year-old children, vocabulary was highly correlated to performance on the low wordlike words ($r = .54$), but not the high wordlike words. For 5-year-olds, both correlations were low and nonsignificant. Why vocabulary no longer correlated to the nonword repetition test is unknown.

These studies have totally failed to support the "phonological work-ing memory causes vocabulary" theory. In the 1995 study (the only study that appears methodologically sound), the two weren't even correlated. Furthermore, because vocabulary is built on an edifice of phonotactically legal words, one would expect that vocabulary would be most strongly (not most weakly) related to the ability to repeat phonotactically probable words (*high wordlike* words).

Dissenting Voices
During this period, other scientists began to investigate the precise nature of the nonword task. It turns out that syllable stress and phonotactic structure have a considerable impact on how well this task is performed. Hulme, Maughan, and Brown (1991) found that memory is strongly af-fected by the phonotactic structure of nonsense words. In this study, two groups of students were compared in memory span and in speech rate while they repeated nonwords that obeyed the phonotactic structure of either Italian or English. The subjects were native English speakers and none spoke Italian. The familiar English phonotactic structure signifi-cantly enhanced both memory span and speech rate. Only the scores on the "Italian" nonwords improved with practice.

Vitevitch et al. (1997) found that ratings on wordlikeness of nonsense words (rating scale of 1–10) were strongly affected by the position of syl-lable stress and by phonotactics. This was an extremely well controlled study in which the nonwords were recorded by a trained phonetician; words were low-pass filtered and subsequently rated for stress patterns by computer. When a second group of subjects was tested on their reaction time to different types of nonwords, reaction time was significantly faster to the nonwords that had the dominant stress pattern and were phonotac-tically legal. Faster processing time reduces memory load. These results illustrate the strong impact of bottom-up or *perceptual-motor* aspects of word recognition combined with top-down influences as well.

The most elegant and well-executed study on this topic was carried out by Dollaghan, Biber, and Campbell (1995). They challenged the hy-pothesis of Gathercole and Baddley in a careful test of the impact of vocabulary on nonword repetition accuracy, pointing out that the non-word repetition test was invalid, because it contained too many real-word fragments. They criticized Gathercole, Willis, and Baddeley (1991) for reporting that only seventeen of their forty nonwords contained a real-word morpheme, when they found that thirty-nine of them did. They felt this considerably weakened Gathercole and Baddeley's argument that nonword repetition accuracy is a measure of phonological memory and is unaffected by vocabulary.

Dollaghan and her colleagues designed a new test to avoid these problems. There were three- and four-syllable nonwords in which primary stress was equally distributed on the initial, second, and third syllables and the number of consonant clusters was controlled. Half of the words contained a real-word morpheme and half did not. For example, the word *fathesis* contains no real-word morphemes, in contrast to *bathesis*.

Previously, the presentation of the nonwords had not been well controlled, and scoring was simply right or wrong. In this study, the procedure was very different. First, words were recorded by a trained female speaker. Next, two trained listeners transcribed the words from the audio recording to make sure they heard the same thing. Agreement was 90 percent. The children (thirty boys in the age range 9–12 years) listened to the tape and repeated the words. Each child's responses were recorded and these recordings were transcribed by a phonetician. A scoring system was worked out to determine which minor mispronunciations would or would not be allowed. The child's response was coded phoneme by phoneme. The score was the number of phonemes correct divided by the number incorrect, and this was tallied over the whole list. There was a reliability check to ensure interrater agreement on the transcription and the scoring. Reliabilities were 87 percent and 89 percent for the two measures.

This is a refreshing example of superb methodology.

The basic findings were that most errors occurred on the unstressed syllables, and were more likely when the entire nonword contained no "real" syllable. Syllable-level errors were extremely rare, and syllable structure was almost always preserved intact (correct number and sequence of consonants and vowels). The source of the errors was misperceived/mispronounced phonemes, with 11 percent of phonemes mispronounced. This is clear evidence of a phonetic component in this task.

A study by Van Bon et al. (1997) supports this conclusion. Dutch good and poor readers were matched on a test of decoding accuracy.

Poor readers did worse on a nonword repetition test, but when scores on a phoneme-detection task were covaried out of the data, the group differences on the nonword task disappeared.

Dollaghan and her colleagues evaluated the impact of vocabulary, or "top-down processing," by classifying 300 errors into four types, scoring each syllable in the nonwords. The most frequent type of error was changing a nonword syllable into a real word syllable (51 percent). Next most frequent was changing a nonword syllable into a different nonword syllable (26 percent). Next came changing a real word syllable for another real word syllable (14 percent). The least common was changing a real word syllable into a nonword syllable (9 percent). The authors noted that this breakdown is highly suggestive of a vocabulary effect, yet this analysis didn't fully pin down the cause of the errors, which could also be due to perception or articulation.

The majority of the errors were consonant errors. Vowel-phoneme errors were studied to rule out the effects of perception and articulation. Vowels are less perceptually confusable and much easier to reproduce. Eighty-four percent of vowel errors were found in the category *nonword to real-word* syllable transformations, with only 2 percent in the opposite category (real to nonword). This is strong evidence of a top-down effect whereby a person's vocabulary affects the way the word is perceived, causing it to be "regularized" toward the closest-sounding real word.

In view of the complexities involved in designing and executing this study, Dollaghan and her colleagues concluded that

contrary to what has been previously thought, nonword repetition tasks are not straightforward to construct, nor to interpret. Basic issues, such as controlling loudness ... and scoring subjects' productions precisely, have rarely been addressed. ...

These data raise a number of questions about the nature of nonword repetition tasks and their use in efforts to assess phonological working memory as a distinct area of psycholinguistic skill. (p. 220)

One might add that they also raise a number of questions about the value of using nonword repetition tasks in reading research.

Whither Nonword Repetition?

The evidence shows that a nonword repetition test is one of the least pure tests available. It correlates to verbal memory, vocabulary, and phonetic analysis, as well as to reading. We will see that it correlates highly to syntax, too (next chapter). Approximately 10 percent of the variance on the test is due to nonverbal IQ. (Verbal IQ was never controlled in any of these studies.) Furthermore, the nonword repetition test has a limited usefulness across the age span, being too difficult at age 3 and 4 and too easy by age 7 or 8. Dollaghan, Biber, and Campbell showed that proper test construction, administration, and scoring are far too complex for this test to be practical in reading research.

Because the nonword repetition test correlates to all major language functions, it's no wonder that it was a marker for a genetic contribution to language in Bishop et al.'s study. This test seems to be the ultimate test embodying Bishop and Edmundson's hypothesis that language is all of a piece, "connected under the skin." A nonword repetition test appears to be one of the best measures of this complete "joining," provided it is properly constructed, administered, and scored. However, it is a *bad test* for the scientific study of specific language functions and whether they have an impact on reading for just this reason.

Summary

One of the central findings in this chapter is that verbal IQ, age, and sex are such dominant contributors to performance on memory tasks that it will never be possible to sort out a specific memory-reading connection unless all these factors are controlled in the same study.

Taken as a whole, research support is most convincing that paired-associate learning is tied to one critically important reading skill: the ability to commit letter-sound correspondences to memory. This has been shown to affect both reading accuracy and reading speed. It is somewhat ironic that this important memory skill has received so little attention from researchers, and that tasks with an indirect or spurious connection to reading have received so much.

By and large, the evidence from the studies of acoustic confusion show that good and poor readers alike are equally "confused" by acoustically similar input. These studies also show that good readers do much better than poor readers on these short-term memory tasks only if verbal

IQ, age, and sex are *not* controlled. The same conclusion can be drawn from the studies on nonword repetition.

In the following chapter, I turn to the connection between reading skill and syntax, a primary language function. Syntax tests are also memory tasks, but of an unusual form. These studies have shown a consistent relationship between performance on syntax tests and reading accuracy, reading fluency, and reading comprehension. One interesting question here is, what type of memory is involved in performance on a syntax test?

SYNTAX AND READING

Syntax is the last general language skill to receive attention from reading researchers. Up to this point, syntax has been described superficially as the grammar domain of general language. This will be remedied here, because we need to understand what aspects of syntax might influence the process of learning to read.

What Is Syntax?

The short answer to this question is that syntax is the structural organization of words in a clause or sentence of a particular language. In English, *syntax* refers specifically to word order in a sentence, and its close cousin *morphology*, to elements within words. A *morpheme* is the smallest unit of sound that represents meaning. It can be a whole word (*strict*, *I*), a prefix or suffix (*de-*, *-ing*), a plural (/s/ /es/), and so forth. English word-order grammar has the following structure: agent-action-object (or subject-verb-object (SVO)). Modern English retains some of its Old English case grammar in the form of inflected verbs (*talk*, *talked*, *talking*) and word fragments (affixes) that represent parts of speech (*happy*, *happily*, *happier*, *happiest*, *unhappy*).

The short answer tells us nothing about how children learn a grammar or even what it is for. Noam Chomsky, the famous linguist, sought to reduce the problem of language acquisition to a set of fundamentals (Chomsky 1965). He began by observing that children would never learn the grammatical structure of a language by hearing the same sentences over and over. No frequency model or statistical model, by itself, could work, for the simple reason that children can understand and produce sentences they have never heard before.

Chomsky's great insight was to reduce the complexity to a basic structure that could be applied to all languages, a *universal grammar*. He coined the term *phrase structure grammar* to describe this. There are two main types of phrases, a noun phrase and a verb phrase, plus additional features or clues. The agent/action/object structure reduces in Chomsky's notation to NP-VP-NP, where a verb phrase = V + NP.

In English, an NP is usually signaled by a marker called an *article*: *a* or *the*. An NP can also be signaled by a descriptor or *adjective*. Adjectives follow articles and precede nouns. These cues are redundant and mutually reinforcing. The first phrase in a sentence is usually a noun phrase and most commonly the subject of the sentence: "*Boats* come adrift from their moorings in these storms." The first phrase plus an article signals a noun and probably the subject of the sentence: "*The boat* came adrift from its mooring." The first phrase plus an article plus a descriptor signals a noun and probably the subject of the sentence: "*The yellow boat* came adrift from its mooring."

Verb phrases typically follow an NP. Most verbs are inflected. Verb descriptors take the suffix *-ly*, and adverbs usually follow verbs: "The car spun wildly." But this isn't always the case: "The leaves swirled and gently floated to the earth." The patterns of order within order provide multiple redundant cues that signal an NP or a VP.

Systematic structural patterns like these, where certain kinds of words occupy slots in a frame and can swap in and out, are known as *recursive combinatorial systems*. For Chomsky, the grammatical nature (not specific structure) of languages is a biological imperative, and the human brain has special "modules" that make fathoming this structure not only possible but inevitable. The debate still rages on this issue. Chomsky viewed language development as a process of acquiring "rules." He knew that young children could never learn rules in the dictionary meaning of the term. But he didn't specify what the child form of these rules might be. Instead, he dodged the issue and put the rule-creating system in the brain, calling it a *language acquisition device*, or LAD for short. He then developed a detailed set of logic rules that took up most of an entire book, rules he believed were instantiated in some form in the brain itself. (For a complete and far more detailed explication of Chomsky's ideas, see Pinker 1994.)

My goal is to get to the root of what children have to be able to do linguistically to master syntax. Children do appear to acquire something rulelike, but this may be deceiving. The rule may simply reflect the internalization of recurrent patterns. For example, 2-year-olds stumble onto something like a rule or pattern for past-tense verbs, called the "add -*ed* rule"—which isn't really that simple, because -*ed* is a convention of our spelling system and not a reality of spoken English. A regular past-tense verb is signaled in one of three ways, and /ed/ is the least common of the three, as in *rioted, turn'd, walk't.* To complicate matters, the most common (Old English) verbs have irregular past-tense forms: *is was, are were, go went, drink drank, run ran, stand stood, think thought.* Pinker (1995) has proposed three main solutions for how young children solve the past-tense problem: (1) hearing the /ed/ /t/ /d/ patterns in parents' speech, and understanding that this is a kind of signal for referencing events in the past; (2) making analogies from irregular-verb families (*blow/blew, grow/grew*); and (3) memorizing other irregular verbs.

We still aren't close to solving the real problem: How does a child know what a noun or a verb is? Obviously, 2-year-olds don't know the words *noun* and *verb*, and no one could possibly explain this. There is another difficulty, because English words are chameleons and often do double or triple duty as nouns *and* verbs *and* adjectives: "He *cut* the branch and got a *cut* on his hand." "She *opened* the window and stared out the *open* window." Yet children learn which words go where in a sentence.

There are other clues besides word order. Words fall into two major grammatical categories. *Open-class words* (nouns, verbs, and adjectives) control sentence structure and are unlimited in number. *Closed-class words* or "function words" are limited in number and act as markers or guides to the structure of a sentence. The role of articles is to signal nouns. Prepositions mark special relationships between persons, objects, and locations. Conjunctions are connectors that link actors or objects, and specify relationships between clauses in the sentence. Open- and closed-class words occupy certain slots in sentences and set up a frame for interpreting the interrelationships between actors, actions, and objects.

I want to propose a simple learning process on the basis of the research and what we know about how mothers guide speech attempts. This process depends on three basic cognitive abilities: vocabulary, categorization, and sequential verbal (phonological) memory. The primary skill in understanding and producing sentences is vocabulary, in the sense of both referential and categorical meaning. A child may never know what a noun, verb, or adjective is, but she will certainly know *words* for persons, animals, places, and things, and *words* for actions and inactions (whether past, present, or future), and *words* for appearances and qualities (colors, size, shape, noisy, quiet).

Infants begin to be aware of perceptual categories (animals, cars, furniture) by age 3–4 months (Quinn and Eimas 1998). By 18 months of age, children know 150 to 200 words (receptive vocabulary), can say 50 to 100 words, and have begun to spontaneously sort objects into like kinds during play (all the marbles here, all the blocks there). Vocabulary builds in tandem with categorizing. As categorizing skill improves, the categories themselves become more detailed: all the green marbles; all the big blocks; all the big, green marbles; all the little, yellow ones. Words are categorized by what they refer to and describe. The "thing" (noun) contains its attribute. "Green" is a property of the marbles; marble is not a property of green. "Big" is a property of the blocks. Verbs are what these persons, animals, or objects do. Places don't "do" anything; they are somewhere you are or somewhere you go. Understanding these distinctions is simply knowing more about reference, like kind, and difference.

To produce a sentence, the child has to order these different kinds of words. At one level she implicitly knows the order, having heard an endless number of correctly produced sentences by the time she gets to the two-word stage. In English, the word for what you are going to talk about usually comes first. And unless it's a proper noun or a pronoun, it usually has an article in front of it. The most important rule of conversations, however, is not a syntactic rule, but the rule that *you must communicate something*. And while mothers rarely correct grammar, they enforce this rule a lot. A 2-year-old won't get by with the sentence "The dog." Mom is going to ask "What dog?" or "What about the dog?"

Some English verbs don't take an object. If Jimmy says "Dog sleeping," this doesn't warrant much comment: "That's nice."

But if Jimmy says "Dog got," he is not going to get away with it. Mom will ask for more information: "What did the dog get?" "Did the dog take your ball?"

Similarly, the child's utterance "Got shoe" will elicit questions like "Whose shoe?" "Where did he take it?" (depending on whether Mom needs to leap into action and rescue the shoe and maybe the dog as well).

These exchanges force Jimmy through the sentence and make him specify what kind of information (not which part of speech) is needed and in what order. The child's first job is to understand the rather simple difference between things and actions. As the child gets good at this (more efficient), more "brain space" becomes available to contemplate extra details: "The dog got daddy's shoe." "The dog got daddy's shoe and ran down the street."

Research carried out by Golinkoff and Hirsch-Pasek (1999) showed that children in the age range 13–20 months process every word in a sentence, understand the agent-action-object relationship, and pay attention to function words. Infants 13–15 months old will direct their gaze correctly to one of two TV monitors—one with a woman kissing some keys and dangling a ball, the other with the same woman kissing a ball, and dangling the key—when asked: "Where is the lady kissing the keys?" By 16–18 months, infants understand who is the object of an action ("Big Bird is tickling Cookie Monster") and will look most often at a video that matches the sentence.

At around 18–20 months of age, children show they rely on function words to help them understand a sentence. In one study, four groups were tested for their responses to sentences with or without the article *the*. The children's job was to find the right picture in a row of pictures. They heard either the full sentence, the sentence with *the* missing, the sentence with *the* replaced by another short English word, or the sentence with *the* replaced by a short nonword. In every case all the information needed to find the correct picture was available (the word *the* is redundant in English). The percent correct is shown in brackets:

Find the dog for me. (86%)

Find dog for me. (75%)

Find was dog for me. (56%)

Find gub dog for me. (36%)

These studies show that toddlers are a lot more verbally precocious than we give them credit for. They also raise the question of which set of verbal skills young children might bring to bear in performing a syntax test. There are various types of syntax tests. In the TOLD sentence-imitation task, the child hears a sentence and has to repeat it verbatim. The sentences are always correct and increase in length and grammatical complexity. In other tests using the same format, the sentences may contain errors. The child is asked if the sentence is right or wrong, and told to repeat it and correct the mistake (Chaney's Syntax A and B). In another version, the child is told ahead of time that every sentence is wrong, and that she must repeat it exactly the same way. Then she is asked to say it the right way. In a *cloze task*, sentences have a missing word the child is expected to supply. Finally, there are receptive-syntax tasks where the child has to point to a picture, or act out a sequence using dolls.

Children need specific kinds of memory skills to do these tasks, as well as a good vocabulary—the more familiar the words, the easier a sentence is to hear and remember. They need sequential memory skills of a special type. Memory for word order isn't enough, though it helps. We don't process sentences on the basis of surface structure (linear word strings), but on the basis of meaning. Syntax is not about simple word order: "The-dog-got-my-blue-ball-and-is-running-down-the-street." Syntactic memory involves parsing the sentence for meaningful units—in other words, knowing how words group together in a phrase structure: "The dog—got—my blue ball—and—is running—down the street." Grouping words into meaningful phrases reduces the memory load. The more the phrase structure of a language has been internalized through listening and practice, the easier it is to remember a novel sentence.

Statistical probabilities—frequency of occurrence—come into play as well, especially with prepositional phrases. This is one reason prepositions are among the hardest words to use correctly in early language acquisition or when learning a foreign language. Is it "We went at the park" or "We went to the park"? Is it "We went on the park" or "We went in the park"?

The above considerations lead us to expect that syntax will be most highly correlated to vocabulary and to verbal memory for several types of utterances: syntactic (phrase) structure, inflectional morphology, and statistical regularities in speech. In short, repeating a sentence verbatim is not a straightforward task, and utilizing syntax does not involve a simple, one-dimensional skill. Nevertheless, memory for natural language is fairly autonomous, and there is no sense of effort in listening to and interpreting speech unless the vocabulary or the syntactic structure is ambiguous or contrived.

A Classic Study on Syntax and Reading

In 1975, Vogel published a small book outlining her research on syntax and reading. As her review of the literature shows, this was a first step in trying to work out the connection between natural language development and reading skill. She viewed syntax and morphology as rule-based systems: "Syntax refers to that body of rules which governs the way words are arranged into sentences.... These rules are based on the most consistent and regular features of the English language which children have internalized as a set of rules gradually approximating adult rules" (p. 5).

Prior to this study, most of the research on syntax and reading had focused on children's errors in reading prose. For example, it was found that children use their knowledge of syntax to guess words in context, that errors in decoding text were largely syntactically correct, and that prose passages written in natural language with simple syntax were easier to read than those written in unnatural language with complex syntactic structures. (Much of this work was related to the whole language movement.)

Almost no research existed on what interests us here: Does variation in natural language development affect reading skill? There was a study by Brittain (1970) showing that a child's mastery of inflectional morphology (plurals, past tense, present participle) was significantly correlated to a composite reading score (word recognition, word attack, comprehension) at age 6 ($r = .36$) and at age 7 ($r = .70$). IQ was controlled, so this was not a factor. These values were identical for boys and girls.

Another important early study was reported by Weinstein and Rabinovitch (1971). The task was to repeat back sentences. Half the sentences used nonsense words for the root words but left English function words and affixes in place. In the other half, the word order was scrambled. Both types of sentence were meaningless, but one set had a strong syntactic structure and the other had none. Good and poor readers at fourth grade were compared on the number of trials they needed to repeat eight sentences of each type correctly. Both reader groups did badly on the scrambled sentences (eighteen and twenty trials), but good readers were far more successful when function words and affixes were in place (ten trials versus seventeen). This was not an IQ effect, because IQ was controlled.

Vogel's study was intended to explore a variety of syntax tests to discover why poor readers might have trouble. Twenty dyslexic boys were selected from twelve elementary schools. They scored at least 1 standard deviation below norms on a standardized test of reading comprehension and on tests for speed and accuracy (Gates-MacGinitie). Each dyslexic boy was matched to a boy with a normal reading score, in age, school, and race. The two groups did not differ significantly in SES or in receptive vocabulary (PPVT). Vogel's choice of research design was a minor tragedy, because her work is otherwise methodologically superior to much of the subsequent research on this topic. (Vogel's data were used for the illustration of the isolated-groups design in chapter 9 (figure 9.1).)

The children were given a battery of tests. These included a test of prosody (melodic inflection), ten tests of syntax and morphology, the PPVT vocabulary test, memory-span tests for words and digits, plus several reading tests (Gates-MacGinitie, Gates-McKillop, and the Wide Range Achievement Test (WRAT)).[1]

As would be expected, in view of the nonoverlapping reading scores, everything was "statistically significant" with the exception of the PPVT scores on which the groups had been matched. Vogel carried out a covariance analysis to examine the connection between memory (WISC digit span, Detroit word span) and syntax. This covariance analysis will be invalid, of course, but as a general observation, *memory span* was a critical factor on about half the syntax tests, particularly those that required verbatim recall (sentence repetition).

---

1. Several of the syntax tests were designed by Vogel. All were provided in an appendix. Descriptive statistics for every test included means, standard deviations, ranges, and reliability coefficients most appropriate for the test (Hoyt's *r*, gamma, Pearson's r, and split-half reliabilities). Means and ranges were solid (almost no floor and ceiling effects) and standard deviations were uniformly low. Reliability coefficients were high. These measures signify carefully designed tests and excellent test administration. These data will be robust and reliable.

Vogel provided us with excellent tools for studying syntax, and in 1977, when the TOLD was published, there was one more. If the world of science was a logical place, future studies on syntax and reading would have built directly on Vogel's efforts. Instead, her work was ignored for a decade. It was briefly resurrected by Bowey in 1986a and more fully in 1994a. But by this time, interest in the connection between natural language and reading skills had taken a backseat to the nature and significance of "metalinguistic awareness," which has muddied the waters.

The Trouble with Metalinguistic Awareness
Metalinguistic awareness was discussed in connection with Chaney's research on language skills in 3-year-olds (chapter 5), but I didn't touch on how it might influence learning to read. In the late 1970s, some researchers (Ehri 1979; Ryan 1980) argued that metalinguistic awareness is critical to decoding accuracy and speed, which in turn will enhance reading comprehension. According to this view, the metalinguistically aware child can consciously anticipate words in a sentence and self-correct decoding errors.

These ideas were given more in-depth treatment by the Australian psychologists Tunmer and Bowey (1984). In subsequent papers by Tunmer and his colleagues, metalinguistic awareness was described as consisting of four domains: phonological, word, syntactic, and pragmatic. Tunmer, Herriman, and Nesdale (1988) cited three "causal" theories of metalinguistic awareness. In one (Marshall and Morton 1978), it develops concurrently with language acquisition as the children monitor auditory feedback from their own speech attempts. In another, it is a product of formal schooling and is largely determined by learning to read (Valtin 1984). In the third theory, proposed by Tunmer and Herriman (1984), metalinguistic awareness is part of a general cognitive aptitude developing in middle childhood, due to a major shift in information-processing capacity. The idea is similar to Piaget's notion of "decentering," which is supposed to emerge during cognitive development in the stage of "concrete operations." The third theory is reminiscent of the claim made by Dolch (Dolch 1948; Dolch and Bloomster 1937), and by Schonell in the 1940s, that children don't have sufficient intellectual maturity to master the alphabet code until age 7.

If the third theory (or even the second) was correct, then what could be said about Chaney's 3-year-olds? Perhaps what they were doing (analyzing the structural properties of speech) was not really metalinguistic. But it is hard to see what else it might be. Chaney's data support the conclusion that metalinguistic awareness develops in tandem with total language experience (not merely from auditory feedback from speech attempts). When a behavior is highly practiced (automatic), it is easier to reflect consciously on that behavior (LaBerge and Samuels 1974; Pribram and McGuinness 1975).

Chaney's discoveries take us far afield from worrying about which of several theories of metalinguistic awareness is right, to a panorama of "metas" that develop concurrently with particular natural or trained behaviors, each reflecting the degree of automaticity of that behavior. These are sliding-scale metas that can't be put in a box. This is not to say that there might not also be global cognitive shifts common to all behaviors that reflect an increase in analytic skill or logical reasoning. It was the shift in logical reasoning during childhood that so intrigued Piaget, and that he was trying hard to pin down. However, the fact that Piaget's model collapsed due to simple changes in the instructions for his tasks is a warning that the concept of metalinguistic awareness may be more problematic than fruitful.

Bowey (1994a) set out a series of constraints that she believed were critical to the assumption that syntax plays a role in reading acquisition or subsequent reading skill. She insisted, however, that the syntax-reading connection must be metalinguistic. Syntax tests must measure "syntactic *awareness*," and be uncontaminated by general (natural) language development. As she noted, if the syntax problem requires a higher linguistic level than has been attained by the child, it is more likely to reflect a general language delay than a metalinguistic problem. This may be true, but pinning down the absolute difference between general and "meta" may be an impossible dream, especially if one derives from the other.

Bowey also pointed out that if syntax tests have too high a semantic or memory load, the results of the study will tell the researcher more about semantics or memory than about syntax. However, it might not be possible to disentangle syntax, semantics, and memory, and Bowey seems to be placing an unnecessary straightjacket on research. Constructing meaning from spoken or written language is a basic function of syntactic analysis. Semantics and syntax can be tightly coupled in a single word, one that can disambiguate the meaning of the entire sentence: "The woman *heard* that she was being evicted." "The woman *heard* in the doctor's office was complaining."

In Chaney's mispronounciation tasks, or in Bowey's error-correction tasks (see below), the errors make the sentences ambiguous or even meaningless, which draws attention to where the error is located. Chaney's data showed that putting scrambled words back into the right word order (Syntax A) was most highly correlated to (1) word meaning (telling real and nonsense words apart), (2) morphology, (3) word segmenting, and (4) phoneme synthesis, in that order. It is unlikely that syntax exists independently of meaning (vocabulary) and sequential verbal memory.

Rather than lay such a heavy burden on task construction, it may be simpler to control for vocabulary and verbal memory after the fact, by subtracting these effects statistically. This is assuming that it is even possible (or reasonable) to strip down syntax to an essence devoid of meaning and memory.

The research on syntax and reading is mixed. Bowey's research is broadly correlational with no isolated groups, and is well controlled and well designed. Other research suffers from the usual methodological problems. None of the studies meet all of McNemar's criteria (chapter 11), and many fail criterion 5 about in-house tests. However, the number of studies on this topic so limited that most of them will be covered here.

Syntax Predicts Reading

There are two opposing positions on the syntax-reading connection—one, that syntax is a significant predictor of reading skill, and two, that syntax has nothing to do with reading. One might wonder how two such extreme positions could be maintained in the face of 15 years of research. This has happened for two reasons. The first has to do with experimenter bias, in which what the experimenters want to prove ends up being what they prove. The other answer is poor methodology, which leads to conflicting results from one study to the next. We begin in Australia with the research supporting the first position.

Australia

In a series of studies, Tunmer and his colleagues explored the relationship between syntactic awareness, age, and reading skill. This work was doomed from the outset by problems with in-house tasks that were not sorted out prior to running the studies. Tunmer's research fails most of McNemar's criteria for valid research, as well as the criteria for in-house tests. The first report (Pratt, Tunmer, and Bowey 1984) sets the pattern for this work. This was essentially a pilot study on whether syntactic-awareness tasks could be performed by 5- and 6-year-olds. Two syntax tasks were developed. Children heard sentences spoken by a puppet with language problems. They were told that the puppet always made mistakes and that their job was to fix the mistakes. In the first task, the puppet made morphological errors (errors within a word). In the second task, the puppet got the word order scrambled, and the children had to put the words back in the right order (for example, "Rode Susan bike the").

In the scoring of the word-order task, children were given considerable leeway, even to using different words. There was no report on interexaminer reliabilities to ensure that scoring was consistent. The results showed that the morphology task was too easy (both age groups performing nearly perfectly). Six-year-olds did significantly better than 5-year-olds on the word-order task. Five-year-olds scored 50 percent correct.

Recall that Chaney's 3-year-olds also did extremely well at fixing morpheme errors, while they failed a similar word-order task (Syntax B). Did Chaney's 3-year-olds and Pratt, Tunmer, and Bowey's 5-year-olds have problems with this task because of developmental differences in syntax, because of developmental differences in metalinguistic awareness, because unscrambling word order is such an unnatural thing to do, or because of the particular task employed or the way it was presented?

After this study, Tunmer and Bowey went in different directions. In Tunmer's research, the persistent use of the isolated-groups design, the use of an unpublished (unnormed? unstandardized?) reading test, problems with task construction, absence of standard deviations and reliability checks on in-house tasks, persistent ceiling and floor effects, and failure to control for guessing created too many problems for this work to be discussed further.

Bowey took extreme care to design or employ reliable tests and to use the appropriate research designs. But even this excellent work was marred by a problem with data transformation, a problem noted by McCauley and Swisher (1984). Raw scores were not transformed into standard scores when they easily could have been. Good data (chronological age) were transformed into bad data (grade level) for no apparent reason.

One of Bowey's goals was to determine whether metalinguistic tasks predicted reading skill in their own right or masked general language ability. This is an intriguing question and very difficult to resolve. In 1986, she developed a new syntax task (Bowey 1986b) to explore this issue. Bowey reported on pilot work to develop this test, and this effort undoubtedly contributed to the fact that the test discriminated well, was effective over a wide age range with a reasonable difficulty level, and produced low standard deviations. The test consisted of thirty ungrammatical statements each containing one wrong word ("Where does this goes?") using simple, familiar vocabulary (low semantic load).

There were 126 children in the study from preschool through fifth grade. The children had to repeat each sentence verbatim (*error imitation*), then say it correctly (*error correction*). Interrater reliability was 97 percent. The children also took the PPVT vocabulary test, an oral reading test, two standardized reading-comprehension tests, and an in-house test of word recognition. A derived score ("syntax control") was calculated to control for the children's tendencies to correct the mistakes in the error-imitation task. This was the most discriminating measure of the three syntax scores, and only these results will be reported.

There were significant differences between age groups on this test. Four-year-olds did relatively poorly (24 percent correct). 5- and 6-year-olds did significantly better and didn't differ from each other (52 percent, 58 percent). There was another spurt at age 7, which remained fairly constant until age 10 (range of 72 to 85 percent). By this time, many of the 10-year-olds scored 100 percent correct.

Correlations were carried out to determine whether syntax predicted reading scores, but the age range was much too broad for this to be meaningful. With age was controlled, syntax control barely correlated to reading skill (values were around $r = .28$). And when grade level was entered first in a regression analysis on reading test scores, it pulled out 59 percent of the variance, and syntax control contributed a mere 5 percent beyond this.

This problem was remedied in the next study by limiting the age range to fourth and fifth grade (Bowey 1986a). In a preliminary analysis, each grade was split into good and poor readers (above and below the mean). Poor readers scored 70 percent correct on the syntax test, and skilled readers in the range 86 to 93 percent. Next, correlations were carried out on all children regardless of reading status. PPVT vocabulary was controlled, but chronological age was not, and these values may be somewhat inflated. Syntax control correlated strongly to word recognition ($r = .65$), to two tests of reading comprehension ($r = .30, .45$), and to the error rate in prose reading ($r = -.42$). Tentatively, it appears that with receptive vocabulary controlled, syntax was significantly correlated to all forms of reading skill.

Bowey and Patel (1988) tackled the question of whether metalinguistic tasks overlap natural language tasks or are independent of natural language. The children were beginning readers in the age range 5:6–7:0. (Children learn to read at age 6 in Australia.) The sentence-imitation test from the TOLD was added (children repeat *correct* sentences that increase in length and syntactic complexity). The TOLD provided legitimacy (construct validity) for Bowey's syntax-control test, which correlated highly to it ($r = .73$).

Bowey and Patel made the assumption that the TOLD and the PPVT measured natural language, and that Bowey's syntax-control task measured metalinguistic awareness, due to the fact that children had to correct the errors in the sentences. Bradley and Bryant's sound-categorization test (odd one out) was added as a metalinguistic phonological-awareness test. Recall that in this test, the child decides which of three spoken words differ in initial, middle, or final sound: *sun, gun, rub*. Reading was measured by the Woodcock word ID and passage-comprehension tests.

Means were appropriate and standard deviations were low, but problems with data conversion persisted. Reading scores were converted to "mastery scores." No computations for "mastery scores" are described in the Woodcock manual, and it isn't clear what these values represent.[2]

---

2. Bowey and Patel's table 1, p. 377, gives word ID and comprehension "mastery scores" as 60.33 and 42.44 respectively. This rules out raw scores—60 is equivalent to a third-grade reading level. It also rules out standard scores: a standard score of 60 is rare, and 40 nearly impossible. Values could represent percentile ranks, but percentile ranks should not be used in statistical analysis.

Raw scores were used for the TOLD and age-equivalent scores for the PPVT, despite the fact that both tests are standardized tests.

Everything was significantly correlated to everything, with values ranging from $r = .30$ to .73. The TOLD and the PPVT (the natural language tasks) were correlated with each other ($r = .56$), as were the two metalinguistic tasks ($r = .47$). Syntax was the highest predictor of word identification, regardless of the test (TOLD and syntax control both at $r = .61$), replicating Bowey 1986a. The two syntax tests seem to be tapping the same skills in word recognition but not in reading comprehension, because the TOLD was a strong predictor of comprehension ($r = .54$) and syntax control was not ($r = .30$).

The purpose of the study was to compare the contribution of natural versus metalinguistic language skills to reading using a multiple regression analysis. The natural language tests (TOLD and PPVT) were entered first, and together accounted for 41 percent of the variance in word ID and 29 percent in reading comprehension. When the metalinguistic tasks were added (syntax control, sound categorization), they made no further contribution. With the order was reversed and the metalinguistic tasks entered first, they accounted for 40 percent of the variance in word ID, and the natural language tasks did not contribute further. In other words, the natural language tasks and the metalinguistic-awareness tasks were *completely interchangeable* in terms of their contribution to word recognition (reading accuracy).

The results were different for reading comprehension. When the metalinguistic scores were entered first, they accounted for 17.4 percent of the variance, and the natural language tasks accounted for a further 12.5 percent. This shows that skills tapped by the TOLD and PPVT are more important than phonological skill for reading comprehension. (Age will be a factor in these results, because it was not controlled.)

Bowey and Patel concluded that "metalinguistic ability did not predict early reading achievement" (p. 379), and that "it is not possible to test a specific metalinguistic contribution hypothesis within a correlational methodology. Rather we must rely on training studies to evaluate such hypotheses" (p. 380). However, if metalinguistic awareness is a *product* of natural language skills, as Chaney has suggested, then training studies are not likely to resolve this issue.

In 1994, Hansen and Bowey provided the most convincing evidence on the connection between syntax and reading, even though, strictly speaking, this study wasn't about syntax. Two hypotheses were tested. One predicted that phonological analysis (using a metalinguistic task) makes a unique contribution to reading, independently of verbal working memory. The other predicted that natural phonological ability underlies the association between phonological analysis, verbal working memory, and reading skill. Because syntax tests like the TOLD have a substantial memory load, Hansen and Bowey decided to treat the TOLD as a memory test rather than a syntax task. I will continue to treat it as a syntax test. Gathercole and Baddeley's nonword repetition test (see the previous chapter) was used to measure working memory, and several memory-span tasks were used as well.

This was a normative correlational study on 77 seven-year-olds (age range 6:10–7:11) who took the following standardized tests (the form of the data is given in parentheses): TOLD sentence imitation (raw scores); PPVT (standard scores); WISC block design (raw scores); Woodcock word ID, passage comprehension, and word attack (W scores). According to the authors, W scores were used because they are "Rasch-based ability scores" that provide a common metric for the three reading tests. This is true, but W scores aren't standard scores.[3]

Other tasks included two types of oddity tasks (odd one out)—one where words shared similar onsets or rimes and the other where words shared middle or final phonemes—plus three memory-span tasks (digit span, word span, and visual sequential memory).

The purpose of the study was to untangle two rival hypotheses using a multiple regression analysis. The phoneme oddity tasks were used as the

3. W scores convert raw scores into a standard metric to make it unnecessary to work with negative numbers when computing standard scores. W scores and raw scores are essentially two versions of the same thing but with different scaling, and neither is corrected for age. In the Woodcock rests, W scores are used in a formula to convert raw scores into standard scores. Age is also a factor in this computation and is converted to a scalar, R. Computing the difference between W and R provides the final numeric value, which is converted (via tables) to a standard score or a percentile score.

Table 14.1

First-order correlations for language tasks and reading

TOLD		Nonword repetition		Vocabulary		Memory span	
Nonword repetition	.61	TOLD	.61	TOLD	.62	TOLD	.51
Vocabulary	.62	Word span	.61	Word span	.39	Nonword	.52
Word span	.51	Digit span	.45	Digit span	.38	All reading	NS
Digit span	.49	Reading comprehension	.47	Nonword repetition	.35		
Reading comprehension	.51	Word ID	.45	All reading	NS		
Word ID	.49	Word attack	.44				
Word attack	.46	Vocabulary	.35				

Note: $N = 77$. Age range: 6:10 to 7:10. Age was not significantly correlated to any measure. All reading tests (word ID, word attack, comprehension) are from the Woodcock Reading Mastery series. Odd-one-out test scores were unreliable and are not reported here. NS = not significant.

Source: Hansen and Bowey 1994.

sole measure of metalinguistic phonological awareness. However, about half the first graders scored at chance (binomial test) on these tests, and Hansen and Bowey also reported large ceiling effects that repeated data transformation did not appear to cure. In addition, age and memory-span scores were not entered into the regression analysis, even though memory span was highly correlated to both the TOLD and nonword repetition. For these reasons, a multiple regression analysis will not be reliable. Instead, I present the results of the first-order correlations (table 14.1).

Age was not significantly correlated to any test and was dropped from the analysis. The TOLD was strongly correlated to the PPVT ($r = .62$), nonword repetition ($r = .61$), all memory-span tasks ($r = .50$), and all reading tasks ($r = .46–.51$). This shows the strong interconnection between syntax, receptive vocabulary, and memory span discussed above. The nonword repetition task had a surprisingly similar profile to the TOLD, except that it was unrelated to vocabulary (contrary to Gathercole and Baddeley's theory). The correlations between syntax and reading were *lower* than those found in Bowey and Patel, and are probably more accurate.

Another study by Bowey (1994b) is in line with the evidence provided throughout this book, that natural language skills are more likely to predict early reading success than phonological-analysis skills, which are fostered by early reading activities and direct instruction. Although the study was designed to investigate different types of phonological tasks, I will focus on vocabulary and syntax.

Ninety-six preschool children, age 5, were given the same tests listed above. Performance on the subsyllable- and phoneme-oddity tasks tended to be at ceiling or at chance, though Bowey did correct for this in the main data analysis. A phoneme-identity test was added in which children had to choose a picture of an object that matched a word onset (consonant cluster) or an initial or final phoneme.

The children were divided into four groups. Group 1 (novices) could read at least one word (average 6.5 words) and knew nineteen letters (by name or by sound). The other three groups were complete nonreaders. They were divided into groups on the basis of their letter knowledge. Group 2 was matched to group 1 on letter knowledge (eighteen or more letters). Group 3 knew six to fifteen letters, and group 4, less than six. As a point of interest, there were more girls in groups 1 and 2 (twenty-eight girls and sixteen boys), equal sexes in group 3, and more boys in group 4 (fifteen boys and nine girls). Groups did not differ in chronological age.

Group 1 (novice readers) and group 2 (nonreaders matched in letter-name/letter-sound knowledge) were compared on the phonological tasks with the PPVT, TOLD, and the WISC-R digit span as covariates. Both the PPVT and the TOLD accounted for significant variance. The digit-span test did not. With these factors controlled, the novice readers scored significantly higher on both the subsyllable-oddity task and phoneme-identity task. Neither group could do the phoneme-oddity task.

When the same analysis was run on the *nonreaders* from groups 2 and 4 (the children with high versus low letter-name knowledge), the PPVT and the TOLD were significant covariates as before. But with this variance subtracted, *no* significant differences were found between the groups on any phonological-awareness task, with all children doing extremely poorly. In other words, general language skills (vocabulary and syntax) accounted for significant variance in letter-name and letter-sound knowledge in the nonreaders, *and phonological awareness accounted for none.*

It appears that the novice readers (group 1) had made a connection between letter knowledge and phonetic segments in words, and nonreaders (groups 2, 3, 4) had not made this connection. Bowey (1994b, 153) suggested four possible explanations:

1) Children high in verbal ability are better able to learn letters, and letter knowledge enhances phonological sensitivity, 2) children high in verbal ability are more phonologically sensitive, and their phonological sensitivity enhances their ability to learn letters, 3) children with high letter knowledge are better at both verbal ability and phonological sensitivity with no causal connection between any two of these abilities, or 4) some combination of these possibilities is true.

Bowey also speculated on the importance of home environment. Children don't spontaneously learn letter names and letter sounds without instruction, and if they come to school with this knowledge, they are likely to have learned it at home or in preschool. The most plausible explanation of these results, based on all the research so far, is a fifth hypothesis: If a child's mother teaches the connection between letters, sounds, and how to use them to decode words, her child is more likely to be in group 1. If the mother teaches only letters, letter names, or letter sounds, divorced from decoding words, this child is more likely to be in group 2 (high letter-name/letter-sound knowledge on the part of nonreaders). If the mother teaches less than that or nothing, or if the child has very low verbal skills, the child will be in group 3 or 4. The home environment needs to be investigated. What goes on there in terms of prereading activities and reading instruction reflects a strong environmental effect on phonological awareness.

Bowey's work is notable for its consistency. Correlational values remain reasonably constant from one study to the next, and as more controls are added to increase reliability, the overall pattern of results strengthens. The evidence is strong that syntactic ability—a skill that combines vocabulary plus memory span plus something unique—is a predictor of reading skill, and that explicit phoneme awareness materializes sometime after reading instruction begins.

Canada

Other research supports a connection between syntax, general language, and reading. Willows and Ryan (1986) tested eighty-eight children in the first through third grades on a battery of tests, including four in-house syntax tests. These included error identification, error correction, and sentence repetition in which both semantic and syntactic errors were included, plus a cloze test ("the moon shines brightly in the _____"), in which the child must supply the missing word. They did not describe how the tests were constructed or provide information on test reliability. Nor were the tests themselves provided. (It would be impossible to replicate this study.) However, means and standard deviations were very respectable.

Reading tests included the standardized Peabody (PIAT) reading-recognition and reading-comprehension tests, Durrell reading fluency, and two in-house tests: a word-recognition test and a reading cloze test modified from the Durrell. Children also took Raven's progressive matrices (nonverbal IQ), the PPVT, and a digit-span test.

Much of the data analyses consisted of intergrade comparisons, which simply showed that children's syntax skills improve with age. I'll focus instead on the multiple regression analyses on word recognition, reading comprehension, and fluency. Age was partialed out at step 1 to correct for the 3-year range, and age contributed the major part of the variance to word recognition (46 percent) and reading comprehension (59 percent). The next tests entered were the Raven's IQ, the PPVT, and digit span, followed by the four syntax tests.

Altogether, age, Raven's IQ, PPVT, and memory span accounted for 62 percent of the variance on the PIAT comprehension test, with 7 percent additional variance due to syntax. For word recognition, the control measures accounted for 50 percent of the variance, and syntax contributed a further 11 percent. The results for the Durrell reading fluency test were interesting. The control variables accounted for 23 percent, and the combined syntax test scores, 19 percent. Willows and Ryan's in-house "listening-cloze" test was the clear winner here. It was the only syntax test that consistently accounted for additional variance on all four reading tests, and it did so with vocabulary controlled (semantic aspects subtracted).

This is the first evidence of a relationship between syntactic skill and *reading fluency*. Fluency was an efficiency measure, based on the time to read several graded passages aloud. Fluency issues are important to understanding the connection between general language and reading, and this study provides the first clue to that connection. We will come back to fluency in the next chapter. However, there is always the possibility that these results were affected by the wide age range, the nonstandardized syntax tests (no reliability measures), and some rather unusual reading tests.

A second study (Siegel and Ryan 1988) didn't solve these problems and only created new ones. The study involved children in grades 1 through 8 with some type of learning disability (math, reading, ADHD). They were compared to 138 normal controls. Sex differences were notable in each of the learning-disabled populations (more boys), but sex ratios weren't matched in the control group (equal sexes). This is another isolated-groups design, made worse by mixing apples and oranges. Because of these problems, I report only the correlations for all groups combined. With age controlled, the highest correlation between reading and any test was to the ITPA test of grammar. This test correlated to word recognition, comprehension, word attack, and nonword spelling, at values ranging from $r = .51$ to $.59$. The ITPA correlated to memory span at $r = .47$. These values are very close to those reported by Bowey.

France

A study by Casalis and Louis-Alexandre (2000) investigated the connection between morphology, phonology, and reading for fifty French children followed from kindergarten to second grade. Although there were problems with some of the tasks (floor effects, absence of reliability checks), some interesting findings appeared. Nonverbal IQ, vocabulary, and age were entered first into a stepwise regression analysis. Together they accounted for 20 to 27 percent of the variance on different reading tests at first and second grade, mainly due to vocabulary. At this point, any test was free to enter. The main correlate of reading accuracy and speed at first grade was a test of phoneme deletion, which accounted for an additional 36 percent of the variance. At second grade, phonology was no longer a factor. Now the major predictors were morphological. Reading accuracy/speed was predicted at second grade by the ability to complete sentences with an affixed pseudoword (16 percent of the variance)—children had to supply a word modified to fit a part of speech.

Reading comprehension (second grade) was predicted by two morpheme tasks: the ability to segment (isolate) morpheme units in words (25 percent of the variance), and receptive morphology (an additional 12 percent of the variance). This study shows that morphology is important to more advanced reading skills, especially reading comprehension, rather than to decoding, and this connection increases with age. (Reading was measured by French standardized tests.)

Taken together, the studies in this section support the hypothesis that performance on tests of syntax and morphology is a consistent and robust predictor of success on a variety of reading tests, including reading comprehension and timed tests of reading fluency. No study is free of flaws, though some come close. The research shows that natural language tasks alone predict aptitude for early readers, and these plus phonological tasks predict reading skill at the beginning-reader stage. Standardized language tests (TOLD, ITPA) are better predictors of reading test scores than in-house tests are, no doubt because they are better constructed tests. And they continue to predict robustly, when age, vocabulary, and memory span are controlled, showing that syntax is much more than just the sum of memory span plus vocabulary. What this "more" might be is unknown. It seems to reflect a special type of structural memory that has not been identified.

Syntax Does Not Predict Reading

As this work was accumulating, other studies seemed to show that syntax was not related to reading and did not distinguish between good and poor readers. Instead, researchers argued that poor performance on general language tasks was due to an underlying phonological-processing problem. Researchers from the Liberman and Shankweiler group (Smith et al. 1989) stated this most emphatically: "All of the poor readers' language-related difficulties are considered to derive from a limitation in phonological processing" (p. 430).

Smith et al.'s study was intended to remedy some deficiencies in previous research by this group (Mann, Shankweiler, and Smith 1984; Shankweiler, Smith, and Mann 1984). These studies showed that good readers had significantly fewer error scores and better comprehension of relative-clause statements than poor readers did. Smith et al. argued that the memory load on the tasks had been excessive. The poor readers did badly because the tasks confounded syntax with memory, and these readers were unable to demonstrate their true syntactic competence. For this reason, Smith et al. reduced the memory load and simplified the task.

Relative-clause sentences force the listener to juggle two actions and sort out who is the actor(s), initiator, and recipient of the actions. These sentences sound odd and unnatural. The four types of sentences used in the study are shown below. The initials indicate the order in which subject + pronoun (SS), or subject + object (SO, OS), or object-object (OO) sits at the head of the sentence. CC is the control sentence in which complexity is avoided by swapping a pronoun for a conjunction:

SS: The girl who pushed the boy tickled the clown.

SO: The boy who the girl pushed tickled the clown.

OS: The girl pushed the boy who tickled the clown.

OO: The boy pushed the girl who the clown tickled.

CC: The girl pushed the boy and tickled the clown.

The children in the study were second-grade good and poor readers with nonoverlapping scores on the Decoding-Skills reading test. PPVT vocabulary was in the normal range. Children did two tasks. In one, they used objects to act out the sentence. In the other, they had to point to one of two pictures that matched a sentence (chance is 50 percent correct).

Standard deviations were higher than the means on both syntax tasks for both reader groups, indicating the data were nonnormally distributed and the tests are invalid. In addition, Smith et al. failed to control for guessing on the picture-matching task. Not surprisingly, no differences were found between good and poor readers on either syntax test.

Nevertheless, Smith et al. argued that these nonsignificant results were clear evidence that the syntax tasks in the previous studies had been too hard. They interpreted this null result as proof of poor readers' *true* syntactic aptitude (nothing to do with invalid tests or methodology). They believed they had provided support for a "processing limitation hypothesis" in which poor readers' problems can be traced almost entirely to a phonological-processing deficit. Their conclusions were riddled with causal language, which I've highlighted:

The aim of this research was to *pinpoint the source* of poor readers' comprehension failures in spoken sentences.... The *processing limitation* hypothesis, but not the syntactic lag hypothesis, *anticipated* that poor readers would achieve a high level of performance on the tasks employed. (p. 445; emphasis mine)

A phonological deficit may also *impose severe limitations* on the operation of verbal working memory.... Let us now spell out how a phonological processing deficit may *result in failure* in sentence comprehension *through its impact* on verbal working memory.... Higher-level processes such as syntactic comprehension *would be compromised* by poor readers' failures to adequately retain phonological information during sentence processing. In effect, *there is a bottleneck that constricts the flow of information from lower levels to higher levels.* (p. 446; emphasis mine)

And this type of argument continues.

This is one of the many examples in reading research where a null result using one task is used to "prove" the validity of a theory based on another task that was not administered in the study.

This study was followed up on a much larger scale with 353 children in the age range 7:5 to 9:5 (Shankweiler et al. 1995). Methodology did not improve. The isolated-groups design appears again, compounded by a variety of learning-disability (LD) diagnoses. There were five groups: normal readers, reading disability, math disability, math plus reading disability, and attention deficit disorder. IQ ranged widely from 80 to over 125, and groups were not matched for IQ. The normal readers had a 14–20 IQ point advantage over every LD group. There was no mention of sex ratios, which will be strongly skewed in the LD groups.

Three composite measures were created from five standardized reading tests. These were word recognition, word attack, and reading comprehension. No explanation was given for how this was done, and this manipulation would rule out the possibility of using standard scores in the data analysis. Children took the Rosner phoneme-awareness test and a test of listening comprehension. A composite memory span was derived from the WISC digit span and in-house word-span and sentence-span tasks, for which no reliabilities were provided.

A new syntax test was designed, which was an expanded version of the one used in the previous study. It contained four types of sentences—relative clauses, passives, adjective control, and pronoun coreference—plus simple control sentences. Only one test item was shown, and there was no information on the number of items in each task. (There is no way to replicate this study.) No standard deviations or measures of test reliability were given for this or the morphology test (see below). From their description, the sentences were considerably more complex than those used previously: "We sought out structures that are considered to be mastered late ... and that our previous research had found to be difficult for children of this age range" (Shankweiler et al. 1995, 150).

Children could get 50 percent correct by guessing on the syntax test, but no corrections for guessing were carried out. I pieced together information from the text and tables on the most likely number of items on the tests and computed binomial tests. These showed that none of the groups scored above chance on the NO response items, and only the normal readers (the children with the high IQs) scored above chance on the YES response items.

A morphology test was developed in which the children supplied a missing word: A child heard "Four. My brother's team placed _____" and was supposed to say "fourth." Half of the items required no phonetic transformation (*four–fourth*), and half of the items did (*Five–fifth*). No other information was provided about other test items, reliabilities, or the number of items.

Anomalies appeared in the correlational data. Vogel, Chaney, and others reported that scores on syntax and morphology tasks are highly correlated. In the study just described, they were not. Not only that, but *one syntax test didn't even correlate to itself!* The correlation between YES and NO responses on the same syntax test was only $r = .19$, a sign of an invalid test.

When an analysis of covariance was carried out to compare good and poor readers, with age, IQ, and listening comprehension as the covariates, there were large and "significant" differences in short-term memory, phoneme awareness, and morphology between the groups. This might be the one valid result if one ignored the research design. Of course, no differences were found between the reader groups on the syntax tests, because most of the children were just guessing.

———

Shankweiler et al. (1995, 155) concluded that while morphological and phonological processing are clearly implicated in reading difficulties, syntax problems are not: "In sum, syntactic abilities per se did not distinguish poor from normal readers after factoring out IQ, nor did syntactic abilities distinguish reading-disabled children from other children with learning problems. The cause of comprehension difficulties in reading and spoken discourse must therefore lie outside syntax itself."

Once more, causality (or anticausality) is inferred from a purely descriptive study in which the methodological problems were monumental. In effect, the two studies from this group showed that if you fail to select subjects randomly from a normal distribution, make the task too difficult, fail to correct for guessing, fail to correct for chronological age and IQ in most of the analyses, and violate the assumptions of statistics, you will prove the null hypothesis.

The last study to be reviewed in this section was carried out by Canadian psychologists Gottardo, Stanovich, and Siegel (1996), who looked at the patterns of correlations between syntax, phonological awareness, memory, and reading. Overall, this was a well-designed study, so it was all the more surprising when critical omissions in data collection and data analysis made the results uninterpretable.

The children were 112 normal third graders, average age 8:9 (estimated age range 17 months). They were given a battery of standardized reading tests, including subtests from the Woodcock, the WRAT, and the Stanford Diagnostic Reading Test, along with the Rosner phoneme-awareness task. The authors provided split-half relability values (Spearman-Brown) on all nonstandardized tests, the only people since Vogel to do so.

Syntax-judgment and error-correction tasks were designed by the authors. The tasks involved noticing errors in clause order, word order, subject-verb agreement, subject-copula agreement, and function words. Children scored significantly above chance on the syntax-judgment task, though reliability was poor (.68). The error-correction task was too difficult. This was obvious from the description of the training protocol and the amount of prompting allowed during the test itself. Examples showed that children frequently substituted new words and misunderstood the task. They were allowed to hear each phrase up to four times during the testing before the item was failed, and were often coached throughout testing: "Say it a different way"; "Make it better." Scoring did not take into account the number of prompts a child received. Interexaminer reliability was not measured, which is critical with such subjective scoring.

The verbal working-memory test was unusual and complex. Children heard a series of short phrases that were either true or false. They had to say "true" or "false," and then remember the last word in each phrase. At a signal, they had to recall these words. In the two-phrase condition, for example, the children heard "Cars have four wheels" (T) and "Fish swim in the sky" (F), then had to respond: *wheels, sky*.

Children scored at chance on these true-false judgments, but did fairly well on the memory component of the task. It appears they were unable to share the processing load of doing two tasks at once and focused exclusively on remembering the words.

Various types of correlational analyses were carried out, but there was one major problem. Neither age nor IQ was controlled in any of them. This was a critical omission, especially in view of Gottardo and her colleague's belief that the Rosner and Simon phoneme-awareness test is a pure reflection of phonological sensitivity. As shown earlier, this test is highly influenced by age and IQ (see chapter 6).

Because the correlations between the Rosner and reading test scores were higher than anything else (range .69–.75), the authors concluded that all the shared variance between reading and the syntax and memory tasks was due to phonological sensitivity: "We found ... that phonological sensitivity was a much more potent unique predictor.... This finding is certainly consistent with the idea that the predictive power of syntactic processing is an epiphenomena [sic] of more basic limitations in phonological processes" (Gottardo, Stanovich, and Siegel 1996, 576, 578).

This conclusion was also based on the finding that when syntax was entered first in a regression analysis, and the Rosner next, it predicted more of the variance in reading than when the order was reversed. And when the Rosner and working-memory scores were entered together, no additional variance was explained by the syntax test. Of course this pattern would be expected when 30 percent of the variance on Rosner-Simon test is due to IQ, and IQ was not controlled.

Quite apart from this, the authors based their conclusion on two false assumptions. First, they assumed that the tasks to measure "phonological-sensitivity," "working-memory," and "syntactic-processing" tasks were pure measures of these constructs, which is not the case. Second, they assumed that any task could be logically prior to any other. However, a complex, highly analytic phoneme-awareness task, on which third graders score only 50 percent correct, is not logically prior to a natural language skill like syntax. Nor did they consider the high cognitive load of their complex memory task.

So far, the "syntax doesn't predict reading" team is batting zero. Due to serious methodological and conceptual problems, this group of studies provides no information about whether syntax does or doesn't play a role in reading, and no evidence that syntax is or is not underpinned by phonological sensitivity.

Why Does Syntax Correlate to Reading?

The best-controlled studies showed that syntax is a consistent predictor of reading skill even with age, nonverbal IQ, vocabulary, and verbal memory span controlled. Syntax is highly correlated to vocabulary and to verbal memory, but it isn't synonymous with them. Vocabulary and verbal memory span jointly explain about 50 percent of the variance on the TOLD sentence-imitation task. What else might contribute to the remaining 50 percent? What skills does a child need to understand and use correct syntax that are independent or different from vocabulary and memory span?

At the moment, there's no answer to this question. A simple-minded hypothesis might be that because syntax is the last rung on the ladder of language development, differences between children in how they perform on a syntax test might reflect normal temporal variation in natural language development. The only way to answer this question would be to follow a large group of children over time and monitor their syntactic development specifically, along with other language measures. As far as I am aware, there are no studies like this in the literature.

Syntactic memory is a different kind of memory from basic memory span, which is measured by lists of unrelated words or digits. Syntactic memory requires active grouping or parsing of phrases on the basis of meaning and grammatical structure, and insight into how words relate to one another within that structure. But if this is indeed a different kind of verbal memory, it is hard to see how it could be measured by anything other than a syntax test!

Finally, while all studies show a connection between the awareness of grammatical structure to reading comprehension and Willows and Ryan's study to reading fluency, no one has endeavored to explain what it is about performance on a syntax test that would predict a child's ability to read isolated words or nonsense words.

NAMING SPEED AND READING

A number of researchers have targeted naming speed or word-finding speed as a possible source of reading problems, reporting significant correlations between naming speed and reading test scores. For most scientists working on this problem, speed of access to words and speech production are inherent properties of individuals and likely to be due to some brain-based trait. Naming speed is considered a pure measure of this property, having nothing to do with learning or environmental factors. This is far from the case, as we will see.

According to these researchers, if it takes too long to recognize a letter and match it to a sound (even if you know it), and takes too long to find words stored in memory, this will lead to inaccurate decoding. Reading speed (fluency) is rarely measured in these studies, because the assumption is that inaccurate decoding produces halting and dysfluent reading.

However, it turns out that there are two types of "dysfluent" readers, those who read slowly because decoding is difficult (speed is caused by accuracy), and those who read slowly even when they decode perfectly. We know a good deal about the first type, and relatively little about the second. Nor do we know the proportion of children whose reading is slow and *inaccurate* versus the proportion whose reading is slow and *accurate*. The latter group are well known to classroom teachers as "word callers," children who read accurately and ponderously, but with such monotony that they rarely comprehend what they read. This group of children has been ignored by the scientific community until recently.[1]

---

1. There is another rare group of children who read accurately *and* fluently but don't comprehend what they read. They are known as *hyperlexics*.

The primary questions the next two chapters seek to address are the following: What is the connection between naming speed and reading? More specifically, is slow naming speed a marker for reading accuracy, reading fluency, or both? Second, what are the characteristics of children who read accurately but slowly?

Naming-Speed Tasks

Naming speed is measured by any task that requires an oral response to something seen or heard that *does not have to be read*. For example, the child sees a card containing pictures of common objects and has to name them as quickly as possible. In previous chapters the tasks used as predictors for reading aptitude were untimed. These were tests like auditory discrimination, phoneme analysis, speech recognition, and nonword repetition, plus general language tasks like vocabulary, verbal memory, and syntax. In the studies discussed in this section, test scores are recorded in seconds or milliseconds instead of number of errors or percent correct (though these are sometimes reported as well).

Timed tests are strongly influenced by age and IQ. Children process input faster and more efficiently as they get older. Kail (1991) reviewed seventy-two studies on visual speeded tasks involving reaction time, search time, and decision time. For the less complex tasks where a child's strategy plays little role, response time decreases with age in a lawful manner. The decrease is nonlinear; it is very rapid in early childhood, slower in middle childhood, and begins to flatten out by age 14. It slowly reaches adult levels by around age 20. This known as an *exponential* function, steep at the beginning, gently curving in the middle, and changing almost imperceptibly at the end. This means that when testing young children, where the slope is steepest, age must be measured in months, not years.

IQ enters the picture because very intelligent children have more efficient brains (process more information faster) than unintelligent children. Obviously, speed and efficiency are not all there is to intelligence, but they are a substantial component of an IQ test. Composite scores of simple speeded tasks, such as reaction time to flashing lights and auditory signals, have been found to be significantly correlated to full-scale IQ.

Of course, IQ tests are timed tests, too. They are timed not only for expediency, but because the original purpose of an intelligence test was to identify severely mentally retarded children, children observed to be too "mentally slow" to profit from normal classroom instruction (Binet and Simon [1905, 1908] 1977). Some IQ subtests are scored as time to completion or items completed in a fixed time interval. Block design, object assembly, and coding are examples from the Wechsler IQ test battery. So it isn't surprising that IQ would correlate to a naming-speed task. The only way to ensure that naming speed is independent of IQ is to disentangle IQ from naming-speed scores statistically.

Changes due to development, plus individual differences in the speed at which these changes occur (partially measured by IQ tests), are not the only factors contributing to speed of processing. Experience is important too. Brain development and organization provide ample evidence of the impact of both biologically determined and experiential factors. One example, already mentioned, is the growth of myelin around nerve fibers that carry messages from one part of the nervous system to another, increasing the propagation rates throughout the nervous system. Myelinization continues until at least 15 years of age (Kolb and Whishaw 1990).

While these anatomical changes are taking place, local processing is carried out by neural networks that "build themselves" with experience, becoming increasingly efficient (burning less glucose) as time goes by. Increasing efficiency due to training and practice translates into finer discrimination, faster processing, and more rapid responding, requiring less effort and less attention to perceptual and motor analysis (Pribram and McGuinness 1975; McGuinness and Pribram 1980; Pribram and McGuinness 1992; McGuinness 1997b).

Networks build from the bottom up, as shown by the fact that the sheer quantity of words spoken to a child has a strong effect on vocabulary growth (Hart and Risley 1995). Once underway, the networks, including their memory systems, exert strong top-down effects, biasing what is heard or seen. As we have noted, children perform best when they are asked to recognize (and repeat) words that occur with high frequency in the language and that were learned early in childhood. Top-down effects go into overdrive when the input is ambiguous or meaningless, as shown in the study by Dollaghan, Biber, and Campbell (1995) on nonword repetition. They found that children relied on both phonetic (perceptual) and vocabulary (long-term memory) skills to reproduce nonsense words.

These facts are critical in interpreting the research literature on speeded tasks and reading. Efficient (fluent, automatic) processing is a reflection of age, individual differences in development, native intelligence (genes), and experience. Any claim that a particular speeded task "predicts" or "causes" reading skill must first account for these aspects of naming speed. Nor do age, intelligence, and experience account for all possible causes or contributors to the connection between performance on speeded tasks and reading. There may be other reasons for the connection, such as the nature of the writing system and the child's decoding strategy.

Having said all this, there does seem to be a small but consistent relationship between certain naming-speed tasks and reading accuracy that survives at least the controls for age and IQ. But whether this is due to naming speed per se is another matter.

Researchers first became interested in naming speed in the early twentieth century. Woodworth and Wells (1911) reviewed research on color and object naming. In these tasks, five colors (red, yellow, green, blue, black), or five geometric shapes, repeat in a random order 100 times. The task is to name the items as quickly as possible. This is known as a *continuous naming-speed* task. Colors were easier (faster) to name than objects, and women had faster color naming speeds than men.

A second type of naming task is *discrete naming speed*. The child sees one symbol or picture at a time and names each item as quickly as possible. The child's score is the average time (in milliseconds) to commence speaking (*voice-onset latency*).

There has been considerable debate over which of the two tasks is best for use in reading research. Advocates of continuous naming tasks point out that they have greater validity because they mimic the act of reading in which decoding lines of text is a continuous process. Advocates of discrete naming tasks argue they are purer, because they aren't contaminated by articulation fluency—the speed to sequence responses from one item to the next.

Because all naming tasks are in-house tasks invented by the researchers, this raises the usual methodological issues to do with test construction, norms, standardization, reliability checks, and so forth. As we will see, the failure to develop tests with the necessary psychometric properties makes it all the more critical that age and IQ are controlled. I should emphasize that, for the most part, the reading tests used in these studies are *untimed tests* of reading accuracy, not tests of reading speed.

Research on Continuous Naming Tasks

Early Days

Rapid naming tests were first introduced into reading research in the 1970s, when M. B. Denckla (1972a, 1972b) designed a set of tasks she called *rapid automatized naming* tasks, RAN for short. All continuous naming tasks will be referred to as RAN from now on. Denckla, a neurologist, became interested in the finding that people with brain damage who suffer from *color anomia* (inability to name colors) sometimes tend to exhibit *alexia* (inability to read) as well. A theory linking color naming to reading was proposed by the famous neurologist Norman Geschwind (Geschwind and Fusillo 1966), who believed there was a connection between color-naming accuracy or fluency, and dyslexia.

Over a period of years, Denckla and her colleague Rudel (Denckla 1972a, 1972b, 1976; Denckla and Rudel 1974a, 1974b, 1976) tested a large number of children on rapid naming tasks, using familiar items. These were patches of colors and pictures of common objects, digits, and letters. Each test consists of a large card on which five items from a set repeat randomly across several rows. The child names the items as quickly as possible and is timed with a stopwatch. The score is the number of seconds it takes to name every item on the card.

Denckla's goal was to establish norms with a broad ability group and then look specifically at poor readers. Her attempt to establish norms was certainly commendable and was absolutely the right thing to do. These studies mark the first *and only* effort in this direction. But the task was never completed. There were not enough children to produce reliable norms, a situation that remains unchanged today.

Nor did Denckla carry out any reliability measures. The lack of stability from one study to the next is illustrated by the average scores for each age group taken from several studies that used Denckla's tests (see table 15.1).

The jitter in the data can be seen at the outset in Denckla's original studies. In 1972a, she reported that it took 154 kindergartners an average of 70 seconds to complete the color-naming task. In the next study, 180 kindergartners took an average of 100 seconds to do it (Denckla and Rudel 1974a). Blachman (1984) reported 81.5 seconds, and Wolf, Bally, and Morris (1986), 57.5 seconds. Given the fact that this is the identical test in all cases, which value is correct?

Table 15.1

Summary table of time in seconds to name 50 items

	Age in years						
Test	5	6	7	8	9	10	13–18
Colors							
Denckla 1972a, 1972b							
Normal K, $N = 154$	70		48	43	45	42	
Normal 7–10, $N = 87$							
Denckla and Rudel							
1974a Normal, $N = 180$	100	68	55	52	42	42	
1974b LD, $N = 128$			60	58	55	54	
Blachman 1984							
Normal, $N = 34$	82	55					
Wolf, Bally, and Morris 1986							
Normal, $N = 72$	58	47	46				
LD, $N = 11$	71	56	57				
Wolff, Michel, and Ovrut 1990							
Normal ($N = 50$)							27
Dyslexic ($N = 50$)							37
Letters and digits							
Denckla and Rudel							
Normal ($N = 180$)							
Letters	91	56	34	30	25	24	
Digits	85	57	34	31	25	24	
LD ($N = 128$)							
Letters			49	39	39	35	
Digits			45	38	38	35	
Wolf et al. 1986							
Normal ($N = 72$)							
Letters	59	34	34				
Digits	56	35	30				
LD ($N = 11$)							
Letters	85	46	46				
Digits	81	47	40				

Also problematic was the high variability between kindergartners *in the same group*, as shown by large standard deviations reported by Denckla and Rudel. There are two reasons for this (apart from test reliability). First, "grade level" is much too coarse a measure of "age," which should be measured in months. Second, not all kindergartners know color names. Differences between the various studies could be a function of home background or SES. Denckla's children lived in Ft. Lee, New Jersey, Blachman's in an impoverished inner city, Wolf's in Waltham, Massachusetts. If family background influences whether children learn color names, the RAN test in not measuring anything "automatic," at least not at this age.

Denckla and Rudel found that variability decreased sharply by age 7. Standard deviations for 6-year-olds ranged from 15 to 27 seconds across the four tasks. At age 7, this range was cut in half (7 to 13 seconds). Not only this, but letter and digit naming speed soon overtook color and object naming speed, no doubt as a consequence of what the children were learning in the classroom. An abrupt shift in naming speed between the ages of 5 and 6, or between 6 and 7, can be seen in every study in table 15.1.

The table illustrates something else equally important: digit and letter naming speeds are identical. In fact, these two tests are used interchangeably in reading research. This tells us that letter names per se have nothing to do with the connection between reading and naming speed. The connection could be due to a number of things. Moms who teach letter names could also teach number names. Learning names for abstract shapes (letters, digits) is a paired-associate memory task, the ability to memorize connections between unrelated pairs of something. Perhaps naming speed taps paired-associate memory.

When Denckla and Rudel compared normal and poor readers (table 15.1), normal readers were faster on all the tasks. The same effect was reported by Wolf. But in view of the unstable values from one group of children to the next, how does one interpret these significant results? Wolf followed children from kindergarten to the end of second grade and identified eleven children as "severely impaired" readers. Yet these severely impaired readers scored identically to the normal kindergartners tested by Denckla and Rudel, as shown in table 15.1. Does this mean that Wolf's impaired readers were normal to start with, or does it mean that all of Denckla and Rudel's kindergartners will turn out to be impaired readers? It is clear that studying the connection between naming speed and reading prior to age 7 is a highly dubious practice.

And there are other concerns. Is a difference of 5 to 10 seconds between good and poor readers in the same study really meaningful? How much does naming speed owe to age, SES, IQ, or sex differences? Denckla and Rudel's group of dyslexic children consisted of 100 boys and 28 girls, but the normal readers had equal sex ratios. Denckla and Rudel, like Woodworth and Wells, reported that girls were significantly faster than boys at naming colors.

Finally, we don't know from Denckla and Rudel's studies what proportion of normal children (unselected) had reading difficulties. These children came from local public schools and would be expected to have a wide range of reading skills. By contrast, the dyslexic children came from special schools or from Denckla's private practice. These children had other problems, including a high rate of development delays in articulation, general language, and motor skills. Denckla reported that nearly 50 percent had neurological "soft signs," including choreiform movements, tremors, and poor reflex-tone asymmetries, along with oculomotor abnormalities like strabismus and nystagmus. Difficulty learning to read is merely one of many problems for these children.

Nor do we know the proportion of the dyslexic children who had abnormally slow naming speeds, or even what constitutes "abnormally slow." Earlier, Denckla (1972b) reported that of the fifty-six children referred to her clinic for reading problems, only five had abnormal color naming speeds (11 percent), along with other abnormalities. This is a very small proportion of poor readers, and these children are not going to be seen very often.

There was one other study on continuous naming speed and reading from this period. Research had shown a connection between reading and memory span (see chapter 13), and Spring and Capps (1974) believed this might be due to a problem with speech-motor encoding. They developed two tests to measure this. The tests to measure speech-motor encoding were virtually identical to Denckla's tests, and included colors, digits, and pictures of objects. Memory was measured by a visual digit-span test. Spring and Capps tested good and poor readers in the age range $7\frac{1}{2}$ to 13 years. Poor readers were slower to name colors, objects, and digits and had poorer short-term memory, with poor recall for early items in the list but normal recall for the last items, as Spring and Capps's theory predicted.

Thus, by the mid-1970s, two sets of studies appeared to show that poor readers had slower automatic naming than good readers. Because naming speed, unlike phoneme awareness, has no obvious connection to reading (i.e., it is unlikely to be caused by learning to read), it seemed reasonable to conclude that naming speed was a property of the child and one of the key markers for dyslexia. The early studies created considerable interest and additional research followed, which is still ongoing. Methodology, by and large, did not improve. The good-reader/poor-reader design has been used almost exclusively. Controls for age, IQ, and sex were seldom seen. Almost no one looked at the experience of the children to find out when or whether they were taught color, letter, and number names. Much of this research is uninterpretable and omitted from this chapter. Instead, I will focus on studies with the *fewest* of these common violations:

The use of an isolated-groups design (good versus poor readers).
No control for sex in matching subject groups.
No information on age, standard deviations, and/or age ranges.
No control for age in the statistical analysis.
No control for IQ in the statistical analysis.
The use of truncated IQ ranges in place of statistical controls. (This involves establishing arbitrary cutoffs for inclusion in a study. It creates nonnormal distributions, could result in unequal variances between reader groups, and guarantees unequal variances between IQ and all other tests.)
Computing correlations on groups with nonoverlapping test scores (nonlinear data).

The rare studies that did control age and IQ didn't begin to appear until the late 1980s. By this time, Blachman (1984) had provided the first test-retest reliabilities for the RAN tests. Kindergartners and first graders were tested twice, 6 days apart, on RAN colors and objects. Test-retest reliabilities for RAN colors and objects were high ($r = .80$) for the 5-year-olds. However, Blachman discovered that only thirteen out of the twenty-eight kindergartners in this inner-city school could identify and name letters. Test-retest reliability for these children was $r = .94$. Reliabilities were excellent for the first graders for colors, objects, and letters,

Table 15.2

Correlations between naming speed and reading skills

	WRAT	Informal reading skills
Kindergarten ($N = 34$)		
Color naming	−.61	−.54
Object naming	−.36	−.40
	WRAT	Coding skills
First grade ($N = 34$)		
Color naming	−.16	−.04
Object naming	−.18	−.04
Letter naming	−.67	−.55

Note: WRAT: letter matching, letter-name knowledge, word recognition. Informal reading skills: letter names, letter sounds. Coding skills: sound-symbol association, reading phonetically regular words.
Source: Data from Blachman 1984.

with values ranging from .88 to .92. These are solid results for such young children and show that the tests themselves don't appear to be responsible for the high variability between the groups of children, as shown in table 15.1. Nor is this variability likely to be due to careless testing or erratic performance on this task. Instead, the naming-speed differences between the groups seem to represent real differences between the populations in the studies; they probably reflect SES, IQ, educational opportunity, and other factors.

Blachman carried out correlations between RAN tests and reading tests. IQ and age were not controlled, but the basic findings are important, as shown in table 15.2.

RAN colors in kindergarten was strongly correlated to standardized reading tests, which, at this age, measured knowledge of letter shapes, letter names and sounds, and the ability to read simple words. No doubt parents who teach colors and color names are likely to teach letters and letter names as well. However, by first grade, RAN colors did not predict reading test scores at all, but RAN letters did. Once again this supports the conclusion that naming speed per se has nothing to do with reading skill.

If it did, color and object naming would be correlated to reading, but they were not. The data suggest that if a child knows a lot about letters or digits, it's much easier to name them in a rapid naming test, and "knowing a lot about letters" has something to do with reading. But we don't know *why* in this case, because age, IQ, and prior experience were not controlled.

Controlling Age and IQ

In the late 1980s we began to get better answers about whether naming tests were really correlated to reading or were masking something else. Spring and Davis (1988) controlled age, verbal IQ, and performance IQ in a study on fifty-six boys and thirty-six girls diagnosed "hyperactive" (age range 9–15 years). Apart from the children's hyperactive status (whatever this might mean), none of them had reading or learning problems. They were given the PIAT word-recognition and comprehension tests, plus RAN digits. Correlations between RAN digits and age were measured in two ways, using either chronological age or age squared. The latter provided the best fit to the RAN scores, showing that age has an exponential relationship to naming speed, exactly as Kail (1991) found with visual speeded tasks. Furthermore, the strength of the correlation followed the same trajectory: strong for the younger children and disappearing at around age 13.

Spring and Davis carried out a series of multiple regressions using the Peabody (PIAT) word-recognition test. Age was controlled prior to data analysis for all measures. Age was partialed out of the RAN test scores, and IQ and reading standard scores (which correct for age) were used. When the WISC-R verbal IQ was entered at step 1, it accounted for a highly significant amount of variance on the PIAT. Performance IQ, entered next, accounted for none. RAN digits entered at step 3 also accounted for a highly significant amount of variance ($p < .001$). Unfortunately, the exact amount of this variance was not provided.

Variance estimates were provided for the PIAT reading-comprehension measure. Comprehension was predicted jointly by word recognition and verbal IQ (33 percent of the variance). RAN digits failed to contribute significantly beyond this. Thus, with age and verbal IQ controlled, RAN accounted for a significant amount of variance in word recognition, but none in reading comprehension. It should also be emphasized that this connection was via *digit* naming speed.

Bowers, Steffy, and Tate (1988) raised concerns about the failure to control age and IQ in naming-speed research, and felt this was causing a great deal of confusion in the field. In most of the research they reviewed, IQ was either not controlled at all or was controlled indirectly, which did not solve the problem. By this, they meant the common practice of using IQ cutoffs for inclusion or exclusion in the study. As they noted, cutoffs don't control for the variability (variance) in the IQ scores between reader groups. The range of scores may be the same, but the distributions of the scores may be quite different. This is a valid argument, but it ignores the far more serious breach of the random-selection requirement, and the fact that the poor-reader/good-reader design *itself* creates unequal variances between groups. It also ignores the fact that restricting IQ range and no other measure means that IQ variance will be unequal to all the other tests, putting statistics off limits in any case.

Nevertheless, the study by Bowers, Steffy, and Tate provides a fascinating glimpse into what happens when researchers limit the range of scores on one measure but not on the remainder. The children were $7\frac{1}{2}$ to $11\frac{1}{2}$ years old and had been referred to a clinic for reading or attention problems. I report only the results from the regression analyses in which all children were combined (see table 15.3).

The table illustrates a series of multiple regression analyses in which IQ was or was not controlled. In the first example, age was entered at step 1 and accounted for 36 percent of the variance in word recognition and 19 percent in word attack. Digit span (short-term memory) was entered next and accounted for an additional 18 percent and 16 percent. Following this, RAN digits accounted for a whopping 28 percent and 17 percent more. RAN colors, substituted at this same step, accounted for only 7 percent and 1 percent of the variance, more evidence that it is the ability to memorize pairs of symbol-name association that is important, and not naming speed per se.

In the second example, IQ tests (WISC-R) were entered at step 2, after age. Performance IQ accounted for no variance in reading test scores. However, verbal IQ (a composite of vocabulary, similarities, information, and comprehension subtests) accounted for 27 percent of the variance in word recognition and 18 percent in word attack. Digit span (step 3) now failed to contribute further, showing that verbal IQ pulled out the variance that connected digit span to reading. RAN digits, entered next, still

Table 15.3

Multiple regression analyses of age, IQ, memory span, and naming speed on reading

	Word identification (%)	Word attack (%)
A. Complete sample $N = 46$		
Step 1 Age	36	19
Step 2 Digit span	18	16
or		
Step 2 Sentence span	19	10
Step 3 RAN digits	28	17
or		
Step 3 RAN colors	7	1
B. Complete sample $N = 46$		
Step 1 Age	36	19
Step 2 Verbal IQ	27	18
Step 3 Digit span	3	4
or		
Step 3 RAN digits	11	7
or		
Step 3 RAN colors	0	0
C. Sample restricted to "average IQ"		
Step 1 Age	41	20
Step 2 Verbal IQ	10	1
Step 3 Digit span	2	10
or		
Step 3 RAN digits	20	12

Note: Results are shown as the "additional variance" added at each step.
Source: Data from Bowers, Steffy, and Tate 1988.

accounted for 11 percent of the variance in word recognition and 7 percent in word attack, support for a connection between performance on the RAN test and reading independent of verbal IQ and digit span. But 11 percent and 7 percent are a far cry from 28 percent and 17 percent, the variance attributable to the RAN before verbal IQ was controlled.

This is a wonderful example of the "blimp effect" in correlational statistics, in which something *not measured* is responsible for inflating the relationship between things that were measured.

In the third example, IQ scores were restricted to mimic the practice of using cutoff scores to select children into the study. Only the data for children scoring in the midrange were used. When verbal IQ was entered at step 2, it barely correlated to reading, accounting for only 10 percent of the variance in word recognition and 1 percent in word attack. Now there was a ripple effect. Restricting the IQ range inflated the variance shared by RAN digits and reading, and it ballooned back up to 20 percent and 12 percent.

This is the best illustration I have seen of the two major problems with correlational statistics: first, correlations can be inflated due to something not measured or controlled, and second, correlations are unstable when there are unequal variances between test scores. This is a clear demonstration of why all test scores should have equal or similar variances (be linear) in order for correlations to be meaningful.

Bowers, Steffy, and Tate found a strong connection between verbal IQ and reading accuracy, but they provided no information on which of the four subtests (vocabulary, similarities, information, comprehension) contributed to this effect. Nor do we know which subtests were responsible for robbing the RAN of its power to predict reading. Because verbal IQ was highly predictive of naming speed, accounting for most of the shared variance in the RAN-reading relationship, it would be interesting to have the answer to this last question.

Ackerman and Dykman (1993) raised similar concerns about controls for age and IQ. They tested eighty-six boys and thirty-three girls ($7\frac{1}{2}$–12 years) referred to a clinic for various learning or attentional problems. All children had IQ scores above 79 on the WISC-R. They were split into three groups: fifty-six children diagnosed with attention deficit disorder with normal reading skills (above 90 on the WRAT), twenty-one poor readers who scored below 90 on the reading tests, and forty-two dyslexics who also scored below 90, but had a discrepancy of 17+ points between reading scores and IQ.

Other differences distinguished the three reader groups. The poor-reader group had significantly lower IQ scores on all three scales (full scale, verbal, performance). The dyslexics' IQ scores did not differ from those of the normal readers. The three groups differed markedly on the WRAT tests of word recognition (103, 83, 74) and spelling (100, 82, 76).

Sex ratios differed as well. Male-to-female ratios were around 2:1 (M:F) in the good- and poor-reader groups but 4:1 in the dyslexic group. So a reading/IQ discrepancy was not the only thing that distinguished these dyslexic children.

The children were tested on a large number of tasks to look at group differences with age and full-scale IQ controlled. The authors used covariance analysis, pooling the data from all the children. As a first step, two covariates (age and IQ) were subtracted from every test score. At step 2, the reader groups were compared. The covariance analysis is reliable to the extent that the combined groups' data are approximately normally distributed. Although group comparisons are unreliable given the research design, I will report them in any case, because they were supported by a multiple regression analysis using all the data from the combined groups.

Articulation Rate Age was a highly significant covariate on all articulation tests. IQ was significant on none, showing that articulation rate is largely due to developmental factors. When the reader groups were compared (with age and IQ statistically controlled), there was no difference between them for three of the five tasks, with only marginal differences on the other two. On the whole, poor readers had no more articulation problems than good readers, a conclusion supported by the multiple regression analysis (see below), and by the studies reviewed in part II.

RAN Tests Age was a highly significant covariate on the all the RAN tasks: digits, letters, and alternating letters and digits. IQ was significant for two of four measures: the alternating task and the combined scores. With age and IQ controlled, group comparisons showed that the dyslexic group (poor reading, normal IQ) was significantly worse on every RAN task (all comparisons, $p < .01$) than the poor and good readers, who did not differ from each other.

The articulation and RAN test results don't support the speech-motor encoding theory proposed by Spring and Capps. Reader groups differed consistently on the RAN tasks but not on the articulation tests. In other words, whatever the connection between RAN and reading might be, it isn't due to natural speech-motor efficiency.

Confrontation Naming The children took the Boston Naming Test, known as a "confrontation naming" test. The child sees pictures of objects and has to name them. This is essentially an expressive vocabulary test, because the objects become more and more obscure as the test proceeds, and the test is scored for accuracy rather than speed. Age and IQ predicted large amounts of variance on this test. With age and IQ controlled, no differences were found between any of the reader groups. This is an important result because a number of well-known studies that failed to control age and IQ are frequently cited as evidence that good and poor readers differ in confrontation naming (Wolf 1984; Wolf and Goodglass 1986; Wolf and Obregon 1992).

Sound Categorization In this test the child identifies the odd one from a list of four spoken words that vary in initial, middle, or final sound. IQ was far and away the major contributor to success on this task ($p < .001$). Age was significant for initial sound (alliteration) and for total scores, but not for middle or final sounds (the sounds that rhyme—*man, can, ban, fan*). However, even with age and IQ controlled, both poor-reader groups were worse than normal readers on this task, and to the same degree. The most discriminating of these tests was for the middle sound (the vowel).

Memory Span Eighteen different memory-span tasks were given, including auditory and visual presentations of digits, letters, and words. Age and IQ were significant for nearly every test. With age and IQ controlled, reader groups did not differ. (Recall that verbal IQ pulls out most of the variance for memory span. See chapter 13.)

Echoic Memory Echoic memory keeps auditory signals lingering in consciousness after they have physically ceased to exist (see chapter 13, this volume; Cowan 1984). How long they last is influenced by loudness, familiarity, meaningfulness, and complexity. Echoic memory isn't simply a passive echo chamber—a "box in the head"—but is a function of auditory neural systems that get input from the rest of the brain.

In the tasks, children heard lists of digits spoken at different rates (slow, medium, fast), and at a signal, had to recall the last three digits they heard. Age was a highly significant covariate for this task, but IQ was not, showing that echoic memory isn't "cognitive." Although the dyslexic

Table 15.4
Summary of the contributions of age and IQ to various tests

Tests with:	Significant differences between reader groups	No significant differences between reader groups
Effects:	RAN all tests +* dyslexics slower	Articulation rate +
Effects:	Odd one out +* all poor readers worse	Boston Naming Test +*
Effects:	Echoic memory + dyslexics worse	Memory span +*

Note: Age significant +. IQ significant *.
Source: Data from Ackerman and Dykman 1993.

group was worse overall, they performed like the controls on the short lists at slow presentation rates.

A summary of the reader-group effects and of which tests were or were not affected by age and IQ is provided in table 15.4.

The authors carried out a regression analysis using the combined data from all the children to find out which tests were the strongest predictors of word recognition (Woodcock word ID). Age and verbal IQ (entered first) accounted for 51 percent of the variance in reading scores. RAN was the next most powerful predictor (14 percent of the variance), followed by echoic memory (5 percent), then by the sound-categorization test (3 percent). A similar pattern was found for word attack (decoding-skills test). Age and verbal IQ accounted for 38 percent of the variance; RAN, 11 percent; echoic memory, 6 percent; and sound categorization, 5 percent. Articulation rate, confrontation naming, and eighteen tests of visual and auditory memory span did not account for any variance in reading.

There is a potential newcomer on the list of reading predictors: echoic memory. An efficient echoic memory (more information, held for longer periods of time) may affect any task that involves matching or comparing auditory information. This is an interesting possibility that Ackerman and Dykman didn't explore.

There are now a number of studies in the literature that show that *pause time* between each articulation period, not articulation rate, is the critical variable in group differences on RAN type tests (Anderson, Podwall, and Jaffe 1984; Obregon 1994; Hulme et al. 1999; Neuhaus et al.

2001), results that support the findings above. Neuhaus et al., using a group of normal first and second graders, found that pause time on the RAN test predicted reading skill, but articulation time did not. The correlations were much stronger for letters than for numbers, and did not hold at all for objects. The relationship was considerably more powerful in first grade, suggesting it is a learning effect (familiarity), more than a word-finding deficit or retrieval problem.

There was one study (D. McGuinness, C. McGuinness, and Donohue 1995) that controlled for sex as well as age and verbal ability. The study involved ninety-four normal first graders with a range of reading aptitudes, with an age range of 6:0 to 7:9 (average 7:0). The majority of the children were from professional families (high SES). They took a variety of tests, including RAN colors and objects, along with the Woodcock word ID and word attack subtests. The authors felt that RAN colors and objects were purer measures of naming speed than letters and digits were, since knowledge of letters and digits is confounded with being taught to read. Both RAN tasks were significantly correlated to reading. RAN color was the stronger predictor, but this was mainly true for girls and only for word recognition (word ID).

Multiple regression analyses were carried out on each reading test for boys and girls separately and for the sexes combined. For the girls, age and receptive vocabulary (PPVT-R) accounted for 28 percent of the variance in word ID. RAN colors was next (12 percent), followed by memory for rhyming words (10 percent). Nothing else was significant. The pattern for the boys was different. Age and vocabulary accounted for 11 percent of the variance, and the LAC test of phoneme awareness for 30 percent. Nothing contributed further. With the sexes combined, only phoneme awareness and the RAN contributed beyond age and the PPVT-R accounting for significant variance on word ID. If boys and girls rely on different skills or strategies in learning to read, as they seem to be doing here, combining the data obscures what's really true.

In the regression analysis on word attack, RAN colors contributed nothing for either sex. Phoneme awareness was by far the best predictor. This led the authors to conclude that RAN colors had more to do with speed of word retrieval than with decoding skill. It should be pointed out that girls and boys did not differ significantly on either RAN colors or RAN objects, but girls were significantly better readers.

The accompanying table summarizes the contribution of the RAN in the multiple regression analyses reported in these studies. Age and verbal IQ/vocabulary were controlled in each case.

	Word recognition	Word attack	Comprehension
Spring and Davis (digits)	$p < .001$	n.a.	n.s.
Bowers et al. (digits)	11%	7%	n.a.
Ackerman and Dykman (digits and letters)	14%	11%	n.a.
McGuinness et al. (colors) (girls only)	12%	0	n.a.

Note: n.a. = not available; n.s. = not significant.

Given the topsy-turvy world of correlational statistics, these results are remarkably consistent. Perhaps the connection between RAN and reading accuracy is *real*. However, the direction of this relationship is unclear. The study by D. McGuinness and her colleagues (1995) was the only study to show a significant effect of RAN colors (a purer measure of naming speed). All other studies found that *only* digits or letters predicted reading test scores. Is this the consequence of early learning, or is it due to some native aptitude that plays a causal role in learning to read?

The group comparisons in the Ackerman and Dykman study showed that there was a subpopulation of poor readers with excessively slow digit naming speeds who were mainly boys. There was another group of poor readers who read almost as poorly, but whose naming speed was normal. But we still don't know how many "slow namers" there are in a normal population or in a population of poor readers.

A comment is in order about the children in these studies. Three of the studies used abnormal populations with serious behavioral or learning problems. The results may be valid only in the light of this fact. They may not apply to children in normal school settings, especially because these extreme populations were heavily weighted toward a preponderance of reading-impaired children and included mostly boys.

In clinical populations like these, the likelihood of undetected language impairments or language delays is strong. Certainly, efficiency of name retrieval, symbol-name associative memory, execution of fluent, sequential speech-motor patterns, plus cognitive control in sequencing responses, are part and parcel of general language skill. Nevertheless, Ackerman and Dykman's results, and those of Neuhaus et al., show that something tapped by RAN digits is outside the bounds of verbal IQ, and articulation rate, and echoic memory. That something—predictable with RAN digits and letters (but not colors or objects)—could reflect either the speed to master symbol-name correspondences or the child's early learning experience.

Longitudinal Research

A 5-year longitudinal study was carried out by Wolf and her colleagues. Eighty-three children entered the study in kindergarten (age range 5–6 years) and were tested each year on RAN digits, letters, and colors. At second grade they were given several reading tests. This study was unusual in giving timed reading tests. The Gates-McGinitie is a timed comprehension test with multiple-choice questions. The Gray Oral Test requires the child to read a series of passages within a time limit; the child's performance is scored for speed and accuracy. The remaining reading tests were in-house word-recognition tests set up in a similar format to the RAN. No information on standardization or reliabilities was provided. The published tests were reported in grade-equivalent scores, which are unsuitable for statistical analysis.

Because longitudinal research is so important and so difficult to do, it is unfortunate that there were too many methodological problems with this study to draw firm conclusions from the data. Age and IQ were never controlled at any point. The authors mentioned that school officials prohibited the testing and use of IQ scores. Nevertheless, PPVT vocabulary scores were available and could have been used instead. The isolated-groups design was superimposed on the data, even though this was a normative sample (normal children). Reader groups were set up at second grade. The numbers were so lopsided (seventy-two good readers, eleven poor readers) that statistics would be out of the question in any case. For these reasons, I will discuss the correlations from the first phase of the study (Wolf, Bally, and Morris 1986; Wolf 1986), when the data from all the children were included.

Blachman had reported that test-retest correlations for the RAN were high across 1 week for kindergartners (64 percent accuracy) and first graders (80 percent accuracy). Wolf, Bally, and Morris did not find this kind of stability over the long term, especially between kindergarten and first and second grade, no doubt because performance on the RAN shifts

Table 15.5

Correlations between grade 2 reading and RAN digits, letters, and colors at three grade levels

	Grade 2 reading test scores		
	Word-recognition speed	Gates comprehension	Gray accuracy and speed
RAN digits (K)	.66	−.51	−.54
RAN digits (1st)	.62	−.54	−.58
RAN digits (2nd)	.55	−.43	−.49
RAN letters (K)	.64	−.55	−.55
RAN letters (1st)	.62	−.54	−.58
RAN letters (2nd)	.51	−.39	−.45
RAN colors (K)	.45	−.47	−.39
RAN colors (1st)	.33	−.37	−.24
RAN colors (2nd)	.20	−.32	−.26

Note: Values will be inflated because IQ was not controlled. Gates and Gray tests are measured in speed, not accuracy, producing negative correlations. Raw scores were used for word recognition. Gates and Gray were converted to grade-equivalent scores.
Source: Data from Wolf, Bally, and Morris 1986.

so dramatically over this time period. They did find that the prediction improved from first to second grade (correlations around .74).

Some curious results appeared in the lag correlations between kindergarten RAN scores and reading at second grade, as shown in table 15.5. Second-grade reading scores were predicted better by *kindergarten* RAN digits ($r = .66$) than by second-grade RAN digits ($r = .55$). This occurred on every reading test, and the same effect appeared for RAN letters as well ($r = .64$). Blachman reported that over half the kindergartners in her study couldn't name any letters. If letter-name knowledge was an issue here, the correlation between letter naming speed and reading will merely reflect how much the child was taught before entering school. In the reading rat race, reading tests really measure accumulated knowledge and practice over time. This means that

• Good readers are good because they get ahead.
• Good readers stay good because they got ahead.

Table 15.6

Correlations between RAN digits (errors and speed) to Woodcock Reading Mastery measured at K, 1st, and 2nd grade

	Reading test scores					
	Fall cohort ($N = 51$)			Spring cohort ($N = 55$)		
	K	1st	2nd	K	1st	2nd
Kindergarten testing						
RAN errors	−.22	−.41	−.68	−.19	−.47	−.48
RAN speed	−.21	−.39	−.43	−.25	−.25	−.33
First-grade testing						
RAN errors		−.42	−.72		−.10	0
RAN speed		−.38	−.82		−.50	−.67

Note: Values will be inflated because age and IQ were not controlled.
Source: Data from Mann and Ditunno 1990.

According to this scenario, RAN test scores not only act as a proxy for age and IQ (they obscure age and IQ effects), but for experience and knowledge as well. The apparent connection between the RAN tests and reading will be an artifact of things not accounted for.

There is other evidence to support this interpretation. Error scores on the RAN tests are rarely reported or used in data analysis. Denckla and Rudel (1974a) recorded the number of children making errors on each of their tests (about 50 percent of 5-year-olds), but did nothing further with the data. Mann and Ditunno (1990) were among the few to look at errors *and* speed in their longitudinal study (see table 15.6). The top figures represent correlations between RAN letters measured in kindergarten to Woodcock reading scores at three grade levels. The bottom figures represent the first-grade RAN testing.

These values are inflated because age and IQ were not partialed out of the data, especially as they found that WPPSI vocabulary and block design were highly correlated to reading.[2]

---

2. Kindergarten testing only. WPPSI vocabulary correlated to first- and second-grade reading for the fall cohort at .44 and .52, and for the spring cohort at .33 and .35. Block design correlated to first- and second-grade reading for the fall cohort at .51 and .40, and for the spring cohort at .39 and .34.

Nevertheless, if one looks at relative values, ignoring absolute values, it can be seen that RAN letter *errors* measured in kindergarten are more highly correlated to subsequent reading scores than RAN *speed*. This is clear evidence that some children knew letter shapes and names better than other children, and knowing them predicted reading up to 2 years earlier. Speed, of course, is confounded with error rate.

The same effect appeared for the first-grade testing in the fall, showing that many children still did not know all their letter shapes and letter names. This pattern disappeared by the time the children were tested at the end of the school year, and errors no longer correlated to reading. Presumably all the children knew their letters by this time (zero errors), at which point naming speed became the stronger predictor of reading skill.

These results show that children come to school with varying degrees of knowledge about letter shapes and letter names. Not every child was consistently accurate until the end of first grade in this Philadelphia suburb. By age 7, the connection between reading and naming speed could reflect either of two things: familiarity and practice with letter/digit names, or a real difference between children in word-finding speed. Articulation rate has been ruled out by Ackerman and Dykman, and by Neuhaus et al.

Research on Discrete Naming Tasks

Discrete naming tasks measure the onset of vocalization after the child looks at a picture, letter, or digit, and says the name. The studies reviewed in this section measured the relationship between discrete naming and reading comprehension. As we saw in the last section, performance on the RAN is not correlated to reading comprehension (Spring and Davis 1988; also see Cornwall 1992).

Perfetti and Hogaboam (1975) asked third- and fifth-grade children to read isolated words as quickly as possible. The children were split into two reader groups based on their scores on the Metropolitan reading-comprehension test. I'll report here only the results for simple words; otherwise this is just another way to show that poor readers can't read. (This study was about more than naming speed, and dealt with the nature of decoding skills.) Naming latency did not differ between the good and poor comprehenders on simple words, while it did so consistently on more difficult words. The authors concluded that discrete naming latency does not predict reading-comprehension skill.

In 1978, Perfetti, Finger, and Hogaboam did a similar study using a variety of discrete naming tasks (colors, digits, pictures, categories, and words). Again, children were divided into reader groups on the basis of reading-comprehension scores. There was no difference between good and poor comprehenders on naming colors, digits, or line drawings of objects. They concluded that vocal-latency measures did not distinguish good from poor readers, and that the only real effect appeared when children had to read something.

Stanovich (1981), one of the major critics of continuous naming tasks, argued that these tasks measure sequential response time, plus the ability to scan rows of print and organize speech production, and that discrete naming is a much purer test of a connection between naming speed and reading. However, this study had too little power (eleven good and eleven poor readers) to resolve this issue. In a second study (Stanovich, Feeman, and Cunningham 1983), 109 normal first graders (average age 7:0) were tested on the Gates and the Metropolitan reading-comprehension tests, as well as on several discrete naming tasks. Only the data from the letter-naming task were reported. This correlated to reading comprehension at $-.38$ (children tested in the fall), and $-.28$ (children tested in the spring). These low values would be even lower if age and IQ had been controlled.

Stanovich and his colleagues concluded that because the correlations were so much weaker than those reported for continuous naming tasks, RAN tests overestimate the relationship between naming speed and reading. This may be true (and the fact that verbal IQ erases a lot of the variance shared between RAN and reading suggests that it is), but finding nothing explains nothing. In the first place, RAN tests didn't correlate well to reading comprehension in the studies reviewed above, and this was the only reading measure used here. The only way to find out if two tests measure different things is to use both tests in the same study.

Continuous and Discrete Naming Tasks Compared

Direct comparisons between the two types of naming tasks appeared in the early 1990s. A longitudinal study was carried out by Bowers (Bowers and Swanson 1991; Bowers 1995) using a variety of discrete and continuous naming tasks, plus tests of phonological awareness, memory, and vocabulary. Reading was measured by word recognition and word attack (Woodcock Reading Mastery). Comprehension was measured in the early part of the study by a group-administered test given by the school (Canadian Test of Basic Skills), and later in the study by the Woodcock passage-comprehension test.

Teachers nominated second graders as being poor and average readers (twenty-five poor and twenty-one average). The proportions of boys and girls were matched in the two groups (ratios around 2:1). There was no information on the children's ages, and age was not controlled in any data analysis, the first of several methodological problems. In sum, the experimental design was invalid, scores were nonnormally distributed, and results will be unreliable. For these reasons, only general trends are reported.[3]

The continuous naming tasks were RAN letters and digits. In the discrete naming test, letters and digits were presented one at a time, either immediately following the previous response or after a delay. Group comparisons showed that good readers were unfazed by this manipulation. The poor readers were 100 ms slower overall and much slower in the immediate-presentation condition.

The combined data for all children were used in a multiple regression analysis, as shown in table 15.7. At the top are the predictors for reading *accuracy*. With vocabulary controlled and the discrete naming task entered first, considerable variance was still accounted for by the RAN. This did not happen in reverse. This means that continuous naming tasks measure what discrete naming tasks measure, and a lot more besides, much as Stanovich suggested.

The bottom of the table shows the results for reading latency, the *speed* with which isolated words were read. Reading speed was accounted

---

3. Reading test scores were computed as percentile ranks, which doesn't maintain the true variance in the raw scores. Standard deviations revealed unequal variances in the groups' reading scores: a range of 8 percentile ranks for poor readers, and 25.4 percentile ranks for good readers. And despite Bowers's beautiful demonstration about the perils of using restricted IQ scores, a PPVT cutoff was set at 7 and below (scaled score), eliminating most of the children on the left side of the bell curve.

Table 15.7

Multiple regression analysis. Percent variance accounted for on reading tests by discrete and continuous naming

	Word ID (%)	Word attack (%)
Grade 2 reading		
Step 1 Vocabulary	11	16
Step 2 Discrete naming	9	2
Step 3 RAN	11	9
Step 1 Vocabulary	11	16
Step 2 RAN	20	10
Step 3 Discrete naming	0	0

Latency to read single words

	Regular spelling (%)	Irregular spelling (%)
Step 1 Vocabulary	1	2
Step 2 Discrete naming	41	46
Step 3 RAN	2	2
Step 1 Vocabulary	1	2
Step 2 RAN	24	32
Step 3 Discrete naming	17	14

Follow-on study Grade 4 reading

	Word ID (%)	Word attack (%)	Comprehension (%)
Grade 2 predictors			
Vocabulary	18	10	25
RAN	14	16	19
Grade 4 predictors			
Vocabulary	17	14	14
RAN only	11	17	7
RAN + discrete naming shared variance	12	0	7

Note: Values will be inflated because age was not controlled and data were non-normally distributed.

Source: Data from Bowers and Swanson 1991; Bowers 1995.

for entirely by discrete naming speed, and the RAN contributed nothing further. Reversing this process shows that half the variance on the RAN tests is due to simple (discrete) naming speed, and the remainder due to something else (pause time or retrieval time). If these results are only marginally reliable, they show that RAN tests are more predictive of reading *accuracy*, and discrete naming tests are measuring reading *speed*.

The children were followed up 2 years later at fourth grade (Bowers 1995). By now a number of good and poor readers had changed places, much as Bishop and Adams found in their study on language-impaired children. For example, six of the original poor readers (scores below the 25th percentile) were now average or good readers. Shifts of this magnitude make the goal of finding reading predictors more precarious than it already is. It also highlights the futility of using the good-reader/poor-reader design as a proxy for a proper correlational study.

The reader groups were reorganized on the basis of their new reading status, which I will designate *dyslexic*, *poor*, and *good*. The poor and dyslexic groups did not differ on IQ (WISC-R) or vocabulary (PPVT-R), and both groups scored well below the good readers. The dyslexic group was also notable for being slow (they were also inaccurate, having been selected for being inaccurate). By contrast, the poor readers performed identically to the good readers on every timed test. The discrete naming task was particularly discriminating, revealing enormous differences between the groups.

Wolff, Michel, and Ovrut (1990) (not to be confused with Wolf) developed a hybrid version of the two naming tasks. It was modeled on the RAN test and behaved like a continuous naming task, except the rate of presentation and the exposure duration of each item was controlled. This meant the child couldn't proceed at his or her own pace.

This study compared adolescent and college-age good and poor readers. Fifty dyslexics were recruited from a special school. Their reading-comprehension scores (Gray-oral) were $2\frac{1}{2}$ to 4 years below grade level. There were two control groups of fifty children each. One group (LD) had other learning difficulties, such as poor study skills and low math skills, but no reading problems. The other group was normal (average) in all respects. IQ range was restricted to 90–110, and groups were matched for age range, SES, and sex ratios. The study also included a group of older dyslexics enrolled in a special residential college and a matched group of college students with normal reading skills.

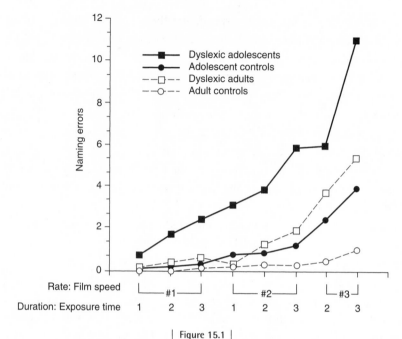

| Figure 15.1 |

Naming errors as a function of film speed and stimulus exposure duration. From Wolff, Michel, and Ovrut 1990.

The automated RAN test was set up as follows. Colors and digits were photographed and made into filmstrips. The film speed was varied at three rates: fast, medium, and slow. A shutter was used to produce three exposure durations of long, medium, and short. The rate and duration of each item were combined in nine ways, ranging from long exposure and slow presentation rate, to brief and fast. The number of naming errors as a function of rate and duration for each group is shown in figure 15.1.

No statistics are necessary here. The dyslexic students were extremely deviant on this task. The other groups didn't differ from each other and were generally unaffected until the fastest film speed. The dyslexics got progressively worse from the outset. There is evidence of an effect of exposure to print. Normal young adults made fewer errors at the fastest rates compared to normal adolescents. Similarly, adult dyslexics performed surprisingly like the adolescent normal readers, and certainly much better than the adolescent dyslexics.

Students were also given the standard version of the RAN test to find out if the same group effects would be seen. The dyslexics were 10 seconds slower on RAN objects and colors than the control groups. Correlations were high between the electronic naming test and the RAN for adolescents ($r = .79$) and adults ($r = .80$). (These within-group correlations are valid.) These results complement previous findings that very poor readers have greater difficulty with speeded tasks. IQ does not appear to be involved here because the IQ range was so restricted.

Wolff, Michel, and Ovrut were the first researchers to attempt to answer the following key question: What is the incidence of slow namers in the normal population and among poor readers? They established two sets of norms using the normal readers' test scores, one for discrete naming and one for the RAN. Using the rather liberal cutoff of 1 standard deviation below the mean, they found that the incidence of slow namers among the normal readers was 12 percent. The incidence for the dyslexic group was 50 percent. Yet when they compared the slow and fast dyslexics, there were no differences in reading accuracy or in IQ. This shows there is no necessary (causal) connection between naming speed and reading accuracy.

Now we have a mystery. There is a dissociation between speed of processing and reading accuracy. If 12 percent of normal readers are slow namers, how are they able to read normally? Or, conversely, if 50 percent of dyslexics have normal naming speeds, why aren't they better readers than the 50 percent of dyslexics who don't? I'll try to answer these questions in the next chapter.

Summing Up

Performance on continuous naming tasks in young children (age 5 and 6) is largely due to familiarity and mastery of color names, as well as letter and digit *shapes* and names. Early experience appears to be largely responsible for the high variability between children in this age range (Denckla and Rudel 1974a). This is confirmed by the fact that naming errors are more highly correlated to reading than naming speed is until the end of first grade (Mann and Ditunno 1990).

Age is also a strong predictor of naming speed for young children and remains a predictor much longer. Spring and Davis (1988) found that there is an exponential relationship between age and naming speed that is significant until around age 13. Verbal IQ is equally important. It accounts for a high proportion of variance in the relationship between naming speed and reading at all ages tested so far, whereas performance IQ does not (Bowers, Steffy, and Tate 1988). This suggests that the naming-speed/reading connection is specific to the language systems of the brain, rather than part of a general speed factor, which is what many of the performance IQ subtests measure.

When experience, age, and verbal IQ/vocabulary are controlled, RAN digits and RAN letters account for about 10 to 14 percent of the variance in decoding accuracy, whereas RAN colors do not (Bowers, Steffy, and Tate 1988). The only discrepant result to this pattern was the finding by D. McGuinness, C. McGuinness, and Donohue (1995) on high-SES girls, whose color naming speeds predicted reading accuracy on real words (word ID) but not on nonsense words (word attack). It is difficult to compare this result on normal children with the studies in this group, because the other children were from clinical populations (LD, ADD, poor readers) with a preponderance of boys.

The fact that RAN digits and letters predict reading so much better than RAN colors and objects do means that naming speed per se is not a factor in learning to read. Also, the fact that RAN digits predict reading just as well as RAN letters do means that letter names per se are not a factor in learning to read. The RAN-reading connection is more general than this, more likely to be due to home instruction and to the speed of paired-associate learning. This is more evidence that paired-associate learning is a key component of decoding skill. (See chapter 13.)

The profile of approximately half of the very poorest readers consists of highly inaccurate decoding coupled with extremely slow naming speeds, with the most deviant performance on rapidly paced *discrete* naming tasks (Bowers and Swanson 1991; Wolff, Michel, and Ovrut 1990). This profile appeared even when the very poor readers did not differ from good readers on full-scale IQ (Wolff, Michel, and Ovrut 1990; Bowers 1995), and when they did not differ on tests of articulation rate and fluency, verbal short-term memory (memory span), and expressive vocabulary (Ackerman and Dykman 1993). The other distinguishing feature of this group is that they are more likely to be boys (4:1 ratio in Ackerman and Dykman's study).

After 30 years of research on what's wrong with poor readers, with good-reader/poor-reader differences and correlations in abundance, we don't seem to be inching toward cause, and now we have an added question, in view of the fact that 12 percent of normal readers are slow namers: When does slow naming speed matter and when doesn't it? The only way to answer this question is to leave the realm of correlational statistics and do some experiments—train slow namers to speed up and see if they can do it without loss of accuracy, and can transfer this aptitude to new text. Studies of this type are reported in *Early Reading Instruction.* They show that the technique of "rereading" has great success if the proper controls are in place. Meanwhile, we go to Austria for new insights about slow readers.

SLOW READERS: HOW SLOW IS SLOW?

Despite the large number of studies on naming speed, there has been no attempt to separate children who read inaccurately and slowly from children who are merely slow. Not even Wolff's analysis helps us here. What is the proportion of readers who are excessively slow but accurate, and does this matter? The answer to this question came by serendipity when slow readers were thrust into the limelight in a search for dyslexic children in Austria (Wimmer 1993).

Slow Accurate Readers

There is no "dyslexia" in Austria, or at least no diagnostic criteria for it. Nevertheless, Wimmer's basic philosophy is that dyslexia is real (a property of the child) and, as such, should be found in Austria like everywhere else. Due to the nature of the German writing system and how reading is taught in Austrian schools, Wimmer believes that dyslexic children will have a different profile from dyslexics in English-speaking countries. As he put it, "The present study is concerned with the nature of dyslexia among children who learn to read the German writing system" (p. 1).

The study had two goals: "to specify the nature of the reading difficulties, and to explore cognitive impairments that may cause the difficulties.... We expected that the German dyslexic children might exhibit similar, or even more serious, impairments of phonological awareness than the English dyslexic children" (p. 3). There is no doubt here that "dyslexia" will be found, and that it is due to an impairment.

The German writing system has a transparent orthography—a nearly one-to-one correspondence between phoneme and grapheme. While some phonemes have more than one spelling, hardly any graphemes represent more than one sound, and this is especially true for vowels. Like English, the German writing system reuses the same vowel letters again and again to stand for different vowel sounds. But unlike English, it consistently marks the vowel letters by a "diacritic"—a symbol that signals a change in pronunciation. (In the words *Baum* ("tree") and *Bäume* ("trees"), the umlaut changes the vowel /ow/ to /oi/.)

Reading instruction is different as well. Austrian children start proper school at age 6. They arrive in the classroom knowing few if any letters, and have little or no awareness of phonemes. All this has to be taught. Instead of the chaotic mix offered to English-speaking children in schools around the world, Austrian children learn the phonemes of their language and the correspondences between these phonemes and their spellings. Letter names are never used. Sight words are never taught. Instead, the child is taught a direct relationship between phonemes and symbols, so there is no interference between letter names and letter-sound correspondences. Children learn to spell by isolating then blending phonemes (letters) into words. They learn to read by translating letter sequences back into phonemes. This is the optimal way to teach any alphabetic writing system, especially one with a nontransparent orthography like English (see McGuinness 1997b, 1998; *Early Reading Instruction*).

Wimmer's first job was to find the poor readers. He asked 60 classroom teachers in Salzburg to refer children who were making unsatisfactory progress in reading or spelling. The teachers identified 120 children. Assuming 25 to 30 children per classroom, 120 poor readers would represent about 7 to 8 percent of children in grades 2 through 4 in the Salzburg schools. When these children were tested for reading and spelling accuracy, they made hardly any mistakes. However, when the reading tests were timed, the children turned out to be exceedingly slow. So far, neither Wimmer nor his colleagues have looked objectively at the practical implications of being slow. There are only anecdotal reports: "Dyslexic children's reading is so slow and laborious that book reading is aversive and learning from text difficult, so that all school activities involving reading are highly problematic for these children" (Landerl, Wimmer, and Frith 1997, 320).

Having discovered these slow but accurate readers, Wimmer set out to find out more about them. He selected the slowest 74 readers out of the 120 referred who were in grades 2 through 4 (7 to 9 years). There were 154 normal readers acting as control groups. Half were the same age, and half read at the same speed but were much younger (reading speed matched). Most slow readers were boys: 80 to 85 percent in second and third grade, and 60 percent in fourth grade. Normal-reader groups had equal sex ratios (50:50).

Apart from the uneven sex ratios, there were other problems with matching the groups. The slow readers had considerably lower WISC vocabulary scores ($p < .001$), a measure of expressive vocabulary. Sex, age, vocabulary, and nonverbal IQ were not controlled in any statistical analysis. Tasks were mainly in-house tests. No information was provided on norms, standard deviations, or reliabilities, and any group differences on these tests must be treated with caution, as must the correlations. The isolated-groups design was front and center. Despite these serious methodological problems, this work is so important that I will report the major trends in the data.

Wimmer developed several reading tests to measure speed and accuracy. The format consisted of left-to-right running text (like a book) that displayed different kinds of words, such as normal text (a story), a series of unrelated words, or digits. Each test had the same format: rows of concrete nouns, rows of function words, compound words, or nonsense words, and so forth.

The children were tested for accuracy and for speed. The reader groups did not differ in accuracy on any text with real words, and while slow readers made more errors reading nonwords, the error rate was so low (8 percent) that it was inconsequential. However, the poor readers were very slow indeed. Fourth-grade slow readers read as slowly as the second-grade normal readers, children with just over 1 year of reading instruction. I converted the data to words per minute to make the scores comparable to other studies in this chapter. Reading speeds for the second and fourth graders set out by the type of text are shown in table 16.1.

One other characteristic of slow readers, documented here and in later studies (Wimmer 1996; Landerl, Wimmer, and Frith 1997; Wimmer and Landerl 1997), is that they do well on phonetic (regular) spelling tests but less well on spelling tests with irregularly spelled words. Irregular spellings are rare in German, so slow readers may not be aware that there *are* unpredictable spellings in the German spelling code.

The main purpose of this study was to compare the reader groups on tests similar to those used in research on English-speaking children.

Table 16.1

Continuous reading speed in words per minute for normal and "slow" Austrian children in grade 2 and grade 4

	Normal readers	Slow readers
Grade 2		
Text	88	41
Content words	72	34
Function words	80	42
Compound words	25	10
Nonwords	28	16
Grade 4		
Text	140	80
Content words	100	67
Function words	100	63
Compound words	51	25
Nonwords	39	23

Note: Data were converted to words per minute from time per word.
Source: Data from Wimmer 1993.

Groups did not differ on most measures. These included a difficult nonword spelling test, a test of nonword repetition, and a digit-span test. Wimmer developed a sound-categorization test (odd one out) consisting of sets of two-syllable words (*Rappe, Kappe, Ratte, Mappe*). This was a difficult task for everyone. Out of ten items, slow readers averaged six correct for the three age groups, and good readers around seven and a half. Slow readers also had marginally more trouble on a vowel-substitution task.

The RAN colors and digits tests were most informative. Slow readers did not differ from normal readers on RAN colors but were much slower on RAN digits. This is illustrated in the accompanying table. Values were converted to words per minute, so a high score is good.

	Second	Third	Fourth
Colors			
Slow readers	56	60	60
Normal readers	61	66	71
Digits			
Slow readers	71	82	79
Normal readers	90	90	107

Children were given a test of visual persistence (iconic memory), the visual analog of echoic memory. Rows of digits flashed briefly on a screen, followed by a pattern, then lines appeared where the digits used to be with a question mark under one of the lines. Children had to remember which digit had been in that location. No differences were found between groups at second and third grade, but slow readers were more inaccurate than normal readers at fourth grade. However, WISC vocabulary was most discrepant for this age group, and this was not controlled.

These results say more about what they didn't show than about what they did. The fact that group differences in naming speed appeared for digits but not for colors shows, once again, that reading slowly has nothing to do with naming speed, supporting studies reviewed in the preceding chapter.

Wimmer did not report reliability estimates for any of his in-house tests, and concern over the test reliability was increased by the correlational data. No table of correlations was provided. Out of thirty-six correlations, Wimmer reported that only six values exceeded $r = .30$. This is very unusual. The highest correlation was between RAN colors and objects (.57), tests that usually correlate at around .70 (Blachman 1984; D. McGuinness, C. McGuinness, and Donohue 1995). The RAN digits test was reported as the strongest predictor of reading speed, but no correlation value was given. Correlations between RAN digits and the other tests were not significant. And there is no question that values would be even lower if age, sex, and vocabulary had been controlled. For these reasons and more, the results from a multiple regression analysis will be unreliable and are not reported.

In follow-up studies to find out more about phonological skills in the slow readers, Wimmer et al. (1991) showed that there was a far greater impact of reading instruction on phoneme-awareness skills than the reverse, once early reading and letter-name knowledge were controlled. Wimmer (1996) tested reading speed for isolated words and nonwords. Fourth-grade slow readers were compared to second-grade normal readers matched for reading speed. The children were asked to read common words, "familiar" nonwords (words with German syllables), and "foreign" nonwords (illegal syllable patterns). There were few differences between the groups, except that slow readers made more errors on the illegal nonwords. Examples were reading *molas* as *malas* (vowel duplication), and *toki* as *koki* (consonant duplication). Wimmer suggested this reflected a "phonological-processing" problem, but this is highly debatable in view of the fact that no group differences were found on the other tasks. Nor is this argument supported by Wimmer, Mayringer, and Landerl 2000, who showed that phoneme awareness measured at the start of school (age 6) had no impact on the children's subsequent reading skill, either for decoding accuracy or fluency.

Mayringer and Wimmer's (2000) study on paired-associate learning was described briefly in chapter 13. The slow readers were 9-year-old boys. They were loosely matched on nonverbal IQ and PPVT vocabulary to boys who were very fast readers (no overlap in reading speed). The children did two tasks. In the first, they were asked to memorize the names of pictures of children that had familiar real names, unfamiliar real names, or made-up names. In the second task, children had to memorize nonsense names of pictures of "fantasy animals."

Slow readers had no trouble learning to match pictures to familiar names, but took much longer to match unfamiliar real names to the pictures; made-up names were even harder. Scores noticeably improved for everyone in the "fantasy-animals" study, probably because the task was more interesting and the names were shorter. By the third trial, the normal readers had an almost perfect score (2.75). Yet at eight trials, slow readers still averaged only 2.25 names correct, and there was little improvement after that.

Mayringer and Wimmer noted that slow readers were able to pronounce the pseudonames perfectly on the first attempt, so they had no problems with auditory perception, phonological short-term memory, or articulation. Slow readers also mastered pairing familiar names with children's pictures as well as normal readers, so their difficulty is not a problem with paired-associate learning per se. They concluded that slow readers had a problem with "learning new phonological forms" and committing them to long-term memory. This conclusion was supported by the fact that most errors were phonological distortions.

However, the slow readers' problem on this task may be more accurately described as a difficulty remembering new *phonotactic* forms, rather than difficulties with German phonology. The nonsense names for children (*sobilo*, *mefose*, *tivami*, and *rofemo*, *kasima*, *felise*) and for fantasy animals (*gelo*, *tafi*, *bosa*, and *sapo*, *lute*, *rika*) are far more like Italian syllable patterns than German. And while the children were able to repeat these words correctly the first time they heard them, these alien syllable patterns have "nowhere to go" in verbal long-term memory. Slow readers, for whatever reason, seem to take longer to set up a "home" for nonstandard syllable patterns, and would be expected to have considerable difficulty learning a foreign language.

Although there are a number of methodological problems with these studies, they opened a veritable Pandora's box of disturbing facts about the notion of dyslexia. They give no credence to the notion that a phonological-processing deficit is the hallmark of dyslexia, a constitutionally determined impairment. The studies also confirm the growing tide of research evidence reviewed in earlier chapters that children with reasonably intact verbal IQs should have no trouble learning to read. Certainly if there were such a thing as a phonological-processing deficit independent of orthography and reading instruction, it ought to afflict Austrian children as well.

Cross-Cultural Studies

The situation did not rest here. Wimmer went on to collaborate with English colleagues on two cross-cultural studies. In a normative study (Wimmer and Goswami 1994), there were eighty-one Austrian and seventy-two English children in approximately second, third, and fourth grade. The children were not screened for reading or any other measure. English children were described as being taught a mix of look-say and phonics, which involved learning letter-sound correspondences for single letters plus word families. No further details were provided.[1]

It was difficult to match the two groups of children. In England, children begin reading instruction at age 4 or 5 and have a head start on the Austrian children, who don't begin until after age 6. The Austrian children were older in this study. The two orthographies differ in the

---

1. This description is very misleading. Reading instruction in the United Kingdom in 1993–1994 was strongly oriented toward whole language due to teacher training and to national and local curriculum guidelines. If phonics was taught, it would have been rarely and unsystematically. See McGuinness 1998.

extreme, as do the teaching methods. One would imagine that it would be hard to interpret any significant differences between the groups. However, the differences were so enormous that none of these details mattered.

The children took the reading tests designed by Wimmer. The first test consisted of rows of digits, the second of number words, and in the third, nonwords were created from the number words by changing one letter. Children were told to read across the rows quickly and accurately. Errors were almost nonexistent for digits, and there were too few errors on number words for any statistical analysis.

The main difference appeared on the nonsense words. The English children did significantly worse at all three grades, making three to five times as many mistakes. The English 9-year-olds made nearly twice as many errors (8.8) as the Austrian 7-year-olds (4.8). And while the children read digits and numbers with equal speed, the English children took over 1 second longer per word to read the nonwords. This means that the English 9-year-olds read at the same rate as Austrian 7-year-olds and made twice as many errors doing it. This is despite the fact that the English 9-year-olds had 4 more years of reading instruction than the Austrian 7-year-olds did.

The 2-year age gap in reading speed between the Austrian and English children is the same as the 2-year gap between the so-called dyslexic Austrian children and their Austrian reading-matched controls. It is this gap that Wimmer uses to define dyslexia. But if Austrian slow readers are dyslexic, as Wimmer asserts, this would mean that *all normal English 9-year-olds* are dyslexic by the same criterion, especially as they've had many more years of reading instruction. However you cut the cake, these results show that dyslexia is entirely relative, tied to a writing system and method of instruction. This is quite apart from the fact that the tests for dyslexia in the two countries aren't remotely the same. Dyslexia in English-speaking countries is defined by reading accuracy, not by speed.

If dyslexia is relative, not independent of the writing system and reading instruction, it is impossible to make a case for a specific impairment due to a constitutional problem.

As a follow on, a comprehensive study was carried out on English and Austrian dyslexics (Landerl, Wimmer, and Frith 1997). In England, the criteria for dyslexia were reading *accuracy* as determined by scores at or below the 19th percentile on a reading test, normal IQ, and persistence of reading problems. The English dyslexics were reading age 4 years below chronological age. Spelling accuracy was at the 8th percentile. The Austrian dyslexics were defined by norms on a reading-*speed* test recently published by the authors, with dyslexics scoring at or below the 12th percentile. Both groups of children were considered severe, and nearly all had received additional help, some of it extensive. Ten of the English children were in special schools. The groups did not differ on nonverbal IQ (Raven's matrices), but there was no mention of verbal IQ, and this was not controlled.

Table 16.2 shows that Austrian dyslexics (as expected) were much more accurate readers than English dyslexics. What was not expected was that the slow Austrian dyslexics would be so much *faster* than the English dyslexics, who read at approximately half the speed. In a 10-minute period, the Austrian dyslexics would be able to read about 500 words compared to 260 for the English dyslexics, and they would misread only 7 percent of the words compared to 40 percent for the English children. The same pattern was found for real words, nonwords, and three-syllable

Table 16.2

A Comparison of reading accuracy and speed between English and Austrian dyslexics

	Words	Nonwords
% Errors, all words		
Austrian	7%	14%
English	40%	52%
% Errors, 3-syllable words		
Austrian	10%	20%
English	53%	70%
Words per minute, all words		
Austrian	50	32
English	26	15
Words per minute, 3-syllable words		
Austrian	35	21
English	15	10

Note: Austrian children: mean age 11:7 (10:7 to 12:7). English children: mean age 10:9 (10:9 to 13:1).
Source: Data from Landerl, Wimmer, and Frith 1997.

words. (No doubt parents of the English dyslexics would be overjoyed if their children read as fluently and accurately as the Austrian dyslexics.)

On the basis of these results, Wimmer suggested that we need to establish two types of dyslexia: "speed dyslexia" and "decoding dyslexia." But why? If there is no decoding dyslexia in Austria, how can there be decoding dyslexia anywhere else? If 100 percent of the Austrian population have no decoding problems, and "speed dyslexics" read twice as fast as dyslexics in England, something is fundamentally wrong with the notion of dyslexia, certainly when defined as an "underlying neurocognitive deficit" (Landerl, Wimmer, and Frith 1997).

The facts are indisputable. There is no validity to a phonological-deficit model of dyslexia. There is no validity to the concept of dyslexia that is independent of sex, verbal IQ, reading instruction, and type of orthography.

However, there are still a number of unanswered questions. What causes children who learn the same transparent orthography with the same excellent reading instruction to be excessively slow readers? And if we find the answer to this question, can anything be done about it?

Causes of Reading Slowly

In a Southern California swimming pool where wannabe Olympic swimmers train, there is a large sign at the end of the pool that reads:

THE ONLY WAY TO SWIM FAST IS TO SWIM FAST.

Would the same advice apply to reading fast? The answer is yes, and fluency-training studies have proven to be highly effective (see Early Reading Instruction). Here, we look at the research on what slow readers do when they read. What are the eyes looking at? How much information can a reader take in at each fixation?

Developmental Aspects of Eye Movements and Perceptual Span

There is no absolute answer to the following question: How fast should one be able to read? Writing is a coded representation of speech, and speech flows at a rate that it optimal for the human brain, which is around 250 to 350 words per minute. One would expect that reading speed should approach a normal speaking rate, or even exceed it, but most adult readers don't read this fast. That reading rate lags so far behind in slow readers appears to be the major reason they're frustrated. They can't extract the information fast enough to process meaning (if indeed Landerl, Wimmer, and Frith are correct in their description of slow readers' problems).

Is there an optimum reading rate? In a review of the literature on eye-movement control, Rayner (1998) provided information on expert readers. These were college students identified as being excellent readers by virtue of high scores on a reading-comprehension test. Despite the similarity of their reading performance, the students had a wide range of reading speeds, with scores ranging from 230 to 382 words per minute (median 315). There appears to be no magic optimum reading speed. It should be emphasized that these expert readers' scores are likely to be higher than those of ordinary readers.

Wimmer's data showed that normal second graders in Austria read about 88 words per minute and fourth graders 140 words per minute. These numbers are comparable to Rayner's (1986) data on American children. Second graders read about 90 words per minute, fourth graders 165, and sixth graders about 200, approaching the slowest good college reader in Rayner's (1998) study (230 wpm). This shows a rapid increase in skill over a 5-year time period, as well as high variability, which does not diminish even in skilled readers.

Rayner also provided information on fixation duration for the same students. The college students were equally variable here as well, with scores ranging from a slow 255 ms to a brisk 190 ms *per word*. These values don't seem that far apart by our sluggish sense of time, which operates on a scale of seconds, but it's a large difference for a brain that computes and transmits messages on a scale of milliseconds. Fixation duration for the children ranged from 237 to 289 ms. Once again the sixth graders overlapped the slowest college students.

Words per minute and fixation duration turned out to be highly correlated when I computed the college students' data ($r = .71$). Rayner pointed out that reading rate in words per minute can be estimated almost completely by three measures: fixation duration, the number of fixations made in a given time interval, and the time it takes the reader to initiate and execute a saccade. A saccadic eye movement takes the reader's eyes from one point of fixation to the next.

Reading is a learned motor skill and eye movements are the major players. There are six pairs of eye muscles. Four pairs control conjunctive movements (eyes moving together up, down, left, right, and diagonally) and two pairs control vergence movements, where eyes move opposite to each other, toward or away from the nose. Reading isn't like a typical motor skill such as playing tennis or the piano where the component parts (arms, legs, fingers) can be inspected and moved around. The skill part of reading is not under voluntary control. It builds indirectly through repetitive acts of analyzing patterns of print, with the only instruction being that eyes look in a left-to-right order and from the top to the bottom of the page. Knowledge of the code is the key, because the reader must find a match for a string of letters to something known and understood before moving on.

In most European alphabets, the young reader has to be *consciously* on the lookout for isolated letters and letter teams at the same time. The letter pair _sh_ decodes as /sh/, not /s/ and /h/. For the beginning reader, this requires some cognitive effort. As the code is mastered, the effort diminishes and begins to run on automatic pilot outside the range of consciousness. The process becomes too fast for us to monitor it, leading people to believe that good readers turn into full-fledged "sight-word" readers, scooping up whole words at a glance—a notion that is completely false. (See *Early Reading Instruction* for a full analysis of this issue.)

Proof that decoding skill is the fundamental process underlying eye-movement patterns comes from studies where children read easy and difficult texts. What is difficult is determined by decoding skill (knowing how the code works), and the length and unfamiliarity of the words. Difficult words produce deviant eye-movement patterns, regardless of age. Eye-movement patterns for difficult-to-read words are noticeably erratic with lots of regressions, causing reading speed to slow. When college students were given difficult text outside their area of expertise, their eye movements looked identical to those of children with serious reading problems (Rayner 1985, 1986). In other words, eye movements are subordinate to higher-order cognitive processing in which the major goal is to make sense of print.

There are other reasons why accurate readers might read slowly. A small number of children have been found to have oculomotor problems that lead to erratic eye-movement control. They are unable to fixate steadily or control eye movements smoothly. Research by Stein (1993; also see McGuinness 1997b, 1998) has shown that problems controlling binocular vergence and tracking can derail a young reader. Vergence movements keep the eyes focused in depth precisely on the surface of the page, while, at the same time, the two eyes scan at precisely the same rate and position. The two groups of eye muscles must work in tandem, eyes consistently converging in one plane (in depth) while moving synchronously in another. Problems with fine-motor control would make reading difficult or impossible, causing letters to bounce around the page and flip over, while the print constantly goes in and out of focus. (Many very poor readers complain about this.)

Vergence control has a long developmental path. Stein, Riddell, and Fowler (1986) reported that only 52 percent of 5- and 6-year-olds had consistent vergence control. This improved slowly, and it wasn't until age 11 that nearly all children were consistent. Obviously, this level of precision isn't necessary for reading—otherwise there would be far more poor readers than there are—but Stein, Riddell, and Fowler found that more poor readers than good readers lagged behind in this developmental process. Problems with eye-movement control might be more common than most people believe, especially because "visual" theories of reading are currently out of favor. Fortunately, oculomotor problems are easy to diagnose, and vision therapies for improving vergence control and binocular tracking appear to be relatively quick and successful (see C. McGuinness, D. McGuinness, and G. McGuinness 1996; McGuinness 1997b).

(Another more controversial theory based on differences in vision physiology between good and poor readers has been put forward by Lovegrove and his group. Due to the highly technical nature of these studies, this is discussed in an addendum to this chapter.)

There is another set of clues in the eye-movement research that might explain why some readers are slow, even though they read accurately. This has to do with the amount of information available at each fixation. Skilled readers have an asymmetric peripheral span. They see about twice as many letters to the right of fixation as to the left. Beginning readers have no asymmetry (of course), and if children are progressing normally, it takes about a year of reading instruction for it to show up. When it finally comes online, this is only the beginning of another period of transition.

Rayner (1986) devised a technique for controlling the number of letters visible in the periphery while the reader reads continuous text. The impact of the number of available letters on reading speed was calculated to find out how far in the periphery the reader could extract useful information. Rayner discovered that children's perceptual spans were smaller than adults' and stayed small until about 12 years of age. Something else was different. The adults actually used all the information available to them, but the children did not. A slight reduction in the number of visible letters to the far right caused a noticeable decline in the adults' reading speed. Children were not seriously affected by this maneuver until the span shrank to eleven letters. They read at nearly the same rate with eleven letters in view as they did with 23, showing they relied almost exclusively on foveal (central) vision and did not take advantage of peripheral cues.

The complex skill called "reading" takes 9 to 13 years to become fully integrated and efficient, and even then it has further to go. When Rayner (1986) measured the *functional* perceptual span for each fixation duration (the amount of information actually obtained by the reader), second graders processed .46 of a word, fourth graders .78, sixth graders .82, and adults, one whole word.

The discovery that peripheral cues are picked up during reading was counterintuitive. It's been known for a very long time, probably since the earliest astronomers, that peripheral vision is useful for spotting dim stars at night (the dark-adapted eye sees best at 20 degrees lateral to fixation), but is decidedly blurred and indistinct when the sun comes up. Yet, somehow, this blurred information is put to use by skilled readers. The first two letters of the following word can be picked up rather well. Beyond that, there is information on word length and pattern marked by ascenders (h, t, b, d) and descenders (j, p, q, y).

Context and syntax come into play as well by priming the brain to estimate in advance what word of that length and pattern, starting with those particular letters, would be likely to fit that slot in the sentence. By activating some words prior to the time the word is fixated, the reader is ahead of the game, having a few possible matches in mind. *Readers do not usually do this consciously* (although it can be done consciously). We aren't aware of making these perceptual and linguistic judgments because they happen too quickly for us to monitor them. Our brain does this for us.

Good readers process nearly every letter in a word while their brain is busily computing probabilities of what words might lie to the right. This means there is bottom-up (code-based) processing going on simultaneously with global pattern recognition (peripheral vision), plus estimations of the statistical likelihood that particular words starting with *those* letters, of *that* shape and length, might appear in certain contexts and sentence slots. (This amazing capacity extends to a preconscious analysis of the syntactic structure of sentences. See *Early Reading Instruction*.)

Summary

At this point, we begin to see the connection between language skills and reading accuracy and fluency, specifically vocabulary and syntax. The top-down effects of vocabulary have been demonstrated many times in this book. Metsala and Walley showed that word frequency and age of acquisition of a word were the strongest factors determining response time to recognize a spoken word. Using context to predict words to the right of fixation involves generative (expressive) vocabulary skills. Wimmer reported that his slow readers had low expressive vocabulary scores.

Reading speed is linked to syntax, one of the few language tests to consistently correlate to reading in properly controlled studies (see chapter 14). Anticipating which words might fall to the right of fixation is more likely to involve syntax than context, because readers will always know where they are in a sentence, and what part of speech is likely to be coming up next. Willows and Ryan (1986) found that performance on syntax tests correlated significantly to a variety of reading tests, with the strongest connection to reading speed or fluency (not accuracy). Rayner (1998) cites forty studies on the impact of syntax on reading fluency and eye movements and describes the "strong impact of sentential context" on reading speed.

Thus, there are various reasons why Wimmer's slow readers are slow. They could be delayed in language development, particularly syntactic development. They could have low verbal IQs. Only one of the many studies from Wimmer's group included a measure of verbal IQ, and large differences between the slow and normal readers were reported. Perhaps they lag developmentally in binocular tracking and convergence. This would cause them to slow down and focus on a smaller set of letters.

They might have more difficulty with paired-associate learning, or they may have begun learning letter-sound correspondences later than the other children.

It is also possible that slow readers develop a habit of using central (foveal) vision exclusively and fail to pick up useful cues in the peripheral visual field that could speed them along. This habit could be caused by any of the things listed above, but it's possible that it's simply a *habit*. It's a habit that is safe because it trades speed for accuracy, a better solution than trading accuracy for speed, a really scary place to be.

This brings us back to the poster on the wall. If you swim slowly you will continue to swim slowly. If you read slowly, you will continue to read slowly. But unlike the swimmer, who is in conscious control of rhythm and speed (swimmers count beats to synchronize arm strokes and kick rate), the slow reader is not in control and doesn't know how to be in control. Just telling a poor reader to read faster doesn't work. Fortunately, there are excellent methods for improving reading speed. These are examined in depth in *Early Reading Instruction*.

Addendum

A popular theory has been put forward that the major cause of dyslexia is due to a malfunction in visual physiology. Lovegrove and his colleagues (see Lovegrove and Williams 1993) have reported a number of studies in which poor readers differ from good readers in "transient" visual-system function, but do not differ on tasks requiring the "sustained" visual system. There are two major visual systems in the brain, which start at the retina and end in the visual cortex. The transient system has a rapid onset and offset to visual input, is responsible for peripheral vision and for seeing in low light, and is highly sensitive to motion. The sustained system operates more slowly. It controls central (foveal) vision, is highly sensitive to detail and color, is not as sensitive to motion, and is blind in low light. The act of reading relies on visual acuity, the primary function of the sustained visual system.

Lovegrove's results are, therefore, paradoxical. Rather than seeking the source of the paradox, Lovegrove prefers the simple view that poor readers have a transient-system deficit. This is another one-cause-fits-all model that fails to consider alternative explanations. One of the main alternatives is that the results are an artifact of sex differences. In an isolated-groups design, which is used exclusively by this group, there are often more girls in the good-reader group and a preponderance of boys in the poor-reader group. This matters because there are striking sex differences in the sensitivity of the two visual systems. The transient system is significantly more sensitive in females. In studies by McGuinness (1976), McGuinness and Lewis (1978), Brabyn and McGuinness (1978), and Brabyn and McGuinness (n.d.), females were found to have greater sensitivity to gross pattern contrasts (lower thresholds for low spatial-frequency input), greater sensitivity to motion (especially low spatial-frequency motion), shorter and less erratic visual persistence in conditions of high luminance, longer visual persistence in the dark, higher sensitivity to long wave lengths, and longer delays in metacontrast masking. Males are generally opposite to the girls in every way in transient-system function. (Males also have higher visual acuity in conditions of normal light.) These sex differences are large and consistent (lawful). The tasks I've listed are identical or similar to those used by Lovegrove in which he finds that *good readers* have greater sensitivity than poor readers.

Lovegrove and his colleagues (Williams, Molinet, and LeCluwse 1989) reported that dyslexic subjects did not experience masking of a central (fixated) target by a peripheral mask. This is what one might expect of children who don't read much. Rayner's data (cited above) showed that sensitivity to peripheral cues during reading takes a long time to set up. However, Lovegrove and Williams prefer an explanation in terms of internal cause, having to do with "transient-on-sustained inhibition," rather than a facility acquired through practice. According to their theory, the transient system is too weak to inhibit attention to a central target in poor readers.

The major difficulty with models like this one, apart from their extremely limited scope, is that they provide no solution and offer no hope. If you have poor visual tracking, it can be trained. If you fail to notice peripheral cues, you can participate in rereading training, or be trained to notice them. But if you have a transient-system deficit, you're stuck with it. It is yet another unfixable, biological marker for "dyslexia." This raises a host of thorny questions like the following. If, as Lovegrove and his colleagues claim, "75% of children with a special reading disability show reduced transient system sensitivity" (p. 316), and transient deficits *cause* reading problems (which is what all this research implies), where do the transient deficits go in countries with a transparent writing system where everyone can read? Why don't they matter there as well? And where do these deficits go after remedial treatment, which we now know can be 100 percent effective in less than 12 hours? (See C. McGuinness, D. McGuinness, and G. McGuinness 1996; McGuinness 1997b.)

SUMMARY: WHAT DO WE KNOW FOR SURE?

The juxtaposition of several research traditions has been both enlightening and disturbing—enlightening because research on language development has been highly productive in resolving major questions about theories of reading acquisition, and disturbing because, with few exceptions, reading research has not. The contrast can be seen at the outset, in how the research problem is tackled.

Research on language development is largely directed to the nature side of the nature-nurture equation. This is entirely appropriate for the study of a species-specific biological trait. Yet the nurture side of the equation is not neglected, and scientists also monitor the role of parents in their children's language development. Researchers like Vihman, Stoel-Gammon, Rescorla, Paul, and many others have documented parents' input during early language acquisition and in studies on late talkers. Hart and Risley made an enormous contribution to our understanding of what "shared environment" means, and to our knowledge of how parents' input influences the acquisition of expressive vocabulary and subsequent language skills.

Reading research has also focused on the nature side of the nature-nurture equation. But this focus is inappropriate. The ability to master a human invention like a writing system doesn't "develop". It is not part of our biological heritage. Reading is a learned skill and needs to be taught. There is a 43 percent functional illiteracy rate in the United States, while most countries with transparent writing systems have marginal illiteracy rates. In Sweden, the rate for 16- to 25-year-olds is a miniscule 3.5 percent (Organization for Economic Cooperation and Development, 1997). In Austria, Wimmer's slow readers were able to decode and spell almost perfectly. If reading was biological, a property of genes, this would mean that people in Sweden, Austria, and the English-speaking countries came from different gene pools, which is patently absurd.

To compound the problem, the important nurture side of the equation has been virtually ignored. Reading researchers have failed to take into account the impact of home environment, the kinds of preliteracy skills taught at home or in preschool, and the type of reading instruction the child has received. These critical environmental factors continue to be ignored even when there is abundant and consistent evidence of their importance. Home instruction in letter-sound correspondences is a major contributor to early reading success, yet this hasn't been accounted for or controlled, even though we have known this for over a decade (Wagner, Torgesen, and Rashotte 1994; Wimmer 1993; Stuart 1995).

This has led to a strange situation in which research on language development provides a truer test of the theories of reading acquisition than the research purported to test these theories. Research on reading has been guided by false assumptions and deductive models that led to a misdirected focus. The emphasis has been on children with reading problems, with the goal of finding out what's wrong with them. This emphasis is underpinned by a belief that the deficiency is *in the child* and not in the environment. A set of unproven assumptions has preempted any rigorous test of the causes of reading success or failure. Causality is assumed to be unidirectional (from the child) despite the fact that causality can't be determined from the descriptive or correlational research that typifies most of this work.[1]

From this platform, or set of premises, it is but one easy step to the additional assumption that the cause of reading difficulties is an inability to process speech at the appropriate level for an alphabetic writing system. Here is the logic: Alphabetic writing systems are designed to map phonemes to visual symbols. Phonemes are difficult to disentangle from the speech stream due to coarticulation. The precursor of explicit phoneme awareness/analysis is speech perception, which develops over childhood.

---

1. An isolated-groups design in which good and poor readers are compared is simply a bogus correlational study.

Therefore, children with reading problems have a deficit in phonological development. This is confirmed by the fact that children with reading problems have more difficulty on phoneme-awareness tasks.

Using this limited, analogical reasoning, researchers believed they could set aside or bypass important issues and critical controls that are essential in science. As noted earlier, if the problem is in the child, then one doesn't have to bother with the environment. If it can be assumed that phonological awareness derives from speech perception, or that speech perception develops in a particular order or manner, this doesn't have to be proven either.

The way this type of reasoning unfolds and sustains itself is illustrated by Liberman and Shankweiler's 1985 paper updating what had transpired since the formulation of their theory in the early 1970s (see chapter 2). Summarizing the earlier work, they wrote: "We know that the child's awareness of phonological structure does not happen all at once, but develops gradually over a period of years" (p. 9).

The I. Y. Liberman et al. (1974, 10) study on tapping syllable beats and phonemes was cited as proof for this claim: "Some 12 years ago, we began to examine developmental trends in phonological awareness.... It was clear from these results that awareness of phoneme segments is harder to achieve than awareness of syllable segments, and develops later, if at all.... It was also apparent that a large number of children may not have attained either level of understanding of linguistic structure even at the end of a full year in school."

After 12 years, Liberman and Shankweiler still did not recognize the true nature of their tasks and what could legitimately be inferred from them, nor that Fox and Routh's results contradicted their position. This statement contains the inference that phonological developmental is untouched by anything that goes on in the classroom. In their view, phonological awareness predicts (causes) reading readiness, and it's the child who becomes ready, not a method of instruction that *makes* the child ready.

Liberman and Shankweiler's paper provided a brief update on subsequent research, including studies that showed unequivocally that appropriate training plays a causal role in learning to read. Yet a simple explanation based on reading *instruction* did not fit their thinking:

There remains some question however, concerning the extent to which phonological awareness, which we have seen to be important for reading success, arises spontaneously, as part of general cognitive development, or whether, alternatively it develops only after specific training or as a spinoff effect of reading instruction....

The question as to whether word-related metalinguistic abilities develop spontaneously or must be taught is *a crucial one*, with obvious implications not only for preschool instruction, but also for the design of literacy teaching programs geared to adults. (p. 11; emphasis mine)

But why would this matter? If you know that phoneme awareness and the alphabet principle can easily be taught in a short period of time, and that this significantly aids children in learning to read and spell, why not just teach it? Why view this as a "crucial" issue?

Later in the paper, the theory was expanded to include different languages and cultures (presumably peoples with nonalphabetic writing systems):

There is now a wealth of evidence pointing to metalinguistic deficiencies in the phonological domain in individual of various ages, languages, and cultural backgrounds, who have difficulty in attaining literacy. We suggest that perhaps it would be reasonable now to consider seriously the possibility that the deficiency in these individuals who are resistant to ordinary methods of literacy instruction may not be limited to metalinguistic awareness, but may reflect a more general deficiency in the phonological domain. (p. 12)

When evidence began to appear that perhaps poor readers had problems with general language functions and short-term memory, these functions were tacked onto the theory as well, along with the assumption that any and all problems stemmed from a single cause: "the failure to exploit the phonological structure in short-term memory" (p. 12).

As the phonological theory turned into dogma and gobbled up more and more territory, a myriad of mini–deductive theories sprouted up under the phonological umbrella, like mushrooms under a tree. These theories drive nearly all the research in the field and have done so for over 30 years.

But what if we treated the scientific evidence (the data) as more important than the theories? At this point I want to shift gears and provide a summary *inductive analysis* of the research reviewed in the preceding chapters. The evidence falls into three main categories:

1. Evidence for or against the notion that phonological awareness develops.
2. Evidence on whether the development of phonological (phoneme) awareness—if this development actually occurs—plays a causal role in learning to read.
3. Descriptive and correlational evidence for whether deficits in other language functions put children at risk for reading and academic problems.

Does Phonological or Phoneme Awareness Develop?

The answer is no. The evidence comes from research on early language development. Findings are consistently negative for the idea that children become more phonologically or phonemically aware with age, and for the theory that children go through stages of awareness from larger to smaller phonetic units (words, syllables, syllable fragments, phonemes) before they can learn to read.

Newborns can discriminate CV syllable contrasts, even when the consonants differ by a mere 40 ms in voice-onset time, as in *ba* versus *pa*. At around 8–9 months, infants begin to distinguish between legal and illegal phoneme sequences in their native language. Consonant sequences are a primary cue for isolating words from the speech stream, the first step in vocabulary building. To a large extent consonant sequences at word boundaries are illegal in the English language, and provide a basic cue for isolating words from phrases. To separate one word from another, infants must be able to split these consonant sequences, and to do this, they must be able to hear inside them—phonemically.

Studies on categorical perception across the age span point to a developmental process, but this developmental process is subphonemic. When consonant contrasts in syllables like *ba-pa*, *ba-ga*, and *ba-da* are gradually made more alike by computer, children's speech perception is more unstable than adults' only at the boundary where one turns into the other.

Children's aptitude is strongly affected by whether these contrasts are embedded in real or nonsense words, or consist of canned or natural speech, evidence of top-down processing. By age 3, children do nearly as well as adults when these consonant contrasts appear in highly familiar words using natural speech. Not only this, they can make these very fine judgments *explicitly* when asked to do so, as shown by Nittrouer and Studdert-Kennedy (1987). And 3-year-olds can do even more. They can blend isolated phonemes into a word and identify that word from among a set of pictures. Chaney (1992) found that 93 percent of lower-middle-class children met the strict criteria for this task, scoring well above chance, with an average score of 88 percent correct. Yet the same children failed simple rhyme-detection and rhyme-production tasks, evidence against the larger-to-smaller theory of phonological development. Nor did children's rhyming skill correlate to reading later in time.

Perception and production of speech are strongly interconnected. Because speech perception is operational at birth, it may play a more dominant role in the development of speech-motor clarity and fluency than the reverse, though the evidence suggests the connection is reciprocal. What is important here is that of all the elements of the language system, speech perception and speech production are the most buffered by nature and least susceptible to enduring impairment, even though they run on very different developmental clocks. Because these language functions are so fundamental, enduring deficits are rare and less likely to be a cause for concern. For this reason they could never play a major role in *any* theory of reading. (Of course, children with such poor speech perception that they are phonologically deaf would be unable to master any writing system.)

Does the Development of Phoneme Awareness Predict Reading Skill?
The answer is no. Obviously if phoneme awareness doesn't develop in the first place, this question makes no sense. But there isn't even evidence that a natural flair for hearing phonemes (a talent) makes much difference either. There is no connection between speech perception and reading, or speech production and reading, as shown in numerous studies. Quite the contrary. A speech-motor delay in the absence of other language problems is, if anything, a positive marker for success in learning to read. In Beitchman's study, 85 percent of the children who had speech-motor problems *only* outgrew this diagnosis and had no more difficulty learning to read

than the normal children. These studies provide no support for I. Y. Liberman and A. M. Liberman's (1989) theory that speech disorders are a marker for reading problems via their connection to speech-perception difficulties. And even if this was true, enduring speech impairments are so rare (being found in only 1 percent of the population) that no theory could be based on them.

In properly controlled studies on categorical perception (subphonemic discrimination), poor readers had trouble only with the most ambiguous consonant contrasts in canned nonsense syllables (Nittrouer 1999; Mody, Studdert-Kennedy, and Brady 1997). This is not something a child would ever need to handle. And even if it was, poor readers' difficulties occur largely because they don't know what to listen for, as Hurford et al.'s (1994) training study showed.

This doesn't mean that phoneme awareness is not important—far from it. Phoneme analysis and sequencing are essential for learning an alphabetic writing system. But the evidence is consistent that proper instruction in an alphabetic writing system has an impact on phoneme awareness, and against the notion that phoneme awareness develops *in order for a child to learn to read an alphabetic writing system!* Instruction in letter-sound correspondences at home or in preschool is strongly correlated to subsequent reading skill (values are as high as $r = .60$). The most important phoneme-analysis skills are segmenting and blending. These skills need to be taught, and they are easy to teach in the context of good linguistic-phonics instruction (see *Early Reading Instruction*).

Do Some Language Problems Put a Child at Risk for Reading Problems?
The answer is maybe. Language researchers, albeit inadvertently, have been more successful than reading researchers in "proving" a connection between general language development and reading skill, though we don't know precisely what this connection is or what it means. This research is so new that the finer points, such as *which* language tasks matter most to what kinds of reading skill, and why, have not been worked out.

One difficulty for language researchers is that they haven't refined their diagnostic protocols or their data sufficiently. The practice of using arbitrary cutoff scores to classify children into two or three categories of language impairment is not a valid method in language research any more than it is in reading research, even though it may be practical in the clinic.

Nor is it helpful to rely on group averages on language tests, because they don't represent the enormous variation among individuals. This is a very complex issue. So far, we have only vague clues about the precise nature of the connection.

A continuing problem is that scientists studying language development have not been able to tease apart normal temporal variation from an impairment. And, given the fact that language development is strongly influenced by the school system (as shown in both Bishop's and Beitchman's longitudinal data), this is not going to be an easy problem to solve. Temporal variation in expressive language is enormous. Development is highly unpredictable until age 5, and only marginally more predictable after this. Children entering a school system exhibit a wide range of language skills, and we urgently need answers to these questions: What constitutes a normal developmental lag and what constitutes an impairment? What specific types of language delay or impairment lead to poor academic outcomes? What role, if any, does teaching practice play in causing otherwise normal children to become reading and language impaired?

There are unresolved issues concerning the connection between verbal IQ subtests, general language tests, and the diagnosis "specific language impairment" (SLI). Is SLI really any different from having a low verbal IQ coupled with a normal performance IQ? If not, why do we need the language tests to measure SLI? I am unaware of any correlational research on these two types of measures. Do the TOLD syntax tests correlate to specific verbal IQ tests, for instance? We need guidelines for which tests are "logically prior," tests most likely to tap developmental factors, and tests least likely to be attributable to cultural factors. It is conceivable that tests that measure the most buffered language functions (receptive and expressive vocabulary, verbal memory, and syntax) are purer measures of innate verbal IQ, than the verbal IQ subtests themselves, especially the comprehension and information subtests that tap cultural knowledge and reflect environmental factors.

Finally, we have the puzzling fact that these language delays or impairments have the greatest impact late in the educational process. This "late effect" could be due to two factors. Poor reading instruction could create confusion about how an alphabet code works, leading to maladaptive decoding strategies. These children would soon fall behind their peers. Children who continue at the appropriate grade for their age will always be reading text well above their level of competence to decode it. This would cause them to be slow readers and would make comprehension difficult and reading a source of frustration.[2]

The second explanation is biological. The late effect could be a consequence of low verbal ability, which would make reading comprehension increasingly difficult as the reading vocabulary exceeds oral comprehension skills. Neither explanation is mutually exclusive. Both factors could be playing a role, and most likely are.

As a start on what is an amazingly complex issue, I looked at the language studies as a whole to find some kind of bottom line—in other words, what Bishop referred to as "base rates" for serious language delays. Beitchman's data provide the best starting point. Out of 1,655 normal five-year-olds, 300 (19 percent) failed the first and second screening and were classified as language impaired based on clinical cutoffs on standardized tests. They were placed in three groups:

Speech impairment only, 6.4 percent
General language impairment only, 8.0 percent
General language and speech impairment, 4.6 percent

A computer analysis of test scores divided the children differently. It identified a highly deviant group, low on all language measures, including a low receptive vocabulary (PPVT = 79). There were 89 children who fit this profile out of the 300 identified by the original screening. This is 29 percent of the language-impaired children, or *5.5 percent of the original sample* ($N = 1,655$). Sex ratios in these impaired groups ranged from 1.6–1.8 boys to 1 girl, about 65 percent boys.

Next, we can look at the risk factors for these groups for continuing language impairment, plus reading and academic problems. Of the 6.4 percent who had a speech impairment, the majority (85 percent) became normal. A speech impairment on its own carries very low risk. Only 1

---

2. I do not mean to imply here that children should be retained in grade until they "catch up." Poor readers need remedial help fast. A good remedial program will get a child caught up to normal levels in about 12 hours. See McGuinness 1997b.

percent of the population ($N = 1,655$) had a speech impairment that subsequently encompassed a general language impairment.

Of the group with the clinical diagnosis of general language impairment (with or without speech-motor problems), 73 percent remained language impaired at age 19. This is a risk factor of 9.2 percent in the general population for a continuing language impairment, plus poor reading and declining academic skills.

Combining the information from the clinical and computer categories, I made the assumption that the proportion of children in the low-language/low-vocabulary group identified by computer analysis remained unchanged, because they appeared to be unchanged at age 12, scoring well below the other three groups on every test. If this is the case, the final risk values at age 5 for a continuing general language impairment plus reading and academic difficulties later on, would break down as follows:

5.5% of the population identified at age 5 with *low general language, low speech, and low verbal IQ* are at very high risk for reading and academic difficulties.

9.2% + 1.0% − 5.5% (low verbal IQ) = 4.7% of the population identified at age 5 with *language delays*, but at least low-normal intelligence, are at some risk for reading and academic difficulties.

This does not account for the additional 9 percent who fit the profile of general language impaired (and reading impaired) by age 19, even though *they had nothing wrong with them* at the start of the study. One must assume they are the victims of the school system, because there seems to be no other explanation.

What do we know about the bottom 5.5 percent? Well, we know a lot. To begin with, we know they represent the far end of a normal distribution for verbal IQ, with scores falling nearly 2 standard deviations below the mean.

Hurford found that 6 percent of the large group of children he studied fit the category "garden variety poor readers" (poor reading, low receptive vocabulary). This group's reading scores could be predicted almost entirely by their receptive vocabulary score (coefficient of .85). When the data were pulled for this group, and the computer analysis run again on the remaining children, vocabulary no longer predicted reading skill.

In a study on 2,000 twin pairs in the United Kingdom, Dale et al. discovered that vocabulary was highly heritable, but only for the bottom 5 percent of the population, and this was mainly true for boys. The heritability coefficient was .90 for boys, but only .40 for girls. Above this cutoff, vocabulary is as likely to be due to shared and unshared environment as to heredity.

Bishop and her group found in their longitudinal study that the worst outcome (highest risk factor) for academic success was a low receptive and expressive vocabulary. This deficit did not appear in isolation but was part of an extensive disability involving most language functions. Bishop's data can't pinpoint incidence, because all the children had language problems. However, the low-IQ group consisted of 22 percent of the children in the study, not far off the proportion of children in the low-language/low-IQ category (29 percent) in Beitchman's study.

So far this is consistent evidence that a general language impairment defined by low verbal IQ/low receptive language puts a child at high risk for reading problems. But what *kind* of reading problems?

Consider that when Wimmer (1993) asked second- through fourth-grade teachers in Salzburg to refer their poorest readers, they identified roughly 7 percent of this population. These very poor readers read perfectly and spelled nearly as well, albeit extremely slowly. Even Down's syndrome children in Italy (verbal IQ 44) were able to read at high levels of accuracy (about 90 percent correct on three difficult reading tests) though they couldn't pass any phoneme-awareness tests or comprehend what they read (Cossu et al. 1993). It isn't known whether they read slowly. One would imagine they did.

These findings have profound implications. As 5.5 percent of children have low language/low receptive vocabulary/low verbal IQ, according to the Canadian demographic data, and this tallies with 5 percent of the 2,000 twin pairs in Dale et al.'s (1998) UK study who had a highly heritable verbal deficit. One would expect to find a similar proportion of these children anywhere in the world, including Austria and Italy. Because all children read accurately in Austria and Italy, this means *no child should ever read inaccurately*. In other words, the inability to read and spell accurately (knowing how the code works) should not be a problem for any child. And if it is, the main culprit is an opaque spelling code in combination with misleading and inadequate instruction.

Cossu, Rossini, and Marshall (1993, 135) put it this way: "These results suggest that it would be worthwhile to pursue the issue further; are there interactions with the nature of the orthography, with the phonological properties of the language, and with the form of reading instruction? The notoriously irregular orthography of English is certainly not an appropriate script on which to demonstrate the value of explicit segmentation skills."

This brings us to the "late effect," the finding that a large proportion of children catch up in middle childhood, only to begin a precipitous slide sometime after the age of 12. The two missing reading skills most likely to influence this effect are fluency and comprehension. Now we have some real scientific questions.

Reading Fluency

Given that Austrian children learn a transparent alphabet and get appropriate reading instruction sufficient for everyone to read (and spell) *accurately*, why are some of these children excessively slow readers? Is there any similarity between the Austrian slow readers and English-speaking children with language impairments who read inaccurately *and* slowly? In other words, are the Austrian slow readers the counterparts of the bottom 5 percent of children who suffer from a genetically determined language difficulty characterized by a low vocabulary and verbal IQ, or do they read slowly for some other reason? (I should remind the reader that *slow* is a relative term. The *average* English child reads as slowly as Wimmer's extremely slow readers.)

Answering these questions would be relatively straightforward, but so far no one has tried. We have a hint of the connection between slow decoding skills and low verbal skills from Wimmer's data. Wimmer (1993) reported that the slow readers in his study scored well below normal readers on the WISC vocabulary test ($p < .001$). However, means and standard deviations were not provided to estimate how many slow readers had low vocabularies or what low vocabulary meant.

There is some evidence from Bowers (1995) and from Wolff, Michel, and Ovrut (1990) that about half of the poor readers they tested had striking deficits in naming speed. Bowers divided eighteen poor readers into very poor readers (below the 25th percentile) and less poor readers (25th to 35th percentile). These groups didn't differ in IQ or vocabulary

(PPVT), though both scored well below the controls. Nevertheless, the very poor readers were much slower than the less poor readers on a variety of naming tasks, while the less poor readers were in the normal range. Wolff, Michel, and Ovrut found a fifty-fifty split for poor readers on naming-speed tasks, half being normal and half very slow indeed.

The studies reviewed in chapter 15 showed that there is a fairly substantial amount of shared variance between naming speed and reading accuracy (10 to 14 percent) after age, sex, and verbal IQ are controlled. But the evidence is consistent that speed per se is not the critical factor for two reasons. First, naming speed for letters and digits far outdistances naming speed for colors and objects after the age of 7, and it is only naming speed for letters or digits that correlates to reading. Second, naming speed for letters and digits is identical, showing that the naming-speed/reading connection is not specific to knowing letters or letter names. This means the critical variable is the common denominator between them: *the efficiency of paired-associate learning* (the time it takes to memorize the sound-symbol pairs and the speed at which they can be retrieved). Of course, if a child is never told what those pairs are, as is typically the case in classrooms around the English-speaking world, the task can never begin, much less be completed.

Wimmer's slow readers certainly did not suffer from poor instruction. They had slower reading speed for other reasons. Perhaps their low verbal skills made it harder to commit sound-symbol pairs to memory. Perhaps they weren't taught digit and letter names (and sounds) at home. Austrian parents typically refrain from teaching any prereading or arithmetic skills before children go to school, and when the children arrive, teachers don't teach letter names. However, Wimmer found that many parents don't obey the rules, and it is quite common for some children to arrive at school knowing letter names *and sounds*. Mann and Ditunno showed that it takes up to 2 years for every child in a typical classroom to score 100 percent correct on a letter-naming task. (If you don't know the names, it's highly unlikely you'll be able to say them quickly!) Children who get a late start won't automate letter-sound knowledge at the same age as the children who started learning this at home.

Other reasons for reading too slowly may be a failure to anticipate words on the basis of syntactic and semantic clues (low verbal ability), or an extreme delay in oculomotor development causing poorly controlled binocular tracking. And it is possible that children get into a habit of reading slowly due to any of the reasons listed above. We know that slow readers can be helped to a great extent by the powerful technique of "rereading," providing it is taught appropriately (see *Early Reading Instruction*). However, we know nothing about individual differences in response to this method.

The origin of slowness is important and well worth addressing, but it isn't the main issue or the main message of the research. For children who learn a transparent alphabet with proper instruction, Wimmer's data show us that reading speed is what the child brings to the table, and we know from observational reports by this group that the primary impact is on reading comprehension. Similarly, Cossu's data on severely mentally retarded children showed that, despite nearly perfect decoding skills, these children did not comprehend what they read.

Oral Comprehension

There are more clues about the "late effect" in the specifics of the language-reading connection. Reading comprehension is almost entirely a function of oral comprehension once decoding skills are well underway. We know from the research reviewed earlier that verbal memory span is connected to reading test scores, with good readers outscoring poor readers in memory for digits, words, and sentences. We also know that paired-associate learning is more efficient in good readers. However, verbal memory is strongly tied to verbal IQ, age, and sex, and these factors are rarely controlled in this research. Verbal memory is part and parcel of a verbal IQ test battery. When age was a focus, as it was in Olson et al.'s longitudinal study, poor readers appeared to have a developmental lag. Memory span increased at a faster rate after age 7 for poor readers than for good readers.

We saw that higher language skills like syntax and morphology were consistently correlated to reading even when age, sex, vocabulary, and verbal memory span had been controlled. These higher-order skills are strongly related to reading speed and reading comprehension as well as to basic decoding (Bowey 1986a; Bowey and Patel 1988; Hansen and Bowey 1994; Willows and Ryan 1986; Casalis and Louis-Alexandre 2000). If these results hold up, one might expect Wimmer's slow readers to do poorly on a syntax test. Syntax links to reading speed via oral comprehension and visual perceptual span. Syntax is one of the primary cues for predicting words that might lie in the periphery as readers scan text (Rayner 1998). Good syntax assists in top-down processing, leading to a faster reading rate and greater ability to access meaning.

As a final comment, Wimmer's cross-cultural studies, in conjunction with Cossu's results on Down syndrome children, rule out the notion of any type of decoding-specific disorder (dyslexia), as does everything else in this book. If there are children at risk for decoding problems, they are at risk mainly in English-speaking countries. An extreme delay in language development, or low verbal IQ, will have a greater impact on children who have to master the English spelling code, because of its complexity and the fact that it is usually badly taught. The children at risk for biological (non-instructional) reasons appear most at risk for being dysfluent readers who fail to comprehend what they read.

In summary, the following factors would be most likely to put young-sters at risk for reading difficulties and academic failure in any country, and they are not mutually exclusive:

- Delayed language development (extreme temporal variation)
- In the bottom 5 percent on vocabulary tests
- Poor verbal memory, which affects: verbal IQ subtests: information, comprehension, digit span, coding, and slow paired-associate learning
- Weak oral-comprehension skills due to delays or impairments with syn-tax, morphology, and semantics
- Being male

We know that when a writing system is properly taught, many of these factors don't matter, at least in the early years when decoding skill has pride of place. Unfortunately, longitudinal studies on children's read-ing acquisition are rare, and usually extend no further than 2 years.

We do know that children taught with a good "linguistic-phonics" program will be a year above controls and national norms initially, and will maintain this advantage over time. Linguistic phonics consists of teaching the forty English phonemes and their most common spellings, along with practice segmenting and blending phonemes in real words, preferably using letters. Johnston and Watson 2003 provided 5-year follow-up data on a large cohort of Scottish children who were taught with a linguistic-phonics approach ("synthetic phonics" in the United Kingdom). These children were a year ahead of controls and national norms at the end of the first year. By age 10, decoding skills were 2 years above national norms. However, reading-comprehension scores followed a very different path, with a modest, and constant, 3-month advantage over this time period. This suggests that decoding is not enough, and something else needs to happen to enhance reading comprehension. There are a few outstanding programs for improving oral and reading comprehension available today. These programs are reviewed in *Early Reading Instruction*.

Some Final Words on Reading Research

"Basic" research on reading, as distinct from "applied" research, constitutes the vast majority of studies in this field. Reviewing this literature in depth, one is struck by three things:

1. The research is so methodologically flawed that few studies are free of problems. These are not trivial methodological issues, but major blunders. The most common paradigm uses a research design (isolated groups) that leads to an uninterpretable outcome, because no statistical tests can be applied to it. This creates a vast amount of noise in the research literature. Properly conducted research is buried under an avalanche of meaningless studies, and here I refer exclusively to studies published in the peer-review journals. The fault may lie in poor training of students in the field, but the real culprits are the editors and editorial boards of the research journals who have failed to set standards and to insist on proper evaluations by informed reviewers. (The same criticism could be leveled at funding agencies.) As a result, instead of solving important problems in the field, many studies have only obscured and compounded these problems.

2. Inductive reasoning is virtually absent in this work. The research is driven by a hodgepodge of deductive theories conjured up via analogies, hunches, or beliefs that have no basis in fact. Few researchers attempt to disprove their theories, a critical omission in science. Taking reasonable steps to disprove one's theory is a fundamental platform of the scientific method, and has been ever since it was formally proposed by Francis Bacon.

Instead, researchers outline their particular deductive theory and set out to prove it. In the written report, other research is selectively cited to weave a framework (a story) for this proof. This research is often cited incorrectly, the author claiming an outcome that never occurred or that wasn't supported by the data. Citations of "commonly known studies" producing "commonly known results" have become mindless and formulaic. And, at the end of the day, if the author's own results (or someone else's) happen to contradict the deductive theory (evidence the theory is wrong), the theory is never changed to accommodate them. Conflicting data are explained away or ignored altogether.

3. Researchers don't build a solid body of knowledge from the ground up, and the field has never moved forward in a productive way. The important spadework in designing appropriate and reliable tests, in establishing norms, in carrying out large-scale correlational studies to identify what is important and what isn't, is rare to nonexistent. There are few meaningful, cumulative, or collaborative efforts in which groups of scientists are fully engaged on a coherent and well-focused problem. We have seen examples in this book of researchers who devote an entire career to a single in-house test that has never been verified as valid or reliable. For these reasons, all the deductive theories conjured up by reading researchers so far have collapsed when proper evidence was brought to bear on them.

This is not a description of science or the scientific method. It is a description of pseudoscience. And what is most startling about this body of work is that the most methodologically flawed research is often the best known and highly regarded.

Contrast this with the research on language development. Here, different research teams tackle common problems systematically and logically. They frequently cooperate in doing the actual research, using or perfecting one another's experimental tools and techniques, and they do this even though they may disagree about what the data imply. The goal in science is to arrive at the truth. The goal is not to protect a theory.

Meanwhile, the critically important applied research on instructional methods has been sidelined since the 1960s. Applied research is out of favor, is not well funded, and when it does appear, is extremely difficult to publish. This is part of a general attitude that research on "what's wrong with children who can't read" is real science (pure research), but research on how to teach children to read is not. Instead, research on new instructional methods in the classroom or clinic often circulates underground in unpublished reports and conference proceedings. There are phenomenal programs available today that only a handful of people know about.

Apart from a few studies that shine like diamonds in a heap of dross, giving us new ways to look at how reading is influenced by language development, the central message of this book is basically this: *The research question "What's wrong with children who can't read?" is a bad question scientifically, logically, and pragmatically, and has been extremely unproductive.*

The applied research is reviewed in *Early Reading Instruction*, and despite the same excess of methodologically weak research, the story told there is much more upbeat. We owe a profound dept of gratitude to the members of the National Reading Panel for wading through the applied material and sorting the wheat from the chaff. The truth is that we do know exactly how to teach reading in all its facets, including decoding, spelling, fluency, reading comprehension, and even spelling. More important, we understand exactly *why* some programs work and others do not.

Appendix 1: Methodological Problems in Studies by Tallal et al.

The Twelve Aphasic Children

Tallal's theory was based on the *average* (group) performance of twelve aphasic children (nine boys, three girls) from the John Horniman School in England. The same twelve children were used in studies by Tallal and Piercy (1973a, 1973b, 1974, 1975). It's not a good idea to base a theory on the performance of the same twelve children, especially children this unusual.

Table A.1 is provided once more to illustrate the test scores for these children in order of the severity of their receptive language scores. The 3-year age range of 6;3 to 9;3 creates problems for data analysis and interpretation, because this was never controlled.

The most unusual thing about these children (not shown in the table) is that their average nonverbal IQ (Raven's matrices) was in the 90th percentile—astonishingly high. Children with this profile are so rare that they are screened into this school from across the country, and the total enrollment at any one time is about twenty-four children. Another unusual thing, seen in the table, was that three children were reading and spelling at or near their age level, and most of the remainder were only 1 year below age. Yet the two best readers had among the worst receptive language skills, evidence that good verbal skills aren't essential for learning to read, certainly when nonverbal ability is this high.

Despite the low-verbal/high-nonverbal profile, the table illustrates the extraordinary variety of the patterns of impairments. Five children had extreme impairments in both receptive and expressive language; seven did not. Four had receptive language scores 4 to 5 years below age. Six had receptive language scores 1 to 2 years below age, and two had no receptive

Appendix A.1

Profiles of twelve aphasic children based on Tallal and Piercy (1973 b)

Age	Receptive Language		Expressive Language		Schonell		Read/Spell
Yrs./ mos.	PPVT	Reynell	Reynell	Renfrew articu- lation	Read	Spell	Yrs. below age
8-4	3-1	3-1	3-6	<3	8-1	7-8	0
8-10	3-7	3-9	0	—	6-6	6-2	−2
8-7	—	4-6	6-0	4-6	7-5	7-5	−1
8-4	4-3	3-6	3-11	<3	8-2	7-9	0
8-8	6-2	4-8	4-8	4-4	7-3	7-7	−1
9-2	6-10	5-6	4-5	4-1	8-0	8-3	−1
9-2	7-7	>6	—	4-6	7-2	7-7	−2
7-9	5-1	>6	3-1	<3	6-5	7-0	−1
9-3	8-2	—	>6	3-6	7-3	7-3	−2
7-3	6-3	6-0	6-0	—	6-4	5-9	−1
6-9	5-10	>6	0	0	5-5	5-2	−1
9-1	12-1	—	—	4-7	8-5	8-3	−8 mos

Note: >6 ceiling (perfect score), — missing data. The language development scores are represented as years-months, set out in order of severity of the receptive language scores.

language deficits at all. Speech problems were by far the most consistent deficit, with nearly every child 4 or more years below chronological age. Two children were mute. Because the most common problem shared by these children was speech-motor problems and not receptive language, this doesn't lend much credence to the "receptive language" component of Tallal's model.

In the studies, the aphasic children were "matched" to twelve normal children in age, sex, and nonverbal IQ, but this is a strange kind of match. Normal children have similar verbal and nonverbal IQ scores. This means that the aphasic children (*extreme low* verbal IQs and *extreme high* nonverbal IQs) were matched to children with *extreme high* nonverbal IQs by design, and *very high* verbal IQs as a consequence. Differences between the groups could just as likely be due to verbal IQ as to language status.

The aphasic children were treated as a group in the data analysis. There is no way to know which type of language impairment is related to auditory perceptual difficulties. Tallal and Piercy (1974) reported, as an aside, that two of the children performed normally on every task, but we don't know who they were.

The Auditory Tasks

Tallal's auditory tasks have virtually defined the field for three decades, despite the fact that they don't meet the minimum requirements for a valid psychophysical test, nor for good test construction. There are no norms. There are no reliability checks that could show whether children perform the same way from the beginning to the end of the test, or from one testing to the next. And quite apart from this, the tasks don't measure what they purport to measure, a problem of construct validity.

There were four auditory-discrimination tasks that mainly measure "difference thresholds." In each case, the children had to tell two speech-like tones apart, make a judgment about them, and push one or two panels in the right order to indicate what they heard. The tasks are as follows:

1. *Identification* (which of the two tones do you hear?). When (or if) the children met a criterion on this test, they went on to the remaining tasks.
2. *Same-different* judgments (are two tones the same or different?).
3. *Repetition* test. Judging a two-tone sequence that can occur in any of four orders: 1–2 or 1–1 or 2–2 or 2–1.
4. *Sequential memory*. The child presses panels for longer tone sequences: 1–1–2–1–2.

Tones vary in presentation rate and in duration. In the repetition test, the two-tone sequences are separated by longer to shorter gaps of silence (428, 305, 150, 60, 30, 15, 8 ms apart), and can range in duration from very short to long. In the study by Tallal and Piercy (1973b), the tones lasted for 250, 175, 125, or 75 ms, at each of the intervals listed above. This is a total of twenty-eight possible combinations. Each combination was presented four times in a test run. This meant the child had to pay attention to 112 tone pairs, make a judgment about each one, and press two panels on each trial (224 panel presses). Long, boring tasks like these encourage children to guess, especially when the structure of the task conspires to make guessing an option (press panel 1 *or* 2).

Tasks with fixed choices are known as *binomial tasks*, tasks where performance is likely to occur by chance. Each child's data needs to be submitted to a *binomial test*, which determines the number of correct responses required to score significantly above chance ($p < .05$) for a given number of test items.[1]

I computed the binomial test for tasks where chance was a factor. On the same-different task, 50 percent would be correct by guessing, but with only four "tries" at each particular tone length and presentation rate, a child must get all four correct to score significantly above chance ($p = .05$). In the repetition test, there are four possible sequences: 1–1, 1–2, 2–1, 2–2 (chance is 25 percent correct). Again, with only four tries for each sequence, a child needs to get three out of four correct to score significantly above chance.

Tallal and Piercy did use the binomial test to estimate the "trials to criterion" for the initial identification test, but none of the data on the remaining tasks were corrected for guessing and will be invalid.

The repetition test is problematic for other reasons. When sounds become too brief and/or the duration between them too short, it becomes impossible to tell them apart (a difference threshold is reached). When someone is asked to make judgments below their sensory threshold, the only option is to guess, which is precisely what the aphasic children did.

Tallal and Piercy (1973b) provided a figure to represent the average scores for the aphasic children for four tone durations (250, 175, 125, 75 ms) plotted as a function of the eight different presentation rates. These "curves" show a steep decline to a nearly right-angle bend and a long plateau starting at around the 150 ms presentation rate. (See figure A.1.) These are not normal sensory (psychophysical) functions, which should

---

1. *Binomial* is Latin for "law of two" and refers to any task (or game of chance) that can be described mathematically by two terms: p and q. p is the probability an event occurring by chance, and $q - p$ is the probability of it not occurring. The binomial test computes the probability of $p \times q \times N$ (the number of items on the test) to a $p = .05$ level, or beyond, based on standard-deviation units. True probability only begins to be reflected at around 200 trials.

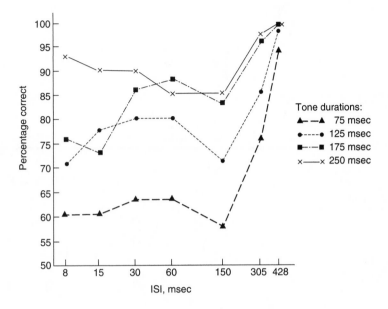

| Figure A.1 |

Effect of tone duration on aphasics' performance on two-element patterns. From Tallal and Piercy 1973b.

be linear or curvilinear. The most logical interpretation of these "functions" is that they reflect the combined scores of two types of children, those who scored nearly perfectly, and those who were just guessing. As the duration of the tones got shorter (250, 175, 125, 75 ms), more and more children dropped to chance at the 150 ms mark. Furthermore, the data below the child's sensory threshold appear to have been used in the statistical analyses, which is invalid.

Methods for measuring difference thresholds have a time-honored history, dating back to Fechner in 1860. Methods for studying temporal judgments were worked out by Klemm in the 1920s. (See Christman 1979). Nordmark (1970) describes many experiments in which tones presented in rapid succession cause the impression of *single* pitch glides rather than sounding like two separate sounds. In short, this is not a new problem.

Glossary

acoustic confusion Refers to memory tasks where similar-sounding words are mistaken for one another, such as lists of rhyming words.

affix General term for any segment (morpheme) added to the beginning or end of a word that changes meaning.

age of acquisition Used in language research to determine the age at which a child (or adult) believes he or she learned each word in a given set of words.

alliteration Words or phrases in which the initial sounds are identical: *picked a peck of pickled peppers*.

alphabet A writing system based on phonemes (individual consonants and vowels).

amplitude A measure in physics for the energy or *power* in a signal. Acoustic signals are measured in decibels, visual signals in candelas or lumens, and so forth. In perception, acoustic power translates to *loudness*, electromagnetic energy to *brightness*, mechanical force on the skin to *pressure*, and thermal energy to *heat*.

basic code Used during initial reading instruction. Each phoneme in the language is represented by its most common or least ambiguous spelling.

bimodal distribution Refers to data that, when displayed in a frequency distribution, show two central tendencies or concentrations of scores instead of one.

binomial test A statistical test that computes a numerical score that will exceed chance (guessing) at a specified level of probability. The computation takes into account the number of items on a test and the number of alternatives for each response.

blending The act of joining a sequence of isolated phonemes into a word: /b/–/l/–/e/–/n/–d/—*blend*.

categorical perception The inability to hear the acoustic transitions between two similar consonant contrasts (*ba-pa*) and the tendency to hear only one or the other.

ceiling effects A situation in which a test or task is so easy that many people get perfect or near-perfect scores.

cloze task A type of syntax task in which a missing element in a phrase has to be supplied: "The moon shines brightly in the _____."

coarticulation Phonemes overlap one another in speech. The phonemes coming later in the word modify the production of phonemes coming earlier in the word, creating a complex acoustic envelope of sounds.

code Any system in which arbitrary symbols are assigned to units within a category. The number symbols 1–10 represent units of quantity. Letters represent units of speech sounds (phonemes).

consonant A phoneme that involves contact and movement between one or more speech articulators. A **voiced consonant** engages the vocal folds. An **unvoiced consonant** does not engage the vocal folds.

consonant blend or **consonant cluster** Two or more consonants in sequence in a word: *str* in *street*.

construct validity The aspect of test design in which items faithfully reflect the construct being measured and not some other construct.

continuous naming speed Measured by a task where items on a list are named as quickly as possible. Scored as the total time to complete all the items on the list. Items consist of anything that doesn't have to be read (colors, pictures of objects, letters, digits).

covariance analysis   A statistical tool to adjust scores on tests given later in time to reflect individual differences in scores at initial testing. For example, intelligence is covaried in order to look at the correlation between initial phoneme awareness (time 1) and subsequent reading scores (time 2), independent of intelligence.

decoding   The act of translating symbols that represent units of something back into those units (translating from letters to phonemes).

diacritic   A special mark or extra letter written above, below, or beside a letter to indicate pronunciation.

difference threshold   In psychophysics, the smallest difference a person can detect between two signals that vary on some dimension (loudness, brightness, duration, pitch, color). Also known as "just noticeable difference."

digraph   Two letters standing for one phoneme: *ch* in *church*.

diphone system   A system of writing in which one symbol represents each consonant-vowel (CV) unit in a language.

diphthong   A vowel sound that elides between two vowels in rapid succession and counts as one vowel (/e/ + /ee/ = /ae/ in *late*).

discrete naming speed   Measured by a task in which each item in a set is named as fast as possible. Recorded in milliseconds by *voice-onset time* for each item.

dyslexia   Greek for "poor reading." Taken to mean a genetic predisposition toward difficulties in learning to read in some countries, like the United States, or simply as poor reading, whatever the cause, in other countries.

echoic memory   Very-short-term auditory memory in which the neural response to a signal outlasts its physical duration.

encoding   The act of transcribing units of a specific category (speech, quantity, music) into a set of arbitrary symbols—for example, transcribing phonemes into their spellings.

explicit awareness   The ability to reflect cognitively on aspects of one's perceptions and behavior that ordinarily lie outside awareness.

expressive language   The totality of spoken language, including articulation, prosody, vocabulary, syntax, and semantics.

expressive vocabulary   A spoken vocabulary. The number of words someone is able to say and also understand.

factor analysis   A complex type of correlational statistics in which the relationships of scores on a variety of tests are explored in geometric space. Tests are sorted according to their similarity to one another (proximity in this space), and factor scores are computed for each test in relationship to every other test. Tests that correlate strongly to each other constitute a "factor." A factor is an abstraction, and it is up to the researcher to determine what the tests that "load" on this factor have in common.

factor loading   The power of a single test in correlational values to represent a factor. As a general rule, factor loadings aren't meaningful unless they are .80 or higher.

first-order correlations   Basic correlational statistics in which every measure is correlated independently to every other measure and the values presented.

floor effects   When a test or task is so difficult that many people score at or near zero.

frequency   In physics, the oscillations of energy (sine waves) in signals. For those signals to which our perceptual systems can respond, frequency translates to *pitch* in the auditory system, and to *color* (frequency over time) and *pattern* (frequency of luminance contrasts over space) in the visual system.

functional illiteracy   A designation of reading difficulty used in national testing in which the reader is unable to find, use, and interpret the meaning of printed text.

gating task   A task that determines the threshold for the recognition of a word or syllable based on hearing fragments of the word. "Gates" chop off portions of the word in a series of steps from an initial fragment until the entire word is presented.

habituation   A property of the nervous system that causes attention to wane and be withdrawn from a repetitive and/or noninformative stimulus.

iconic memory   Very-short-term visual memory in which the neural response to a signal outlasts its physical duration.

implicit sensitivity   Sensory processing that goes on outside the capacity for conscious reflection.

incidental memory   Memory measured by a task in which people are first asked to assess the items, and then are unexpectedly asked to recall them. If the incidental task is meaningful (evaluative), recall is better than if the task is meaningless. It is also superior to intentional recall, where people are told ahead of time to memorize the items.

inferential statistics   A family of statistical tests used for experimental research designs in which causality can be inferred by exposing randomly selected groups to different treatment conditions. Includes t-tests as well as the ANOVA family of statistics.

intentional memory   Memory measured by a task in which the subjects are told ahead of time to memorize the items for recall.

isolated-groups design   A research design in which two or more groups of subjects are selected to represent different segments of a normal distribution on a measure of interest. Statistics cannot be applied to this design because the mathematics of probability prohibits nonrandom selection of groups, along with other factors.

item analysis   In test construction, an analytic technique to determine the power and reliability of individual items to measure a construct, such as which items produce consistent or inconsistent responses, and which are too easy or too difficult.

lag correlations   First-order correlations in which the subjects are tested at time 1 on one or more tests, and scores are correlated to tests given later in time. Lag correlations are often used to infer causality based on the principle that time does not run backward. This assumption is insufficient to infer causality from correlations.

lateral variation   The extent of natural biological variation in any trait at a specific time in development, including adulthood.

linear   In mathematics, this means "terms of the first degree," values that are in an arithmetic relationship (can be added, subtracted, multiplied, or divided). In statistics, it refers as well to the distribution of the data that should be of the same form (normal).

mean length of utterance   The average length of spoken phrases in spontaneous, natural speech.

memory span   What an individual can hold in mind and repeat in the short term.

metalinguistic   Literally "above or beyond language." Used to refer to tasks or to a process in which higher-order cognitive analysis is brought to bear on one's own language expression or analysis.

morpheme   The smallest unit of a word that conveys meaning (*boat* contains one morpheme; *boating* contains two morphemes).

morphology   A division of grammar in which morphemes determine grammatical form.

multiple regression analysis   A complex form of correlational analysis in which the common variance in a group of tests is selectively subtracted from every test in a series of steps, with correlations on the remaining tests being recomputed at each step. Useful for determining what residual correlations remain when important measures like age and IQ have been controlled (partialed out).

myelin   A fatty sheath that grows around the nerve fibers and speeds information transmission from one part of the brain to another. Myelin rates of growth vary for each sensory modality and the motor system. Myelinization is not complete until around age 15.

nonsense words   Words with no meaning that obey the legal syllable structure of the language.

nonword repetition test   A test in which the children hear a series of spoken nonsense words and are asked to repeat each one in turn.

normal distribution   A mathematical distribution of a series of measurements in which the form of the distribution can be entirely determined by the mean and the standard deviation. The distribution takes the form of a bell.

onset   A technical term that refers to the initial consonant or consonants that precede a "rime." *str* in *street* is an onset.

ontogeny   The biological development of an individual.

opaque alphabet   An alphabetic writing system in which there are multiple spellings for the same phoneme.

orienting   A property of the nervous system in which an organism is alerted to any signal or event that is *sudden, novel, of high interest*, or represents potential *danger*. An orienting reflex engages the whole body and mind. There are changes in physical and sensory orientation, plus changes in the autonomic nervous system (heart rate, blood flow, adrenaline).

orthography   "Standard spelling." The patterns of permissible spellings for sounds in words in a writing system.

paired-associate learning   A type of learning that requires memorization of arbitrary pairs of something (letter symbols for phonemes).

partial out   An expression used in correlational statistics to refer to a procedure in which a measure that is correlated to other measures (shared variance) is statistically subtracted. The data can then be recomputed with this particular measure "partialed out." An example would be to subtract common variance due to age or IQ from a group of measures.

percentile rank   A conversion of a test score from a standardized test to reflect the level at which this score exceeds a percentage of the population. A percentile score of 90 means this person exceeded 90 percent of the population.

perceptual span   In eye-movement research, this is the distance in the periphery from central visual focus within which people can see and/or use information. In reading research this is measured by the number of letters to the left or right that influence speed of decoding.

phase A technical term used to describe the interrelationship of the sine/cosine components of mechanical, electrical, and thermal energy. The brain preserves these interrelationships, which provides coherence and certain qualitative aspects of perceptual experience. Mathematically, phase is described by a Fourier coefficient.

phoneme The smallest unit of speech that people can hear; corresponds to consonants and vowels.

phoneme awareness The ability to hear and remember the order of phonemes in words.

phonetic Speech sounds in words.

phonics A generic term for any reading method that teaches a relationship between letters and phonemes.

phonological awareness The ability to hear and remember a variety of units of sound within words: syllable, syllable fragment (onsets/rimes), phoneme.

phonology A system of speech sounds that make up a language.

phonotactics The permissible or legal phoneme sequences in words in a particular language.

phylogeny The evolutionary patterns or lines of descent of an organism.

place of articulation The place in the mouth where articulators make contact to stop or alter the flow of air during the production of consonants.

prefix A morpheme (unit of meaning) added to the front of a root word: _unhappy_.

proactive interference In memory experiments, a situation where items coming earlier in a list interfere with memory for later items, causing intrusion errors. Proactive interference is enhanced when items are too similar or lack novelty, and when there are multiple lists that come at too fast a pace.

probability (1) The likelihood of a particular event or occurrence as a function of a total range of possibilities (*a* is the most probable spelling for the sound /a/ in *cat*). (2) A mathematical term reflecting the likelihood of a particular value occurring by chance.

productive language Spoken language. Same as *expressive language*.

prosody The general term for variations in the acoustic properties of speech for a given language that carry meaning indirectly, such as fluency, melody, stress patterns, and inflection.

rapid automatized naming (RAN) A task where people are asked to *name* a small set of items that repeat in a random sequence as quickly as possible. Items are anything that don't have to be read (colors, digits, letters).

recall memory Memory retrieved from a long-term memory store without the benefit of prompts or clues. (An essay test involves recall memory.)

receptive language The understanding of spoken language.

receptive vocabulary The number of spoken words that someone can understand.

reciprocal causality Mutual causation. The effect of a cause acts back on what caused it. Applies to the mutual interplay between speech production and speech recognition.

recognition memory Memory retrieved from a long-term memory store that is assisted by prompts and clues. (A multiple-choice test involves recognition memory.)

reliability In test construction, a reliable test is one where people score similarly on different parts of the test and on different occasions.

rime A technical term for the final portion of a word that sounds like other words (rhymes). An example is *and* in *band, bland, brand, hand*.

segmenting In reading instruction, the process of separating individual phonemes in sequence: *frame*—/f/ /r/ /ae/ /m/.

semantic or **semantics** The content or sequence of words in phrases that conveys meaning. In linguistics—the study of how language represents meaning.

shared environment A term used in studies on heredity. It explains significant portions of correlations between parents and offspring that cannot be attributable to heredity (genes) and are, therefore, likely to be due to common environmental factors.

shared variance In correlational statistics, the amount of variance (standard deviation, or s.d.^{2}) that is shared between two measures—what is common between them.

short-term memory The number of items that can be recalled from a list of meaningless items (unrelated words, digits).

sight words Printed words that children are asked to memorize visually as random strings of letters.

spatial frequency A technical term in vision research that refers to the brain's capacity to process luminance contrasts over space in terms of their sine/cosine patterns.

specific language impairment In the speech and hearing sciences, a designation for a condition in which performance IQ is normal, but certain language skills are seriously deficient as determined by cutoffs on various language tests.

spectral analysis An electronic device that can break down complex signals into their sine/cosine components. In auditory psychophysics, the signals break down to time, frequency (formant spectrum), and amplitude.

speech gestures The articulatory patterns used in speech for a particular language.

speech recognition The ability to recognize speech sounds and words sufficient to respond to them in a meaningful (nonrandom) way.

Responses include sucking on a nipple, head nod, obeying requests, speaking, and so forth.

speech spectogram A paper printout of speech elements measured electronically, which represents *time*, speech *formant components* (frequencies), and *loudness*.

speech synthesizer An electronic device that can produce humanlike speech.

spelling alternatives All possible spellings of each phoneme.

standard deviation A measure of the variance (variability) in a set of scores that represents the square root of the sum of the squared differences of each score from the mean. Abbreviated s.d.

standardized test A test administered to a very large number of people (normed) over a wide age range, in which test scores are "standardized" to fit a normal distribution. This is often converted to a standard metric, with a mean of 100 and s.d. of 15. Individual test scores take into account age (in months) and the distance from the mean in standard-deviation units.

standard score A score derived from a standardized test that takes into account a person's performance relative to his or her age and population norms (see *standardized test*).

statistical power The number of scores on a particular test or task. The greater the number, the more likely there will be a normal distribution. This translates into the number of subjects in a study: large number = high power = more reliable result.

suffix A morpheme added to the end of a root word (*happiest*).

syllable A speech unit contained within a word, or constituting a whole word, that contains one vowel plus any consonants. *I* and *straight* are one-syllable words, *basket* and *triumph* are two-syllable words, and so on.

syntax The aspect of a grammar that refers to phrase structure, specifically word order.

template   Used in cognitive psychology to refer to some type of representation in the brain that exactly mirrors a percept, as in a "replica" or a "neural copy."

temporal variation   Natural biological variation that is reflected in differential rates of development in children of the same age.

transparent alphabet   An alphabetic writing system in which there is rarely more than one spelling for the same phoneme.

variance   Technically: the standard deviation squared. Also refers to "amount of variability" in the data.

voice-onset time or **voice-onset latency**   The time in milliseconds to begin speaking after seeing or hearing a stimulus. Measured by a highly sensitive voice key that is activated by speaking.

vowel   A phoneme in which the articulators do not stop or curtail the flow of breath. All vowels are voiced.

vowel + *r*   A category of vowels in English in which the sound /r/ is either a vowel on its own (*her* contains the sounds /h/ /r/), or forms a diphthong with another vowel (*for* contains the diphthong /oe/ + /r/). The are nine such vowels in English.

whole language   A philosophy that holds that learning to read is similar to the acquisition of natural language. Children learn to read by exposure, by reading along with the teacher, and by guessing words using the context, pictures, and other cues.

word attack   A type of reading test that consists entirely of pronounceable nonsense words.

word family   A group of words sharing the same ending sounds that are spelled the same and rhyme (*bright, night, fight, sight*).

word frequency   The number of times a word appears in a very large corpus of words. Usually refers to frequency in print.

word-identification test   A type of reading test in which a child decodes unrelated words one at a time.

word-recognition test   Same as above.

working memory   A memory system that allows organisms to "keep things in mind" for a limited period of time, including perceptions, thoughts, and feelings. Operationally, this term is nearly synonymous with "attention span" or "span of consciousness."

writing system   A systematic mapping of the elements of a unit of speech onto a set of arbitrary symbols so that every word in the language can be represented. No writing system marks whole words. Writing systems mark one of four sound units (and only one): syllable, CV diphone, consonants only, or consonants and vowels (phonemes).

Some Common Acronyms for Standardized Tests:

CELF-R   Clinical Evaluation of Language Fundamentals–Revised

PPVT-R Peabody Picture Vocabulary Test–Revised (receptive vocabulary)

TOAL   Test of Adolescent Language

TOLD   Test of Language Development

TROG   Test for Reception of Grammar

WAIS   Wechsler Adult Intelligence Scale

WISC   Wechsler Intelligence Scale for Children

WRAT   Wide Range Achievement Test

References

Ackerman, P. T., and Dykman, R. A. 1993. Phonological processes, confrontation naming, and immediate memory in dyslexia. *Journal of Learning Disabilities*, *26*, 597–609.

Adams, M. 1994. *Beginning to Read*. Cambridge, MA: MIT Press.

Anderson, S. W., Podwall, F. N., and Jaffe, J. 1984. Timing analysis of coding and articulation processes in dyslexia. *Annals of the New York Academy of Sciences*, *433*, 71–86.

Aram, D. M., Ekelman, B. L., and Nation, J. E. 1984. Preschoolers with language disorders: 10 years later. *Journal of Speech and Hearing Research*, *27*, 232–244.

Aram, D. M., and Nation, J. E. 1975. Patterns of preschool language disorders. *Journal of Speech and Hearing Research*, *18*, 229–241.

Aram, D. M., and Nation, J. E. 1980. Preschool language disorders and subsequent language and academic difficulties. *Journal of Communication Disorders*, *13*, 159–170.

Aslin, R. N., Saffran, J. R., and Newport, E. L. 1998. Computation of conditional probability statistics by 8-month-old infants. *Psychological Science*, *9*, 321–324.

Bacon, F. [1620] 2004. *Novum Organum*. In Graham Rees and Maria Wakely, eds., *The Oxford Francis Bacon: The Instauratio Magna Part II: Novum Organum and Associated Texts*. Oxford: Oxford University Press.

Baddeley, A. D., and Hitch, G. 1974. Working memory. In G. A. Bower, ed., *The Psychology of Learning and Motivation*. New York: Academic Press.

References

Baddeley, A. D., Thomson, N., and Buchanan, M. 1975. Word length and the structure of short-term memory. *Journal of Verbal Learning and Verbal Behavior, 14*, 575–589.

Beitchman, J. H., Brownlie, E. B., Inglis, A., Wild, J., Ferguson, B., Schacter, D., Lancee, W., Wilson, B., and Mathews, R. 1996. Seven-year follow-up of speech/language impaired and control children: Psychiatric outcome. *Journal of Child Psychology and Psychiatry, 37*, 961–970.

Beitchman, J. H., Brownlie, E. B., Inglis, A., Wild, J., Mathers, R., Schacter, D., Krill, R., Martin, S., Ferguson, B., and Lancee, W. 1994. Seven-year follow-up of speech/language impaired and control children: Speech/language stability and outcome. *Journal of the American Academy of Child and Adolescent Psychiatry, 33*, 1322–1330.

Beitchman, J. H., Hood, J., Rochon, J., Peterson, M., Mantini, T., and Majumdar, S. 1989. Empirical classification of speech/language impairment in children: I. Identification of speech/language categories. *Journal of the American Academy of Child and Adolescent Psychiatry, 28*, 112–117.

Beitchman, J. H., Nair, R., Clegg, M., and Patel, P. G. 1986. Prevalence of speech and language disorders in 5-year-old kindergarten children in the Ottawa-Carleton region. *Journal of Speech and Hearing Disorders, 51*, 98–110.

Beitchman, J. H., Wilson, B., Brownlie, E. B., Walters, H., and Lancee, W. 1996. Long-term consistency in speech/language profiles: I. Developmental and academic outcomes. *Journal of the American Academy of Child and Adolescent Psychiatry, 35*, 804–814.

Benton, A. L. 1964. Developmental aphasia and brain damage. *Cortex, 1*, 40–52.

Bernstein, L. E., and Stark, R. E. 1985. Speech perception development in language-impaired children: A 4-year follow-up study. *Journal of Speech and Hearing Disorders, 50*, 21–30.

Biddle, B. J., and Martin, M. M. 1987. Causality, confirmation, credulity, and structural equation modeling. *Child Development, 58*, 4–17.

Binet, A., and Simon, T. [1905, 1908] 1977. *The Development of Intelligence in Children*. Reprinted from the translation of E. S. Kite in D. N. Robinson, ed., *Significant Contributions to the History of Psychology, 1750–1920, vol. 4. Washington, DC: University Publications of America.*

Bishop, D. V. M. 1983. *Test for the Reception of Grammar*. (TROG.) Manchester, UK: University of Manchester.

Bishop, D. V. M. 1991. Developmental reading disabilities: The role of phonological processing has been overemphasised. *Mind and Language, 6,* 97–101.

Bishop, D. V. M. 2001. Genetic influences on language impairment and literacy problems in children: Same or different? *Journal of Child Psychology and Psychiatry, 42,* 189–198.

Bishop, D. V. M., and Adams, C. 1990. A prospective study of the relationship between specific language impairment, phonological disorders and reading retardation. *Journal of Child Psychology and Psychiatry, 31,* 1027–1050.

Bishop, D. V. M., Bishop, S. J., Bright, P., James, C., Delaney, T., and Tallal, P. 1999. Different origin of auditory and phonological processing problems in children with language impairment: Evidence from a twin study. *Journal of Speech, Language, and Hearing Research, 42,* 155–168.

Bishop, D. V. M., Carlyon, R. P., Deeks, J. M., and Bishop, S. J. 1999. Auditory temporal processing impairment: Neither necessary nor sufficient for causing language impairment in children. *Journal of Speech, Language, and Hearing Research, 42,* 1295–1310.

Bishop, D. V. M., and Edmundson, A. 1987. Language-impaired 4-year-olds: Distinguishing transient from persistent impairment. *Journal of Speech and Hearing Disorders, 52,* 156–173.

Blachman, B. A. 1984. Relationship of rapid naming ability and language analysis skills to kindergarten and first-grade reading achievement. *Journal of Educational Psychology, 76,* 610–622.

Bond, G. L., and Dykstra, R. 1967. The cooperative research program in first-grade reading instruction. *Reading Research Quarterly, 2,* 1–142.

Bond, G. L., and Dykstra, R. 1997. The cooperative research program in first-grade reading instruction. (Reprint of the 1967 paper.) *Reading Research Quarterly, 32,* 342–427.

Bowers, P. G. 1995. Tracing symbol naming speeds' unique contributions to reading disabilities over time. *Reading and Writing: An Interdisciplinary Journal, 7,* 189–216.

Bowers, P. G., Steffy, R., and Tate, S. 1988. Comparison of the effects of IQ control methods on memory and naming speed as predictors of reading disability. *Reading Research Quarterly, 23,* 304–319.

Bowers, P. G., and Swanson, L. B. 1991. Naming speed deficits in reading disability: Multiple measures of a singular process. *Journal of Experimental Child Psychology*, *51*, 195–219.

Bowey, J. A. 1986a. Syntactic awareness in relation to reading skill and ongoing reading comprehension monitoring. *Journal of Experimental Child Psychology*, *41*, 282–299.

Bowey, J. A. 1986b. Syntactic awareness and verbal performance from preschool to fifth grade. *Journal of Psycholinguistic Research*, *15*, 285–308.

Bowey, J. A. 1994a. Grammatical awareness and learning to read: A critique. In E. M. H. Assink, ed., *Literacy Acquisition and Social Context*. New York: Harvester Wheatsheaf.

Bowey, J. A. 1994b. Phonological sensitivity in novice readers and nonreaders. *Journal of Experimental Child Psychology*, *58*, 134–159.

Bowey, J. A., Cain, M. T., and Ryan, S. M. 1992. A reading-level design study of phonological skills underlying fourth-grade children's word reading difficulties. *Child Development*, *63*, 999–1011.

Bowey, J. A., and Patel, R. K. 1988. Metalinguistic ability and early reading achievement. *Applied Psycholinguistics*, *9*, 367–383.

Boysson-Bardies, B. de, Halle, P., Sagart, L., and Druand, C. 1989. A cross-linguistic investigation of vowel formants in babbling. *Journal of Child Language*, *16*, 1–17.

Boysson-Bardies, B. de, and Vihman, M. M. 1991. Adaptation to language: Evidence from babbling and first words in four languages. *Language*, *67*, 297–319.

Brabyn, L. B., and McGuinness, D. 1979. Gender differences in response to spatial frequency and stimulus orientation. *Perception and Psychophysics*, *26*, 319–324.

Brabyn, L. B., and McGuinness, D. n.d. Sex differences in visual metacontrast masking. Unpublished manuscript.

Bradley, L., and Bryant, P. E. 1983. Categorizing sounds and learning to read—a causal connection. *Nature*, *301*, 419–421.

Bradley, L., and Bryant, P. E. 1985. *Rhyme and Reason in Reading and Spelling*. Ann Arbor: University of Michigan Press.

Brady, S. 1997. Ability to encode phonological representations: An underlying difficulty of poor readers. In B. A. Blachman, ed., *Foundations of Reading Acquisition and Dyslexia*. Mahwah, NJ: Lawrence Erlbaum Associates.

Brady, S., Mann, V., and Schmidt, R. 1987. Errors in short-term memory for good and poor readers. *Memory and Cognition, 15*, 444–453.

Brady, S., Shankweiler, D., and Mann, V. 1983. Speech perception and memory coding in relation to reading ability. *Journal of Experimental Child Psychology, 35*, 345–367.

Brandt, J., and Rosen, J. J. 1980. Auditory phonemic perception in dyslexia: Categorical identification and discrimination of stop consonants. *Brain and Language, 9*, 324–337.

Brittain, M. M. 1970. Inflectional performance and early reading achievement. *Reading Research Quarterly, 6*, 34–48.

Brown, J. 1959. Information, redundancy and decay of the memory trace. In *The Mechanisation of Thought Processes*. National Physics Laboratory Symposium, No. 10.

Bruce, D. J. 1964. The analysis of word sounds by young children. *British Journal of Educational Psychology, 34*, 158–170.

Bryant, P. E., Bradley, L., Maclean, M., and Crossland, J. 1989. Nursery rhymes, phonological skills and reading. *Journal of Child Language, 16*, 407–428.

Byrne, B., and Shea, P. 1979. Semantic and phonetic memory codes in beginning readers. *Memory and Cognition, 7*, 333–338.

Calfee, R. C., Lindamood, P. C., and Lindamood, C. H. 1973. Acoustic-phonetic skills and reading: Kindergarten through twelfth grade. *Journal of Educational Psychology, 64*, 293–298.

Campbell, J. R., Donahue, P. L., Reese, C. M., and Phillips, G. W. 1996. *National Assessment of Educational Progress 1994: Reading Report Card for the Nation and States*. Washington, DC: Office of Educational Research and Improvement, U.S. Department of Education.

Casalis, S., and Louis-Alexandre, M. 2000. Morphonological analysis, phonological analysis, and learning to read French: A longitudinal study. *Reading and Writing, 12*, 303–335.

Case, R., and Kurland, D. M. 1980. A new measure for determining children's subjective organization of speech. *Journal of Experimental Child Psychology, 30*, 206–222.

Case, R., Kurland, D. M., and Goldberg, J. 1982. Operational efficiency and the growth of short-term memory span. *Journal of Experimental Child Psychology, 33*, 386–404.

Chall, J. 1967. *Learning to Read: The Great Debate*. New York: McGraw-Hill.

Chaney, C. 1992. Language development, metalinguistic skills, and print awareness in 3-year-old children. *Applied Psycholinguistics, 13*, 485–514.

Chaney, C. 1994. Language development, metalinguistic awareness, and emergent literacy skills of 3-year-old children in relation to social class. *Applied Psycholinguistics, 15*, 371–394.

Chaney, C. 1998. Preschool language and metalinguistic skills are links to reading success. *Applied Psycholinguistics, 19*, 433–446.

Chomsky, N. 1965. *Aspects of the Theory of Syntax*. Cambridge, MA: MIT Press.

Christman, R. J. 1979. *Sensory Experience*, 2nd edition. New York: Harper and Row.

Cohen, N. J., Barwick, M. A., Horodezky, N. B., Vallance, D. D., and Im, N. 1998a. Language, achievement, and cognitive processing in psychiatrically disturbed children with previously identified and unsuspected language impairments. *Journal of Child Psychology and Psychiatry, 39*, 865–877.

Cohen, N. J., Menna, R., Vallance, D. D., Barwick, M. A., Im, N., and Horodezky, N. B. 1998b. Language, social cognitive processing and behavioral characteristics of psychiatrically disturbed children with previously identified and unsuspected language impairments. *Journal of Child Psychology and Psychiatry, 39*, 853–864.

Conrad, R. 1964. Acoustic confusions in immediate memory. *British Journal of Psychology, 55*, 75–84.

Conrad, R., and Hull, A. J. 1964. Information, acoustic confusion, and memory span. *British Journal of Psychology, 55*, 429–437.

Cooper, S. 1995. *The Clinical Use and Interpretation of the Wechsler Intelligence Scale for Children*. 3rd ed. Springfield, IL: Charles C. Thomas.

Cornwall, A. 1992. The relationship of phonological awareness, rapid naming and verbal memory to severe reading and spelling disability. *Journal of Learning Disabilities*, *25*, 532–538.

Corso, J. F. 1959. Age and sex differences in thresholds. *Journal of the Acoustical Society of America*, *31*, 498–507.

Cossu, G., Rossini, F., and Marshall, J. C. 1993. When reading is acquired but phonemic awareness is not: A study of literacy in Down's syndrome. *Cognition*, *46*, 129–138.

Coulmas, F. 1989. *Writing Systems of the World*. Oxford: Blackwell.

Cowan, N. 1984. On short and long auditory stores. *Psychological Bulletin*, *96*, 341–370.

Dale, N. 1898. *On the Teaching of English Reading*. London: J. M. Dent and Co.

Dale, P. S., Simonoff, E., Bishop, D. V. M., Eley, T. C., Oliver, B., Price, T. S., Purcell, S., Stevenson, J., and Plomin, R. 1998. Genetic influence on language delay in two-year-old children. *Nature Neuroscience*, *1*, 324–328.

Daniels, P. T., and Bright, W. 1996. *The World's Writing Systems*. New York: Oxford University Press.

Darwin, C. [1892] 1958. *The Autobiography of Charles Darwin and Selected Papers*. Ed. F. Darwin. New York: Dover.

DeCasper, A. J., and Fifer, W. P. 1980. Of human bonding: Newborns prefer their mothers' voices. *Science*, *208*, 1174–1176.

DeCasper, A. J., and Spence, M. J. 1986. Prenatal maternal speech influences newborns' perception of speech sounds. *Infant Behavior and Development*, *9*, 133–150.

De Moivre, A. 1738. *The Doctrine of Chances*, 2nd ed. London: Woodfall.

Dempster, F. N. 1981. Memory span: Sources of individual and developmental differences. *Psychological Bulletin*, *89*, 63–100.

Denckla, M. B. 1972a. Color-naming defects in dyslexic boys. *Cortex*, *8*, 164–176.

Denckla, M. B. 1972b. Performance on a color task in kindergarten children. *Cortex*, *8*, 177–190.

Denckla, M. B., and Rudel, R. 1974a. Rapid "automatized" naming of picture objects, colors, letters and numbers by normal children. *Cortex, 10,* 186–202.

Denckla, M. B., and Rudel, R. 1974b. Rapid "automatized" naming (R.A.N.): Dyslexia differentiated from other learning disabilities. *Neuropsychologia, 14,* 471–479.

Denckla, M. B., and Rudel, R. 1976. Naming of object-drawings by dyslexic and other learning disabled children. *Brain and Language, 3,* 1–15.

Denenberg, V. H. 1999. A critique of Mody, Studdert-Kennedy, and Brady's "Speech perception deficits in poor readers: Auditory processing or phonological coding?" *Journal of Learning Disabilities, 32,* 379–383.

Denes, P. B., and Pinson, E. N. 1993. *The Speech Chain,* 2nd ed. New York: W. H. Freeman.

Dolch, E. W. 1948. *Problems in Reading.* Champaign, IL: Garrard Press.

Dolch, E. W., and Bloomster, M. 1937. Phonic readiness. *Elementary School Journal, 38,* 201–205.

Dollaghan, C. A., Biber, M. E., and Campbell, T. F. 1995. Lexical influences on nonword repetition. *Applied Psycholinguistics, 16,* 211–222.

Dunn, L. M., and Dunn, L. 1982. *Peabody Picture Vocabulary Test–Revised.* Circle Pines, MN: American Guidance Services.

Ebbinghaus, H. [1885] 1964. *Memory.* New York: Dover.

Edwards, J., Fourakis, M., Beckman, M. E., and Fox, R. A. 1999. Characterizing knowledge deficits in phonological disorders. *Journal of Speech, Language, and Hearing Research, 42,* 169–186.

Efron, R. 1963. Temporal perception, aphasia, and *deja vu. Brain, 86,* 403–424.

Ehri, L. C. 1979. Linguistic insight: Threshold of reading acquisition. In T. G. Waller and G. E. Mackinnon, eds., *Reading Research: Advances in Theory and Practice,* vol. 1, 63–114. New York: Academic Press.

Eimas, P. D., Siqueland, E. R., Jusczyk, P. W., and Vigorito, J. 1971. Speech perception in infants. *Science, 171,* 303–306.

Eisenson, J. 1968. Developmental aphasia: A speculative view with therapeutic implications. *Journal of Speech and Hearing Disorders, 33,* 3–13.

Eliot, L. 1999. *What's Going On in There?* New York: Bantam Books.

Elkonin, D. B. 1963. The psychology of mastering the elements of reading. In J. Simon and B. Simon, eds., *Educational Psychology in the U.S.S.R.* London: Routledge.

Elkonin, D. B. 1973. U.S.S.R. In J. Downing, ed., *Comparative Reading.* New York: Macmillan.

Elliott, L. L. 1986. Discrimination and response bias for CV syllables differing in voice onset time among children and adults. *Journal of the Acoustical Society of America, 80,* 1250–1256.

Elliott, L. L., and Hammer, M. A. 1988. Longitudinal changes in auditory discrimination in normal children and children with language-learning problems. *Journal of Speech and Hearing Disorders, 53,* 467–474.

Elliott, L. L., Hammer, M. A., and Scholl, M. E. 1989. Fine-grained auditory discrimination in normal children and children with language learning problems. *Journal of Speech and Hearing Research, 32,* 112–119.

Elliott, L. L., Longinotti, C., Meyer, D., Raz, I., and Zucker, K. 1981. Developmental differences in identifying and discriminating CV syllables. *Journal of the Acoustical Society of America, 70,* 669–677.

Erdelyi, M. 1974. A new look at the New Look: Perceptual defense and vigilance. *Psychological Review, 81,* 1–25.

Erdelyi, M., Buschke, H., and Finkelstein, S. 1977. Hypermnesia for Socratic Stimuli: The growth of recall for an internally generated memory list abstracted from a series of riddles. *Memory and Cognition, 5,* 283–286.

Fechner, G. T. [1860] 1966. Elements of Psychophysics. D. H. Howes and E. G. Boring, eds., H. E. Adler, trans., New York: Holt Rinehart and Winston.

Fenson, L., Dale, P. S., Reznick, J. S., Thal, D., Bates, E., Hartung, J. P., Pethick, S., and Reilly, J. S. 1993. *MacArthur Communicative Development Inventories: User's Guide and Technical Manual.* San Diego: Singular Publishing Group Inc.

Fisher, R. A. [1925] 1970. *Statistical Methods for Research Workers.* Oxford: Oxford University Press.

Fletcher, J. M., Francis, D. J., Rourke, B. P., Shaywitz, S. E., and Shaywitz, B. A. 1992. The validity of discrepancy based definitions of reading disabilities. *Journal of Learning Disabilities, 25,* 555–561.

Fletcher, J. M., Shaywitz, S. E., Shankweiler, D. P., Katz, L., Liberman, I. Y., Stuebing, K. K., Francis, D. J., Fowler, A. E., and Shaywitz, B. A. 1994. Cognitive profiles of reading disability: Comparison of discrepancy and low achievement definitions. *Journal of Educational Psychology, 86,* 6–23.

Fowler, A. E. 1991. How early phonological development might set the stage for phoneme awareness. In S. A. Brady and D. P. Shankweiler, eds., *Phonological Processes in Literacy.* Hillsdale, NJ: Lawrence Erlbaum Associates.

Fox, B., and Routh, D. K. 1975. Analyzing spoken language into words, syllables, and phonemes: A developmental study. *Journal of Psycholinguistic Research, 4,* 331–342.

Friederici, A. D., and Wessels, J. M. I. 1993. Phonotactic knowledge and its use in infant speech perception. *Perception and Psychophysics, 54,* 287–295.

Galton, F. 1886. Family likeness in stature. *Proceedings of the Royal Society, 40,* 42–72. (Table III, p 68).

Gathercole, S. E. 1995. Is nonword repetition a test of phonological memory or long-term knowledge? It all depends on the nonwords. *Memory and Cognition, 23,* 83–94.

Gathercole, S. E., and Baddeley, A. D. 1989. Evaluation of the role of phonological STM in the development of vocabulary in children: A longitudinal study. *Journal of Memory and Language, 28,* 200–213.

Gathercole, S. E., and Baddeley, A. D. 1990. The role of phonological memory in vocabulary acquisition: A study of young children learning new names. *British Journal of Psychology, 81,* 439–454.

Gathercole, S. E., Willis, C. S., and Baddeley, A. D. 1991. Differentiating phonological memory and awareness of rhyme: Reading and vocabulary development in children. *British Journal of Psychology, 82,* 387–406.

Gathercole, S. E., Willis, C. S., Baddeley, A. D., and Emlie, H. 1994. The Children's Test of Nonword Repetition: A test of phonological working memory. *Memory, 2,* 103–127.

Gelb, I. 1963. *A Study of Writing.* Chicago: University of Chicago Press.

Geschwind, N., and Fusillo, M. 1966. Color-naming defects in association with alexia. *A. M. A. Archives of Neurology, 15,* 137–146.

Gibbs, D. P., and Cooper, E. B. 1989. Prevalence of communication disorders in students with learning disabilities. *Journal of Learning Disabilities, 22,* 60–63.

Godfrey, J. J., Syrdal-Lasky, A. K., Millay, K. K., and Knox, C. M. 1981. Performance of dyslexic children on speech perception tests. *Journal of Experimental Child Psychology*, *32*, 401–424.

Goldstein, D. 1974. Learning to read and developmental changes in covert speech and in word analysis and synthesis skill. *Dissertation Abstracts International*, *35*, 1B–606B.

Golinkoff, R. M., and Hirsh-Pasek, K. 1999. *How Babies Talk*. New York: Penguin/Dutton.

Goodell, E. W., and Studdert-Kennedy, M. 1993. Acoustic evidence for the development of gestural coordination in the speech of 2-year-olds: A longitudinal study. *Journal of Speech and Hearing Research*, *36*, 707–727.

Goswami, U., and Bryant, P. 1990. *Phonological Skills and Learning to Read*. Hove, UK: Lawrence Erlbaum Associates.

Gottardo, A., Stanovich, K. E., and Siegel, L. S. 1996. The relationships between phonological sensitivity, syntactic processing, and verbal working memory in the reading performance of third-grade children. *Journal of Experimental Child Psychology*, *63*, 563–582.

Hall, J. W., Wilson, K. P., Humphreys, M. S., Tinzmann, M. B., and Bowyer, P. M. 1983. Phonemic-similarity effects in good versus poor readers. *Memory and Cognition*, *11*, 520–527.

Hammill, D., Brown, V., Larsen, S., and Wiederholt, J. 1994. *Test of Adolescent/Adult Language–3*. (TOAL). Austin, TX: Pro-Ed.

Hansen, J., and Bowey, J. A. 1994. Phonological analysis skills, verbal working memory, and reading ability in second-grade children. *Child Development*, *65*, 938–950.

Hart, B., and Risley, T. R. 1992. American parenting of language-learning children: Persisting differences in family-child interactions observed in natural home environments. *Developmental Psychology*, *28*, 1096–1105.

Hart, B., and Risley, T. R. 1995. *Meaningful Differences*. Baltimore, MD: Paul H. Brookes.

Helfgott, J. A. 1976. Phonemic segmentation and blending skills of kindergarten children: Implications for beginning reading acquisition. *Contemporary Educational Psychology*, *1*, 157–169.

Henry, L. A., and Millar, S. 1991. Memory span increase with age: A test of two hypotheses. *Journal of Experimental Child Psychology*, *51*, 459–484.

Holligan, C., and Johnston, R. S. 1988. The use of phonological information by good and poor readers in memory and reading tasks. *Memory and Cognition*, *16*, 522–532.

Hull, F. M., Mielke, P. W., Timmons, R. J., and Willeford, J. A. 1971. The National Speech and Hearing Survey: Preliminary results. *ASHA*, *3*, 501–509.

Hulme, C., Maughan, S., and Brown, G. A. 1991. Memory for familiar and unfamiliar words: Evidence for a long-term memory contribution to short-term memory span. *Journal of Memory and Language*, *30*, 685–701.

Hulme, C., Newton, P., Cowan, N., Stuart, G., and Brown, G. 1999. Think before you speak: Pauses, memory search, and trace reintegration processes in verbal memory span. *Journal of Experimental Psychology: Learning, Memory, and Cognition*, *25*, 447–463.

Hulme, C., Thomson, N., Muir, C., and Lawrence, A. 1984. Speech rate and the development of short-term memory span. *Journal of Experimental Child Psychology*, *38*, 241–253.

Hurford, D. P., and Sanders, R. E. 1990. Assessment and remediation of a phonemic discrimination deficit in reading disabled second and fourth graders. *Journal of Experimental Child Psychology*, *50*, 396–415.

Hurford, D. P., Schauf, J. D., Bunce, L., Blaich, T., and Moore, K. 1994. Early identification of children at risk for reading disabilities. *Journal of Learning Disabilities*, *27*, 371–382.

Jakobsen, R. [1941] 1968. *Child Language, Aphasia, and Phonological Universals*. The Hague: Mouton.

Jamieson, D. G., and Rvachew, S. 1992. Remediating speech production errors with sound identification training. *Journal of Speech-Language Pathology and Audiology*, *16*, 201–210.

Johnson, C. J., Beitchman, J. H., Young, A., Escobar, M., Atkinson, L., Wilson, B., Brownlie, E. B., Douglas, L., Taback, N., Lam, I., and Wang, M. 1999. Fourteen-year follow-up of children with and without speech/language impairments: Speech/language stability and outcomes. *Journal of Speech, Language, and Hearing Research*, *42*, 744–760.

References

Johnston, R. S. 1982. Phonological coding in dyslexic readers. *British Journal of Psychology, 73*, 455–460.

Johnston, R. S., and Watson, J. 2003. Accelerating the development of reading, spelling and phonemic awareness skills in initial readers. *Reading and Writing.*

Jorm, A. F. 1983. Specific reading retardation and working memory: A review. *British Journal of Psychology, 76*, 311–342.

Jorm, A. F., Share, D. L., Maclean, R., and Matthews, R. 1986. Cognitive factors at school entry predictive of specific reading retardation and general reading backwardness: A research note. *Journal of Child Psychology and Psychiatry, 27*, 45–54.

Juel, C., Griffith, P. L., and Gough, P. 1986. Acquisition of literacy: A longitudinal study of children in first and second grade. *Journal of Educational Psychology, 78*, 243–255.

Jusczyk, P. W. 1998. *The Discovery of Spoken Language.* Cambridge, MA: MIT Press.

Jusczyk, P. W., and Aslin, R. N. 1995. Infants' detection of sound patterns of words in fluent speech. *Cognitive Psychology, 29*, 1–23.

Jusczyk, P. W., Cutler, A., and Redganz, N. 1993. Preference for the predominant stress patterns of English words. *Child Development, 64*, 675–687.

Jusczyk, P. W., Houston, D. M., and Newsome, M. 1999. The beginnings of word segmentation in English-learning infants. *Cognitive Psychology, 39*, 159–207.

Jusczyk, P. W., Luce, P. A., and Charles-Luce, J. 1994. Infants' sensitivity to phonotactic patterns in the native language. *Journal of Memory and Language, 33*, 630–645.

Kail, R. 1991. Developmental change in speed of processing during childhood and adolescence. *Psychological Bulletin, 109*, 490–501.

Kaufman, A. S. 1979. WISC-R Research: Implications for interpretation. *School Psychology Digest, 8*, 5–27.

Kaufman, A. S., Harrison, P. L., and Ittenback, R. F. 1990. Intelligence testing in the schools. In T. B. Gutkin and C. A. Reynolds, eds., *Handbook of School Psychology*, 2nd ed. New York: Wiley.

Kirk, S., McCarthy, J., and Kirk, W. 1968. *The Illinois Test of Psycholinguistic Abilities*. (ITPA.) Rev. ed. Urbana: University of Illinois Press.

Kolb, B., and Whishaw, I. Q. 1990. *Fundamentals of Human Neuropsychology*. New York: W. H. Freeman.

LaBerge, D., and Samuels, S. J. 1974. Toward a theory of automatic information processing in reading. *Cognitive Psychology*, *6*, 293–323.

Landerl, K., Wimmer, H., and Frith, U. 1997. The impact of orthographic consistency on dyslexia: A German-English comparison. *Cognition*, *63*, 315–334.

Lenneberg, E. 1967. *Biological Foundations of Language*. New York: Wiley.

Leonard, L., Newhoff, M., and Mesalam, L. 1980. Individual differences in early child phonology. *Applied Psycholinguistics*, *1*, 7–30.

Levitt, A. G., Utman, J., and Aydelott, J. 1992. From babbling towards the sound systems of English and French: A longitudinal two-case study. *Journal of Child Language*, *19*, 19–49.

Liberman, A. M., Cooper, F. S., Shankweiler, D. P., and Studdert-Kennedy, M. 1967. Perception of the speech code. *Psychological Review*, *74*, 431–461.

Liberman, A. M., and Mattingly, I. G. 1985. The motor theory of speech perception revised. *Cognition*, *21*, 1–36.

Liberman, I. Y. 1973. Segmentation of the spoken word and reading acquisition. *Bulletin of the Orton Society*, *23*, 65–77.

Liberman, I. Y., and Liberman, A. M. 1989. Phonology and learning to read. In I. Y. Liberman and D. Shankweiler, eds., *Phonology and Reading Disability: Solving the Reading Puzzle*. Ann Arbor: University of Michigan Press.

Liberman, I. Y., and Mann, V. A. 1981. Should reading instruction and remediation vary with the sex of the child? In A. Ansara, N. Geschwind, A. Galaburda, M. Albert, and N. Gartrell, eds., *Sex Differences in Dyslexia*, 151–167. Towson, MD: Orton Dyslexia Society.

Liberman, I. Y., and Shankweiler, D. 1985. Phonology and the problems of learning to read and write. *Remedial and Special Education*, *6*, 8–17.

Liberman, I. Y., Shankweiler, D., Liberman, A. M., Fowler, C., and Fisher, F. W. 1974. Explicit syllable and phoneme segmentation in the young child. *Journal of Experimental Child Psychology*, *18*, 201–212.

Lincoln, A. J., Dickstein, P., Courchesne, E., Elmasian, R., and Tallal, P. 1992. Auditory processing abilities in non-retarded adolescents and young adults with developmental receptive language disorder and autism. *Brain and Language, 43*, 613–622.

Lindamood, C. H., and Lindamood, P. C. 1969. *Auditory Discrimination in Depth*. Allen, TX: DLM Teaching Resources.

Lindamood, C. H., and Lindamood, P. C. 1971. *Lindamood Auditory Conceptualization Test*. Boston: Teaching Resources.

Lovegrove, W. J., and Williams, M. C. 1993. Visual temporal processing deficits in specific reading disability. In D. M. Willows, R. S. Kruk, and E. Corcos, eds., *Visual Processes in Reading and Reading Disabilities*. Hillsdale, NJ: Lawrence Erlbaum Associates.

Lowe, A. D., and Campbell, R. 1965. Temporal discrimination in aphasoid and normal children. *Journal of Speech and Hearing Research, 8*, 313–314.

Luce, P. A. 1986. Neighborhoods of words in the mental lexicon. In *Research on Speech Perception*. Technical Report No. 6. Bloomington: Speech Research Laboratory, Indiana University.

Lyons, G. R., and Moats, L. C. 1997. Critical conceptual and methodological considerations in reading intervention research. *Journal of Learning Disabilities, 30*, 578–588.

Maccoby, E. E., and Jacklin, C. N. 1974. *The Psychology of Sex Differences*. Stanford, CA: Stanford University Press.

Mandel, D. R., Jusczyk, P. W., and Pisoni, D. B. 1995. Infants' recognition of the sound patterns of their own names. *Psychological Science, 6*, 315–318.

Mann, V. A. 1984. Longitudinal prediction and prevention of early reading difficulty. *Annals of Dyslexia, 43*, 117–136.

Mann, V. A. 1993. Phoneme awareness and future reading ability. *Journal of Learning Disabilities, 26*, 259–269.

Mann, V. A., and Ditunno, P. 1990. Phonological deficiencies: Effective predictors of future reading problems. In G. T. Pavlidis, ed., *Perspectives on Dyslexia*, vol. 2, 105–131. New York: Wiley.

Mann, V. A., and Liberman, I. Y. 1984. Phonological awareness and verbal short-term memory. *Journal of Learning Disabilities, 17*, 592–599.

Mann, V. A., Liberman, I. Y., and Shankweiler, D. 1980. Children's memory for sentences and word strings in relation to reading ability. *Memory and Cognition*, *8*, 329–335.

Mann, V. A., Shankweiler, D., and Smith, S. T. 1984. The association between comprehension of spoken sentences and early reading ability: The role of phonetic representation. *Journal of Child Language*, *11*, 627–643.

Marshall, J. C., and Morton, J. 1978. On the mechanics of EMMA. In A. Sinclair, R. J. Jarvella, and W. J. M. Levelt, eds., *The Child's Conception of Language*, 225–239. Berlin: Springer-Verlag.

Marshall, W. H., Talbot, S. A., and Ades, H. W. 1943. Cortical responses of the anesthetized cat to gross photic and electrical afferent stimulation. *Journal of Neurophysiology*, *6*, 1–15.

Mattys, S. L., Jusczyk, P. W., Luce, P. A., and Morgan, J. L. 1999. Phonotactic and prosodic effects on word segmentation in infants. *Cognitive Psychology*, *38*, 465–494.

Mayringer, H., and Wimmer, H. 2000. Pseudoname learning by German-speaking children with dyslexia: Evidence for a phonological learning deficit. *Journal of Experimental Child Psychology*, *75*, 116–133.

McArthur, G. M., Hogben, J. H., Edwards, V. T., Heath, S. M., and Mengler, E. D. 2000. On the "specifics" of specific reading disability and specific language impairment. *Journal of Child Psychology and Psychiatry*, *41*, 869–874.

McCauley, R. J., and Swisher, L. 1984. Psychometric review of language and articulation tests for preschool children. *Journal of Speech and Hearing Disorders*, *49*, 34–42.

McCracken, G., and Walcutt, C. C. 1963. *Basic Reading*. Philadelphia: Lippincott.

McGuinness, C., McGuinness, D., and McGuinness, G. 1996. Phono-Graphix: A new method for remediation of reading difficulties. *Annals of Dyslexia*, *46*, 73–96.

McGuinness, D. 1972. Hearing: Individual differences in perception. *Perception*, *1*, 465–473.

McGuinness, D. 1976. Away from a unisex psychology: Individual differences in visual sensory and perceptual processes. *Perception*, *5*, 279–294.

McGuinness, D. 1985. *When Children Don't Learn*. New York: Basic Books.

McGuinness, D. 1986. The sensory-motor cogs in cognition. In F. Klix and H. Hagendorf, eds., *Human Memory and Cognitive Capabilities*. Amsterdam: Elsevier Science Publishers.

McGuinness, D. 1997a. Decoding strategies as predictors of reading skill: A follow-on study. *Annals of Dyslexia*, 47, 117–150.

McGuinness, D. 1997b. *Why Our Children Can't Read*. New York: Simon and Schuster/Free Press.

McGuinness, D. 1998. *Why Children Can't Read*. London: Penguin Press.

McGuinness, D. 2004. *Early Reading Instruction*. Cambridge, MA: MIT Press.

McGuinness, D., and Lewis, I. 1978. Sex differences in visual persistence: Experiments on the Ganzfeld and afterimages. *Perception*, 5, 295–301.

McGuinness, D., McGuinness, C., and Donohue, J. 1995. Phonological training and the alphabet principle: Evidence for reciprocal causality. *Reading Research Quarterly*, 30, 830–852.

McGuinness, D., Olson, A., and Chaplin, J. 1990. Sex differences in incidental recall for words and pictures. *Journal of Learning and Individual Differences*, 2, 263–286.

McGuinness, D., and Pribram, K. H. 1978. The origins of sensory bias in the development of gender differences in perception and cognition. In M. Bortner, G. Turkewitx, and J. Tizard, eds., *Cognitive Growth and Development: Essays in Honor of Herbert G. Birch*, 3–56. New York: Brunner/Mazel.

McGuinness, D., and Pribram, K. H. 1980. The neuropsychology of attention: Emotional and motivational controls. In M. C. Wittrock, ed., *The Brain and Educational Psychology*, 95–139. New York: Academic Press.

McNemar, Q. 1949. *Psychological Statistics*. New York: Wiley.

Mehler, J., Jusczyk, P. W., Lambertz, G., Halsted, N., Bertoncini, J., and Amiel-Tison, C. 1988. A precursor of language acquisition in young infants. *Cognition*, 29, 144–178.

Menn, L. 1971. Phonotactic rules in beginning speech. *Lingua*, 26, 225–251.

Merzenich, M. M., Schreiner, C., Jenkins, W., and Wang, X. 1993. Neural mechanisms underlying temporal integration, segmentation, and input sequence representation: Some implications for the origin of learning disabilities. In P. Tallal, A. M. Galaburda, R. R. Llinas, and C. von Euler, eds.,

Annals of the New York Academy of Sciences, 682, 1–23. New York: New York Academy of Sciences.

Metsala, J. L. 1997. An examination of word frequency and neighborhood density in the development of spoken-word recognition. *Memory and Cognition, 25*, 47–56.

Metsala, J. L., and Walley, A. C. 1998. Spoken vocabulary growth and the segmental restructuring of lexical representations: Precursors to phonemic awareness and early reading ability. In J. L. Metsala and L. C. Ehri, eds., *Word Recognition in Beginning Literacy*. Mahwah, NJ: Lawrence Erlbaum Associates.

Mody, M., Studdert-Kennedy, M., and Brady, S. 1997. Speech perception deficits in poor readers: Auditory processing or phonological coding? *Journal of Experimental Child Psychology, 64*, 199–231.

Morais, J. 1991. Constraints on the development of phonemic awareness. In S. A. Brady and D. P. Shankweiler, eds., *Phonological Processes in Literacy*. Hillsdale, NJ: Lawrence Erlbaum Associates.

Morley, M. E. 1972. *The Development and Disorders of Speech in Childhood*. Edinburgh: Churchill Livingstone.

Mullis, I. V. S., Campbell, J. R., and Farstrup, A. E. 1993. *National Assessment of Educational Progress 1992: Reading Report Card for the Nation and States*. Washington, DC: Office of Educational Research and Improvement, U.S. Department of Education.

Murphy, R., Menyuk, P., Liebergott, J., and Schultz, M. 1983. Predicting rate of lexical development. Paper presented at the conference of the Society for Research in Child Development, Detroit.

Myers, P. I. 1987. Assessing oral language. In D. D. Hammill, ed., *Assessing the Abilities and Instructional Needs of Students*. Austin, TX: Pro-Ed.

Nation, K., and Hulme, C. 1997. Phonemic segmentation, not onset-rime segmentation, predicts early reading and spelling skills. *Reading Research Quarterly, 32*, 154–167.

National Reading Panel. 2000. *Report*. Washington, DC: National Institute of Child Health and Human Development.

Nelson, K. 1998. *Language in Cognitive Development*. Cambridge: Cambridge University Press.

Neuhaus, G., Foorman, B. R., Francis, D. J., and Carlson, C. D. 2001. Measures of information processing in rapid automatized naming (RAN) and their relation to reading. *Journal of Experimental Child Psychology*, *78*, 359–373.

Newcomer, P., and Hammill, D. 1977. *Test of Language Development*. (TOLD.) Austin, TX: Empiric Press.

Newcomer, P., and Hammill, D. 1988. *Test for Adolescent and Adult Language*. (TAAL.) Austin, TX: Pro-Ed.

Nittrouer, S. 1993. The emergence of mature gestural patterns is not uniform: Evidence from an acoustic study. *Journal of Speech and Hearing Research*, *36*, 959–971.

Nittrouer, S. 1995. Children learn separate aspects of speech production at different rates: Evidence from spectral moments. *Journal of the Acoustical Society of America*, *97*, 520–530.

Nittrouer, S. 1999. Do temporal processing deficits cause phonological processing problems? *Journal of Speech, Language, and Hearing Research*, *42*, 925–942.

Nittrouer, S., and Crowther, C. S. 1998. Examining the role of auditory sensitivity in the developmental weighting shift. *Journal of Speech, Language, and Hearing Research*, *41*, 809–818.

Nittrouer, S., Crowther, C. S., and Miller, M. E. 1998. The relative weighting of acoustic properties in the perception of [s] + stop clusters by children and adults. *Perception and Psychophysics*, *60*, 51–64.

Nittrouer, S., and Miller, M. E. 1997. Predicting developmental shifts in perceptual weighting schemes. *Journal of the Acoustical Society of America*, *101*, 2253–2266.

Nittrouer, S., and Studdert-Kennedy, M. 1987. The role of coarticulatory effects in the perception of fricatives by children and adults. *Journal of Speech and Hearing Research*, *30*, 319–329.

Nittrouer, S., Studdert-Kennedy, M., and McGowan, R. S. 1989. The emergence of phonetic segments: Evidence from the spectral structure of fricative vowel syllables spoken by children and adults. *Journal of Speech and Hearing Research*, *32*, 120–132.

Nittrouer, S., Studdert-Kennedy, M., and Neely, S. T. 1996. How children learn to organize their speech gestures: Further evidence from fricative-vowel syllables. *Journal of Speech and Hearing Research*, *39*, 379–389.

Nordmark, J. O. 1970. Time and frequency analysis. In J. V. Tobias, ed., 55–83. *Foundations of Modern Auditory Theory*. New York: Academic Press.

Nova, S., and Rescorla, L. 1994. A comparison of interactional style between SELD and normal mother-child dyads in a picture box reading task. Unpublished manuscript.

Obregon, M. 1994. Exploring Naming Timing patterns by Dyslexic and Normal Readers on the Serial RAN Task. Unpublished master's thesis, Tufts University.

O'Donnell, L., Granier, M. J., and Dersh, J. J. 1991. Does handedness affect children's coding performance on the WISC-III? Poster at American Psychological Association conference, San Francisco.

Olson, R. K., Davidson, B. J., Kliegl, R., and Davies, S. 1984. Development of phonetic memory in disabled and normal readers. *Journal of Experimental Child Psychology*, 37, 187–206.

Organization for Economic Cooperation and Development. 1995. *Literacy, Economy, and Society*. Ottawa: Statistics Canada.

Otto, W. 1961. The acquisition and retention of paired associates by good, average, and poor readers. *Journal of Educational Psychology*, 52, 241–248.

Paul, R., and Jennings, P. 1992. Phonological behavior in toddlers with slow expressive language development. *Journal of Speech and Hearing Research*, 35, 99–107.

Paul, R., Looney, S. S., and Dahm, P. S. 1991. Communication and socialization skills at ages 2 and 3 in "late-talking" young children. *Journal of Speech and Hearing Research*, 34, 858–865.

Pearson, P. D. 1997. The first grade studies. A personal reflection. *Reading Research Quarterly*, 32, 428–432.

Perfetti, C. A., Finger, E., and Hogaboam, T. 1978. Reading skill and the role of verbal experience in decoding. *Journal of Educational Psychology*, 70, 717–729.

Perfetti, C. A., and Hogaboam, T. 1975. Relationship between single word decoding and reading comprehension skill. *Journal of Educational Psychology*, 67, 461–469.

Piaget, J. [1964] 1993. Development and learning. In M. Gauvain and M. Cole, eds., *Readings on the Development of Children*, 25–33. New York: Scientific American Books. W. H. Freeman.

Pinker, S. 1994. *The Language Instinct*. New York: William Morrow.

Pinker, S. 1995. Language acquisition. In L. R. Gleitman and M. Liberman, eds., *An Invitation to Cognitive Science: Language*, vol. 1, 135–182. Cambridge, MA: MIT Press.

Plomin, R., and Dale, P. S. 2000. Genetics and early language development: A UK study of twins. In D. V. M. Bishop and L. B. Leonard, eds., *Speech and Language Impairment in Children: Causes, Characteristics, Intervention and Outcome*, Hove, UK: Psychology Press. 35–51.

Plomin, R., Fulker, D. W., Corley, R., and DeFries, J. C. 1997. Nature, nurture, and cognitive development from 1 to 16 years: A parent-offspring adoption study. *Psychological Science, 8*, 442–448.

Polka, L., and Werker, J. F. 1994. Developmental changes in perception of non-native vowel contrasts. *Journal of Experimental Psychology: Human Perception and Performance, 20*, 421–435.

Pratt, C., Tunmer, W. E., and Bowey, J. A. 1984. Children's capacity to correct grammatical violations in sentences. *Journal of Child Language, 11*, 129–141.

Preisser, D., Hodson, B., and Paden, E. 1988. Developmental phonology: 18–29 months. *Journal of Speech and Hearing Disorders, 53*, 125–130.

Pribram, K. H. 1971. *Languages of the Brain*. Englewood Cliffs, NJ: Prentice-Hall.

Pribram, K. H. 1991. *Brain and Perception*. Hillsdale, NJ: Lawrence Erlbaum Associates.

Pribram, K. H., and McGuinness, D. 1975. Arousal, activation and effort in the control of attention. *Psychological Review, 82*, 116–149.

Pribram, K. H., and McGuinness, D. 1992. Attention and para-attentional processing: Event-related potentials as tests of a model. *Annals of the New York Academy of Sciences, 658*, 65–92.

Quinn, P. C., and Eimas, P. D. 1998. Evidence for a global categorical representation of humans by young infants. *Journal of Experimental Child Psychology, 69*, 151–174.

Raaymakers, E., and Crul, T. 1988. Perception and production of the final /s-ts/ contrast in Dutch by mis-articulating children. *Journal of Speech and Hearing Disorders, 53*, 262–270.

Rayner, K. 1985. The role of eye movements in learning to read and reading disability. *Remedial and Special Education, 6,* 53–60.

Rayner, K. 1986. Eye movements and the perceptual span in beginning and skilled readers. *Journal of Experimental Child Psychology, 41,* 211–236.

Rayner, K. 1998. Eye movements in reading and information processing: 20 years of research. *Psychological Bulletin, 124,* 372–422.

Reed, M. A. 1989. Speech perception and the discrimination of brief auditory cues in reading disabled children. *Journal of Experimental Child Psychology, 48,* 270–292.

Renfrew, C. E., and Geary, L. 1973. Prediction of persisting speech defect. *British Journal of Disorders of Communication, 8,* 37–41.

Rescorla, L. 1989. The language development survey: A screening tool for delayed language in toddlers. *Journal of Speech and Hearing Disorders, 54,* 587–599.

Rescorla, L., and Fechnay, L. 1996. Mother-child synchrony and communicative reciprocity in late-talking toddlers. *Journal of Speech and Hearing Research, 39,* 200–208.

Rescorla, L., and Ratner, N. B. 1996. Phonetic profiles of toddlers with specific expressive language impairment (SLI-E). *Journal of Speech and Hearing Research, 39,* 153–165.

Rescorla, L., and Schwartz, E. 1990. Outcome of toddlers with expressive language delay. *Applied Psycholinguistics, 11,* 393–407.

Richardson, S. O. 1989. Specific developmental dyslexia: Retrospective and prospective views. *Annals of Dyslexia, 39,* 3–23.

Roberts, J., Rescorla, L., Giroux, J., and Stevens, L. 1998. Phonological skills of children with specific expressive language impairment (SLI-E): Outcome at age 3. *Journal of Speech, Language, and Hearing Research, 41,* 374–384.

Rohl, M., and Pratt, C. 1996. Phonological awareness, verbal working memory and the acquisition of literacy. *Reading and Writing, 8,* 327–360.

Rosner, J., and Simon, D. P. 1971. The Auditory Analysis Test: An initial report. *Journal of Learning Disabilities, 4,* 40–48.

Roswell-Chall Auditory Blending Tests. 1959. New York: Essay Press.

Rvachew, S., and Jamieson, D. G. 1989. Perception of voiceless fricatives by children with a functional articulation disorder. *Journal of Speech and Hearing Research*, *54*, 193–208.

Ryan, E. B. 1980. Metalinguistic development and reading. In L. H. Waterhouse, K. M. Fischer, and E. B. Ryan, eds., *Language Awareness and Reading*. Newark, DE: International Reading Association.

Sattler, J. M. 1992. *Assessment of Children. WISC III and WIPPSI Supplement*. San Diego: Jerome M. Sattler.

Schatschneider, C., Francis, D. J., Foorman, B. R., Fletcher, J. M., and Mehta, P. 1999. The dimensionality of phonological awareness: An application of item response theory. *Journal of Educational Psychology*, *91*, 439–449.

Schonell, F. J. 1945. *The Psychology and Teaching of Reading*. London: Oliver and Boyd.

Sekular, R., and Blake, R. 1994. *Perception*, 3rd ed. New York: McGraw-Hill.

Semel. E., Wiig, E. H., and Secord, W. 1986. *Clinical Evaluation of Language Fundamentals—Revised*. (CELFR.) San Diego: Psychological Corp.

Shankweiler, D., Crain, S., Katz, L., Fowler, A. E., Liberman, A. M., Brady, S. A., Thornton, R., Lundquist, E., Dreyer, L. Fletcher, J. M., Stuebing, K. K., Shaywitz, S. E., and Shatwitz, B. A. 1995. Cognitive profiles of reading-disabled children: Comparison of language skills in phonology, morphology, and syntax. *Psychological Science*, *6*, 149–156.

Shankweiler, D., Liberman, I. Y., Mark, L. S., Fowler, C. A., and Fischer, F. W. 1979. The speech code and learning to read. *Journal of Experimental Psychology: Human Learning and Memory*, *5*, 531–544.

Shankweiler, D., Smith, S. T., and Mann, V. 1984. Repetition and comprehension of spoken sentences by reading-disabled children. *Brain and Language*, *23*, 241–257.

Share, D. L., Jorm, A. F., Maclean, R., and Matthews, R. 1984. Sources of individual difference in reading acquisition. *Journal of Educational Psychology*, *76*, 1309–1324.

Shaywitz, B., Holford, T. H., Holahan, J. M., Fletcher, J. M., Stuebing, K. K., Francis, D. J., and Shaywitz, S. E. 1995. A Matthew effect for IQ but not for reading: Results from a longitudinal study. *Reading Research Quarterly*, *30*, 894–906.

Siegel, L. S., and Ryan, E. B. 1988. Development of grammatical-sensitivity, phonological, and short-term memory skills in normally achieving and learning disabled children. *Developmental Psychology, 24,* 28–37.

Smith, C., and Tager-Flusberg, H. 1982. Metalinguistic awareness and language development. *Journal of Experimental Psychology, 34,* 449–468.

Smith, S. T., Macaruso, P., Shankweiler, D., and Crain, S. 1989. Syntactic comprehension in young poor readers. *Applied Psycholinguistics, 10,* 429–454.

Snowling, M., Goulandris, N., Bowlby, M., and Howell, P. 1986. Segmentation and speech perception in relation to reading skill: A developmental analysis. *Journal of Experimental Child Psychology, 41,* 489–507.

Spring, C., and Capps, C. 1974. Encoding speed, rehearsal, and probed recall of dyslexic boys. *Journal of Educational Psychology, 66,* 780–786.

Spring, C., and Davis, J. M. 1988. Relations of digit naming speed with three components of reading. *Applied Psycholinguistics, 9,* 315–334.

Stanovich, K. E. 1981. Relationships between word decoding speed, general name-retrieval ability, and reading progress in first-grade children. *Journal of Educational Psychology, 73,* 809–815.

Stanovich, K. E. 1986. Matthew effects in reading: Some consequences of individual differences in the acquisition of literacy. *Reading Research Quarterly, 26,* 7–29.

Stanovich, K. E., Cunningham, A. E., and Cramer, B. B. 1984. Assessing phonological awareness in kindergarten children: Issues of task comparability. *Journal of Experimental Child Psychology, 38,* 175–180.

Stanovich, K. E., Feeman, D. J., and Cunningham, A. 1983. The development of the relation between letter-naming speed and reading ability. *Bulletin of the Psychonomic Society, 21,* 199–202.

Stanovich, K. E., Nathan, R. G., and Vala-Rossi, M. 1986. Developmental changes in the cognitive correlates of reading ability and the developmental lag hypothesis. *Reading Research Quarterly, 21,* 267–283.

Stanovich, K. E., Nathan, R. G., and Zolmna, J. E. 1988. The developmental lag hypothesis in reading: Longitudinal and matched reading-level comparisons. *Child Development, 59,* 71–86.

Stanovich, K. E., and Siegel, L. S. 1994. Phenotypic performance profile of children with reading disabilities: A regression-based test of the phonological-core variable-difference model. *Journal of Experimental Psychology*, *86*, 24–53.

Stark, J. A. 1967. A comparison of the performance of aphasic children on three sequencing tests. *Journal of Communication Disorders*, *1*, 31–34.

Stark, R. E., and Tallal, P. 1979. Analysis of stop consonant production errors in developmentally dysphasic children. *Journal of the Acoustical Society of America*, *66*, 1703–1712.

Stark, R. E., and Tallal, P. 1981. Selection of children with specific language deficits. *Journal of Speech and Hearing Disorders*, *46*, 114–122.

Stark, R. E., Tallal, P., and Curtiss, B. 1975. Speech perception and production errors in dysphasic children. *Journal of the Acoustical Society of America*. Supplement 1, 57, 524A.

Stein, J. F. 1993. Visuospatial perception in disabled readers. In D. M. Willows, R. S. Kruk, and E. Corcos, eds., *Visual Processes in Reading and Reading Disabilities*. Hillsdale, NJ: Lawrence Erlbaum Associates.

Stein, J. F., Riddell, P., and Fowler, M. S. 1986. The Dunlop Test and reading in primary school children. *British Journal of Opthalmology*, *70*, 317.

Stoel-Gammon, C. 1985. Phonetic inventories, 15–24 months. A longitudinal study. *Journal of Speech and Hearing Research*, *28*, 506–512.

Stoel-Gammon, C. 1989a. From babbling to speech: Some new evidence. Conference report, Child Phonology Conference, Evanston, IL.

Stoel-Gammon, C. 1989b. Prespeech and early speech development of two late talkers. *First Language*, *9*, 207–224.

Stoel-Gammon, C. 1991. Normal and disordered phonology in two-year-olds. *Topics in Language Disorders*, *11*, 21–32.

Stothard, S. E., Snowling, M. J., Bishop, D. V. M., Chipchase, B. B., and Kaplan, C. A. 1998. Languge-impaired preschoolers: A follow-up into adolescence. *Journal of Speech, Language, and Hearing Research*, *41*, 407–418.

Strange, W., and Jenkins, J. J. 1978. Role of linguistic experience in the perception of speech. In R. D. Walk and H. L. Pick, eds., *Perception and Experience*. New York: Plenum.

Stuart, M. 1995. Prediction and qualitative assessment of five- and six-year-old children's reading: A longitudinal study. *British Journal of Educational Psychology*, *65*, 287–296.

Studdert-Kennedy, M., and Mody, M. 1995. Auditory temporal perception deficits in the reading impaired: A critical review of the evidence. *Psychonomic Bulletin and Review*, *2*, 508–514.

Tallal, P. 1980. Auditory temporal perception, phonics, and reading disabilities in children. *Brain and Language*, *9*, 182–198.

Tallal, P., Miller, S., and Fitch, R. H. 1993. Neurological basis of speech: A case for the preeminence of temporal processing. In P. Tallal, A. M. Galaburda, R. R. Llinas, and C. von Euler, eds., *Annals of the New York Academy of Sciences*, *682*, 27–47. New York: New York Academy of Sciences.

Tallal, P., and Newcombe, F. 1978. Impairment of auditory perception and language comprehension in dysphasia. *Brain and Language*, *5*, 13–24.

Tallal, P., and Piercy, M. 1973a. Defects of non-verbal auditory perception in children with developmental aphasia. *Nature*, *241*, 468–469.

Tallal, P., and Piercy, M. 1973b. Developmental aphasia: Impaired rate of non-verbal processing as a function of sensory modality. *Neuropsychologia*, *11*, 389–398.

Tallal, P., and Piercy, M. 1974. Developmental aphasia: Rate of auditory processing and selective impairment of consonant perception. *Neuropsychologia*, *12*, 83–93.

Tallal, P., and Piercy, M. 1975. Developmental aphasia: The perception of brief vowels and extended stop consonants. *Neuropsychologia*, *13*, 69–74.

Tallal, P., Sainberg, R. L., and Jernigan, T. 1991. The neuropathology of developmental dysphasia: Behavioral, morphological and physiological evidence for a pervasive temporal processing disorder. *Reading and Writing: An Interdisciplinary Journal*, *3*, 363–377.

Tallal, P., and Stark, R. E. 1978. Identification of a [sa] to [sta] continuum by normally developing and language-delayed children. *Journal of the Acoustical Society of America*, *64*, 50.

Tallal, P., and Stark, R. E. 1981. Speech acoustic-cue discrimination abilities of normally developing and language-impaired children. *Journal of the Acoustical Society of America*, *69*, 568–574.

Tallal, P., Stark, R. E., and Curtiss, B. 1976. Relation between speech perception and speech production impairment in children with developmental dysphasia. *Brain and Language*, *3*, 305–317.

Tallal, P., Stark, R. E., and Mellits, D. 1985. The relationship between auditory temporal analysis and receptive language development: Evidence from studies of developmental language disorder. *Neuropsychologia, 23,* 527–534.

Tees, R. C., and Werker, J. F. 1984. Perceptual flexibility: Maintenance or recovery of the ability to discriminate non-native speech sounds. *Canadian Journal of Psychology, 38,* 579–590.

Thal, D. J., Oroz, M., and McCaw, V. 1995. Phonological and lexical development in normal and late-talking toddlers. *Applied Psycholinguistics, 16,* 407–424.

Tincoff, R., and Jusczyk, P. W. 1999. Some beginnings of word comprehension in 6-month-olds. *Psychological Science, 10,* 172–175.

Trehub, S. E., and Henderson, J. L. 1996. Temporal resolution in infancy and subsequent language development. *Journal of Speech and Hearing Research, 39,* 1315–1320.

Trehub, S. E., Schneider, B. A., and Henderson, J. L. 1995. Gap detection in infants, children, and adults. *Journal of the Acoustical Society of America, 98,* 2532–2541.

Tunmer, W. E., and Bowey, J. A. 1984. Metalinguistic awareness and reading acquisition. In W. E. Tunmer, C. Pratt, and M. L. Herriman, eds., *Metalinguistic Awareness in Children: Theory, Research and Implications,* 144–168. Berlin: Springer-Verlag.

Tunmer, W. E., and Herriman, M. I. 1984. The development of metalinguistic awareness. In A. Sinclair, R. J. Jarvella, and W. J. M. Levelt, eds., *The Child's Conception of Language,* 12–35. Berlin: Springer-Verlag.

Tunmer, W. E., Herriman, M. L., and Nesdale, A. R. 1988. Metalinguistic abilities and beginning reading. *Reading Research Quarterly, 23,* 134–158.

Urbach, P. 1987. *Francis Bacon's Philosophy of Science.* Peru, IL: Open Court.

Valtin, R. 1984. Awareness of features and functions of language. In J. Downing and R. Valtin, eds., *Language Awareness and Learning to Read,* 227–260. New York: Springer-Verlag.

Van Bon, W. H. J., and Van Der Pilj, J. M. L. 1997. Effects of word length and word likeness on pseudoword repetition by poor and normal readers. *Applied Psycholinguistics, 18,* 101–114.

Vandervelden, M. C., and Siegel, L. S. 1995. Phonological recoding and phoneme awareness in early literacy. A developmental approach. *Reading Research Quarterly*, *30*, 854–875.

Vellutino, F. R., Harding, C. J., Phillips, F., and Steger, J. A. 1975. Differential transfer in poor and normal readers. *Journal of Genetic Psychology*, *126*, 3–18.

Venezky, R. L. 1999. *The American Way of Spelling*. New York: Guilford Press.

Vihman, M. M. 1993. Variable paths to early word production. *Journal of Phonetics*, *21*, 61–82.

Vihman, M. M., Ferguson, C., and Elbert, M. 1986. Phonological development from babbling to speech: Common tendencies and individual differences. *Applied Psycholinguistics*, *7*, 3–40.

Vitevitch, M. S., Luce, P. A., Charles-Luce, J., and Kemmerer, D. 1997. Phonotactics and syllable stress: Implications for the processing spoken nonsense words. *Language and Speech*, *40*, 47–62.

Vogel, S. 1975. *Syntactic Abilities in Normal and Dyslexic Children*. Baltimore, MD: University Park Press.

Wagner, R. K., Torgesen, J. K., Laughon, P., Simmons, K., and Rashotte, C. A. 1993. Development of young readers' phonological processing abilities. *Journal of Educational Psychology*, *85*, 83–103.

Wagner, R. K., Torgesen, J. K., and Rashotte, C. 1994. The development of reading-related phonological processing abilities. *Developmental Psychology*, *30*, 73–87.

Wallach, L., Wallach, M. A., Dozier, M. G., and Kaplan, N. W. 1977. Poor children learning to read do not have trouble with phoneme recognition. *Journal of Educational Psychology*, *69*, 36–39.

Walley, A. C., and Metsala, J. L. 1990. The growth of lexical constraints on spoken word recognition. *Perception and Psychophysics*, *47*, 267–280.

Walley, A. C., and Metsala, J. L. 1992. Young children's age-of-acquisition estimates for spoken words. *Memory and Cognition*, *20*, 171–182.

Walley, A. C., Smith, L. B., and Jusczyk, P. W. 1986. The role of phonemes and syllables in the perceived similarity of speech sounds for children. *Memory and Cognition*, *14*, 220–229.

Weinstein, R., and Rabinovitch, M. S. 1971. Sentence structure and retention in good and poor readers. *Journal of Educational Psychology*, *62*, 25–30.

Weismer, S. E., Murray-Branch, J., and Miller, J. R. 1994. A prospective longitudinal study of language development in late talkers. *Journal of Speech and Hearing Research*, *37*, 852–867.

Werker, J. F., Gilbert, J. H., Humphrey, K., and Tees, R. C. 1981. Developmental aspects of cross-language speech perception. *Child Development*, *52*, 349–355.

Werker, J. F., and Lalonde, C. E. 1988. Cross-language speech perception: Initial capabilities and developmental change. *Developmental Psychology*, *24*, 672–683.

Werker, J. F., and Logan, J. S. 1985. Cross-language evidence for three factors is speech perception. *Perception and Psychophysics*, *37*, 35–44.

Werker, J. F., and Tees, R. C. 1983. Developmental changes across childhood in the perception of non-native speech sounds. *Canadian Journal of Psychology*, *37*, 278–286.

Werker, J. F., and Tees, R. C. 1984a. Cross-language speech perception: Evidence for perceptual reorganization during the first year of life. *Infant Behavior and Development*, *7*, 49–63.

Werker, J. F., and Tees, R. C. 1984b. Phonemic and phonetic factors in adults' cross-language speech perception. *Journal of the Acoustical Society of America*, *75*, 1866–1878.

Werker, J. F., and Tees, R. C. 1987. Speech perception in severely disabled and average reading children. *Canadian Journal of Psychology*, *41*, 48–61.

Williams, M., Molinet, K., and LeCluwse, K. 1989. Visual masking as a measure of temporal processing in normal and disabled readers. *Clinical Vision Sciences*, *4*, 137–144.

Willows, D. M., and Ryan, E. B. 1986. The development of grammatical sensitivity and its relationship to early reading achievement. *Reading Research Quarterly*, *21*, 253–266.

Wimmer, H. 1993. Characteristics of developmental dyslexia in a regular writing system. *Applied Psycholinguistics*, *14*, 1–33.

Wimmer, H. 1996. The nonword reading deficit in developmental dyslexia: Evidence from children learning to read German. *Journal of Experimental Child Psychology*, *61*, 80–90.

Wimmer, H., and Goswami, U. 1994. The influence of orthographic consistency on reading development: Word recognition in English and German children. *Cognition*, *51*, 91–103.

Wimmer, H., and Landerl, K. 1997. How learning to spell German differs from learning to spell English. In C. A. Perfetti, L. Rieben, and M. Fayol, *Learning to Spell*. Mahwah, NJ: Lawrence Erlbaum Associates.

Wimmer, H., Landerl, K., Linortner, R., and Hummer, P. 1991. The relationship of phonemic awareness to reading acquisition. More consequence than precondition but still important. *Cognition*, *40*, 219–249.

Wimmer, H., Mayringer, H., and Landerl, K. 2000. The double-deficit hypothesis and difficulties in learning to read a regular orthography. *Journal of Educational Psychology*, *92*, 668–680.

Wolf, M. 1984. Naming, reading, and the dyslexias: A longitudinal overview. *Annals of Dyslexia*, *34*.

Wolf, M. 1986. Rapid alternating stimulus naming in the developmental dyslexias. *Brain and Language*, *27*, 360–379.

Wolf, M., Bally, H., and Morris, R. 1986. Automaticity, retrieval processes, and reading: A longitudinal study in average and impaired readers. *Child Development*, *57*, 988–1000.

Wolf, M., and Goodglass, H. 1986. Dyslexia, dysnomia, and lexical retrieval. *Brain and Language*, *27*, 360–379.

Wolf, M., and Obregon, M. 1992. Early naming deficits, developmental dyslexia, and a specific deficit hypothesis. *Brain and Language*, *42*, 219–247.

Wolff, P. H., Michel, G. F., and Ovrut, M. 1990. Rate variable and automatized naming in developmental dyslexia. *Brain and Language*, *39*, 556–575.

Wolpaw, T., Nation, J. E., and Aram, D. M. 1976. Developmental language disorders: A follow-up study. *Illinois Speech and Hearing Journal*, *12*, 14–18.

Woodcock, R. W. 1987. *Woodcock Reading Mastery Tests—Revised*. Circle Pines, MN: American Guidance Service.

Woodworth, R. S., and Wells, F. L. 1911. Association Tests. In J. R. Angell, H. C. Warren, J. B. Watson, and A. H. Pierce, eds., *The Psychological Monographs*. No. 57. Princeton, NJ: Psychological Review Company.

Yopp, H. K. 1988. The validity and reliability of phonemic awareness tests. *Reading Research Quarterly*, *23*, 159–177.

Zimmerman, I. L., Steiner, V. G., and Evatt-Pond, R. L. 1979. *Preschool Language Scale*. Rev. ed. Columbus, OH: Merrill.

Author Index

Subject Index